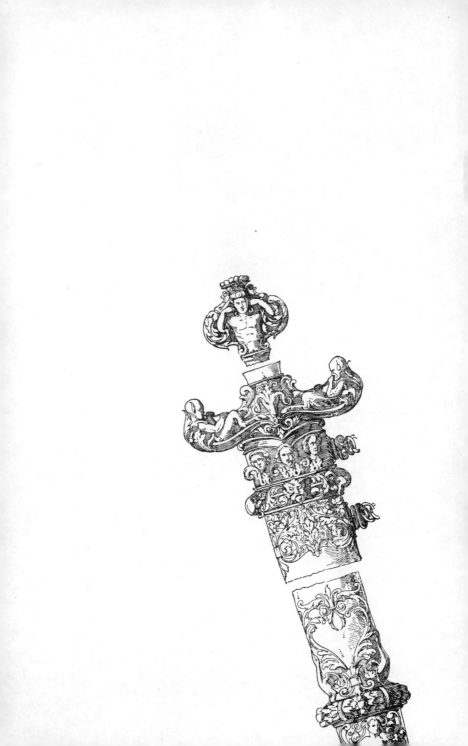

handbook
of ornament

a grammar of art industrial and
architectural designing in all its branches for practical
as well as theoretical use by

Franz Sales Meyer

300 plates and numerous illustrations in the text

Dover Publications, Inc., New York

Published in Canada by General Publishing Company, Ltd., 30 Lesmill Road, Don Mills, Toronto, Ontario.

Published in the United Kingdom by Constable and Company, Ltd., 10 Orange Street, London WC2H 7EG.

This Dover edition, first published in 1957, is an unabridged and unaltered republication of the English translation of the last revised edition.

DOVER *Pictorial Archive* SERIES

International Standard Book Number: 0-486-23480-0
Library of Congress Catalog Card Number: 77-72183

Manufactured in the United States of America
Dover Publications, Inc.
180 Varick Street
New York, N.Y. 10014

HANDBOOK OF ORNAMENT

Author's Preface.

Strictly speaking, the present "Handbook of Ornament" is a re-issue, in book form, of my "Collection of ornamental forms" published in folio size under the title "Ornamentale Formenlehre".

The reasons which induced me to publish this "Handbook" were the following. Owing to the nature of the case, the text of the "Formenlehre", which forms an essential though not the chief part of that work, had to be printed on separate sheets, which is always a source of inconvenience in practical use; and for this reason many critics, who in other respects passed an unexpectedly favourable and very flattering judgment on my work, expressed the wish that the text should be issued in a more convenient book form. On the other hand it was clear that the text could have no value except for those who already possessed the plates, and as the price of the collection, owing to its size and style, is not inconsiderable, and as plates on a reduced scale are quite sufficient for all who desire to use the work merely for study, and not directly for purposes of design, the author and publisher arranged to combine text and plates in the "Handbook" in such a way that the plates, on a greatly-reduced scale, might be printed with the text. They hope in this way to have met the wishes that have been expressed, and while offering to teachers a convenient aid, to have produced a work which from its wealth of text and illustrations and its comparatively trifling price, may prove of very general utility.

As a companion to the "Ornamentale Formenlehre" it was necessary that the Handbook should retain the general plan and main divisions of that work; but this did not exclude partial alterations, and particularly an enlargement of the descriptive text. These have accordingly been made, as will be seen on a careful comparison. But in making them there has been no sacrifice of the principle of giving everything that is important and essential, with the utmost conciseness and the omission of all digressions.

I take this opportunity of thanking all those who have rendered the publication of this work possible and have supported me with their kind assistance, and I now present the book to the public, in the hope that it will meet with a hearty reception and favourable criticism.

Carlsruhe, March 1888.

FRANZ SALES MEYER.

PREFACE TO THE FOURTH EDITION.

Scarcely four years have elapsed since the first edition of this book was placed in the hands of the public. Its unexpectedly favourable reception continues to recommend it. As my critics, to whom my best thanks are due, have made no suggestions for improvement in it, the "Handbook", apart from some trifling corrections, has remained essentially the same. May it continue to win new friends in school and home.

Carlsruhe, February, 1892.

THE AUTHOR.

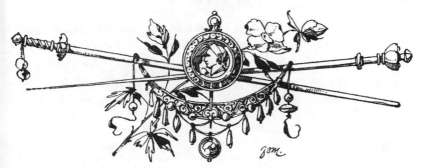

Introduction.

[The term "ORNAMENT", in its limited sense, includes such of the Elements of Decoration as are adapted, or developed, from Natural Foliage. These differ from the Geometrical elements, inasmuch as they are *organic* i. e. possessing stems, leaves, flowers, &c., while the latter are *inorganic.*

When merely drawn on paper, &c., and unapplied — a foliated element is considered in the abstract as "Ornament". When applied to beautify an object — it becomes an "Element of Decoration".

The term "DECORATION" signifies the art or process of applying the various Elements to beautify Objects. It is also used to denote the completed result. Thus the artist, who is occupied in the "decoration" of a vase, may represent ornament upon it; and the ornament is then the "Decoration" of the vase.

The "ELEMENTS" of Decoration are: Geometrical-lines, Ornament, Natural-foliage, Artificial Objects, Animals, and the Human Figure. These may be considered as the "ingredients"; and they are mixed, and applied, on various arrangements or "Features", according to certain acknowledged "recipes" which are termed "Principles".

The "PRINCIPLES" of Decoration are not included in this Handbook, as the limits of it allow only a brief notice of such Elements as have been in general use during the successive Historic-epochs.]

Wherever the hand of man has produced any Decoration, be it

original Invention, or only the arbitrary Variation of some familiar fundamental idea, the following will invariably be the case:

(a) The decoration is produced by arranging and joining Dots and Lines, or by combining and dividing Geometrical Figures, in accordance with the laws of rhythm, regularity, symmetry, &c.;

(b) It arises from the attempt of the decorator to represent the Objects of the external world. Nearest at hand for imitation, is organic Nature with the Plants, Animals, and Human form. But inorganic Nature also offers models: e. g. the forms of Crystallisation (snow-flakes), and the Phenomena of nature (clouds, waves, &c.). Rich sources are also opened-up by the Artificial Objects which are fashioned by man himself.

It is obvious that all kinds of Elements may be used in combination: Geometrical may be united with Natural forms; and so on. Moreover it was easy for human imagination to combine details taken from nature into monstrous forms not found in nature, e. g. the Sphinx, Centaur, Mermaid, &c.; and Animal and Human bodies with plant-like terminations.

If we collect, into groups, the bases or motives of decoration, omitting what is non-essential and detached, we arrive at the classification given in the following pages.

Decoration is applied to countless objects; and the style may be very varied without being arbitrary; being determined, firstly, by the aim and the material of the object to be decorated, and, secondly, by the ideas ruling at different periods and among different nations. It is therefore obvious that it has a comprehensive and important domain. A knowledge of it is indispensable to artists; and it is an instructive and sociologically interesting factor of general culture.

The peculiarities which arise from the reciprocal relation of material, form, and aim, more or less modified by the ideas of the Age and the natural characteristics of the Nation, are termed the "Style" of that Period and Nation. The mention, of the Century and the Nation, gives a convenient method of labelling works of Art, which is now well understood; e. g. — "17th century, Italian".

The majority of works on ornament, arrange their material according to Periods and Nations; but the present Handbook, following the principles laid down by Semper, Bötticher and Jacobsthal, is based on a system which is synthetic rather than analytic; and intended more to construct and develope from the Elements than to dissect and deduce. It contains three main divisions:

Division I treats of the "Elements of Decoration", or motives of which it is formed. Geometrical motives formed by the rhythmical arrangement of dots and lines, by the regular section of angles, by the formation and division of closed figures, are followed by the forms of Nature which are offered for ornamental imitation by the vegetable and animal kingdoms, and by the human frame. These in their turn are followed by Artificial Objects, or forms borrowed from Art, Technology, and Science, and usually met-with in the class of trophies, symbols, &c.

Division II, "Ornament applied to Features", arranges them according to their functions, and the reciprocal relation between the construction of the object and the application of the ornament. The division falls into five sub-divisions: A. Bands (bordering, framing and connecting forms); B. Free Ornaments (forms whose construction expresses a termination or cessation); C. Supports (types of ornament which express the principle of weight-bearing); D. Enclosed Ornament suitable for the enlivenment of a defined bordered field, (panels); E. Repeating Ornament (the decoration of surfaces which, disregarding the limits of space, are developed, on a geometrical or organic basis, into "patterns").

Division III, shows the application of decoration to vase-form, metal objects, furniture, frames, jewelry, heraldry and writing, printing, &c.

Further details, as to the groups and divisions, will be found in the "Table of the Arrangement of the Handbook" which follows this introduction.

The illustrations, numbering almost 3,000, and comprised on 300 full-page plates, represent the styles of the most various periods and nations. A comparatively large share of attention has been devoted to the Antique, because it is in that Period that form usually finds its clearest and most beautiful expression. Next to that in importance is the Renascence with its wealth and freedom of form. The space, devoted to the creations of the Middle Ages, is more limited. From the styles of the Decadence, only a few examples have been admitted, for the sake of comparison and characterisation. Modern times, as a rule, have only been taken into account, where forms arose which do not occur in the historic styles.

The illustrations have been partly taken direct from the originals; and partly — as was almost unavoidable — reproduced from other Books; for the leading idea of the present work is not to offer anything new, but to arrange what is already known, in a manner suitable both to the subject and to the aim of a Handbook. Where the author was acquainted with the source, which he regrets was not always the case, the authority has been mentioned in the text.

Each division and sub-division is prefixed by a few remarks on style and history, characteristics, motives, symbolism, aim, and application. These are followed, so far as is necessary and practicable, by notes on the places where the objects illustrated were discovered, where they are now preserved, and on their material and size. Hints as to construction, are given only where the construction cannot at once be inferred from the figure.

Readers who use this book for purposes of tuition, will find in the Author's "*Ornamentale Formenlehre*"* the Plates on a scale of $2\,^1/_2$ times the size of this Handbook, together with the requisite hints for the use of the work in schools.

---

* Franz Sales Meyer: *Ornamentale Formenlehre;* Three hundred folio plates, in a portfolio.

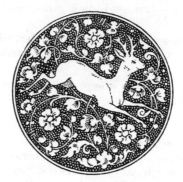

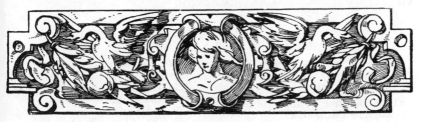

TABLE

SHOWING THE ARRANGEMENT OF THE CHAPTERS AND PLATES.

DIVISION I.

THE ELEMENTS OF DECORATION.

DIVISION II.

ORNAMENT APPLIED TO FEATURES.

DIVISION III.

DECORATED OBJECTS.

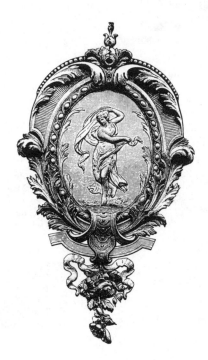

DIVISION I.

THE ELEMENTS

OF

DECORATION.

A. Geometrical Elements, & Motives.

B. Natural Objects:

    a. Plant organisms (Flora of ornament).

    b. Animal organisms (Fauna of ornament).

    c. Human organism.

C. Artificial Objects (Trophies, Symbols, etc.).

F.S.M.

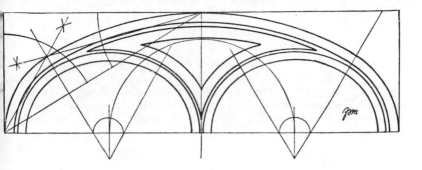

A.

GEOMETRICAL ELEMENTS AND MOTIVES.

Geometrical Ornament is the primordial or oldest of the Elements of Decoration. The implements of savages, and the tattooing of the Indians, prove this. The seam, with the thread running slant-wise from one piece to the other, may have been the original for the Zigzag line; and woven-work, of warp and woof of every kind, the original for Reticulated patterns; and the plaited hair that of the Plaited band. The revolutions of a fork-like instrument led to the discovery of the Circle; the combination of dots, at regular intervals, to the Polygon or Pointed-star. The gradual developement of these original geometrical forms, rising from stage to stage with the growth of culture and knowledge, led finally to geometrical artistic forms such as we see in Moorish panelled ceilings, in Gothic tracery, in guilloche-work, and the like. The developement of geometry into a science, with its theorems and proofs, also came to the assistance of art. As evidence of this, we need only refer to the construction of the ellipse from given lengths of axes.

The majority of all geometrical ornaments may be divided into three groups. They are either continuous and ribbon-like (bands), or in enclosed spaces (panels), or in unlimited flat patterns. In every case the foundation of the geometrical ornament will be a certain division, a subsidiary construction, or a network. We will begin with the last; and pass in turn to the ribbon motives, the flat patterns, and the figure motives.

NETWORK. (Plate 1.)

The systems of subsidiary lines required in geometrical patterns, e. g.: parquets, mosaics, window-glazing, &c., are termed Nets. The name explains itself. They may be of very various kinds. The most frequent are quadrangular and triangular reticulations, combined of single squares or equilateral triangles. A special network, resembling the plait of a cane chair, is required for some Moorish patterns.

PLATE 1. NETWORK.

1. Ordinary quadrangular. Equal divisions are set off in one direction, parallels are drawn through the points of division, and the former cut by a line at an angle of 45°. The points, where these diagonals cut the parallels, mark the divisions in the opposite direction.
2. Oblique quadrangular. The divisions are set-off on a vertical line and the parallels are then drawn at an angle of 45° on each side of the points of division.
3. Straight, with alternate divisions. Construction similar to No. 1.
4. Oblique quadrangular, with alternate divisions. Construction similar to No. 2.
5. Moorish Diapers.
6. Enlarged detail to No. 5.
7. Triangular net. It is based on the construction of the equilateral triangle; and may be arranged in two attitudes, as shown in figs. 8 and 9.

8 and 9. Enlarged details to fig. 7.

BAND MOTIVES. (Plates 2—4.)

Plates 2, 3 and 4 contain a number of band motives. These are made by the joining of regularly-placed points: those in Plate 2 are joined by straight lines; those in Plate 3 by arcs; and those in Plate 4 by a combination of both.

Each of the plates contains, beneath the motives, specimens of their application, taken from different styles.

PLATE 2. BAND MOTIVES, IN STRAIGHT LINES.

1, 7, 8 and 14. Greek.
2. Zigzag lines.
15. Moorish plaited band.
6 and 16. These examples may be illustrated by folded strips of paper.

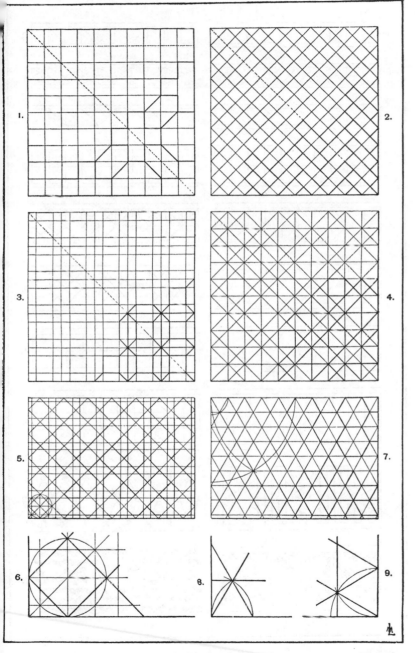

Network. Plate 1.

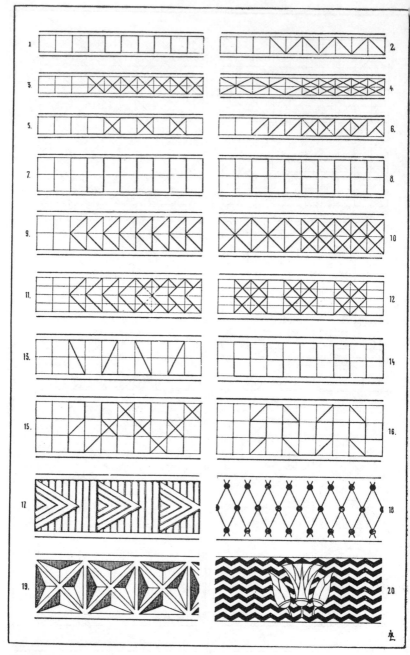

Plate 2.   Band Motives.

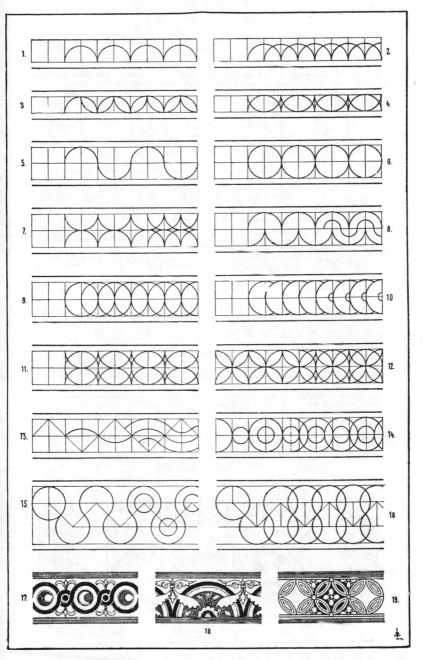

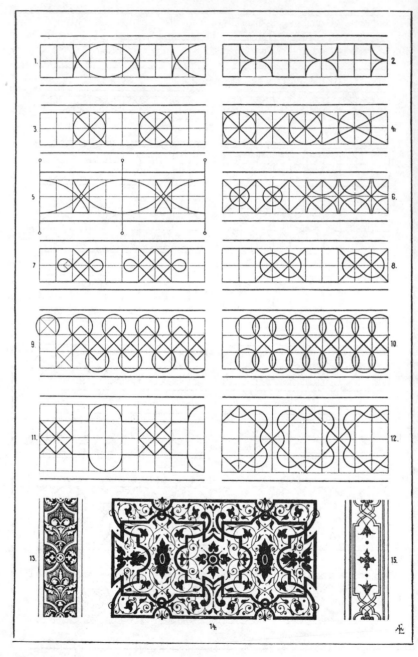

Plate 4.   Band Motives.

71 and 19. Carvings in basrelief from the implements of savages.
18. Greek vase painting, Motive: the seam.
20. Waves with lotus, Egyptian wall-painting, (Owen Jones).

PLATE 3. BAND MOTIVES, IN ARCS.
5 and 13. Undulate lines.
10. Motive of the "strung coin" pattern (coins threaded on a cord).
17. Romanesque ornament from an evangeliarium written for Charle-
    magne, 8th century, Library of the Louvre, Paris.
18. Romanesque mural painting, Swedish church.
19. Chinese damaskeened ornament from a vase, (Racinet).

PLATE 4. BAND MOTIVES, MIXED.
13. Romanesque glass painting, church of S. Urban, Troyes.
15. Frieze, house, Beaune, 17th century, (Racinet).

    N. B. Where two arcs are joined: it is necessary, in order to avoid a
break, that the two centres and the point of junction should be in the
same straight line.

DIAPER PATTERNS. (Plates 5—7.)

    Plates 5, 6 and 7 give a selection for flat patterns. Almost all
the constructions may be referred to the quadrangular or the triangular Net. The examples in Plate 5 show junctions in a straight
line; those in Plate 6 are composed of arcs; and in Plate 7 the
regularly-placed points are joined by mixed lines.
    The designs may be used as patterns for parquet flooring, window
glazing, and similar work, without further enrichment. They are at
the same time available as construction-lines for the further developement of richer patterns for mural and glass painting, carpets, tapestry,
ceilings, &c., as shown by the examples of application appended to
the simple motives.

PLATE 5. DIAPER PATTERNS, &c., WITH STRAIGHT LINES.
4 and 6. Roof-covering may be considered as the motive.
10.   The natural motive is the cell of the honey bee.
13—15. Designs for coffer ceiling, by Sebastian Serlio, 16th century,
        (Formenschatz).

PLATE 6. DIAPER PATTERNS, WITH ARCS.
1, 4 and 7. Scale motives.
10. Romanesque glass painting, Cathedral, Bourges, (Racinet).

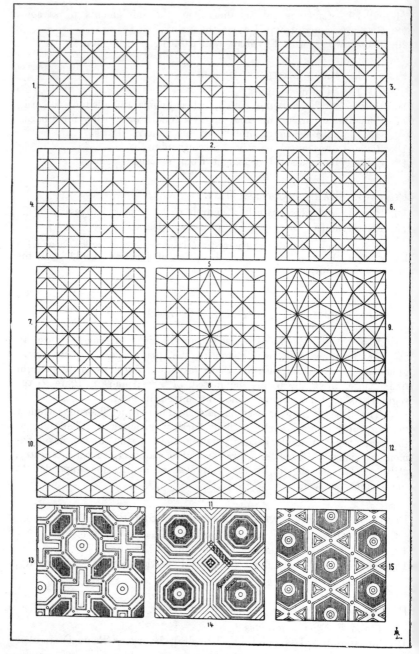

Plate 5.   Diaper Patterns.

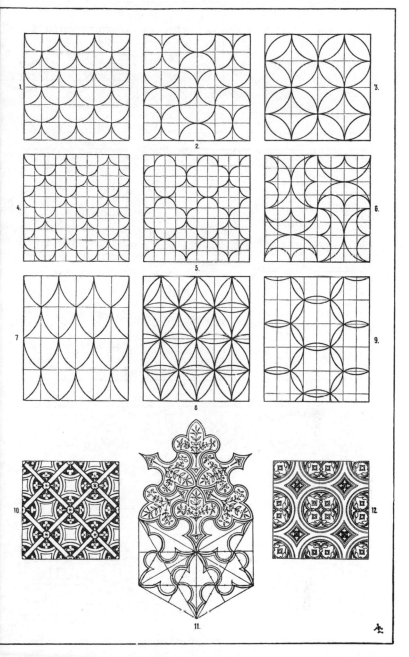

Diaper Patterns. Plate 6.

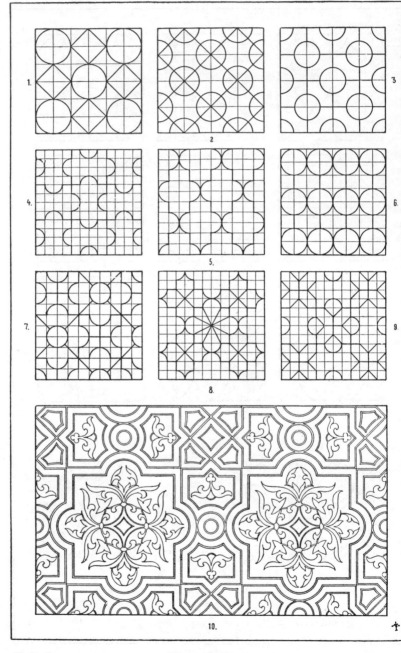

Plate 7.   Diaper Patterns.

11. Mural painting, Assisi, (Vorbilder für Fabrikanten und Hand-
    werker).
12. Old Italian mural painting, San Francesco, Assisi, (Hessemer).

PLATE 7. DIAPER PATTERNS, WITH MIXED LINES.
10. Old Italian mural painting San Francesco, Assisi, (Hessemer).

THE SECTOR, THE POLYGON, AND THE STAR.

Polygons and Stars are of frequent occurrence in ornamental
design. The Sector is the foundation of Rosettes. The Polygon and
the Star are often used as Frames to Ornaments. They also serve
as compartments in coffer Ceilings and composite ornamental designs.
In this case, they are frequently divided into smaller figures, as will
be seen in the following plates.

Plate 8 gives the shape, and construction of those which most
frequently occur; followed by some examples of their application.

PLATE 8. RADIATING FIGURES, &c.
1—4. The Sector, produced by the regular division of circles.
5.   The Square, described obliquely in a circle.
6.   The Square formed by the juxtaposition of right angles and
       cutting-off the lengths for the sides.
7.   The regular Octagon, described obliquely in a circle.
8.   The regular Octagon, described in the square by measuring
       half diagonals from its angles.
9.   The regular Triangle and Hexagon, formed by measuring the
       radius, as chords, six times round the circumference.
10.   The regular Duodecagon, formed by applying the radius
       to the circle from the ends of two diameters at right angles
       to each other.
11—12. The regular Pentagon and Decagon, formed by a construc-
       tion based on the theorem of the "Golden Mean", as shown
       in the figures.
13.   The regular five-pointed Star, formed by joining the alter-
       nate points of five points placed at equal distances in the
       circumference of a circle. Known in the history of magic
       and witchcraft as the Pentagram or "Pentacle".
14.   The regular six-pointed Star, formed by joining alternate
       points placed at equal distances in the circumference of a
       circle.

15—16. Regular eight-pointed Star, formed by combining every second or third of eight points placed at equal distances in the circumference of a circle.

17—18. Regular ten-pointed Stars, formed by joining every second or third of ten points placed at equal distances in the circumference of a circle.

The pointed Stars may also be formed by producing to a sufficient distance the sides of ordinary regular polygons; and, conversely, each star contains a simpler star, as well as the regular polygon of the same number of sides.

19.   Star, formed by a suitable combination of corresponding points regularly placed on the circumferences of two concentric circles.

20.   Uraniscus, the star-like decoration of a Greek coffer ceiling. From the Propylaea in Athens. Gold on a blue ground.

21.   Back of a modern chair, carved in basrelief.

22.   Ornamentation of a semi-regular pointed star. Arabic, 16th century, (Prisse d'Avennes).

THE SQUARE, AND ITS SUBDIVISIONS.   (Plates 9 and 10.)

The regular four-sided figure or Square, with its equal sides and angles, is a fundamental form of frequent occurence. It may be divided into compartments in various ways; the principal auxiliary lines for this purpose being the Diagonals (or oblique lines connecting the angles), and the Diameters (or lines connecting the centre of each side). Where the square is divided for a ceiling, floor or similar object: a border is made round the enclosed space. In most cases, a large central compartment is retained; and this may be a square, either parallel or oblique to the other; or may be a circle, an octagon, &c.

The Subdivisions of Plate 9 follow the richer divisions of Plate 10.

PLATE 9.   THE SQUARE.
1—15. The simple Subdivisions.

PLATE 10.   THE SQUARE.
1—8. Richer and more complicated Subdivisions.

6.   Panelling of Ceiling, inn, Nuremberg, Modern.

8.   Panelling of ceiling, Massimi Palace, Rome, by Baldassare Peruzzi, Italian Renascence, (Letarouilly).

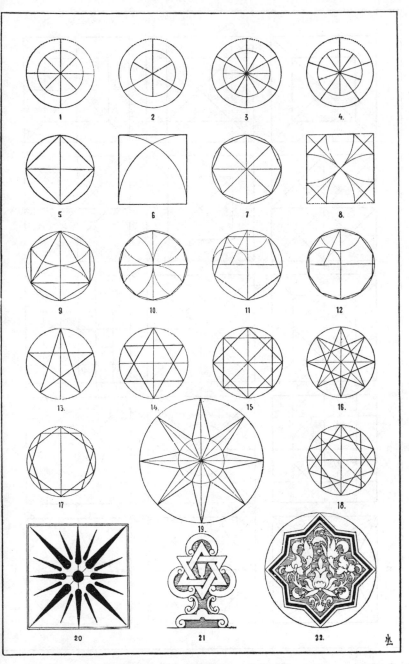

The Sector, the Polygon, and the Star. Plate 8.

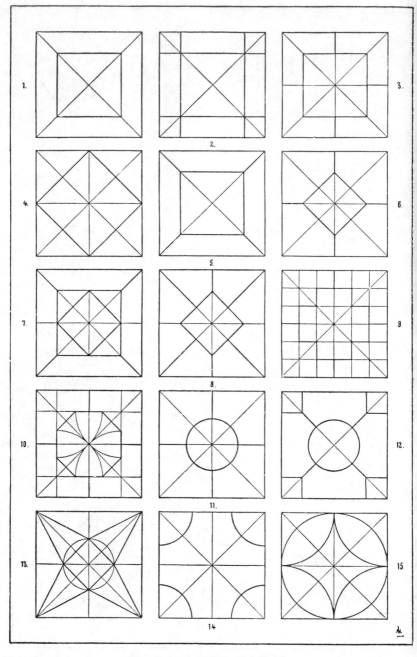

Plate 9. The Square, and its Subdivision.

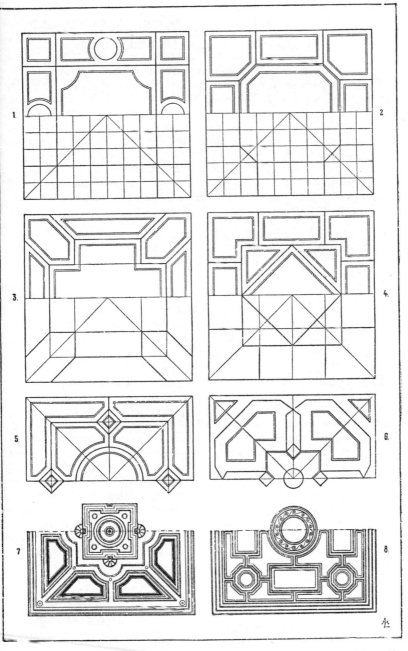

The Square and its Subdivision.　　　Plate 10.

THE SUBDIVISION OF THE OCTAGON, TRIANGLE, AND HEXAGON. (Plates 11 and 12.)

Next to the square: the regular polygons most frequently occurring in ornamentation are the Octagon and the Hexagon. The Triangle, Pentagon, Decagon and Duodecagon are, for obvious reasons, less common; while the other regular polygons are scarcely used at all. Sometimes the semi-regular polygons also appear. These are formed by cutting-off equal triangles from the angles of a regular polygon in such a manner that the resulting figure has long and short sides alternately, and the angles all lie on the circumference of a circle.

Diagonals and Diameters with series of lines in the manner of pointed stars, are the readiest auxiliaries for dividing regular and semi-regular Polygons.

PLATE 11. THE OCTAGON.

1—8. The best-known Subdivisions.

PLATE 12. THE TRIANGLE, THE HEXAGON, &c.

1— 5. Simple Subdivisions of the Equilateral triangle.
6—13. The best-known Subdivisions of the regular Hexagon.
14.   Subdivisions of a regular Pentagon.

THE OBLONG, AND ITS SUBDIVISION. (Plates 13—16.)

The right-angled plane figure with unequal pairs of sides, known as an Oblong, is the most usual of all fundamental forms. Ceilings, floors, walls, doors, wainscoting, panels of furniture, table-tops, book-covers, and numbers of other objects, have an oblong shape. The difference in the lengths of the sides adapts itself to all possible conditions: the Oblong approaching the square on the one hand and the Band or Border on the other; so that the divisions are very various; as will be seen by a glance at the examples. As a rule, the diagonal is not used as an auxiliary line, but is replaced by the mitral-line of the angle, as this latter alone gives equal breadths of the Border. When the Oblong approaches the Square, a distorted square subdivision is sometimes resorted-to, (Compare Pl. 16, fig. 2).

PLATE 13. THE OBLONG.

1—6. The usual subdivisions.
7.   Mosaic, flooring, Italian, 16th century, (Storck).

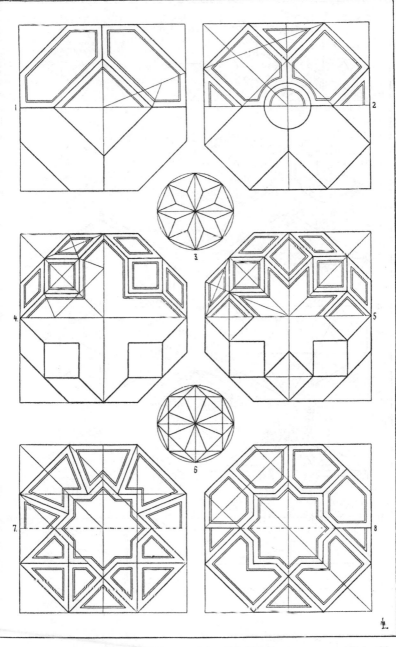

The Octagon, and its Subdivision.   Plate 11.

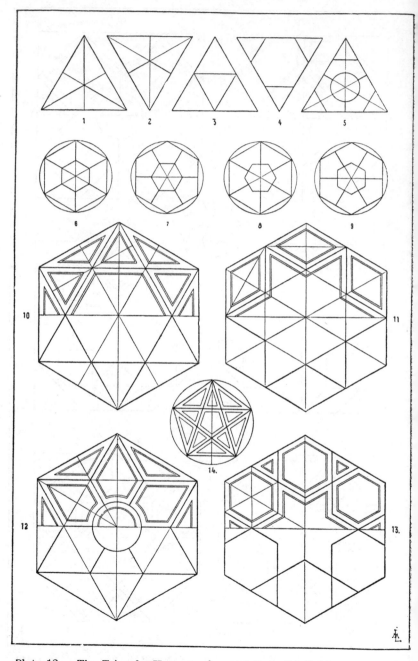

Plate 12.   The Triangle, Hexagon, &c., and their Subdivision.

THE SUBDIVISION OF THE RHOMBUS, AND THE TRAPEZIUM.
(Plate 17.)

Rhombus or "Lozenge" is the name usually given to the equilateral foursided figure with pairs of unequal angles. The principal
auxiliary lines of these figures are the diagonals. The subdivision
generally leaves an oblong or hexagonal panel in the centre.

The Trapezium is a four-sided figure with unequal sides. The
Parallel Trapezium has two parallel sides which are unequal and two
equal sides which are not parallel (Pl. 17, figs. 5 to 8). The Symmetrical Trapezium has two pairs of adjacent equal sides (Pl. 17,
figs. 9 and 10). Any other irregular four-sided rectilinear figure is
a Trapezoid. Some suitable subdivisions are given on Plate 17.
Definite directions for the Trapezoid can scarcely be given; its subdivision is seldom easy, and varies with each particular case. The
general principle is: — Endeavour to cut-off projecting angles by means
of triangles in such a way as to leave a portion of the entire figure
regular or symmetrical. This is, however, a matter of artistic taste;
and more easily learnt than taught.

Among other applications of the symmetrical or parallel Trapezium is that to Cupolas of Domes: the lines are indeed curves
on a bent surface; but this causes very little alteration in the subdivision.

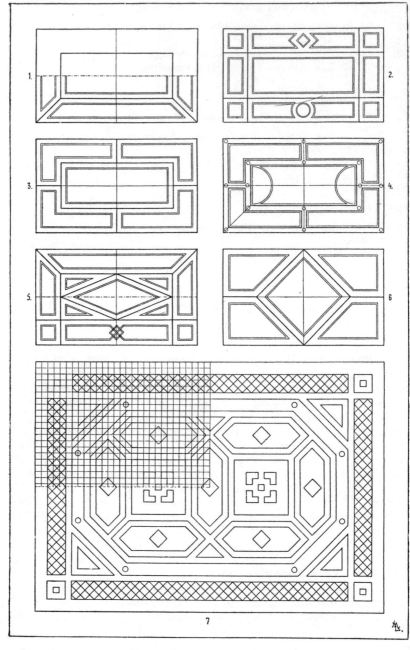

Plate 13.   The Oblong, and its Subdivision.

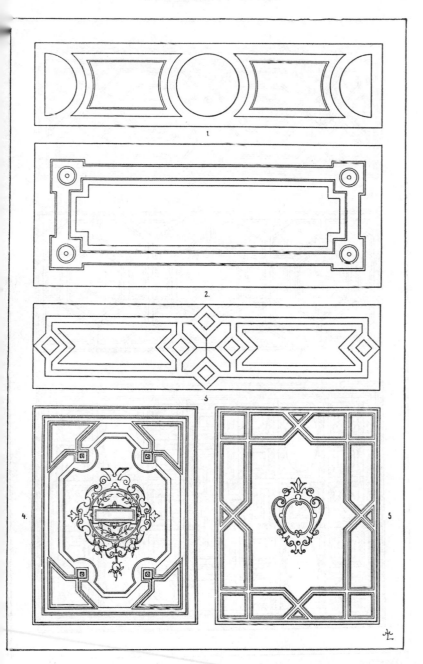

1

2.

3

4.   5

The Oblong, and its Subdivision.   Plate 14.

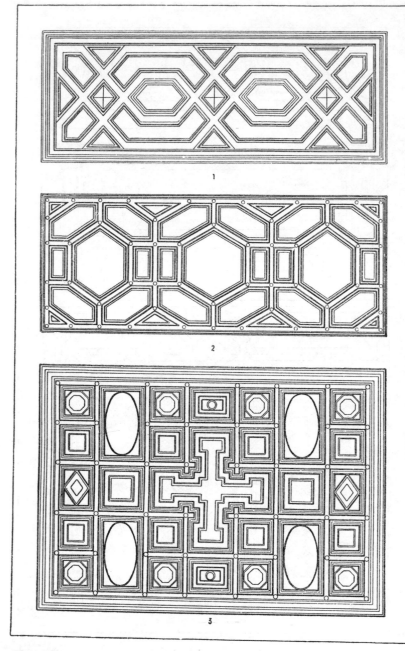

Plate 15.   The Oblong, and its Subdivision.

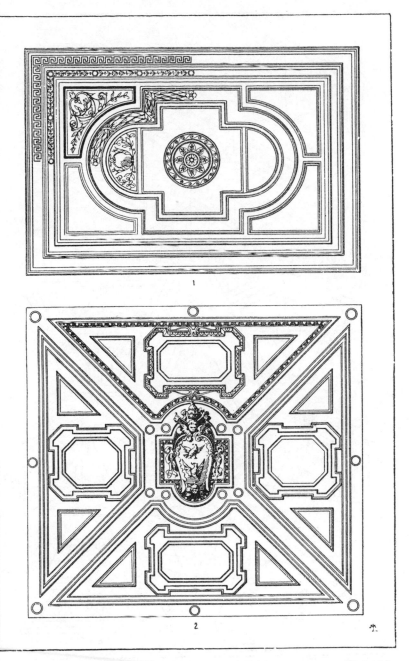

1

2

The Oblong, and its Subdivision.   Plate 16.

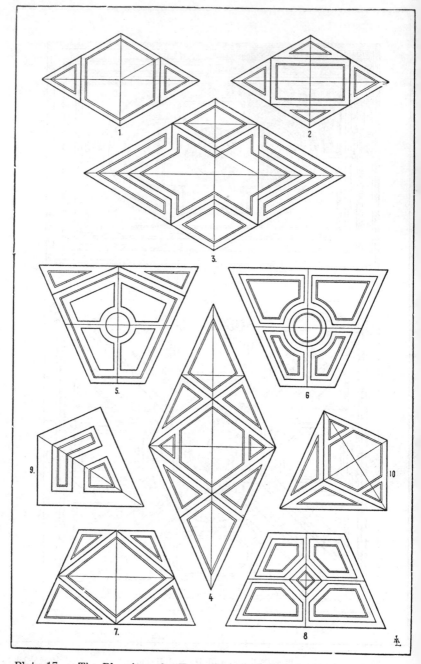

Plate 17.   The Rhombus, the Trapezium, and their Subdivision.

PLATE 17. THE RHOMBUS, AND THE TRAPEZIUM.

1— 4. Subdivision of the Rhombus.
5— 8.   „   „   „ Parallel Trapezium.
9—10.   „   „   „ Symmetrical Trapezium.

THE CIRCLE, ITS SUBDIVISION, AND INTERSECTIONS.
(Plate 18.)

The Circle is often used in ornamentation as a fundamental form. No good result is produced (as a rule) by dividing it merely by radii or other straight lines; and it is therefore usually divided by means of curved lines or of a combination of arcs and straight lines. By describing circles to cut each other: motives may be obtained, as shown by figures 3 and 7, the latter of which is the basis of a Roman mosaic pavement found in Pompeii (Figure 17).

That circles which cut each-other form of themselves an effective pattern—is shown by the engine-turned ornament, which is produced by machinery and applied to the decoration of Watch-cases, and to the plates from which Bank notes, Share certificates, &c. are printed.

Ornamentation by means of arcs plays a conspicuous part in Gothic tracery, which will be treated-of in the following chapter.

PLATE 18. THE CIRCLE.

1—12. Different divisions and intersections.
13—16. Tracery in the Gothic style.
17.   Centre of a mosaic pavament, Pompeii, (Kunsthandwerk).

GOTHIC TRACERY. (Plate 19.)

In the forms of Tracery, the Gothic style evolved and brought to perfection a characteristic decoration by means of arcs of circles. And although the results have something stiff and mechanical, when compared with the ornaments taken direct from nature in other styles, it cannot be denied that they possess a great originality, and richness of form.

Tracery was chiefly applied to stone, and wood; in architecture, and furniture; for galleries, windows, and panels, &c.

Well-known forms are the circles (figs. 13—16 of Plate 18 showing 2, 3, 4 and 6 foliations), the trefoil (Plate 19, figs. 3 and 4),

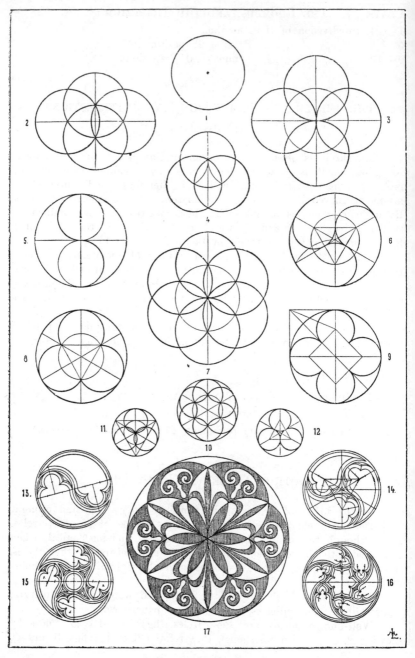

Plate 18.   The Circle, and its Subdivision.

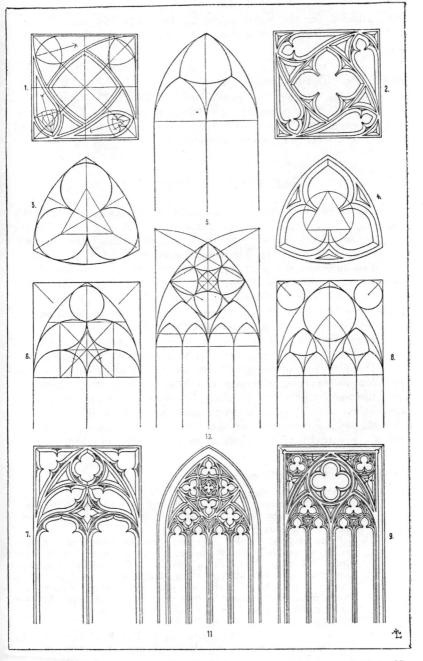

Gothic Tracery. Plate 19.

the quatrefoil (in the centre of fig. 2), the cinquefoil, &c. The projecting points are termed cusps, the voids between the cusps are
termed foils.

PLATE 19.   TRACERY.

1—11. Gothic tracery, for panels and windows. The figures give
partly the fundamental construction, partly the further developement. Thus figures 1 and 2, 3 and 4, 6 and 7, 8 and
9, 10 and 11, belong together.

THE ELLIPSE. (Plate 20.)

The Ellipse is a figure, whose radius of curvature is continually
changing. It has the peculiar quality that, if any point on the
circumference be joined with the two foci, the sum of the two connecting lines is invariable, and always equal to the longitudinal axis.

The three-centred arch is an approximate construction to an
elliptic curve. It is composed of a number of arcs, which is not
possible in the case of the ellipse. As regards beauty of line it can
never be a substitute for the Ellipse; but its easier construction has,
notwithstanding, caused it to be used for many purposes.

The expression "Oval" for the ellipse, is erroneous. Oval is
derived from "ovum" (egg), and therefore means an egg-shape.

The Ellipse is of comparatively late appearance in art, the construction presupposing a certain knowledge of Geometry, which was
not possessed by primitive peoples. Afterwards it became of common
application, as will be seen from many passages of this Handbook.
The Ellipse is a very popular shape for ceilings, panels, boxes, and
dishes. Figure 15 affords hints as to the manner of subdividing it.

PLATE 20.   THE ELLIPSE, &c.

1—2.   Construction by means of 8 points.
          When the square with its diagonals and transversals is projec-
          ted as an Oblong, the circle described in it becomes an Ellipse.
3.   Construction from the Foci.
          From the ends of the conjugate axis, describe circles with a
          radius of one half the transverse axis; the points where these
          circles cut each other will be the foci. Now divide the trans-
          verse axis into two unequal parts, and from the foci as centres
          describe circles having these unequal parts for their radii; the
          points of intersection will be four points of the Ellipse. Another
          division will give another four points, and so on.
4.   Construction by means of Tangents.
          Construct an Oblong with sides of the lengths of the transverse
          and conjugate axes respectively; draw the transversals, that is,

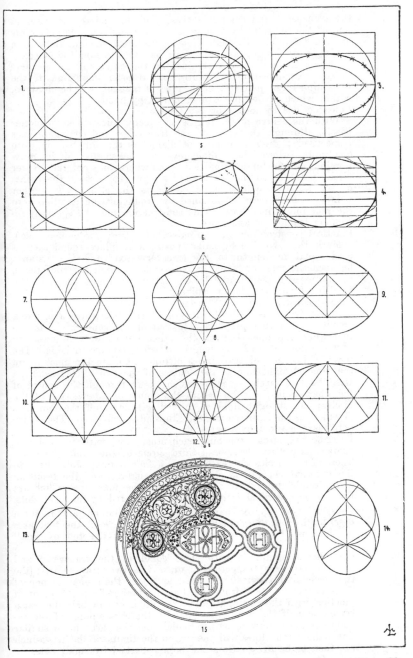

The Ellipse, and its Subdivision.   Plate 20.

the transverse and conjugate axes; join the ends of the axes in one of the quarters by a diagonal; and set-off a number of points on this diagonal. Through these points draw straight lines from the opposite angle, and also parallels to the longitudinal axis. Now join the points thus obtained on the outside of the quarters in the way shown in the figure; and transfer these lines to the remaining three quarters; and a series of tangents will be obtained, within which the ellipse can be drawn by hand.

5. Constructions by means of two Circles.

With the centre of the Ellipse as a centre describe two circles passing through the ends of the transverse and conjugate axes respectively; draw a number of diameters through two opposite quadrants; where these diameters cut the smaller circle, draw parallels to the longitudinal axis; and where they cut the greater circle, parallels to the transverse axis (or vice versa); the points of the parallels will then be points on the ellipse. The other points required may be obtained by producing the parallels into the remaining quadrants. This construction may be specially recommended for practical use.

6. Practical construction on a larger scale (centres, garden-beds, &c.).

Mark the two foci by nails, posts, &c.; place round them a cord equal in length to the transverse axis plus the distance between the foci, and tied at both ends; stretch the cord tense, by means of a pencil, and let the latter run round the foci: the resulting figure will be an Ellipse.

7—12. Several constructions for Ellipsoids.

In constructions 7—9 the length of the transverse axis has a definite, invariable proportion to that of the conjugate axis, so that when the one is given the other immediately follows. In constructions 10—12 the length of each axis is variable. The point of junction of two circles of different diameter must lie on the same straight line as the centres of the two circles.

7. Describe two circles each of which passes through the centre of the other. Join the centres with the points of intersection of the circles: the straight lines so formed will mark-off the four arcs of which, as the figure shows, the Ellipsoid is composed. The centre points are marked by small dots.

8. Describe two circles touching each other, and with the point of contact as centre, describe a third circle of the same diameter. These three circles cut each other in four points. Join these to the external centres as shown on the figure; and the resulting four straight lines will again mark-off the four arcs which are then to be described from the points indicated by the small dots.

9. Construct two squares, having one side in common, and in them describe the four diagonals; these will then mark-off the four arcs which must then be drawn from the points denoted by small dots.

10. Construct a rectangle with sides equal to the transverse and longitudinal axes respectively; draw the two transversals (the transverse and longitudinal axes) and join their ends in one of the quarters. Cut-off from this line, beginning from the point of junction with the conjugate axis, the difference of half the transverse and half the conjugate axis; on the centre point of the remaining piece draw a perpendicular and the three more similar lines; these four lines will then show the limits of the arcs which are then to be drawn from the points marked by small dots.

11. Construct an Oblong with sides equal to the transverse and longitudinal axes respectively, and draw the two transversals. Measure the half of the transverse axis upon half the longitudinal axis, and ascertain the difference; halve this difference. This half difference must now be taken four times along the transverse axis from the centre point of the Ellipsoid, and three times along the longitudinal axis. The four required points will thus be obtained. The straight lines connecting them will give the points of junction of the arcs.

12. Construction from eight centres.

Construct an Oblong whose sides are equal to the major and minor axes respectively; draw the transversals, and join their ends in one of the quarters. From the nearest angle, draw a perpendicular to this diagonal; the points where this perpendicular cuts the two axes will be two of the required centres. Two more are obtained by symmetrical transference. From these four points describe circles with a radius = $\frac{1}{2}$ (CB-DA); the points where they cut each other internally will give four more centres. If the centres thus found be joined by means of straight lines, as shown on the figure, the latter will mark the points where the eight arcs will meet.

13—14. Construction of Ovals or egg-shaped figures. The construction of such figures usually consists in combining a semi-circle with a semi-ellipse.

13. Draw in a circle two diameters at right angles to each other, and two intersecting chords of a quadrant; these when produced will determine the points where the various arcs meet. The centres of these latter lie on the ends of the diameters.

14. The construction of the lower half is the same as in fig. 7. The centre of the upper lies in the intersection of tangents to the lower and upper circles.

15. Example of the subdivision and decoration of an ellipse, (Storck's Zeichenvorlagen).

THE THREE-CENTRED ARCH.

The Three-centred arch, which was often used in the Transition period between the Gothic and the Renascence, may be considered as a semi-ellipsoid; and it may be described by one of the methods shown on Plate 20 (see also the Head-piece to this Section, on page 3).

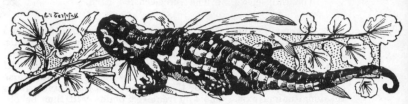

B.

NATURAL FORMS.

a. The Organisms of Plants (Flora of Ornament).

In nearly every style the plant-world has been used in patterns. Leaves, sprays, flowers, and fruits, either singly or combined, have been adapted in ornament. The direct imitation of nature, retaining form and color as much as possible, leads to the naturalistic conception; the construction of an ornament according to the rules of rhythm and symmetry, with a stricter observance of regularity — is known as the artificial method.

The selection of the comparatively few plants from the luxuriant field of the plant-world was partly determined by beauty of form (the outline of the leaf, the delicacy of the spray, &c.) and partly by the fact that they possess (or did at some time possess) a symbolic meaning.

The plates which illustrate this section will first exhibit the Akanthos; and then such plant-forms as are less used or only found in certain styles. They will first be presented as they exist in Nature; and then as they were modified in the various styles.

THE AKANTHOS LEAF. (Plates 21—23.)

Of all the ornamental designs which have been borrowed from plants; the Akanthos is the most popular. Since its introduction by the Greeks, it recurs again and again in every Western style. A symbolical significance has never attached to the Akanthos; its frequent and varied application is due to the ornamental possibilities and beautiful serration of its leaves. It grows wild in the South of Europe, but in more northern latitudes is only found in our botanical gardens. There are many varieties of the plant, of which we may mention the following: *Akanthos mollis*, with broad, blunt tips to the leaves; *Akanthos spinosus*, with pointed lobes terminating in spines, and comparatively narrow leaves. The conception and treatment of the margin and shape of the leaf, is the principal characteristic of the different styles. The Greek foliage has pointed leaf-edges; in the Roman style, the tips of the leaves become rounder, broader, to some extent with more vigorous curves; the Byzantine and Romanesque styles, again, return to stiffer, less delicate forms. The Gothic style, which used the foreign Akanthos in addition to a number of native plants, adopted in the early period, round, bulbous forms; later Gothic, on the contrary, preferred bizarre, long-extended, thistle-like foliage: in both cases the general conception is more or less naturalistic, but the details are usually idealised beyond recognition. The Renascence, which revived Antique ornament, developed the Akanthos, and particularly the Tendril, to the highest degree of perfection; in the following styles formalism degenerates in this direction. Modern ornamental art seeks its models in almost every style; and its creations have generally no pronounced, specifically Modern character.

PLATE 21.   THE AKANTHOS, AND ARTIFICIAL LEAF.

1. Leaf of Akanthos Mollis, (Jacobsthal).
2. Akanthos calyx, the leaves and flower of Akanthos Mollis, naturalistically treated, (Jacobsthal).
3. Leaf of Akanthos Mollis, (Raguenet).
4. Leaf of Akanthos Spinosus, (Gewerbehalle).
5. Cup, corona of a Greek Stele, (Raguenet).
6. Overlap of leaf, Roman candelabrum, Vatican.
7. Greek leaf, displayed, (Jacobsthal).
8. Roman leaf, Capital of a column, Pantheon, Rome, the spoon-like roundings of the points of the leaves, as well as the deep incisions, are characteristic; and designed to look well at a distance.

PLATE 22.   THE ARTIFICIAL LEAF.

1. Leaf, Roman capital, (Raguenet).
2. Leaf displayed, as it is often used on Roman reliefs, e. g.: somewhat more richly developed, on the so called Florentine Pilaster, Uffizi, Florence, (Jacobsthal).
3. Byzantine leaf, Sta. Sofia, Constantinople, (Raguenet).
4. Romanesque leaf, St. Denis, (Lièvre).

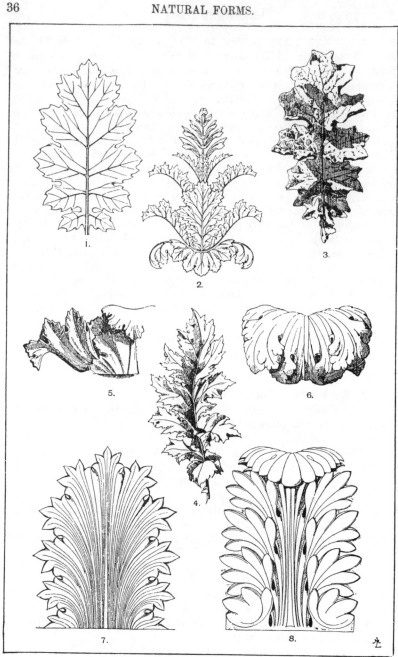

Plate 21.   The Akanthos Leaf, and the Artificial Leaf.

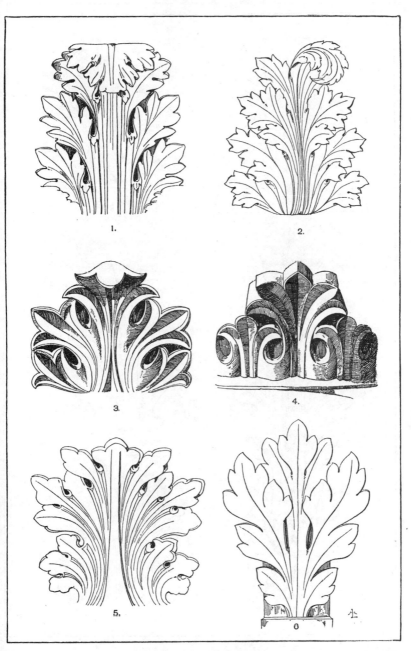

The Artificial Leaf.   Plate 22.

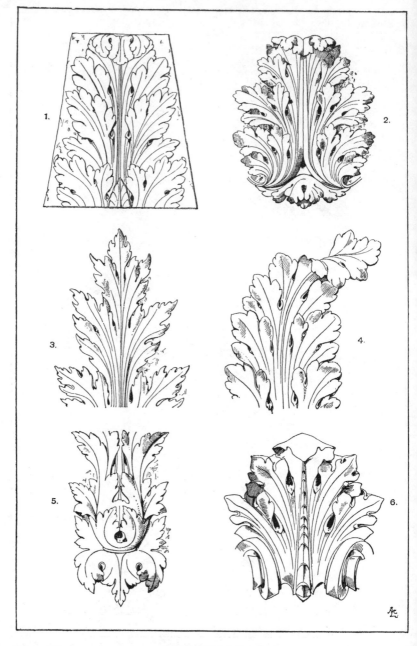

Plate 23.   The Artificial Leaf.

5. Romanesque leaf, monastery of St. Trophimus, Arles, XII. century, (Raguenet).
6. Gothic leaf, (Lièvre).

PLATE 23.   THE ARTIFICIAL LEAF.

1. Leaf, French Renascence, St. Eustache, Paris.
2. Leaf, style of Louis XVI, (Raguenet).
3. Leaf, French Renascence, church, Epernay, (Lièvre).
4. Leaf, French Renascence, (Gropius).
5. Modern Leaf, Louvre, Paris, (F. A. M. Cours d'ornement).
6. Modern Leaf, Theatre, Monte Carlo, Monaco, (Raguenet).

ARTIFICIAL FOLIAGE.   (Plates 24—26.)

The Scroll is a purely artistic invention, the natural plant having no tendrils. Flowers and calices, such as frequently occur in artificial foliage, are usually developed with serrated edges, composed to recall natural models, (Comp. Plate 25, figs. 2 und 3). Artificial foliage is often combined with forms from plants, e. g.: laurel, oak, ivy, ears of wheat, &c., (Comp. Plate 26, figs. 2 and 4). What was said above of the Akanthos leaf, holds good here too, for the differences of execution in the various styles. The greatest luxuriance and the highest elegance were attained by the Italian Renascence, (Comp. Plate 25, fig. 5). It is characteristic of the Louis XVI. epoch that the lines which form the scroll are somestimes flattened, and, so to speak, make elliptic spirals, (Comp. Plate 26, fig. 4).

PLATE 24.   ARTIFICIAL FOLIAGE.

1. Ornament, summit of the monument of Lysikrates, Athens.
2. Cup, Roman.
3. Roman ornament, the so called "Medicean Pilaster", (Artificial foliage of a large size).
4. Fragment of a Greek relief, (F. A. M., Cours d'ornement).

PLATE 25.   ARTIFICIAL FOLIAGE.

1. Roman ornament, marble Biga, from the style of the ornament it must have been an imitation of an original in bronze.
2. Roman ornament, from the so called "Florentine Pilaster", a richly decorated marble relief in the Uffizi, Florence, (Jacobsthal).
3. Romanesque frieze, St. Denis, (Lièvre).
4. Early Gothic, Notre Dame, Paris, (Lièvre).
5. Renascence ornament, relief on the tomb of Hieronimo Basso, Sta. Maria del Popolo, Rome, by Sansovino, (Gropius).

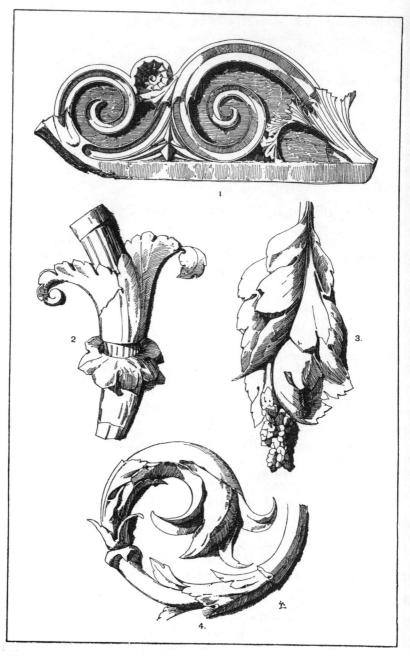

Plate 24.   Artificial Foliage.

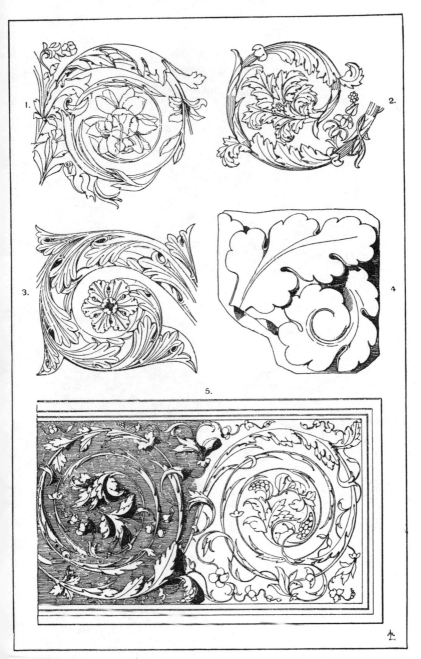

Artificial Foliage. Plate 25.

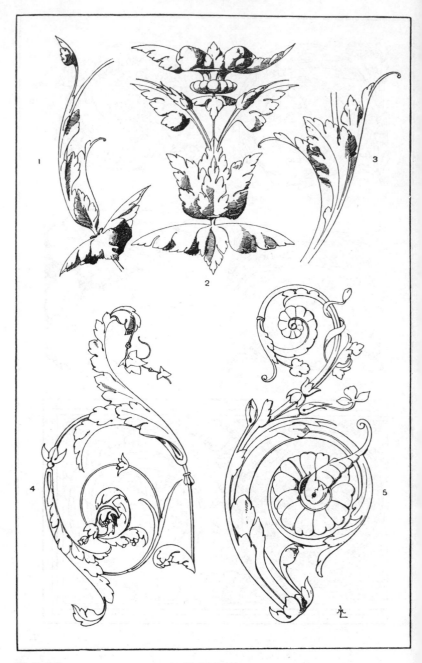

Plate 26.   Artificial Foliage.

PLATE 26. ARTIFICIAL FOLIAGE.

1—3. Details from a relief on the lectern, cathedral, Limoges, (Lièvre).
4. Ornament, Louis XVI. style, (F. A. M., Cours d'ornement).
5. Modern French ornament, (F. A. M.).

THE LAUREL, AND THE OLIVE. (Plates 27, 28.)

The Laurel and the Olive owe their introduction into ornamentation to their symbolical significance. Both played a conspicuous part in the tree worship of the ancient Greeks. The Laurel was sacred to Apollo. It was the symbol of atonement; singers and conquering heroes were crowned with it; and in a similar sense it is still used as a symbol of glory.

The Olive was sacred to Athene; Olive branches were the prize of victory et the Olympian games. In Rome the victorious, Laurel-crowned heroes were met on their return home by slaves bearing wreaths of Olive boughs. The Olive branch is the symbol of peace.

PLATE 27. THE LAUREL, &c. FROM NATURE.

1. Laurel *(Laurus nobilis)*. Evergreen; blossoms yellowish white; fruit ball or egg shaped, blue black.
2. Olive *(Olea europea)*. Evergreen; blossoms small, white; fruit oval, greenish, or black.

PLATE 28. THE LAUREL, &c.

1—2. Branches, Greek vase, conventional painting, (Owen Jones).
3. Branches, beaker, in the silver treasure, Hildesheim, Roman, Original of chased silver, museum, Berlin.
4. Fragment, Roman marble relief.
5. Branch, intarsia panel, Palazzo Ducale, Mantua, (Meurer).
6. Branch, spanrail, Louis XVI. style, (Lièvre).
7. Band, French Renascence.

THE VINE. (Plates 29, 30.)

Although the Vine does not occur frequently, it is not an unpopular element of artistic decoration. The Antique and Medieval styles, in particular, show a certain preference for the vine.

In Antiquity the Vine *(Vitis vinifera)* is the attribute of Bacchus. Vine leaves and Ivy, sometimes in connection with Laurel, encircle the brows of Bacchantes, and adorn their drinking-vessels and utensils, the thyrsus, kantharos, &c.

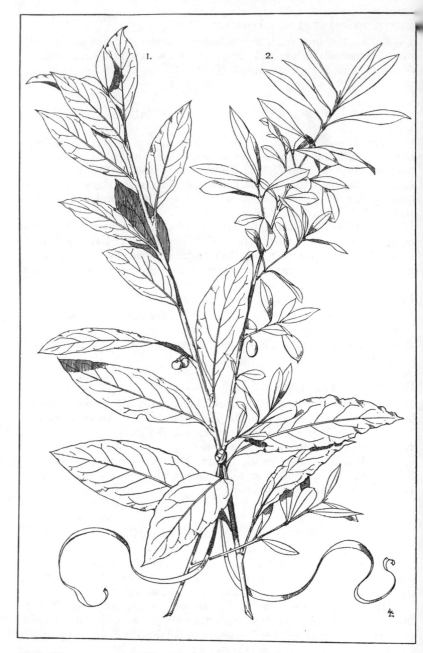

Plate 27.   The Laurel, and the Olive.

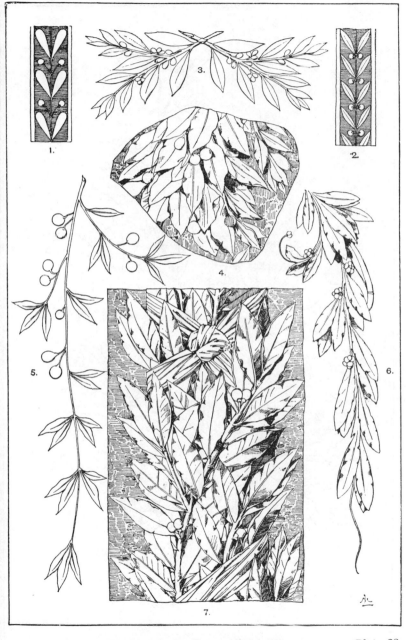

The Laurel, the Bay, and the Olive.   Plate 28.

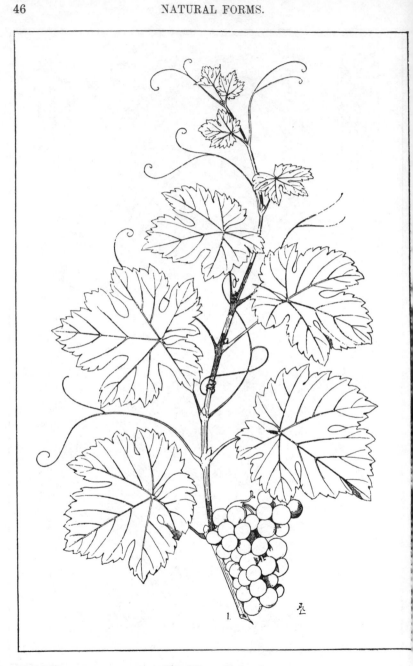

Plate 29.   The Vine: Natural.

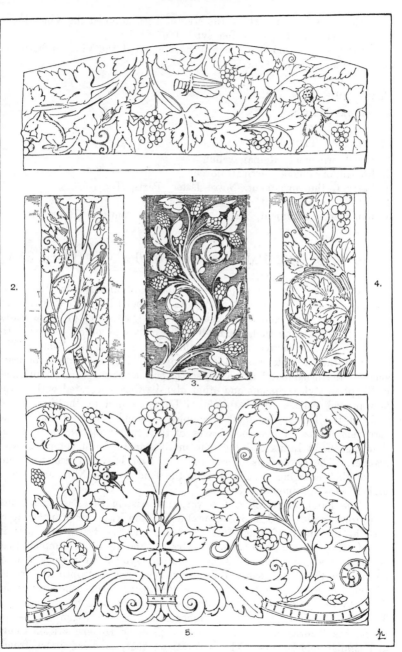

The Vine: Artificial. Plate 30.

The ecclesiastical art of the Middle Ages adopted the Vine, together with ears of Corn, as the symbol of Christ.

Later styles, and Modern art, have adopted the Vine in both the antique and medieval senses.

PLATE 29. THE VINE.

1. Natural branch.

PLATE 30. THE VINE.

1. Scroll ornament, Roman relief.
2. Roman ornament, vertical Border.
3. Early Gothic ornament, Notre Dame, Paris, (Lièvre).
4. Renascence ornament, Italian pilaster.
5. Renascence ornament, frieze, Venice, 16th century, (Grüner).

THE LOTUS, THE PAPYRUS, AND THE PALM.   (Plate 31.)

The Lotus and the Papyrus are plants of ancient oriental civilisation; and play an important part in the social life of the Egyptians, Hindoos, Assyrians, and other nations. The dried stalks of these water plants were used as fuel, or made into mats and other plaited articles; their roots served as food; the pith as wicks for lamps. The paper of the ancients was made of Papyrus. This explain sits appearance in the ornamental art of these nations, and its special luxuriance, in Egyptian style. Spoons and other utensils were decorated with Lotus flowers and calices; the capitals of Columns imitate the flowers or buds of the Lotus: the shaft resemples a bound group of stalks; the base reminds us of the root leaves of these water plants; their mural Painting shows Lotus and Papyrus motives in the most comprehensive manner. The Lotus was sacred to Osiris and Isis, and was the symbol of the recurring fertilisation of the land by the Nile, and, in a higher sense, of immortality.

The Palm, of which a few varieties exist in the East and South of Europe, is also used in ornamental art. Palm leaves or branches were used at the entry of kings into Jerusalem, at the feasts of Osiris in Egypt, at the Olympian games in Greece, and in the triumphal processions of ancient Rome. They were the symbol of victory and of peace. In this latter sense they have been received into the ritual of the Christian church. The late Renascence and following styles down to the present day have made a decorative use of palm leaves. The symbolic significance in a higher sense, as the token of eternal peace, has secured for the Palm leaf a place in Modern art on tombs and similar monuments. The decorative effect, of dried palm fronds

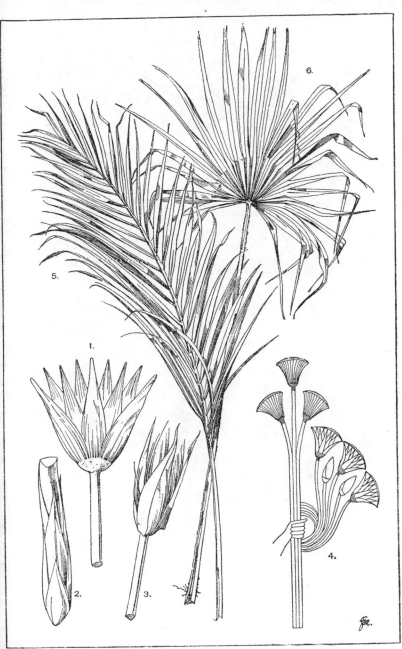

The Lotus, the Papyrus, and the Palm.   Plate 31.

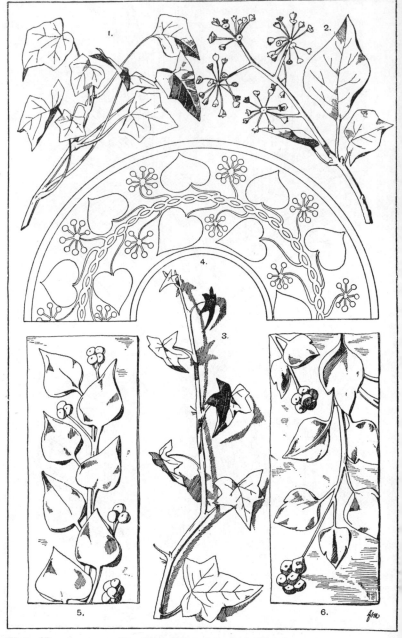

Plate 32.   The Ivy: Natural, and Artificial.

along with tufts of grasses and the like, has brought them into fashion as a finish to the artistic adornment of rooms.

PLATE 31.   THE LOTUS, &c., FROM NATURE.

1.   Lotus flower *(Nymphaea Nelumbo* — Indian water lily).
2 and 3.   Lower end and half-opened bud of the Papyrus plant *(Cyperus Papyrus L. — Papyrus antiquorum* Willd).
4.   Idealised Lotus and Papyrus, Egyptian mural painting, (Owen Jones).
5.   Frond of an Areca Palm *(Areca rubra* — in Asia as a tree, the so called *Pinang).* The species Chamaedorea and Phoenix have similar fronds.
6.   Leaf of a Fan Palm *(Corypha australis).* The species *Latania, Chamaerops, Borassus,* &c., have a leaf of similar shape.

THE IVY.   (Plate 32.)

The Ivy *(hedera helix)* is indigenous to the East, North Africa, South and Central Europe, and England.   It is an evergreen climbing shrub which develops into a tree under favourable circumstances.   In ancient times it was sacred to Bacchus.   Beakers for filtering wine were made of ivy wood.   As an attribute of Bacchus it is found twined round the thyrsus which the bacchantes flourished in their hands in processions and dances.   The Ivy is a common decorative ornament on ancient vases.   It was also the symbol of friendship, especially of the weaker with the stronger.   Ivy leaves are of very various shapes.   Usually broad and five-lobed, they appear at the ends of young shoots in long pointed, lance-like forms.   Flowering twigs have leaves without indentations, heart-shaped, with elliptic or oval tapering.   The latter forms in particular were adopted by Antique art.

PLATE 32.   THE IVY.

1. Spray with broad-lobed leaves, from Nature.
2. Spray with elliptic tapering leaves, after blooming, from Nature.
3. Spray with lanceolate leaves, from Nature.
4. Decoration of the neck of a Greek Hydria, Campana collection, (L'art pour tous).
5. Upper part of a pilaster like-panel, Antique.
6. Fragment of decoration, Roman column, Vatican, Rome.

The Corn, the Hop, the Convolvulus, and the Bryony.
(Plates 33, 34.)

Seeing how important agriculture has been in all ages, it was impossible that decorative art should neglect the ears of Wheat, although their comparatively scanty ornamental possibilities prevented any very extensive application. Combined with other motives, ears of Corn have been made use of in various styles. In ecclesiastical art they have a symbolical significance (See what was said of the Vine).

The Hop *(Humulus lupulus)* is a well known indigenous plant of civilisation, and also occurs wild in marshy woods. Its picturesque qualities indicate it as well adapted for ornamental use. In combination with ears of Barley, it is applied in Modern art to the decoration of Beer-mugs, the walls of Inns, &c.

The Convolvulus *(Convolvulus)*, an indigenous climbing plant of ornamental appearance, is frequently used in Modern art.

The Bryony *(Bryonia)* has delicate tendrils and beautifully in- dented leaves, which afford a fertile motive, so that it is astonishing that this, and other allied plants have hitherto found comparatively little favor in decorative art.

Plate 33. The Corn, &c.

1. Ears of Oats *(Avena sativa)*.
2. Ears of Rye *(Secale cereale)*.
3. Ears of Wheat *(Triticum vulgare)*.
4. Ears of Spelt *(Triticum spelta)*.
5. Ears of the common Barley *(Hordeum distichum)*.
6. Ears of the battledore Barley *(Hordeum zeokriton)*.
7. Field Convonvulus *(Convolvulus arvensis)* with red flowers. The hedge Convolvulus *(Convolvulus sepium)* has a similar habit and white flowers. (The group has been sketched freely from a cast from nature, by Bofinger of Stuttgart.)

Plate 34. The Hop, &c.

Hops and Bryony (drawn from pressed plants).

Various Leaves.   (Plate 35.)

Plate 35 presents a series of various leaves, whose general orna- mental possibilities have either secured or deserve to secure for them a place in art.

The Oak, the king of our indigenous trees, the symbol of power

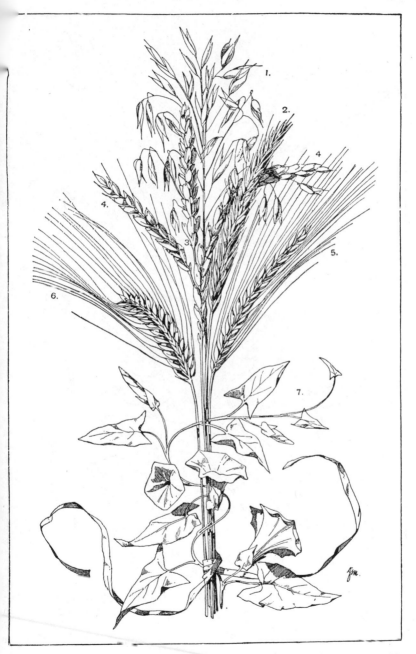

The Corn, and the Convolvulus.   Plate 33.

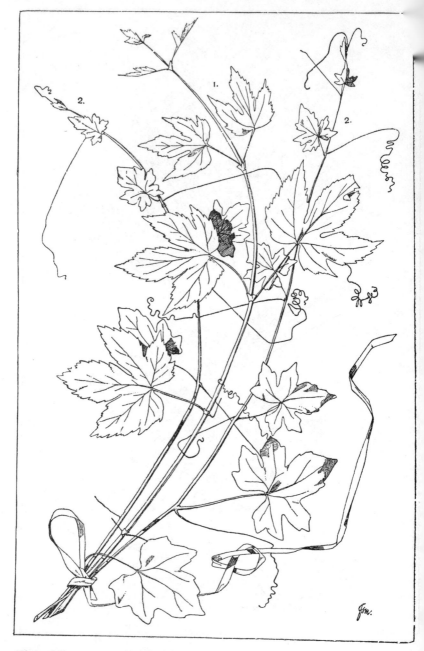

Plate 34.   The Hop, and the Bryony.

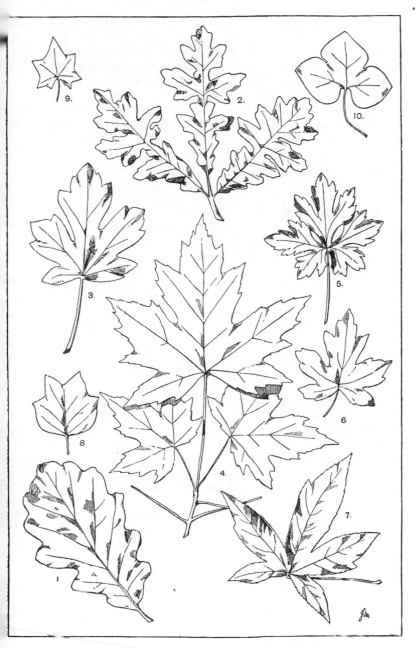

Various Leaves.   Plate 35.

and strength, in antiquity the tree of Jupiter, has from time to time been used in every western style. Oak foliage, and perhaps almost as frequently the leaves of the Maple, are often used in early Gothic, where we meet them on friezes, cornices, and columns. The frequent recurrence of oak leaves, in certain works of the Italian Renascence, is due to the fact that the Oak was the crest of the family of della Rovere (*Rovere* = winter oak; two members of which family ascended the papal chair, as Sixtus IV. and Julius II.). Oak, sometimes alternating with laurel, is a usual ornament of medals and coins.

PLATE 35. OAK LEAVES, &c.

1. Leaf of the winter Oak *(Quercus sessiliflora)*.
2. Spray of the bitter Oak *(Quercus cèrris)*.
3. Leaf of the Maple *(Acer campestre)*.
4. Spray of the sugar Maple *(Acer plantanoides)*.
5. Leaf of a species of Ranunculus.
6. Leaf of the oriental Amber tree *(Liquidamber orientale)*.
7. Leaf of the American Amber tree *(Liquidamber Styraciflua)*.
   (This tree furnishes the Storax or Styrax, a kind of resin.)
8. Leaf of the Tulip tree *(Liriodendron tulipifera)*.
9. Leaf of the climbing Mikania *(Mikania scandens)*.
10. Leaf of the Liverwort *(Hepatica triloba)*.

VARIOUS FLOWERS. (Plates 36, 37.)

It need scarcely be said that flowers, these most beautiful products of the plant world, have in all ages been exceedingly popular in ornamental art. In flat as well as in relief ornament they are used in the most manifold forms, as bouquets, garlands, wreaths, &c. Flower-painting for decorative purposes (fans, tapestry, &c.) has developed into a distinct branch of art. Flowers, with their natural developement from a centre, are the most obvious models for the formation of Rosettes (rosette = little rose). The Rosettes on the well-known sarcophagus of Scipio, the rosette Bosses on the doors of the Antique and the Italian Renascence, are striking examples of this.

The realm of Flowers is so extensive that we must confine ourselves to a few examples.

Plate 36 gives a variety of single flowers (drawn from casts from nature by J. G. Bofinger of Stuttgart): Plate 37 shows a bouquet of flowers.

PLATE 36. VARIOUS FLOWERS.

1. Alpine Rose *(Rhododendron)*.

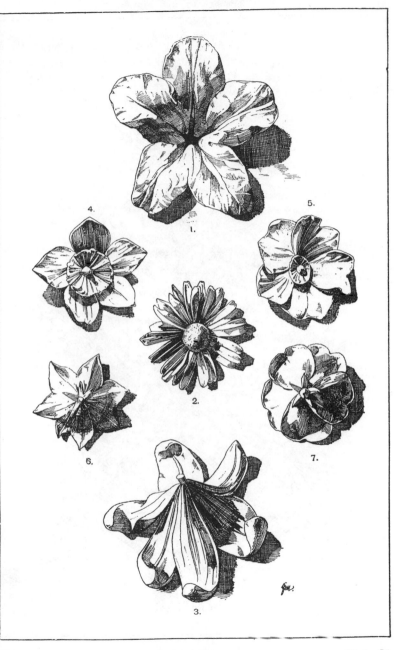

Various Flowers. Plate 36.

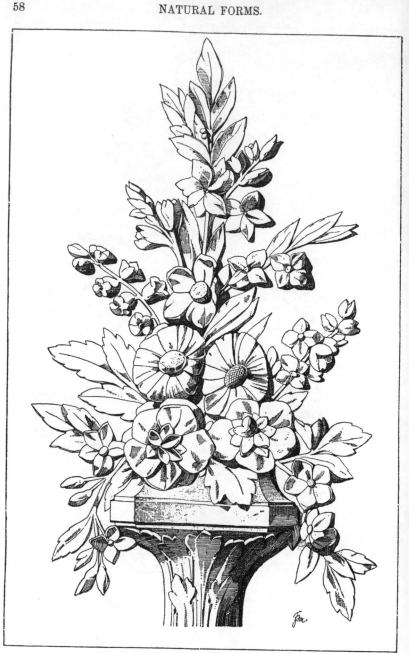

Plate 37.   Various Flowers.

2. Chrysanthemum.
3. White Lily *(Lilium candidum)*.
4. Hellebore *(Helleborus)*.
5. Wild Rose *(Rosa canina)*.
6. Blue-bell *(Campanula)*.
7. Wild Rose, seen from the back.

PLATE 37. VARIOUS FLOWERS.

Bouquet, carving, Louis XVI. style, (F. A. M., Cours d'ornement).

THE FRUIT FESTOON. (Plates 38—40.)

Fruit, tied in a bunch with leaves and flowers, was a popular decorative motive of the Roman, Renascence, and later styles. We may mention the hanging clusters as a decoration of pilaster and similar panels; and the clusters hanging in a curve and known as Festoons. In these cases: flowing ribbons fill up the empty spaces. The plates give examples of both kinds.

Festoons of fruits hanging in deep curves between rosettes, candelabra, skulls of animals, &c., are common in the Roman style. The origin of this style of decoration is to be sought in the circumstance that Festoons of real fruit were hung as a decoration on the friezes of the temples, alternating with the real Skulls of slaughtered sacrificial animals, in connection with the Candelabra, Tripods, and other sacrificial Instruments. This style of decoration was then transferred from sacred to secular architecture, revived by the Renascence in more or less altered forms, and has remained in use to the present time. In the Roman style the empty space above the centre of the curve is often filled by Rosettes, Masks, and Figures. These features were usually replaced by heads of Angels on the ecclesiatical buildings and tombs of the Italian Renascence.

PLATE 38. THE FRUIT FESTOON.

1. Cluster, Libreria, Cathedral, Siena, Italian Renascence.
2. Cluster, tomb of Louis XII. St. Denis, French Renascence.
3. Cluster, Modern.
4. Festoon, tomb of Cardinal della Rovere, St. Maria del Popolo, Rome, Italian Renascence.

PLATE 39. THE FRUIT FESTOON.

1. Festoon, between skulls, Roman.
2. Festoon, Roman mortuary tablet, Vatican.

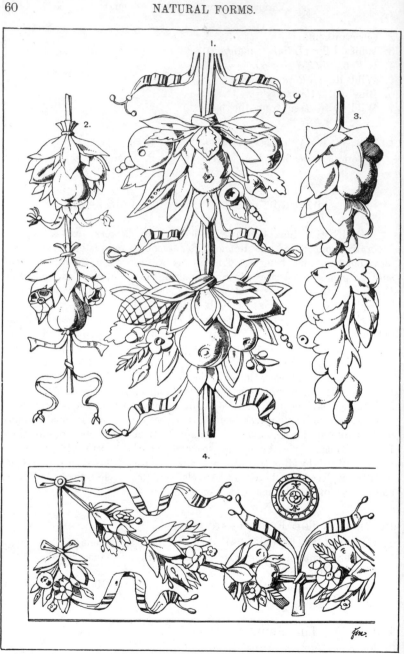

Plate 38.   The Fruit Festoon.

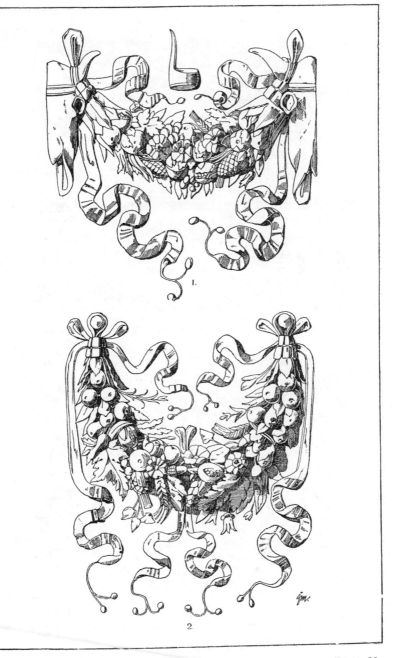

The Fruit Festoon.

Plate 39.

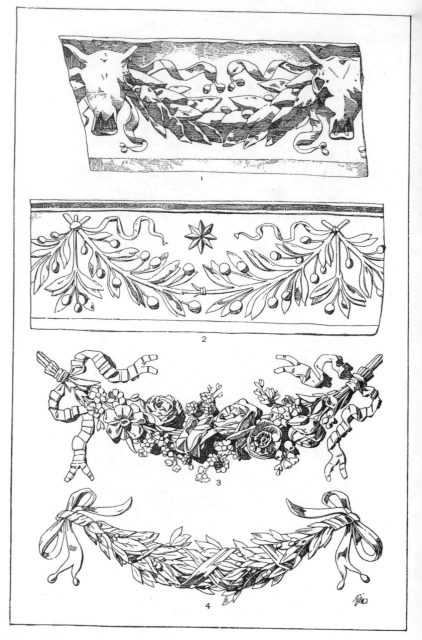

Plate 40.   The Leaf, and Flower Festoon.

PLATE 40. THE LEAF FESTOON, &c.

1. Festoon between skulls, Roman.
2. Festoon, tomb of Beatrice and Lavinia Ponzetti, Sta. Maria della Pace, Rome, Renascence, by Baldassare Peruzzi.
3. Festoon, Louis XVI. style.
4. Festoon, Modern, Paris, (Raguenet).

---

b. Animal Organisms (The Fauna of Ornament).

By the side of the Flora, stand the Fauna of ornament. The use of Animals, in natural or idealised forms, is considerable; but, compared with that of Plant-forms, it is less extensive. The reason of this is obvious: that greater difficulties stood in the way of the adaptation of animal forms than in the use of plant motives. The absence of Animals in the Mahometan styles is due to religious maxims which forbade or limited the use of representations of living Beings.

Following the same direction as was taken in the Flora, we shall find that the principal representations from the Fauna are not, as might be supposed, those of domestic animals such as the horse, the dog and the like, but that the selection was guided first by the symbolic character, and next by the ornamental possibilities of each.

If we disregard the more accidental naturalistic use of animals, such as enliven scroll ornaments in the shape of butterflies, birds, reptiles, and other animals, and confine our attention to those independent forms of animal ornament which have become typical; they will be found to diminish to a comparatively small number, the most important of which will here be treated in detail. Of the mammalia we have first to mention the Lion, Tiger and Panther, the Ox, the Horse, and the Goat; the Delphin also finds a place. The Eagle is the only bird which has been generally used. Then come the fantastic forms of fabulous animals: the Griffin, the double headed Eagle, &c.

THE LION. (Plates 41—44.)

The Lion (Felis leo) holds the first rank in ornamental fauna. His strength, his courage, and his nobility, have assured him from the earliest times the Title of "King of Beasts". His majestic stature, his compact, proportionate build, his striking muscles, offer grateful problems to art. Lying, walking, sitting, fighting, conquering or conquered, he is an often-used motive.

Lion scenes and lion hunts are common subjects on the palaces of the Assyrian kings. Characteristic, natural movements, and a distinctive rendering of the muscles, give these idealised representations a peculiar charm and a certain grandeur.

The Lion was used in the Egyptian religion. The fact that the annual overflow of the Nile, so fertilising and of such immense importance for the land, occurred at the time when the sun entered the sign of the Lion, brought the animal into relation with water; and led to representations on pails and other vessels for water, &c. Egyptian art usually idealises the Lion till he is unrecognisable; it represents him at rest; and the simple, severe treatment of the mane (not unlike a stiff ruff) gives him somewhat of the appearance of the Lioness, which does not posses one.

Among the Greeks and Romans the Lion was considered as the guardian of springs, of gates, and temples; hence his appearance at fountains, on flights of steps, over gates, and on monuments. The sleeping Lion is the symbol of the fallen hero. (The lion of the Piraeus, the tomb of Leonidas, and the tombs of Halicarnassus, may be quoted as evidence.)

In Christian art: the symbolism of the Lion is various: as the emblem of the Redeemer (the Lion of the Tribe of Judah), as the emblem of the evil principle and of the enemies of the church as well as of the Devil himself (the enemy who goeth about as a roaring lion, seeking whom he may devour), as the attribute of the evangelist St. Mark, and of other saints. Hence his frequent appearance on the vessels, and other articles of religious use, &c.

In consequence of the crusades in the 12th century, he was introduced into Heraldry, in which he became the most popular animal figure. As a heraldic creature he was severely idealised, (see Division III, under Heraldry).

In the Renascence period, the Lion is represented in all of the foregoing uses.

In the Rococo period, there was little skill, and little understanding, for the figure of the Lion.

Modern art follows the example of the Antique and the Renascence; and thus it comes that in the present day the Lion enjoys the lion's share in decoration.

It is remarkable that in all ages, when representing the Lion, Artists have given to his countenance something of a human type, by using the oval eye of man, instead of the round Cat-like eye, (Compare, Plate 47, fig. 1).*

Plates 41—43 show the Lion in naturalistic treatment, and also the conventional treatments of the various epochs; Plate 44 is devoted to heraldic treatments.

---

* An exhaustive article, entitled "Der Löwe in der Kunst," by Const. Uhde, will be found in the "Gewerbehalle," 1872. pp. 81 et seqq.

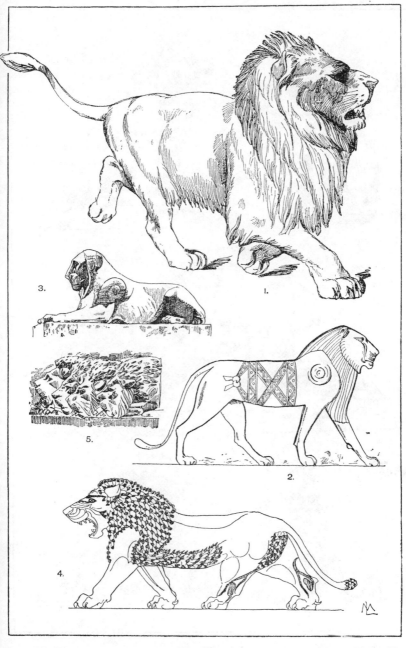

The Lion. Plate 41.

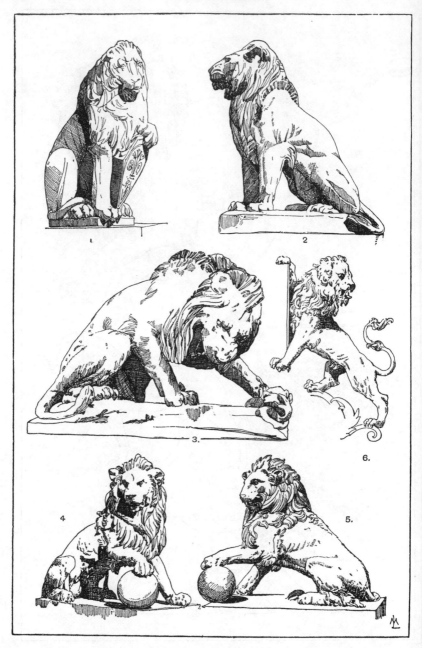

Plate 42.   The Lion.

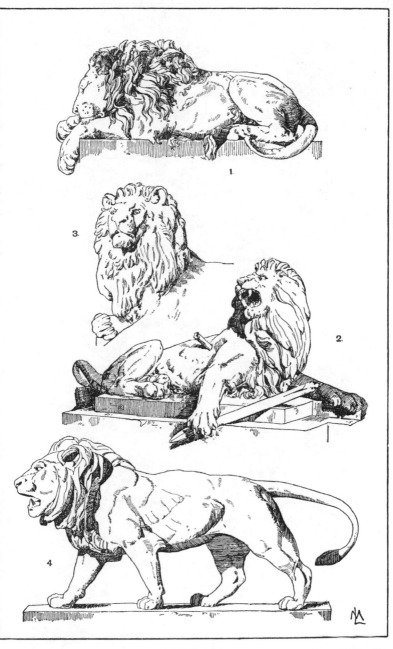

The Lion. Plate 43.

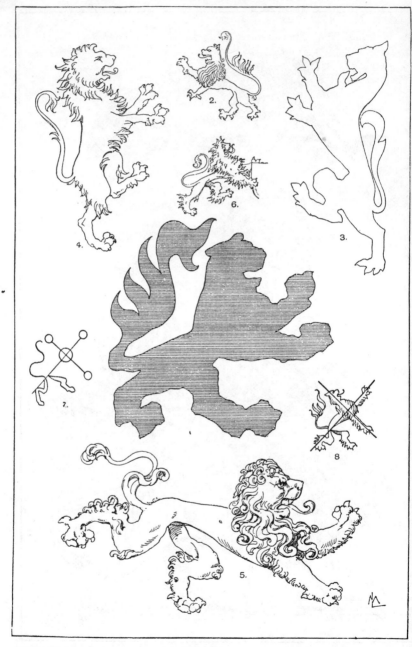

Plate 44. The Lion.

PLATE 41. THE LION.

1. Walking Lion, from Nature, (Münchener Bilderbogen).
2. Egyptian Lion, relief with sunken outlines, temple, Dachel, (Raguenet).
3. Egyptian Lion, Capitol, Rome, (Raguenet).
4. Assyrian Lion, glazed clay slabs, royal palace, Khorsabad, 6th century B. C.
5. Heads of slaughtered lions, Assyrian bas-relief, British Museum.

PLATE 42. THE LION.

1. Lion supporting a shield (called "il Marzocco"), by Donatello, National Museum, Florence, Italian, 15th century.
2. Lion, front of the Louvre, Paris, Modern, by Barye, (Baldus, Raguenet).
3. Lion, Tuileries, Paris, Modern, (Baldus, Raguenet).
4 and 5. Lion, in front of the palace of the Cortes, Madrid, Modern, (Raguenet).
6. Lion supporting a shield, Modern, (Raguenet).

PLATE 43. THE LION.

1. Sleeping Lion, monument to Pope Clement XIII., St. Peter's, Rome, by Canova.
2. Wounded Lion, Kriegerdenkmal, Hannover, by Professor Volz, of Carlsruhe.
3. Head of the Companion of the above.
4. Walking Lion, Modern, French.

PLATE 44. THE LION.

1. Lion, in pavement, town hall, Lüneburg.
2. Lion, shield of Johann of Heringen, register of the university of Erfurt, 1487, (Heraldische Meisterwerke).
3. Lion, coat of arms, Inlaid marble work, Sta. Croce, Florence. Italian Renascence, (Teirich, Eingelegte Marmorornamente).
4. Lion, coat of arms, Intarsia panel, Sta. Maria Novella, Florence, Italian Renascence, (Meurer, Flachornamente).
5. Lion, tomb in Wertheim, German, 16th century, by Johann of Trarbach.
6. Lion supporting a shield, mural decoration, Modern, (Heraldische Meisterwerke).
7 —8. Heraldic Lions, Albrecht Dürer.

THE GRIFFIN, AND THE CHIMAERA. (Plates 45 and 46.)

In addition to the imitations of natural animals there have been, from the earlist times, various fabulous Monsters, which were composed of parts of several different animals.

Centaurs, Sphinxes, the Assyrian human Lions, Lion and Eagle men, combine the human and the animal body. The combination, of different animal-forms with one another, leads to Monsters, the chief representatives of which are the Griffin, and the Chimaera. The Griffin is the union of a Lion's body with the head and wings of an Eagle. The fore extremities may belong either to the Lion or the Eagle. As the Lion with water, so the Griffin is associated in Antiquity with fire; hence his frequent appearance with Candelabra on friezes, &c. In Heraldry the Griffin is the symbol of wisdom, and watchfulness.

There are other combinations; e. g. the Chimaera, the Hippogriff, the Ichthyogriff, &c., which may be seen in Pompejan decoration.

PLATE 45. THE GRIFFIN.

1. Greek Griffin, Fragment, Museum, Naples.
2. Roman Griffin, Fragment.
3. Griffin, Renascence.

PLATE 46. THE GRIFFIN, &c.

1. Head of an Assyrian eagle-headed Personage, ⎫
2. Head of an Assyrian lion-headed Personage, ⎬ British Museum.
   ⎭
3. Roman Chimaera, Vatican.
4. Sitting Griffin, support of a seat, Castle of Gaillon, French Renascence, (F. A. M., Cours d'ornement).
5. Winged Lion, tomb of Loys de Breszé, Rouen cathedral, 1535—1544.
6. Winged Lioness, as supporter, Louvre, Paris, Modern, (Baldus).
7. Sitting winged Lioness, Casa S. Isidora, Santiago, Chili, Modern, French, (Raguenet).

THE LION HEAD. (Plates 47, 48.)

The Lion head has been still more extensively applied than the entire figure of the Lion. It is found in countless examples: — as a Gargoyle on the temples of the Antique, as a Spout on vessels, with a ring in the jaw as a Handle and Knocker on the doors of the portals of the Middle Ages and the Renascence; and as a purely decorative element like Bosses and Rosettes. The Antique created a

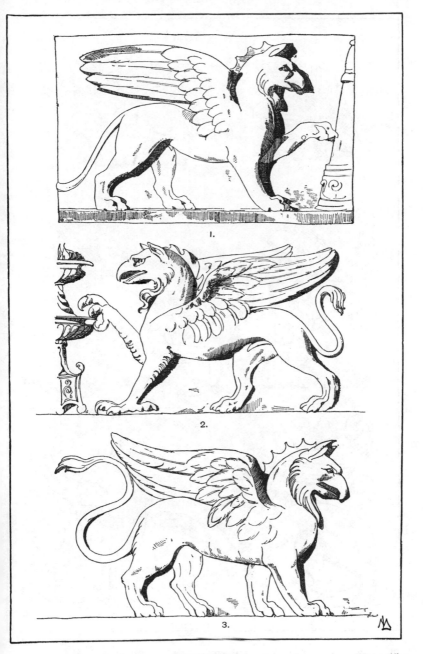

1.

2.

3.

The Griffin. Plate 45.

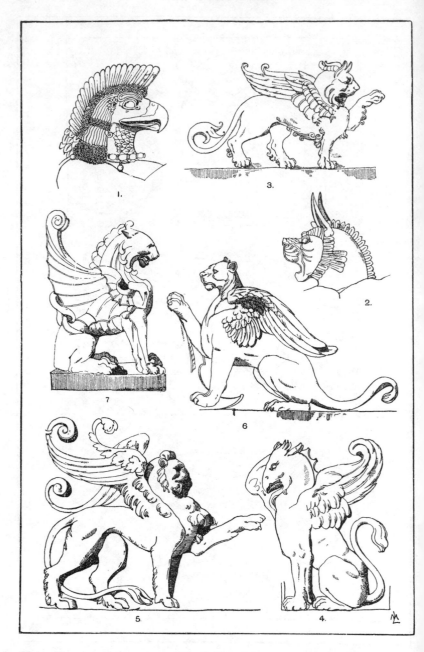

Plate 46. The Griffin, &c.

remarkable form by the direct union of the Lion head with one leg, to form the support of a Table, (See Division II, Supports, Plates 143 and 144).

PLATE 47. THE LION HEAD.

1. Head, prospectus of Dr. Schubert's Naturgeschichte.
2. Head, painting by Paul Meyerheim.
3. Gargoyle, Metapontum, Greek, (Gropius, Archiv.).
4. Gargoyle, terracotta, Athens, (Gropius).
5. Gargoyle, Parthenon, Athens.
6 and 7. Front and side view of an antique head, Vatican.

PLATE 48. THE LION HEAD.

1. Door knocker, Cathedral, Mainz, Romanesque.
2—3. Heads, in basrelief, by Ghiberti, Medallions inside the bronze doors, Baptistry, Florence, Italian Renascence, (Gropius).
4. Head, fountain of the sacristy, San Lorenzo, Florence, Italian Renascence.
5. Head, in medallion, Italian Renascence.
6. Head, Heidelberg castle, German Renascence.
7. Gargoyle, Opera House, Paris, Modern, French, Architect Garnier, (Raguenet).
8. Head, Modern, French, Architect Garnier, (Raguenet).
9. Head, in profile, Modern, French, by the sculptor Cain of Paris, (Raguenet).
10. Head, by Liénard, Modern, French.
11. Head, by Prof. Volz, of Carlsruhe.

THE LION HEAD, GOAT HEAD, &c. (Plates 49, 50.)

The Tiger *(Felis tigris)* and the Panther *(Felis pardus)* are sometimes found in antique works. Amorini, Bacchantes, and Maenads, gambol about on them or drive in carriages drawn by these creatures; and decorate themselves and their utensils with their skins.

Panther and Tiger heads, as well as the head of the Lynx *(Felis lynx)*, find from time to time similar application to the Lion head. Ram heads are a favourite form of corner ornament for the cornices of altars, and tripods; or serve, like the skulls of Oxen, as objects from which to hang festoons. The decorative use in both cases is connected with the use of the Ram as a sacrificial animal, (Compare p. 71).

Instead of real animal heads we sometimes meet with fantastic forms which may be described as Chimaera heads.

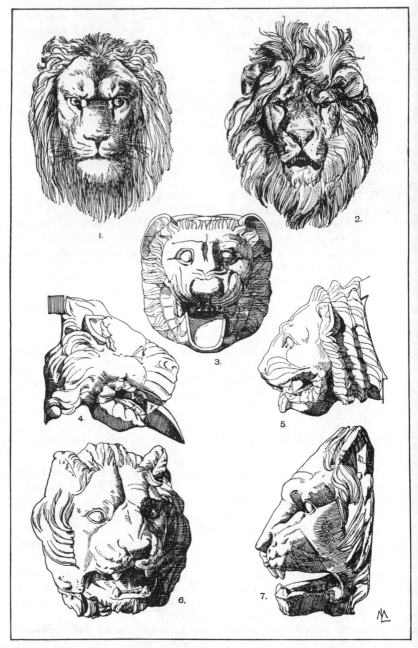

Plate 47.   The Lion Head.

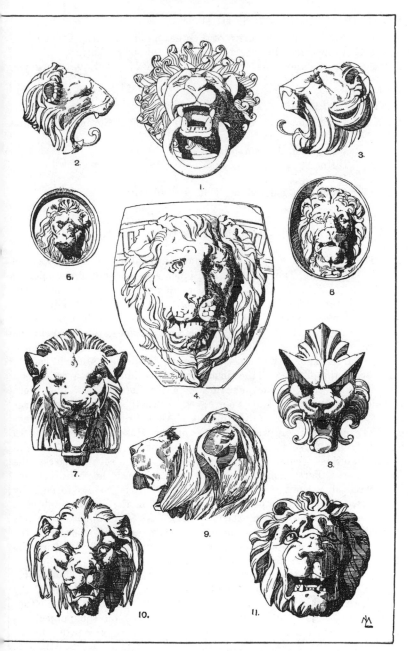

The Lion Head. Plate 48.

PLATE 49. THE PANTHER HEAD, &c.

1 and 2. Front and side view of Panther head, Modern, French.
3 and 4. Front and side view of Tiger head, from Nature.
5 and 6. Front and side view of Lynx head, Antique Gargoyle, Vatican.

PLATE 50. THE RAM HEAD, &c.

1 and 2. Front and side view of Chimaera head, Corner of antique three-sided altar.
3.   Ram head, Roman altar.
4.   Ditto.
5.   Ditto.
6 and 7. Front and side view of Ram head, Late Renascence.

HEADS OF VARIOUS ANIMALS. (Plate 51.)

The Horse *(Equus)* offers certain difficulties in the way of artistic imitation. The legs, for example, are too thin for rendering in Statues, except in Metal. This circumstance presents less hindrance to representations in bas-relief. As an isolated figure the Horse seldom occurs; he is more frequent in groups forming teams of two, three, and more *(biga, triga, quadriga)*, intended to be the crowning feature of monumental edifices (San Marco, Venice; Brandenburger Thor, Altes Museum, Berlin; Propylaea, Munich) mostly along with the figure of the man who leads him (Horse-tamers on the Monte Cavallo, Rome) or rides him (Statue of the Condottiere Bartolommeo Colleoni 1476, Venice; the colossal statues in the Burghof at Vienna; the Grosser Kurfürst, the Alter Fritz, the battle scenes by Kiss and Wolff on the staircases of the Museum at Berlin). In bas-relief: the horse is, almost without exception, represented only in profile (hunting scenes from the ancient Assyrian royal palaces, the frieze of the Parthenon). In grottesque Painting: he furnishes the fore parts of various monsters, the hinder parts being formed by fish tails, or in some other way. The use of the horse head as a medallion, on Stables, Riding-schools, Prize-cups, and numerous objects connected with sport, is common in Modern art. In Heraldry: the Horse occurs in a few cases (Shield of Stuttgart). In Japan: the Horse is symbolical; and is connected with the hours.

Still less adapted to ornamental purposes is the Ox; and representations are therefore exceedingly rare. The same is true of the Dog, the Pig, the Fox, the Stag, the Hare, &c., whose forms, either entire or as heads, are only used symbolically, on such objects as have some connection with Hunting (hunting weapons, powder horns, targets).

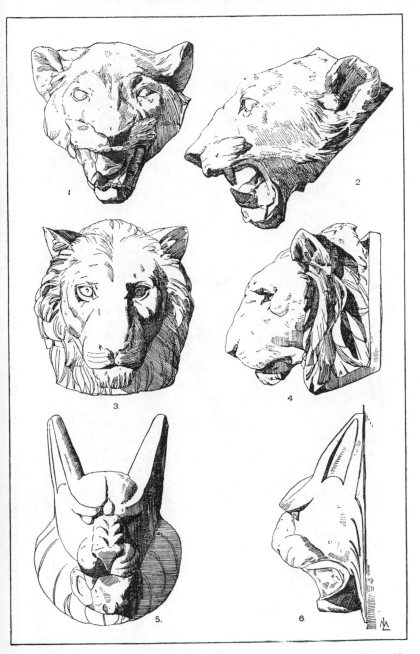

The Panther Head, &c.   Plate 49.

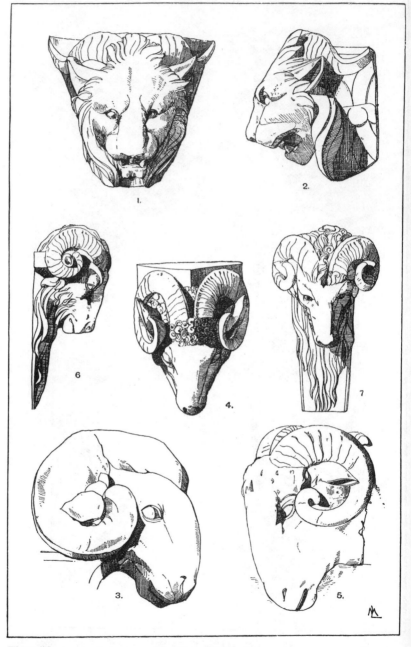

Plate 50. The Ram Head, &c.

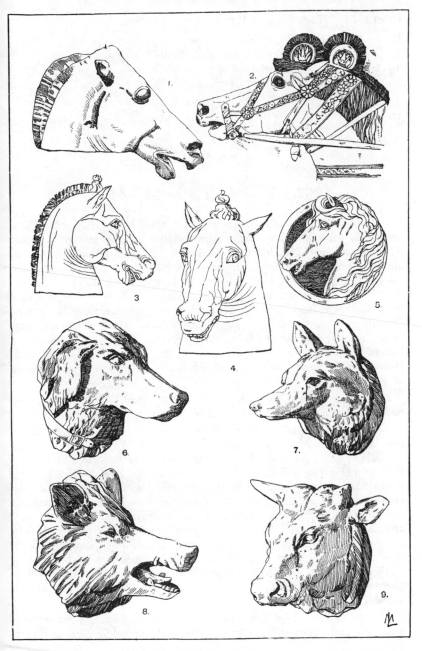

The Horse Head, &c. Plate 51.

PLATE 51. THE HORSE HEAD, &c.

1.   Horse head, Parthenon, Athens.
2.   Horse head, Assyrian basrelief, British Museum.
3—4. Antique Horse head.
5.   Horse head, Modern, German.
6.   Head of a hunting Dog, ⎫
7.   Head of a Fox,   ⎪
8.   Head of a Boar,   ⎬ by Habenschaden, of München.
9.   Head of an Ox,   ⎭

THE EAGLE. (Plates 52—54.)

Like the lion among quadrupeds, the Eagle *(Aquila, Falco fulvus)* is the most important representative of the feathered tribes. His size and strength, his majestic flight, his keen vision, distinguish him above all other birds. He has been used in decorative art since the earliest times, e. g. in the Persian, Assyrian, and Egyptian styles.

With the Greeks: he was the companion of Zeus, whose thunderbolts he keeps and guards; he carried off Ganymede on his wings. The Romans used him in the apotheoses of their emperors; and chose him for the standards of their legions. Napoleon I., imitating Roman caesarism, granted his armies the French Eagle in 1804. Hence the frequent appearance of the Eagle on trophies, and emblems of war.

In ecclesiastical àrt: the Eagle is the symbol of the evangelist S. John, whom he either accompanies, or symbolises independently.

The Eagle appears in Heraldry at a very early period, about the time of Charlemagne. Next to the Lion he is the most-used heraldic creature (e. g. the United States, Germany, Austria, Prussia, and France under the second empire, all possess the Eagle). His heraldic forms vary considerably from the natural one. Blue excepted, he appears in all the tinctures. The double-headed Eagle is a Byzantine invention. The heraldic eagle is a highly ornamental figure, so that, from the middle ages up to the present time, he has been employed not only for heraldic, but also for purely decorative purposes: he is seen in manifold forms in intarsia, cut or etched in metal, cut in leather, embroidered, woven, and painted; on weapons and tools, furniture, ceilings, and walls, (See the Heraldic treatment in Division III, Heraldry).

Our figures show him, natural as well as idealised, in various positions and conceptions; plate 53 shows his heraldic forms, (Comp. plate 284).

PLATE 52. THE EAGLE.

1. Young Eagle, in a scutella (dish), Roman.
2. Roman Eagle, pedestal of Trajan's column, Rome, (Raguenet).
3. Roman Eagle, Vatican, Rome, (Raguenet).
4. Roman Eagle in an oak garland, Bas-relief originally in Trajan's Forum, now in SS. Apostoli, Rome, (De Vico, Trenta tavole, &c.).
5. Sitting Eagle, modern, (Gerlach, Das Gewerbemonogramm).

PLATE 53. THE HERALDIC EAGLE.

1. Romanesque Eagle, Germanisches Museum, Nuremberg.
2. Eagle, Gothic style, Viollet-le-Duc, (Dictionnaire de l'architecture).
3. Eagle, Gothic style, oil painting, Germanisches Museum, Nuremberg.
4. Eagle, Gothic style, by Albrecht Dürer, (Hirth, Formenschatz).
5. Eagle, Renascence, by Albrecht Dürer, (Hirth).
6. Eagle, Renascence, (Hirth).
7. Eagle, Renascence, by Wenderlin Dietterlin, (Hirth).
8. Eagle, Modern, German, (Heraldische Meisterwerke).

PLATE 54. THE EAGLE.

1. Eagle, as Akroter, Flora pavillion, Louvre, Paris, Architect Lefuel, (Baldus).
2. Eagle, in a laurel garland, Modern, German, by Rauch.
3. Eagle, with olive branch, in medallion, Louvre, Paris, (Baldus).
4. Eagle, high relief, by Rauch, on monument, Berlin.
5. French Eagle, Modern, new Opera House, Paris, Architect Garnier, (Raguenet).
6. Flying Eagle, from Nature, (Raguenet).
7. Eagle, from nature.

THE WING. (Plate 55.)

As the small scale of the preceding plates does not admit of the details of the Wing being fully shown; and as draughtsmen, as well as modellers, are often called-upon to design winged shapes (besides the Eagle, Angels, Amorini, Genii, Grottesques, the Caduceus of Mercury, the symbolic Wheel of the railroad, &c,: we have thought it advisable to add a plate showing the details of the Wings on a somewhat larger scale. They are taken from nature; but will be found helpful for idealised renderings.

PLATE 55. THE WING.

1. Wing of a duck.
2. Wing of a wild goose.

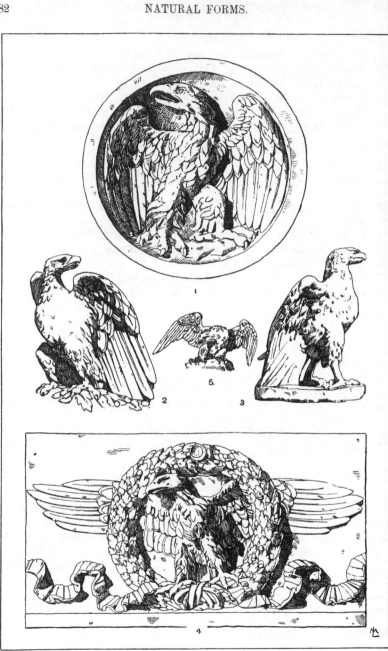

Plate 52.   The Eagle.

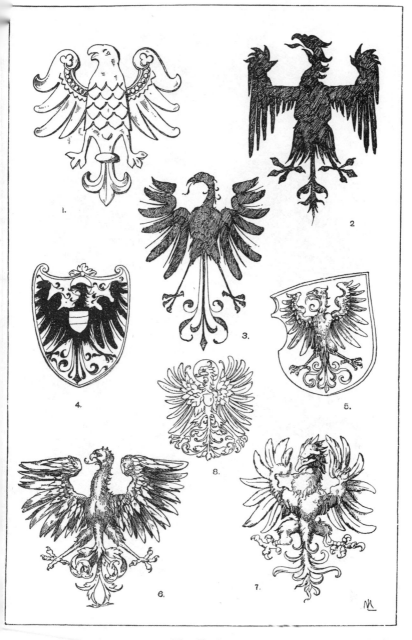

The Eagle. Plate 53.

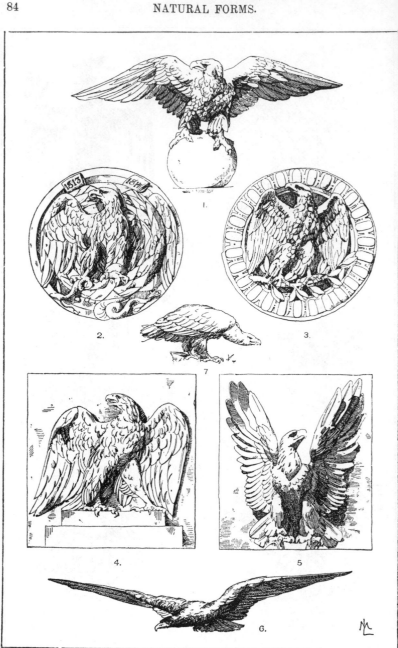

Plate 54.   The Eagle.

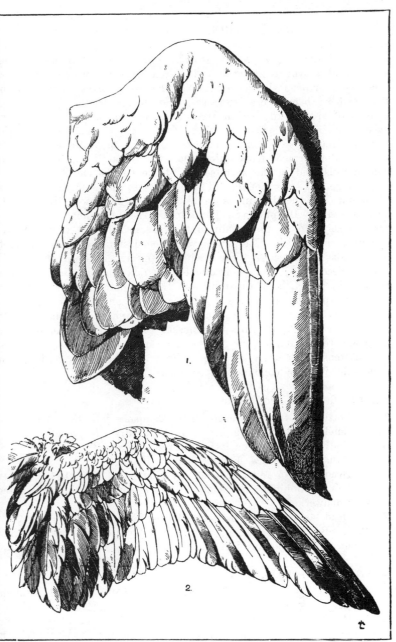

The Wing. Plate 55.

The Dolphin. (Plates 56—58.)

The Dolphin *(Delphinus delphis,* French, *dauphin)* has enjoyed
an unusual share of attention. This sea mammal, which has sometimes been erroneously classed among the fishes, lives in the seas of
the northern hemisphere, swarms round ships, swims in shoals, and
is fond of sport. In ancient times the Dolphin enjoyed, and enjoys
even now in some parts, a kind of veneration which protects him
from persecution. We meet him occasionally on Antique coins, on
Graeco-italic terracottas, on Pompeian mural paintings, on furniture
and utensils, and in the architecture of the Greeks and Romans.

Guigo IV. of Viennois (1140) took to himself the title of
"Dauphin", and the Dolphin as crest. One of his successors, Humbert II.,
surrendered the Dauphiny in 1349 to Charles of Valois, in exchange
for a legacy and on the condition that the heir to the throne should
always bear the title "Dauphin"; which condition was faithfully kept.
This is the explanation of the frequent appearance of the Dolphin in
French decoration; but its frequent appearance in Italian decoration.
is due to its artistic capabilities. The Dolphin is often used in
pilasters, panels, in intarsias, in ceilings and mural paintings,
in enamel, in niello work, and in typographical ornaments. In
modern styles the Dolphin often masks the spouts of fountains. In
symbolic representations he is the companion of Nymphs, Nereids,
and Tritons, and of Arion, Aphrodite, and Neptune, with whose
trident he is often combined in ornament.

Plate 56. The Dolphin.

1.   Portion of frieze, Graeco Italic, Campana collection, Paris.
2.   Shield of the French kings, 15th century, (Raguenet).
3.   Castle at Blois, French Renascence, (Raguenet).
4.   Italian Renascence, Louvre, Paris, (Raguenet).
5.   Head, from a relief, French, by Clodion (1738—1814).
6.   Pair of Dolphins, by Schinkel, (Vorbilder für Fabrikanten und
      Handwerker).
7.   Head, as spout, by Barbezat, Paris, (Raguenet).
8—9. Heads, as spouts, face and profile, (Hauptmann, Moderne Orna-
      mentale Werke im Stile der Italienischen Renascence).

Plate 57. The Dolphin.

1.   Frieze, Sta. Maria dell' Anima, Rome (1500 to 1514), Italian,
      (Raguenet).
2.   Panel ornament, French Renascence.
3.   Choir seats, Certosa near Pavia, Italian Renascence, (Teirich,
      Meurer).

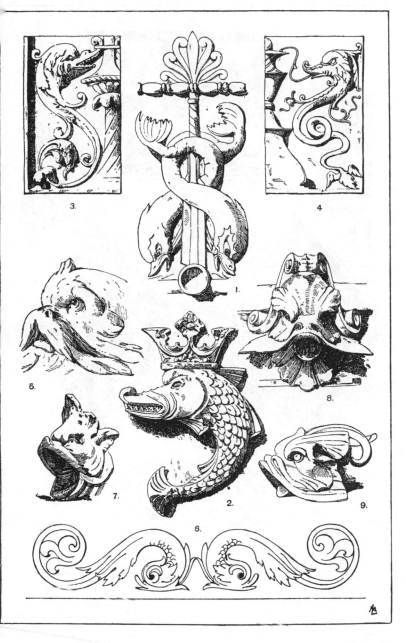

The Dolphin.

Plate 56.

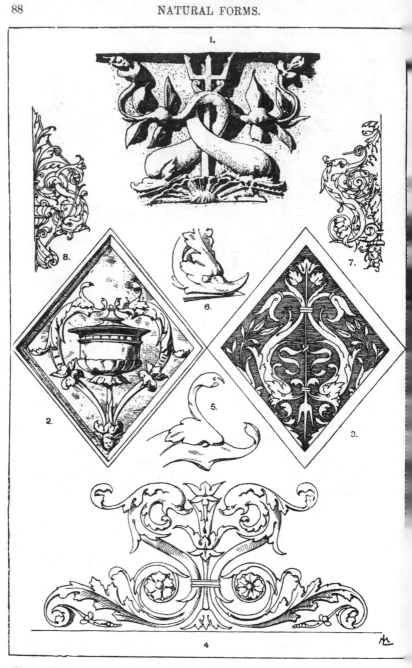

Plate 57.   The Dolphin.

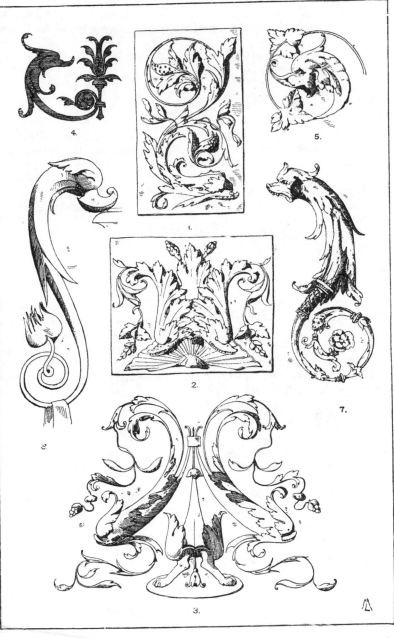

The Dolphin.

Plate 58.

4.   Part of Frieze, Rome, Arco della chiesa nuova, Italian Re-
      nascence, (Weissbach und Lottermoser, Architektonische Motive).
5—6. Heads.
7—8. Parts of Address by German artists, to king Humbert of Italy,
      by Director Götz.

PLATE 58. THE DOLPHIN.

1. Panel, Venetian Renascence.
2. Lower part of panel, Ducal Palace, Venice, Italian Renascence.
3. Part of frieze, Sta. Maria della Pace, Rome, by Bramante, 1504,
   Italian.
4. Part of Majolica Tile, Sta. Caterina, Siena, Italian Renascence.
5. Head, cathedral, Limoges, French Renascence.
6. Handle of a vessel, pilaster, by Benedetto da Majano, Italian Renascence.
7. Pen drawing, by Lucas von Leyden (1527).

THE SHELL. (Plate 59.)

Among molluscs: the Nautilus *(Nautilus Pompilius)* and various
shells, principally of the family of the Trochoidae, are placed on feet;
and, elegantly mounted in metal, serve as Drinking-vessels.

The Scallop shell is used as the top of cylindrical niches, as a
waterbasin in the form of a shallow dish, and as a decorative background for vases and busts. It was extensively employed for these
purposes in the later Renascence.

PLATE 59. THE SHELL.

1. Nautilus, from nature.
2. Snail *(Turbo marmoratus)*, from a Renascence drinking-vessel.
3. Exterior of the Scallop *(Ostrea Jacobaea — Pecten Jacobaeus)*,
   from nature.
4. Interior of the Scallop, after Jost Amman, (Hirth, Formenschatz).
5. Scallop design, Louis XVI. style, lower end of a panel.
6. Scallop design, by the sculptor Lehr, of Berlin.
7. Scallop design, for the decoration of a niche.

THE SERPENT. (Plate 60.)

The Serpent is occasionally used for symbolic and decorative
purposes. It is developed ints an antique Bracelet, and to a Handle
for vessels, a pair twine round the Staff of Mercury (the Caduceus,

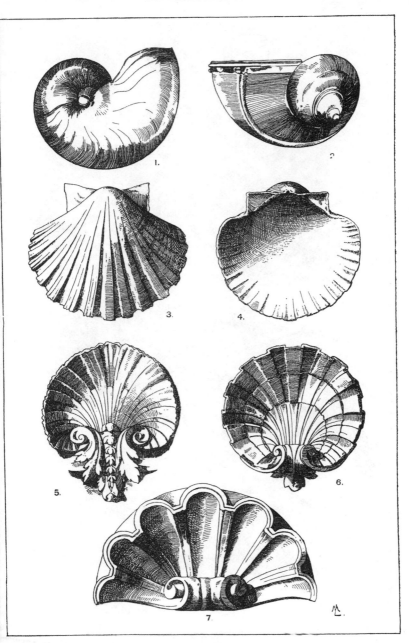

The Shell. Plate 59.

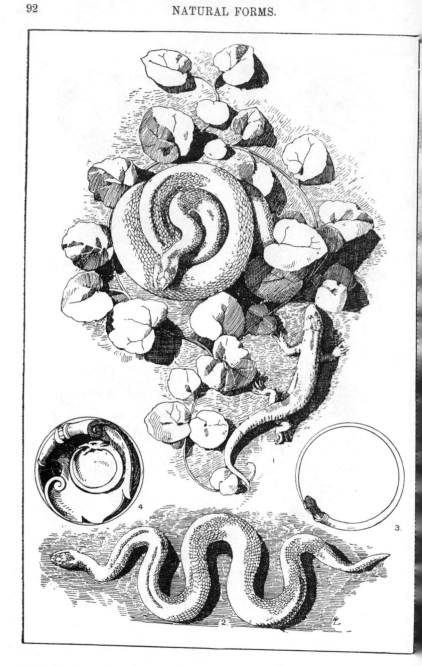

Plate 60.   The Serpent, &c.

comp. plate 76), and a single one round the staff of Esculapius. Coiled in a circle with tail in mouth it is the symbol of Eternity on tombs, it is used in mythology, and is an indispensable accompaniment of the symbols of Envy and Dissension; and the hair of Medusa is represented as composed of Serpents (Plate 65).

In ecclesiastical art: the Serpent is the symbol of Wickedness, Sin, and Temptation (the scene in Paradise); it appears under the feet of the Virgin Mary with an apple in its mouth. In Heraldry: it is represented devouring a child, on the shield of the Visconti, of Milano.

PLATE 60. THE SERPENT.

1. Cast from life of a Viper *(Vipera berus — Pelias berus)* with a Lizard *(Lacerta viridis — Lacerta agilis)*, by J. Eberhard of Heilbronn.
2. Cast from life of a Viper, by J. Eberhard of Heilbronn.
3. Antique bracelet in the form of a Viper, Pompeii.
4. The Snake as the symbol of Eternity, (Gerlach, Allegorien und Embleme).

---

c. *Human Organism.*

The human form has been, and is destined to be a favoured object of representation in art. The desire, to depict for contemporaries and to transmit to posterity, the great Deeds of individuals and the epoch-making Achievements and fate of whole races and nations, is universal among mankind; as also the attempt to reproduce the Portraits of celebrated Persons. Even the supernatural powers, his Gods, man represents in the form of men. The "Lord of creation" can give to the beings he venerates no more ideal form than his own, which he holds to be the most developed*. The Christian conception has arrived at the same result by the reverse process: "God created man in his own image." Virtues, Vices, Passions, Sciences and Arts, Ages, Seasons and Hours, Elements, Rivers, Countries, Hemispheres, and many other things receive symbolic expression; and are pictorially rendered by human figures. And the human body is often represented, without any meaning, and solely (decoratively)

---

* Mortals, however, opine that the Gods had an origin man-like;
Feel and have voices like men, like men have a bodily fashion.
Oxen and lions, no doubt, if they had but hands and a chisel,
Pencils as well, to depict the figure divine, would do likewise:
God for the horse were a horse, and God for the oxen were ox-like,
Each would think God like himself and give to his God his own
image.
Xenophanes of Colophon. 600 B. C.

on account of its beauty of form. All these delineations, which fall within the domain of high art, lie beyond the scope of this work. We have only to deal with the human figure so far as it has been received into decoration: we have only to occupy ourselves with "conventionalised" man. This includes the applications of the human face, more or less true to nature or with arbitrary accessions; masks and caricatures; grottesques, those strange combinations of human with animal or plant elements; and also the applications of the upper half of the human body as the starting-point of ornament; half-lengths as commencements of ornaments; those mixtures of human and animal shapes in which the upper half falls to the share of man, e. g.: — sphinxes, centaurs, &c.

The Mask. (Plate 61.)

The Mask, strictly so-called, is an artificial, hollow face, intended to be placed in front of, and to conceal the human countenance so as to make the wearer unrecognisable, or to characterize him in some special way. The use of the Mask dates back to the popular Harvest games of the earliest Greek period. From these games the mask is believed to have been transferred to the ancient Theatre, in which the actors all appeared masked. Different classes of Masks were recognised: tragic, comic, &c. Definite types of Masks were connected with definite characters and "persons". The mouth-openings of these Masks were unnaturally large and shaped like a bell-mouth, so as to reinforce the voice of the speaker; in Latin the mask is termed "persona" (from personare = to sound through). From theatrical, the Masks passed to artistic use, e. g. in the mural paintings of theatres and secular edifices (Pompeian decorations), on Bacchic vessels and other utensils (various beakers in the silver treasure of Hildesheim). The Renascence and the following styles have at times used Masks in decoration, altering and exaggerating the forms. In particular the Mask is often used for the decoration of the keystones of door and window arches. We may also mention the beautiful, freely-treated Heads of dying warriors by Schlüter on the arsenal at Berlin; and the Masks in Antique style on the new Opera House in Paris, by Garnier.

Plate 61. The Mask.

1.   Bacchus, Graeco Italic, fragment of a vessel or utensil.
2—3. Heads, goblet (Hildesheim treasure), Roman, Berlin Museum.
4.   Keystone, Graeco Italic, terracotta, Campana collection.
5.   Part of Frieze, Graeco Italic, Campana collection.
6.   Silenus, handle of Etruscan vessel.
7—8. Decoration, Pompeii.

9.   Satyr, Italian Renascence, by Sansovino, over a Festoon in
        Sta. Maria del Popolo, Rome.
10.   Dying warrior, by Schlüter, Berlin arsenal, 1697.

THE GROTTESQUE MASK. (Plates 62—64.)

Masks and Caricatures pass into each other, so that it is difficult to draw a strict line between them. The French language expresses this connection clearly, by using the related words "masque"
and "mascaron."

Under Masks are usually classed the delineations of beautiful
countenances, either true to nature or idealising it. Caricatures are
faces grinning, deformed, distorted by accessories, or terminating in
foliage.

The Antique, which had no love whatever for the depicting of
the ugly and bizarre, only used Caricatures in its oldest periods, in
the so-called Archaic style.

The Middle Ages frequently employed Caricatures.

The Renascence and Barocco styles, as well as our most Modern,
art, often apply Caricatures to keystones, to consoles, as spouts and
handles, on shields and cartouches, in capitals and panels, on the
backs of chairs, and in general on carved furniture, on stove-tiles, &c.
We possess a number of excellent Caricatures from the hand of the
youthful Michelangelo, who treated this form with predilection, and
with the breadth characteristic of his genius.

PLATE 62. THE GROTTESQUE MASK.

1.   Etruscan, terracotta, Campana collection, (F. A. M., Cours
        d'ornement).
2.   Grottesque, Italian Renascence, Venice.
3.   Grottesque, tomb of the cardinal Sforza, Sta. Maria del Popolo,
        Rome, Italian Renascence, by Sansovino.
4.   Single Grottesque, from frieze, Italian Renascence, by Michel-
        angelo, San Lorenzo, Florence.
5.   Part of capital of pilaster, French Renascence, tomb of Louis XII,
        St. Denis.
6—7.   Modern French Grottesques.

PLATE 63. THE GROTTESQUE MASK.

1.   Carved bench, Italian Renascence, Bargello, Florence.
2—3.   Female, metal shields, German Renascence.
4.   Akroter, Tribunal de Commerce, Paris.
5.   Grottesque, Louvre, Paris, (Baldus).

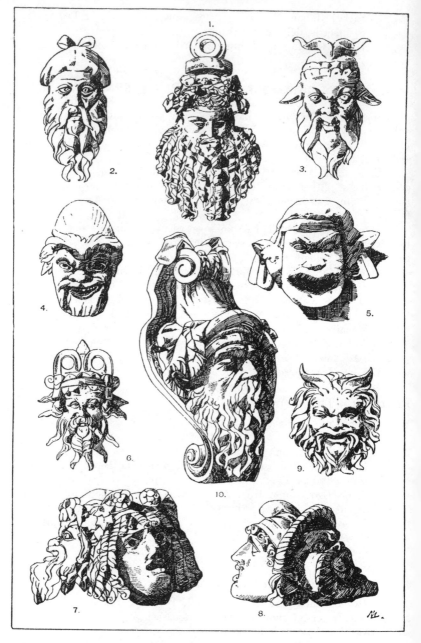

Plate 61. The Mask, &c.

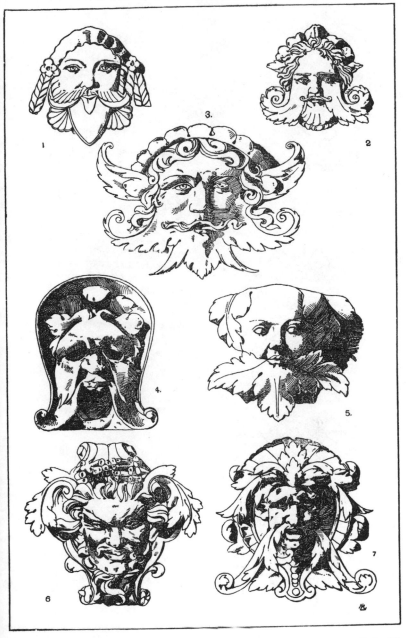

The Grottesque Mask.

Plate 62.

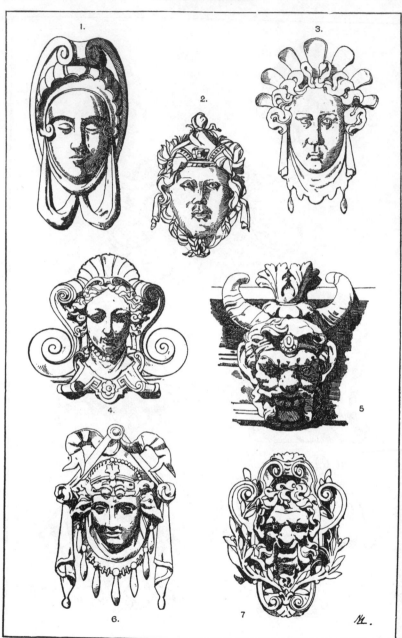

Plate 63.   The Grottesque Mask.

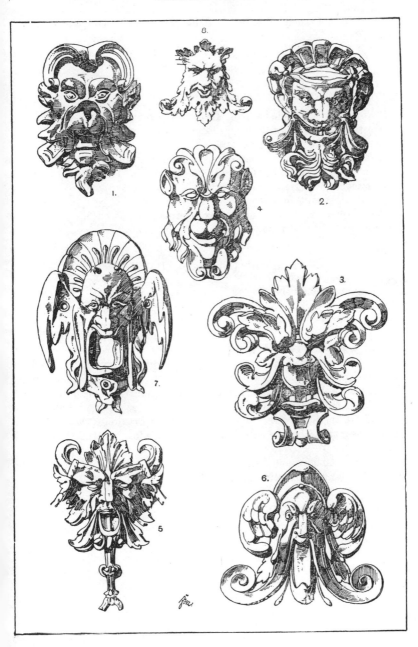

The Grottesque Mask.   Plate 64.

6.   Modern French, Theatre de Bellecour, Lyons, Architect Chatron, (Raguenet).
7.ˑ   Modern French, Ministry of War, Paris, Architect Bouchot, (Raguenet).

PLATE 64. THE GROTTESQUE MASK.

1. Grottesque, by Michelangelo, Italian Renascence, (Raguenet).
2. Grottesque, castle of Ecouen, French, 1538, (Raguenet).
3. German, 16th century, (Lessing).
4. Grottesque, German Renascence, Gemanisches Museum, Nuremberg.
5. Grottesque, pedestal of a column, tomb in Pforzheim, German Renascence, by Hans von Trarbach.
6. From the spout of a can, German Renascence.
7. Grottesque, escutcheon of a lock, German Renascence.
8. Grottesque, modern panel, Sculptor Hauptmann.

THE MEDUSA HEAD. (Plate 65.)

Unique among the masks is the head of Medusa. Medusa, in mythological tradition one of the three Gorgons, whose Head Perseus cut-off, to present it to Athene as an ornament for her shield. It is employed in ancient art as a decoration for breastplates and shields, on and above doors and gates, and on the ground of paterae and dishes. The expression is that of the rigidity of death; its look is meant to petrify; the hair is interlaced with serpents; serpents wind themselves in knots beneath her chin; and small wings are often added.

The Archaic art represented the Gorgon as ugly, terrible, and disgusting; the later Greek conception, under Praxiteles, was of stern, grand, beauty, (the so called Rondanine Medusa in the Glyptothek at Munich).

In the Modern and Renascence styles, the head of Medusa is only decorative; and it is seldom employed.

PLATE 65. THE MEDUSA HEAD.

1. The Farnese dish (Onyx Patera), Museum, Naples, Roman.
2. Centre of antique Patera, Roman.
3. Medallion, probably modern, French.
4. Tympanum, Tuileries, Paris, (Baldus).

THE GROTTESQUE. (Plate 66.)

Grottesques (from *grotto*) are fantastic, often really ugly monsters, produced by the combination of human, animal, and plant organisms in the freest and most arbitrary manner. Squatting, winged female figures without arms; human bodies with fishtails, with endlessly long, winding necks, with extremities terminating in foliage, are types of this style of ornamentation. The origin of the Grottesque must be sought in the decorative painting of the Romans. Pompeii offers copious material. Various painters of the Italian Renascence, among them Rafael, revived and used the antique Grottesque painting (Rafael's loggie), after the discovery of the grottesque painting in the thermae of Titus at Rome, (from these vaults or Grottoes is derived the name grottesque).

The Grottesques are a striking example of the playful and artistic feeling of the Ancients; and stand in great contrast to the coarse attempts at the comic to be found in Medieval art. From decorative painting the grottesques passed to the plastic art of the Renascence. The revival of Italian decorative painting in modern art has led to the retention of these forms also.

PLATE 66. THE GROTTESQUE.

1. Part of pilaster, Italian Renascence, by Benedetto da Majano.
2. Part of pilaster, tomb of Louis XII., St. Denis, French Renascence.
3. Part of pilaster, Palazzo magnifico, Siena, Italian Renascence, by Barile.
4—5. Parts of ornamental columns, Palazzo Guadagni, Florence, (Schütz).
6. Italian majolica pavement, Siena, Italian Renascence, (L'art pour tous).
7. Stall in San Severino, Naples, Italian Renascence, by Bartolommeo Chiarini and Bernadino Torelli da Brescia, (Schütz).
8. Stall, San Agostino, Perugia, Italian Renascence.

THE HALF-FIGURE. (Plates 67—68.)

From Antique times up to the present day, Half-figures have been popular as startings for ornaments. The upper part of the human body undergoes little variation from its natural forms. Below the breast or the stomach, often defined by a girdle, there is developed a sort of inverted foliage-cup, from which the scroll ornament grows. Half-figures are found not only in the flat and in bas-relief, but also in round plastic art, in this latter case as brackets for lamps, torchholders, doorknockers, &c.

PLATE 67. THE HALF-FIGURE.

1—2. Panels, Roman Altar.
3. Part of a Roman relief.

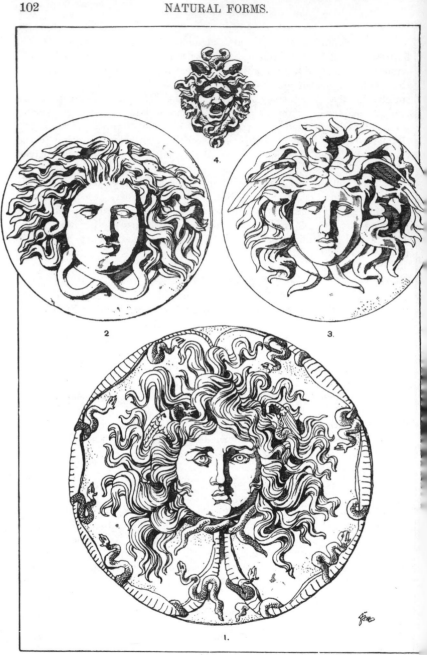

Plate 65. The Medusa Head.

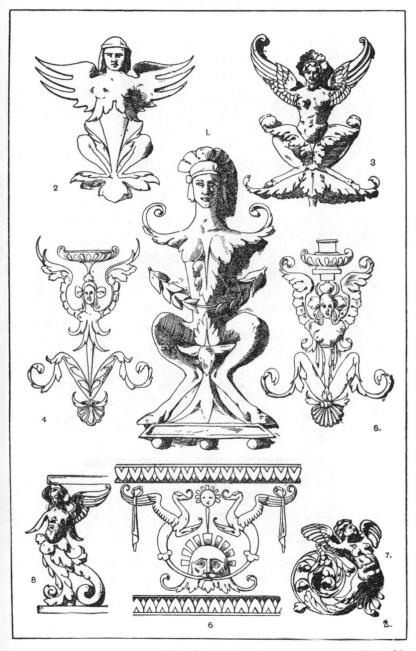

The Grottesque.   Plate 66

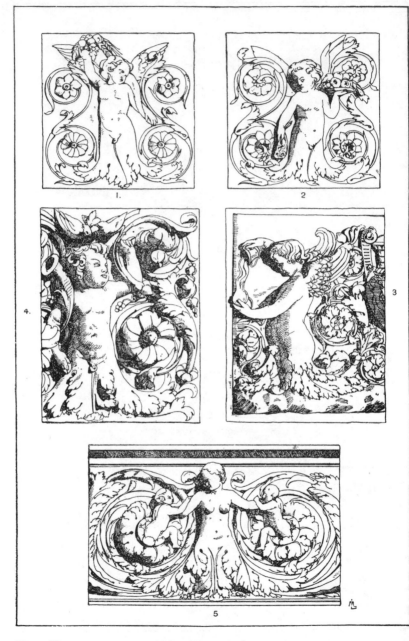

Plate 67.   The Half-Figure.

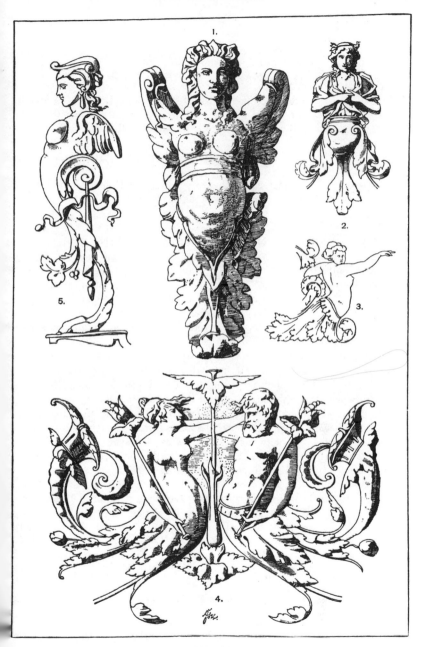

The Half-Figure.   Plate 68.

4.   Socle of Altar, cathedral of Orvieto, Italian Renascence, (Gewerbehalle).
5.   Part of relief, Italian Renascence.

PLATE 68. THE HALF-FIGURE.

1. Bracket, 1750, Italian, South Kensington Museum, London, (Arundel Society, Objects of art).
2. Decoration on ceiling, Castle of S. Angelo, Rome, Italian Renascence.
3. Sketch, by Polidore da Caravaggio, 16th century, Italian, Louvre, Paris.
4. Centre of a relief, lectern, cathedral, Limoges, French Renascence.
5. From basrelief, by J. Verchère, Modern, French.

THE SPHINX, AND THE CENTAUR. (Plate 69.)

The Sphinx is an imaginary combination of the Human bust with the body of the Lion. It was originally an Egyptian invention. The colossal Sphinx of Memphis was begun under Cheops; it is hewn from the living rock, partly supplemented by masonry, and is more than 150 feet long. The bust is generally a Woman's; but in some cases it is a Ram head. The Sphinx is the guardian of temples and tombs, in front of which it is frequently ranged in avenues. In the Roman period: wings are added, probably through Assyrian influence; and the crouching position is sometimes exchanged for the half-erect. The Renascence uses Sphinxes in painting (as double sphinx also, with a single head and double body), and in free shapes as fire dogs, &c. The Barocco period adorns gardens and portals with crouching Sphinxes, (the castle garden at Schwetzingen contains a considerable number).

Centaurs are imaginary wild monsters, with the fore part of a Man and the hinder part of a Horse. Among the Greeks, the Centaur originally symbolised the Thessalian race of equestrian renown. Mythology recounts their struggles with the Lapithae. Later delineations, such as the mural paintings of Pompeii, depict the Centaurs less wild, tamed to the service of Dionysos, and sporting with Amorini and Bacchantes. The decorative capabilities of these fantastic figures has ensured them renewed application in later styles; and they are sometimes used in modern decoration.

PLATE 69. THE SPHINX, AND THE CENTAUR.

1.   Crouching Sphinx, Egyptian, Louvre, Paris, (Raguenet).
2.   Crouching Sphinx with ram head, Egyptian, (Raguenet).
3.   Lower corner of an antique candelabrum, Roman.

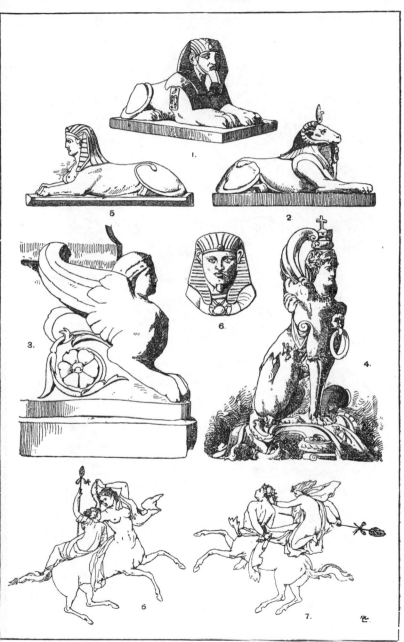

The Sphinx, and the Centaur.   Plate 69.

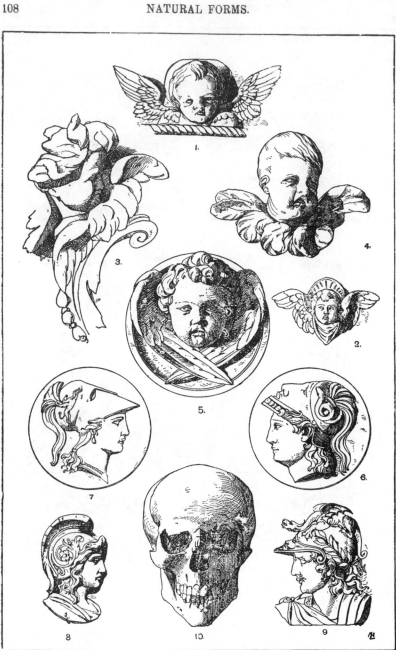

Plate 70. The Cherub Head, &c.

4. Sitting Sphinx, Modern, French, Andiron, by the sculptor Piat, (L'art pour tous).
5. Crouching Sphinx, modern.
6—7. Centaurs and Bacchantes, Mural paintings, Pompeii, (Chefs d'oeuvre de l'art antique).

MISCELLANEOUS HEADS. (Plate 70.)

Angel-faces, winged, youthful heads, with a circular or disc-like halo, are first met-with in the Byzantine style, as a result of the activity of ecclesiastical artists. In the early Italian Renascence, the rendering is charmingly naive (Lucca della Robbia may be specially mentioned); they adorn friezes and arches, fill medallions, and are found in borders. They occur often on Tombs; and they are also much used in Modern ecclesiastical decoration.

The profiles of Minerva, Mars, Apollo, frequently occur in medallions.

The Skull or Death's head, the gruesome grinning relic of departed life, and emblem of Decay and Death, finds its place in the Dances of Death, at one time so popular; also on the shield of Death (Albrecht Dürer), on Monuments, Tombs, &c. It is generally represented in front view, and often over two crossed bones.

PLATE 70. THE CHERUB HEAD, &c.

1. Cherub, Early Italian Renascence.
2. Cherub, candelabrum, Certosa near Pavia, Italian Renascence.
3. Frame, Germanisches Museum, Nuremberg.
4. Column of the Plague, Vienna, Barocco.
5. Modern, medallion, by Prof. Heer, Carlsruhe.
6. Minerva, Berlin Museum, Modern.
7. Minerva, Modern.
8. Warrior, Louvre, Paris, (Baldus).
9. Mars, from Lièvre, Les Arts Decoratifs.
10. Skull, from nature.

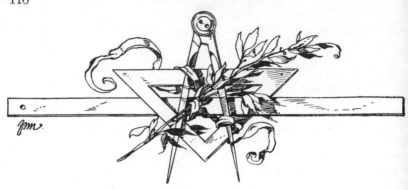

C.

ARTIFICIAL OBJECTS.

Besides Geometrical elements, and those copied from organic Nature: ornamental art avails itself of Artificial objects, either alone or in combination with the two first-named classes. But this does not include the accidental use of all kinds of articles in symbolic work, and the still-life painting, but only the vessels, tools weapons instruments, shields, knots, ribbons, &c., which are used as decoration, or blended with it.

It is easy to understand how the vessels of religious rites passed into the decoration of religious edifices, temples, and churches. In the Antique style: the altars, tripods, candelabra, sacrificial axes sprinklers, &c.; in the Christian styles: the symbol of the cross, marks of priestly dignity, the instruments of the Passion, &c., decorate friezes, walls, and panels, (Comp. Plate 75, figs. 2 and 6).

Decorative groups of hunting and warlike implements and o tools, &c., are termed Trophies: the devices of guilds and companie are Symbols.

The following chapters will treat of these things in detail, along with other designs, of somewhat rarer occurrence, which also belong to this section.

THE TROPHY. (Plates 71 and 72.)

It was the custom of the Greeks to hang on the trunks o trees, the weapons which the flying enemy had left behind on th field of battle. These tokens of victory, or Trophies, have also found a place in decoration. The Romans erected artificial, symbolical Trophies of stone or bronze in the form of columns, pyramids, and similar architectural structures. Since their time Trophies have been used not only to decorate all monuments connected with war and victory, e. g. arsenals, the offices of the ministry of war, guard-houses, barracks, and weapons, especially shields; but they have been used up to the present time for purely decorative purposes, as elegantly-arranged and prettily-grouped weapons of war, in the architecture of the pilasters of castles, town-halls and tombs, in the intarsias of the Renascence, on woven fabrics and tapestries, as vignettes; and, above all, in plastic ornament.

It was also natural that Trophies should also be formed of hunting-weapons, which have much similarity with weapons of war, and also of objects connected with the navy. The original meaning of the word ($\tau\varrho o\pi a\iota o\nu$ = token of victory, from $\tau\varrho o\pi\acute{\eta}$, turning, flight) has, it must be admitted, been lost sight of in these applications.

PLATE 71. THE TROPHY.

1— 6. Decoration of chased metal dish, Renascence.
7— 8. Decoration of clock panel, French Renascence, Louis XIII style, (Lièvre).
9—10. Panels of door, Otto-Heinrich portion of the Castle, Heidelberg, German Renascence, (Pfnor).

PLATE 72. THE TROPHY.

1. Panel, tomb of Galeazzo Pandono, San Domenico maggiore Naples, Italian Renascence, (Schütz).
2. Part of Panel, Italian Renascence.
3. Part of Panel of a stall, Dordtrecht, Dutch Renascence.
4. Pedestal of monument to a Margrave, Pforzheim, by Hans von Trarbach, German Renascence.
5—6. Panels, Quay front, Tuileries, Paris, (Baldus).
7. Part of design for a monument, by J. Ch. Delafosse.

THE SYMBOL. (Plates 73—77.)

The grouping of tools and instruments, to symbolise some special idea, leads to the design of Symbols. Thus we find, disregarding those of war and hunting, which we have treated of as trophies, Symbols of art, both of Art in general and of the special arts: Music, Painting, Sculpture, Architecture, &c.; Symbols of Science,

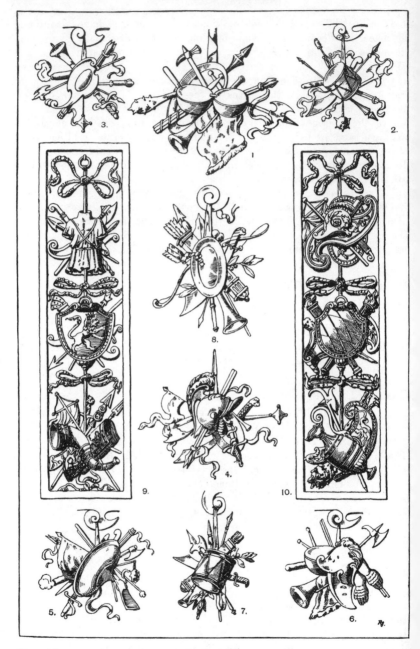

Plate 71.   The Trophy.

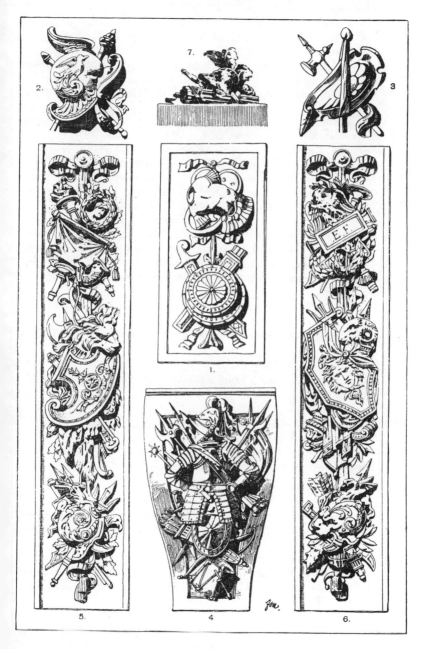

The Trophy.

Plate 72.

either as a whole or for individual sciences: Mathematics, Astronomy,
Chemistry, &c.; of Commerce, of Technical Science, and finally of
Handicrafts and Trades.

Singing, for example, is symbolised by a lyre with or without
sheets of music: Music by violins, flutes, horns, Pan's pipes, &c.;
Dancing by the tambourine and castagnettes; Acting by masks; Painting by brush and palette; Sculpture by the hammer, chisel, and
works of sculpture, busts, torsi; Architecture by square, straight-edge
and compasses, usually in combination with capitals. The Railroad
and Steam are symbolised by a winged wheel, the Telegraph by coils of
wire, which radiate lightning. Trade is represented by casks and bales
of goods on which the caduceus (a staff round which winged serpents
are twining — the attribute of Mercury) is resting; Agriculture has
the plough, the sickle, the scythe, &c., Vine culture the vine press.

The different Trades have chosen their Symbols partly from their
tools, partly from their finished products. The Guilds and Companies
of past centuries introduced a certain system into these outward and
visible signs; a large number of guild pictures, some of them very
beautiful and ingenious, are preserved in the industrial art museums
of modern times.

A far more detailed and extensive treatment of Symbols than can
be given in the present work will be found in Gerlach's *Allegorien
und Embleme,* to which we are indebted for a number of illustrations.

PLATE 73. THE SYMBOL.

1.   Angle ornament, hall of the Ministry of State, Louvre, Paris,
      (Baldus).
2.   Louvre, Paris, (Baldus).
3.   Symbol of the violin makers' guild, Klingenthal, 1716, (Gerlach,
      Allegorien und Embleme).
4—5. Pilaster panels, by the sculptor Fomilini of Florence, Modern.
6—9. Medallions, by the sculptor Lehr of Berlin, Modern.

PLATE 74. THE SYMBOL.

1.   Carved wood Door-head, French, 18th century, (L'art pour tous).
2—3. Symbols of sculpture and painting, by the sculptor Hauptmann,
      Dresden, Modern.
4.   Part of Exhibition-programme, München, 1876, by R. Seitz.
5.   Address-card of an ink factory, by Prof. Hammer of Carlsruhe.
6.   Title to an edition of Goethe's works, by Dir. Götz of Carlsruhe.

PLATE 75. THE SYMBOL.

1. Part of Panel, court of Ducal palace, Venice, Italian Renascence,
   (Schütz).

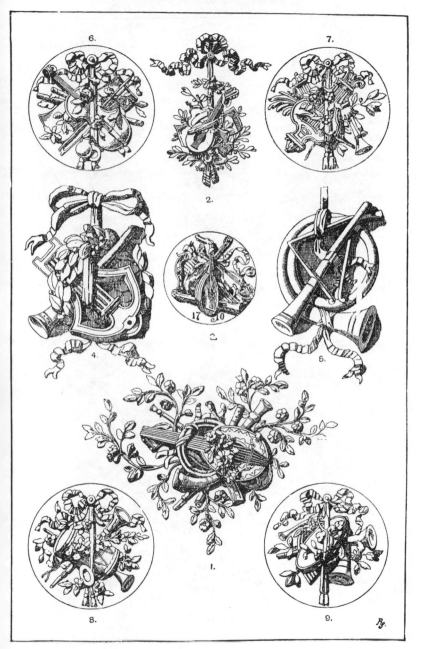

The Symbol.

Plate 73.

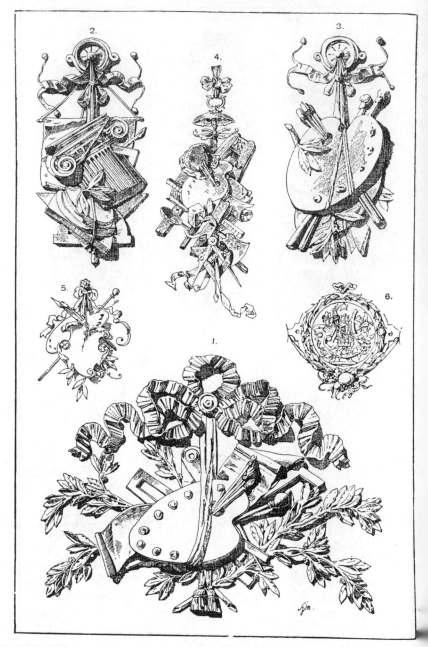

Plate 74.   The Symbol.

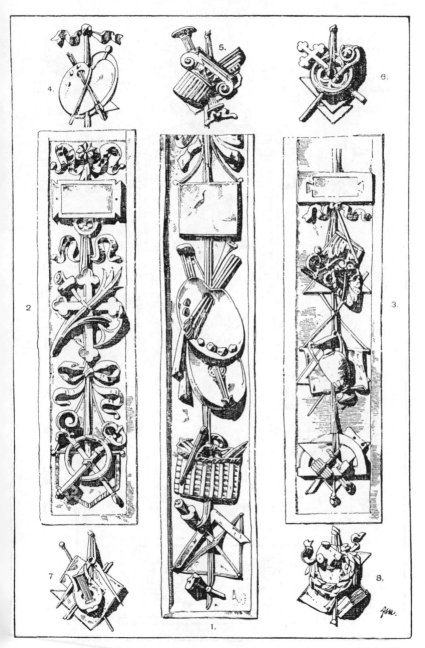

The Symbol. Plate 75.

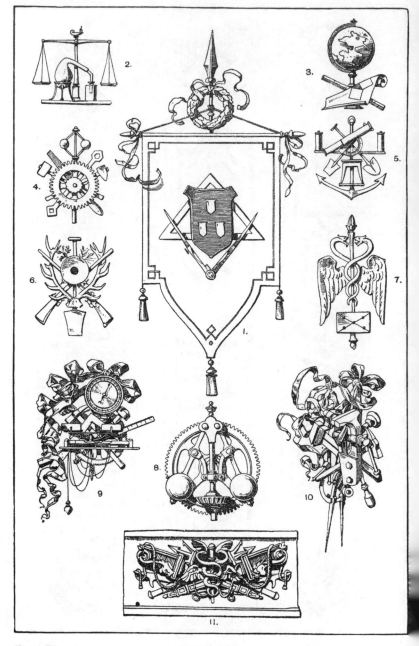

Plate 76. The Symbol.

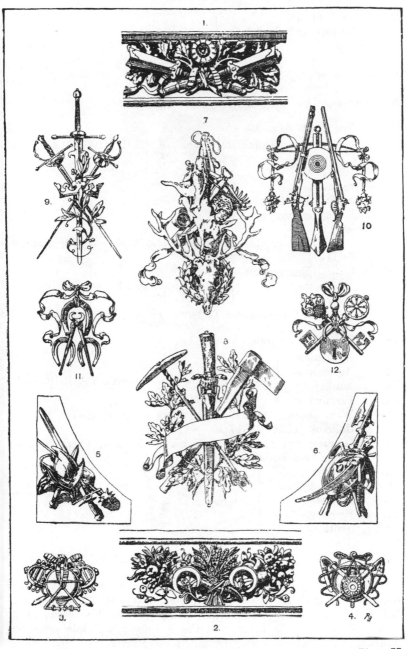

The Symbol.

Plate 77.

2. Ecclesiastical art,
3. Architecture and Sculpture,
4. Painting,   In Pilasters, by the sculptor
5. Antique art,   Hauptmann, Modern, staircase of
6. Christian art,   Museum, Dresden.
7. Art,
8. Sculpture,

PLATE 76.   THE SYMBOL.

1. Banner, of the architectural school of the Polytechnicum, Carlsruhe.
2. Chemistry.
3. Mathematics.
4. Mechanical Engineering.
5. Civil Engineering.
6. Forestry.
7. Post and Commerce, Polytechnicum at Carlsruhe, Designed by
   G. Kachel.
8. Mechanical Engineering,
9. The Mechanic,   (Gerlach, Allegorien und Embleme).
10. Smithery,
11. Navigation and Commerce, Tuileries, Paris, (Baldus).

PLATE 77.   THE SYMBOL.

1.   Navigation,
2.   Agriculture,
3.   Music,   Court front of the Tuileries, Paris, (Baldus).
4.   Farming,
5—6. War, Border of a copper plate engraving, by Heinrich
      Goltzius (1558—1617).
7.   Hunting and Fishing, by Stuck of Munich, (Gerlach, Alle-
      gorien und Embleme).
8.   Forestry,
9.   Sword-making,
10.   Musketry,   (Gerlach).
11.   Farriery,
12.   Smithery.

THE RIBBON.   (Plates 78—79.)

Ribbons are not used alone, but are frequently employed as a
decoration of garlands and festoons (comp. plates 38, 39, 40), of symbols (comp. plates 71—77), or they are Labels to bear some motto
(comp. plate 78). The Ribbons of the Antique are simple, often terminating in a ball or acorn like knob; the Middle Ages, particularly

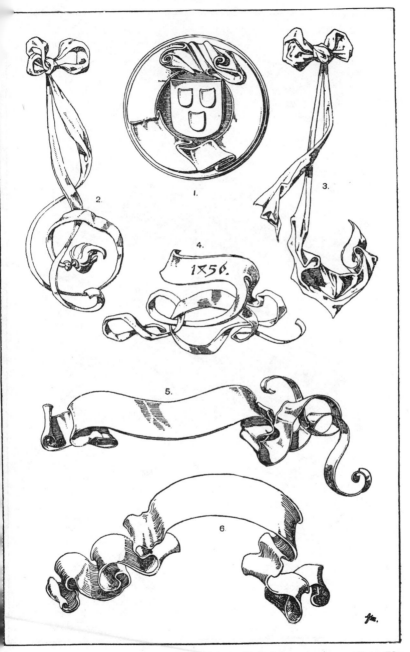

The Ribbon, and the Label. Plate 78.

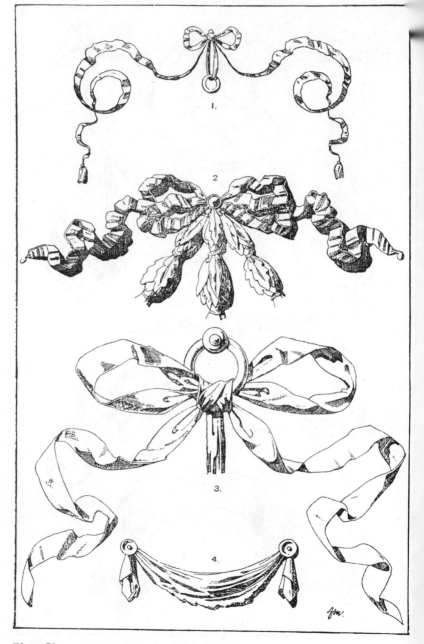

Plate 79.   The Ribbon.

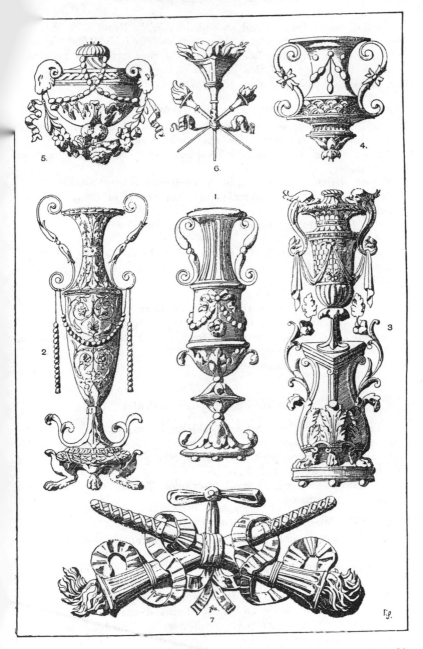

Miscellaneous objects.   Plate 80.

the Gothic, make them curled and quaint; in the Renascence they developed in various free and elegant styles, often divided at the e like a pennon. In the Louis XVI. style they are often peculia crinkled, but in spite of this mannerism they are not without a ce tain decorative charm, (Comp. plates 78 and 79).

PLATE 78. THE RIBBON, AND THE LABEL.

1. Label for motto, on the seal of the town of Schiltach, Gothic, Inscription on the scroll: "S. opidi schilttach".
2. Ribbon, from Jost Amman's Wappen- und Stammbuch, German Renascence.
3. Ribbon, painting by B. Zeitblom, Carlsruhe gallery, Gothic.
4. Label for motto, old Germain painting, School of Cologne, Carlsruhe gallery.
5. Label for motto, triumphal car, by Hans Burgkmair, 1473—1530, German, (Hirth).
6. Label for motto, Albrecht Dürer's "Der Eülen seyndt alle Vögel neydig und gram," German Renascence, (Hirth).

PLATE 79. THE RIBBON.

1. Ribbon and knot, After Daniel Mignot, German Renascence.
2. Ribbon and knot, the Louis XVI. style, (Lièvre).
3. Ribbon and knot for a bunch of fruit, after Prof. Sturm of Vienna, (Storck's Zeichenvorlagen).
4. Drapery Festoon, (Raguenet).

MISCELLANEOUS OBJECTS. (Plate 80).

Finally, among the artificial objects which are used in decoration, especially of pilasters, we may mention those forms like candelabra and vases, from which ornaments, like growing plants, usually rise, (Comp. plates 80 and 131).

Cornucopias, Torches, small inscription Tablets, and many other objects, are introduced.

PLATE 80. MISCELLANEOUS OBJECTS.

1. Vase, window pilaster of the Cancelleria, Rome, by Bramante, Italian Renascence, (De Vico).
2. Vase, pilaster of a door, San Angostino, Rome, (De Vico).
3. Vase, lower part of a panel, Italian Renascence.
4. Vase, tomb of Louis XII., St. Denis, French Renascence.
5. Vase, Louis XVI. style, (F. A. M., Cours d'ornement).
6. Crossed Torches, upper part of pilaster, by Benedetto da Majano, Italian Renascence.
7. Crossed Torches, Renascence.

DIVISION II.

ORNAMENT

APPLIED TO FEATURES.

A. Bands.
B. Free Ornaments.
C. Supports.
D. Enclosed Ornaments, or Panels.
E. Repeating Ornaments, or Diapers.

INTRODUCTION.

The second division of the Handbook deals with ornament a. applied in decorative Features. They will be arranged according to their function, and treated in accordance with the mutual relations of the decorative form and its application.

Every one acquainted with Decoration, must have been struck by the fact that on certain Objects and on certain parts of them the decoration invariably appears to have been modelled on the same principle, no matter how much the selected motives may vary from each other or belong to special styles. In decoration, as elsewhere, there is a right and a wrong use for everything; each object, even the very smallest, requires its own proper Form and Decoration, and the artist who understands style will give these, though in many cases unconsciously; artistic instinct guiding one man where another must study laboriously.

Be this as it may, the relations are there. A socle ornament cannot be reversed and used as a frieze without modification; a column, which looks beautiful and even delicate on monumental architecture, may produce a clumsy effect if reduced and applied to furniture; no one finds fault with the 20 or 24 flutings of it in architecture, but half of them would more than suffice for the smaller Cabinet. And so on. The achievements of those periods, in which the intimate connection between form, aim and material was either unknown or forgotten, are what might be expected. The Empire Style, which copied the Antiqne at the instance of an august personage; and, in so doing, produced work which is classical in respect of its mannerisms; is an example. A Greek temple and an arm chair are two different things; each has its own peculiarities; and must be fashioned and decorated in accordance therewith.

It were an insoluble problem to give a formula for each case; and to attempt to do so lies beyond the scope of this Handbook. But we will attempt to bring together some important groups from the entire field; and by means of them to illustrate the principles of design.

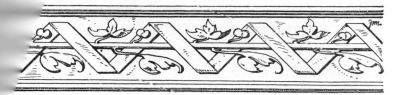

A.

BANDS.

The group of Bands includes all those ornamental forms which are used to give expression to the ideas of bordering, framing, and connecting.

The motives are partly geometrical, partly organic, chiefly plant-forms; artificial forms being more rarely used.

The Band has no "up" or "down"; but only an onward or an outward tendency. It has no limitation in regard to length; but is generally a narrow, ribbon-like ornament.

The proper application of Bands is to the enclosing of ceilings, walls, floors, panels, on certain architectural constructions, on the abacus and the plinth of columns, and as a running ornament round the shaft of the latter. They are further used as the hem or border of garments, carpets and other textiles; as borders in typography, on the rims of plates or dishes, or to separate the ground from the rim, &c.

The principal ornaments in this group are: the Fret; Chain and Interlaced patterns (Guilloche); Foliated bands in the various forms of Rosette, Palmette, Flower, Leaf, and Scroll bands, &c.

The Evolute Spiral band (Plate 97) stands to a certain extent on the borderline between Bands and Free ornaments.

Leaf patterns, and the Egg-and-tongue which has been developed from them, are not Bands at all, in the strict sense of the word. They express the mediation between the support and the weight, for which reason they are used as the enrichment of Mouldings. They are here included among bands in order to avoid an independent group for the sake of the one plate. As a matter of fact, they do often appear as bands (the Egg-and-tongue as a decoration of plates, medallions, &c).

THE FRET BAND. (Plates 81—84.)

The Greek Fret (or Meander border) is, as it name indicat
specifically Greek ornament, and no doubt of textile origin.
accomodation to the rectangular network suggests this.

The name "meander" is said to be derived from a river of As
Minor, the Maeandros, now the Menderes, which flows in sinuou
curves. Although the forerunners of the Greek border are to be
found in the Assyrian and Egyptian styles, it was Greek vase-painting
and architecture which gave rise to the variations of the pattern;
architecture also employed it plastically. Among other applications
in the Roman style it was used for mosaics on floors and often —
contrary to the principles of style of flat ornaments — in those
parallel perspective representations in which it seems as if it were a
plastic ornament, (Plate 83. 8).

The Middle Ages seldom used the Fret (one example will be
found on Plate 83. 9); but similar forms are common in the Chinese
and Japanese styles (Plate 84. 7).

The Renascence revived the Fret in its ancient application; made
new combinations; and sometimes interlaced it with plant motives
(Plate 83. 10). Although very commonplace, the fret still has a good
effect when it is applied in the proper manner.

Its construction is very simple. In general — although not always —
the breadth of the broad lines or ornament is equal to the distance
between them; we therefore draw a square network as shown on
Plate 1, fig. 1, then draw all the horizontal lines (the measure-
ment of the lengths and the observance of the rhythmic regularity
peculiar to each Greek pattern are the only difficulties), and then join
their ends by means of perpendiculars, (Plates 81 and 82).

Centres are formed by arranging the axis at a suitable place, and
reversing the pattern, (Plate 84. 6 and 10).

Angle junctions may be similarly arranged by cutting the pattern
diagonally to the square net at a suitable place, and reversing as
before, (Plate 84. 3, 4 and 6)   The angle-treatment of Current Frets
is more difficult (Plate 84: figs. 1, 2, and 5).

The end of a Fret with only one row may be formed by cutting
the pattern short at a suitable spot; where two or more rows run
parallel to or cross each other, they may be combined so as to form
proper endings (Plate 84. 11).

The pattern is sometimes carried round a circle; but this is an
arrangement which is quite out of accordance with its character.

The square network is not always applicable to cases in which the
Fret has to be repeated within a given length. In this case the divisions of length are either elongated or compressed by drawing the
auxiliary lines at a greater or less angle than 45^0 (this is shown on
Plates 81 and 82).

81. UNSYMMETRICAL OR CURRENT FRETS: GREEK VASE
PAINTINGS.

Ordinary, simple patterns.

Elongated pattern.

Raking pattern.

10. Patterns which are interrupted by rosettes, stars, &c.

-9. Abnormal pattern, formed by fragments, instead of a contin-
nous line.

PLATE 82. RECIPROCATING FRETS.

1--4. Ordinary, simple patterns.
5. Double pattern, Greek.
6. Intersecting pattern, Louvre, Paris.
7 and 10. Fragmentary pattern, Greek, and modern.
7 and 9. Symmetrical double pattern, Greek.
7—10. Ornamented patterns.

PLATE 83. INTERSECTING FRETS, &c.

1—6. Ordinary patterns, Greek vase paintings.
7. Abnormal pattern, Japanese metal vessel.
8. Pattern in parallel perspective, Roman mosaic pavement.
9. Mediaeval folded-tape pattern, resembling the Fret, (Racinet)
10. Pattern ornamented with laurel, Louvre, Paris.

PLATE 84. ENDS, ANGLES, AND CENTRES, OF FRETS.

1, 2 and 5. Free, unsymmetrical angle treatment.
3, 4, 6, 7 and 8. Symmetrical angles.
9 and 10. Centre treatments.
11—14. Ends of patterns.
Antique motives, except No. 7 (Chinese), and No. 8 (Modern).

THE CHAIN BAND. (Plate 85.)

The basis of the design is the Chain. The Chain Band is therefore cemposed of circular, elliptical, square, or lozenge shaped links,
which are either represented all in front view (as in 1, 2, 4 and 8),
or alternately in profile (as in 3, 5, 6, and 7).

The Chain pattern probably occurs sporadically in every style.

That Chain-bands have not been more frequently used, although
hey are a simple and effective mode of decoration, may be due to
he fact that the chain appeared to a certain degree to be too force-
ul, too vigorous in its effect. At any rate, delicacies of artistic feel-

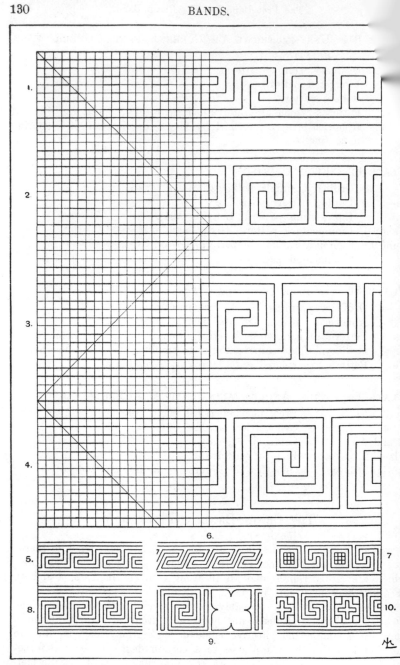

Plate 81.　　　　　　　The Fret Band.

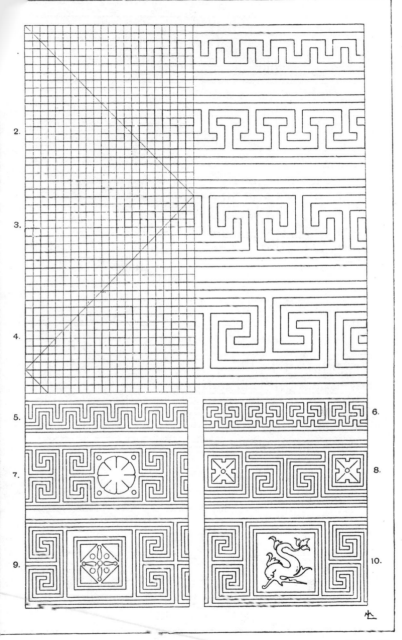

The Fret Band. Plate 82.

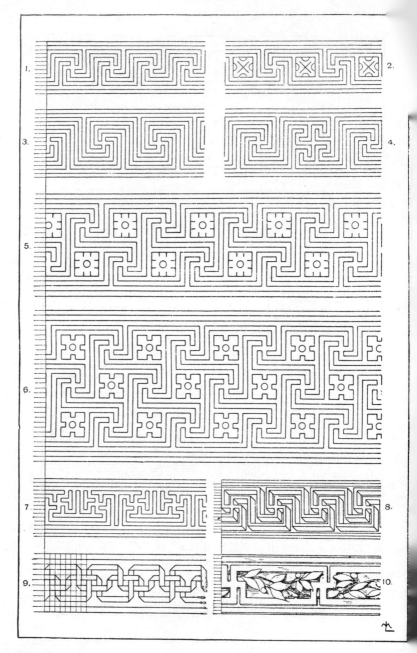

Plate 83.   The Fret Band.

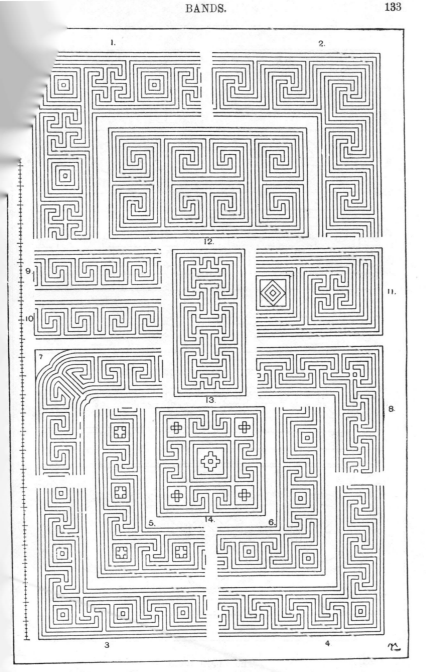

The Fret Band.

Plate 84.

BANDS.

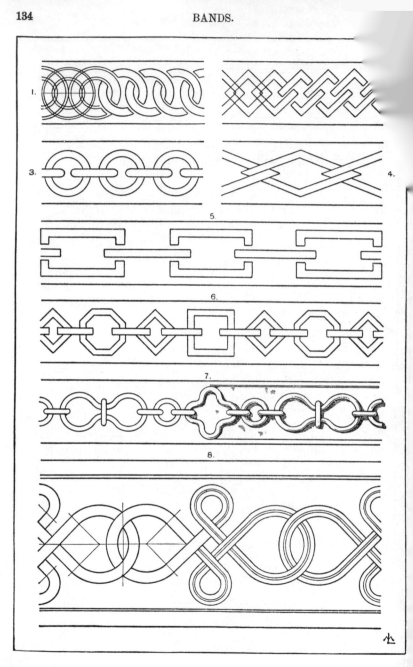

Plate 85. The Chain Band.

have found expression elsewhere, and often unconsciously, point to this conclusion.

construction of such bands is simple; and in the case of illustrated may be understood from the plate itself.

85. THE CHAIN BAND.

. Modern decorative painting.

8. Carved wooden ceiling, Townhall, Jever, German, Renascence.

THE INTERLACEMENT BAND. (Plates 86—90.)

The Interlacement Band includes all those bands which are formed of a number of lines interlaced or plaited together. They are usually symmetrical to the longitudinal axis; and may be produced indefinitely. The principle is that the interlacing broad lines shall pass over and under one-another alternately.

Rope patterns are used as borders in painting, in textiles, in pottery, intarsia, and the ornamentation of manuscripts; in architecture on the under sides of stays and beams, on archivolts (the arches of doors and windows), in the soffits of arches, sometimes in a frieze, and often as the enrichment of the torus moulding.

Interlacement patterns are used in all styles, though in some they are more popular than in others. And in this ornament the individuality of each style is very strongly marked.

In the Antique: the ornament consist of wavy interlacing bands round regularly-placed knobs or eyes. The wavy lines are composed of arcs or of arcs and straight lines, in which latter case the arcs make tangential junctions with the straight lines (Plate 86). In flat ornament the interlacing lines are distinguished from each-other by shading or by colour; in plastic ornamentation they are fluted or channelled.

The Interlacement patterns of the Middle Ages — chiefly of the Byzantine and Romanesque periods — make use of Antique forms; adding to them the angular bend (Plate 87. 1—3).

In the so called Northern styles — Celtic, Anglo-saxon, Norman, Scandinavian, and Old Frankish: it is the most conspicuous ornament. Here we meet extremely complicated and richly combined interlacings, mostly freely drawn, without the aid of the compasses. It is characteristic, and remarkable in regard to these styles, that the same band appears in sections of different colours in their ornament. The works of Owen Jones and Racinet contain numerous examples, mostly from old illuminated manuscripts: our Plate 87 (4—8) reproduces some of the simplest (reconstructed with the compasses).

The Moorish style favours a peculiar interlacement. racteristic that the bands, which are always straight, make 90^0 or 135^0, and are adapted to a network as shown on fig. 5. Here, too, we find the alternate colouring of the single Numerous examples will be found in Owen Jones, Racinet, and d'Avennes, *"L'Art Arabe"*, a selection from these being give. Plate 88, figs. 1—6.

The other Oriental styles exhibit greater variety in this respe and also employ round forms, (Plate 88. 7 und 8).

The Renascence developed great variety. Besides the traditiona forms of the Antique, peculiar constructions appear, chiefly to be met-with in the arts of inlaying, on book-cover decoration, in pewter chasing, and typographical borders, (Plate 89).

Modern art borrows from all styles; and, as was also the case in the Middle Ages and the Renascence, intersperses its patterns with foliage, (Plate 90).

PLATE 86. THE INTERLACEMENT BAND.

1—3. Ordinary antique patterns, single, double, and triple.
4—6. Elongated antique patterns, single, double, and triple.
7.　　Antique pattern, doubly interlaced, with unequal waves.
8.　　Antique pattern with two rows, terracotta painting.

> Construction: First mark the centres of the eyes: in 2 and 3 these lie on the points of intersection of a triangular net; in 5 and 6 on those of a diagonal square net. The rest will be understood from the figure.

PLATE 87. THE INTERLACEMENT BAND.

1.　　Romanesque patterns, decoration of archivolt, Segovia.
3.　　Byzantine pattern, Sta. Sofia, Constantinople.
4—7. Northern patterns, Manuscript ornaments of the 8th and 9th century, (Racinet)

PLATE 88. THE INTERLACEMENT BAND.

1—6. Simple Moorish patterns, Alhambra, Granada.
7.　　Persian pattern, metal vessel, (Racinet).
8.　　Russian Oriental pattern, (Viollet le Duc, "L'Art Russe").

PLATE 89. THE INTERLACEMENT BAND.

1—3. Patterns, wood and ivory inlaid work, Italian Renascence.
4.　　Pattern, by Domenico de Fossi, of Florence, 16th century (Raguenet).
5.　　Intarsia pattern, Sta. Maria in Organo, Verona; in the original the interstices are enriched by plant sprays.

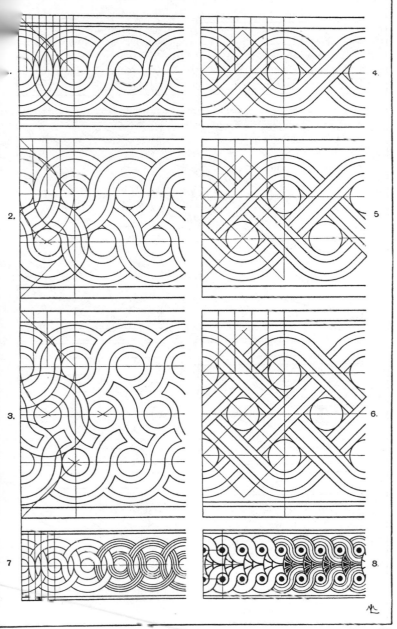

The Interlacement Band.

Plate 86.

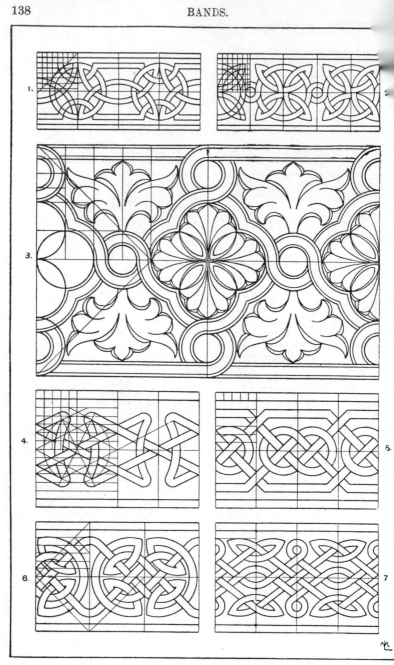

Plate 87.   The Interlacement Band.

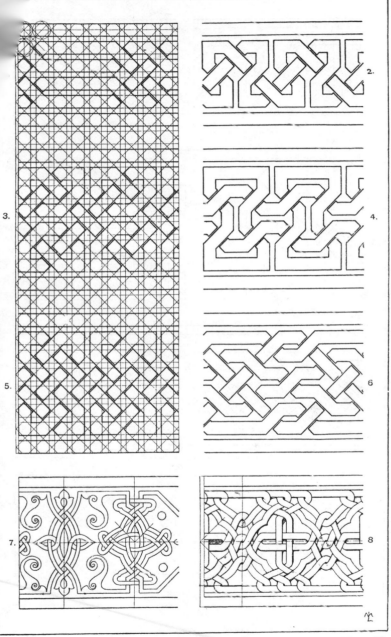

The Interlacement Band. Plate 88.

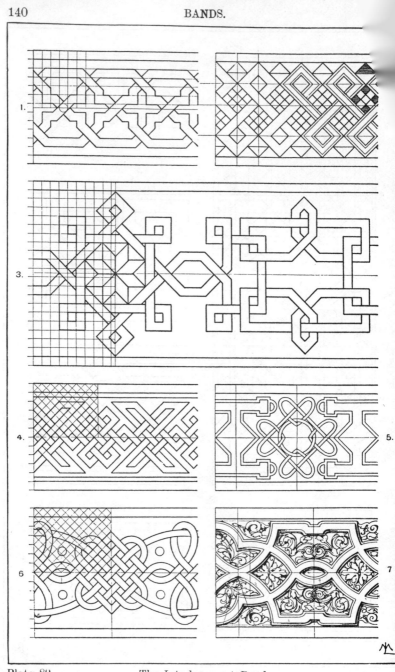

Plate 89.   The Interlacement Band.

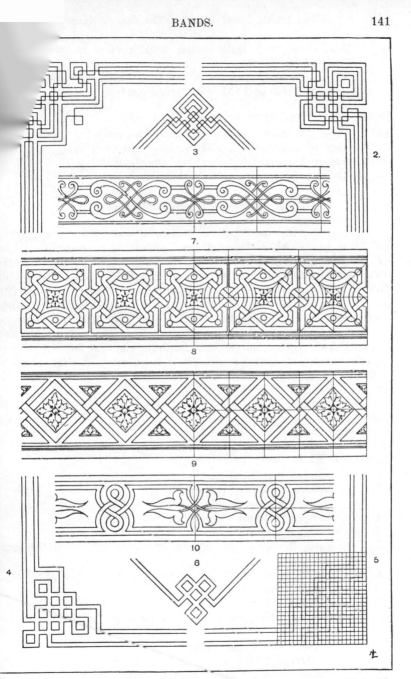

The Interlacement Band. Plate 90.

6.   Title border of a mathematical work, printed in Par.
      Finé, 1544, (Hirth).
7.   Soffit ornament, entrance of the Otto Heinrich buildin
      delberg, 1556 to 1559, (Musterornamente).

PLATE 90. THE INTERLACEMENT BAND.

1—6. Angles of Border, Modern French, (Raguenet).
7.   Edge of a modern Damask border, (Gewerbehalle).
8—9. Modern borders, (Bötticher, "Ornamentenbuch").
10.   Modern wood intarsia, (Gewerbehalle).

THE ROSETTE BAND. (Plate 91)

The term "Rosette Band" is a general name for rosette, spray
and other bands, when the rosette is the leading characteristic. The
single rosettes, which are similar to conventional roses seen in front-
view, are either in immediate juxtaposition (Plate 91. 1 and 3), or
divided by channels (Plate 91. 2), by calices (Plate 91. 5, 7, 12),
or by stalks and sprays (Plate 91. 4, 6, 10, 11). The Rosette bands
are either current, that is, they have a definitive direction sideways;
or they are entirely without direction, that is, they are symmetrical,
not only from top to bottom but also from right to left. By allow-
ing the rosettes to overlap we get a band more or less identical
with the so called Strung-coin, or "money-moulding", (Plate 91.
13 and 14).

Rosette bands are especially common in the Assyrian style, in
Antique vase painting, in the Medieval enamels (Cologne enamel),
in the Indian style, in the Renascence, and in the Modern styles.

PLATE 91. THE ROSETTE BAND.

1.   Antique vase painting.
2.   Modern decorative pattern.
3.   Antique bronze shield.
4 and 6. Antique patterns, after Jacobsthal.
5.   Neck of a Greek hydria.
7.   Latin Evangeliarum, written by Godescald for Charlemagne,
         8th century, (Racinet).
8.   Enamel ornament, the great reliquary, Aachen, (Racinet).
9.   Indian enamel border, (Prisse d'Avennes).
10.   Indian carving, (Owen Jones).
11.   Intarsia border, Sta. Maria in Organo, Verona, 1499, (Muster-
         ornamente).
12.   Popular Renascence pattern.
13.   Pattern, Persepolis.
14.   Plastic border, Louis XVI. style, (Raguenet).

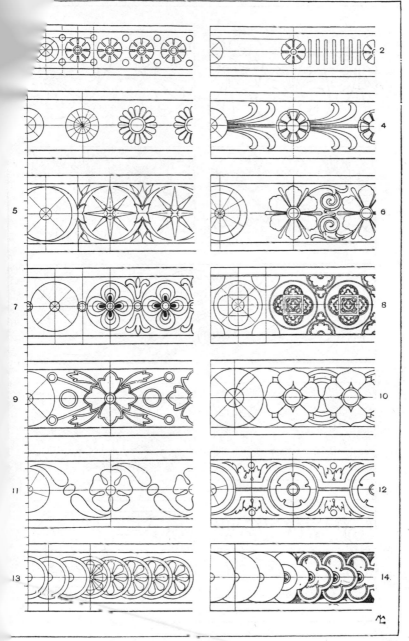

The Rosette Band. Plate 91.

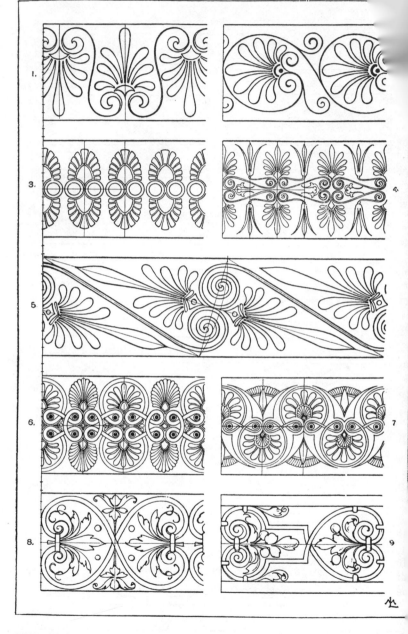

Plate 92.   The Palmette Band.

THE PALMETTE BAND. (Plate 92.)

The Palmette is a specifically Greek kind of ornament. Like the fingers of an outspread hand (*palma*, the palm of the hand) a group, 1 in number, of narrow, entire leaves is combined into a symmetrical ornament. The centre leaf is the largest; and the leaves diminish gradually as they approach the sides. The tips of the leaves lie on a regular curve. The lower ends of the leaves are disconnected, divided from each other by slight intervals, and usually spring from a tongue-shaped leaf. The delicate sensitiveness of Greek artistic feeling finds a striking expression in this ornament. It is applied in manifold ways, e. g: as Antefixes and Akroters, as Cornice-decoration (comp. the group of Free ornaments), and as Palmette borders. In rare cases the Palmette ornaments are in juxtaposition without anything between them — this is usually the case on the Lekythos (a Greek vessel for Oil, &c.) Plate 92. 3 — in the majority of cases the palmettes are connected or bordered by spiral bands (Plate 92. 1. 2 &c.).

Palmette ornaments are of frequent occurrence on Greek vessels, and on the friezes of their architecture. Where they occur in later styles: it is only sporadically; and the severe classical beauty is not retained.

PLATE 92. THE PALMETTE BAND.

1. 2, 3 and 5. Paintings, Greek, terracotta vessels.
4. 6 and 7.   Greek, friezes.
3.   Intarsia, Italian Renascence.
9.   Modern, wrought iron trellis.

THE VERTEBRATE BAND, &c. (Plates 93—96.)

Leaf bands are generally numerous in all styles; and as varied as are the modes of their application. The leaved stalk, with or without flowers, fruits, &c., is the simplest natural motive. The various plants are used as a basis, partly with, partly without, symbolical reference. The Antique chiefly availed itself of the laurel, olive, and ivy; the Middle Ages used the vine, clover, thistle, and maple; the Renascence shows the Artificial leaf. To these traditional patterns: Modern art has added some others which are specially adapted for naturalistic representation, such as the convolvulus, the passion-flower, the hop, &c.

Thus we find in the Antique: a succession of buds (Plate 93. 1); straight stalks with leaves, either attached or free (Plate 93. 2, 3); or undulating stalks, with leaves, fruit, or flowers (Plate 93. 4, 5, 6).

The latter mode was retained in the Medieval style; in the Rou esque style the stalks are more compressed, and the lobes of leaves fully rounded (Plate 93. 7, 8); in the Gothic style the forr are thin and extended, the latter slit and pointed. Extremely comm are the two forms depicted on Plate 94. 7 and 8. Characteristic the late Gothic is the example 13, Plate 94; this kind of ornamen ation is excellently adapted for simple wood-carving and stampec leather-work.

The Oriental conception, in textile fabrics and by the engraved and inlaid metal-work, is shown (Plate 94. 1—4).

Intarsia technique, leather-stamping, weaving, and the ornamentation of manuscripts offered the Renascence opportunity to make use of, and to vary the floral border with advantage (Plate 95). Interlacement and floral patterns are frequently combined in the same example (Plate 95. 5 and 6).

As examples of Modern art, the naturalistic borders figured on Plate 96. 9—11. are given.

When the main-stem runs longitudinally along the centre of the Band, like the vertebral column in the skeletons of animals, then the arrangement is termed Vertebrate. When the main-stem oscillates from side to side (as in Plate 93. 4, 5, & 8), then the arrangement is termed Undulate.

PLATE 93. THE VERTEBRATE BAND, &C.

1—6. Paintings, Greek, terracotta vessels.
7—8. French, mural paintings, 13th century, (Racinet).
9. Glass window, Cathedral, Bourges, 14th century, (Racinet).
10. Medieval.
11. Intarsia, Sta. Maria in Organo, Verona, 1499.
12. Modern, plate-border.

PLATE 94. THE UNDULATE BAND.

1—3. Persian, metal vessels, (Racinet).
4. Indian.
5. Byzantine, glass mosaic, San Marco, Venice, (Musterornamente)
6. Portion of Romanesque initial, 13th century, Berlin Museum
7. Romanesque, portal of cathedral, Lucca, (Musterornamente)
8. Gothic flat carving, end of 15th century, (Musterornamente)
9. Medieval, mural painting, Swedish church.
10. French, mural painting, 13th century, (Racinet).
11. Early Gothic, French.
12. Gothic, manuscript ornamentation.
13. Late Gothic, flat carving, 15th century, (Musterornamente).

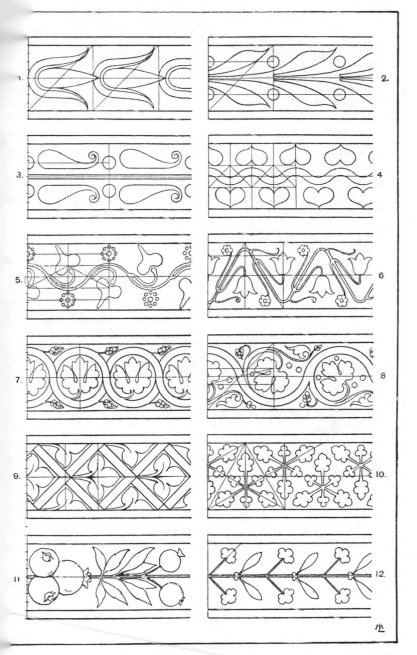

The Vertebrate Band, &c.

Plate 93.

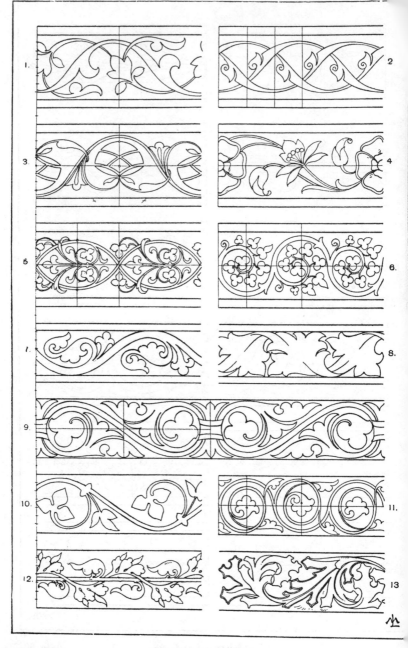

Plate 94.   The Undulate Band, &c.

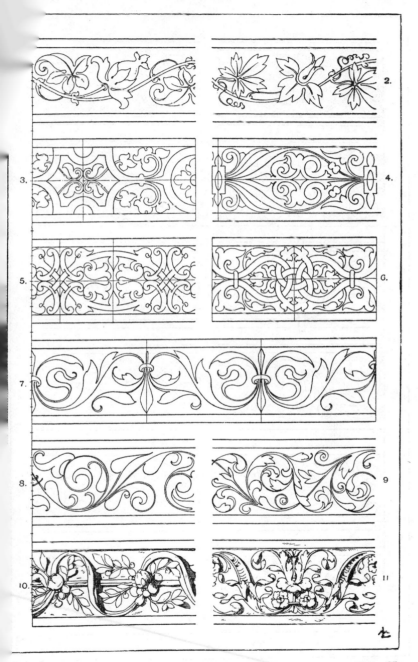

The Undulate Band, &c. Plate 95.

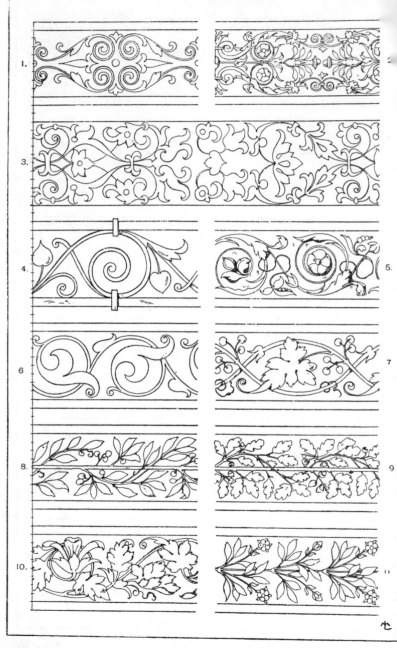

Plate 96. The Undulate Band, &c.

E 95. THE UNDULATE BAND, &C.

2. Leather stamping, 16th century, Schwäbisch Hall, (Muster-ornamente).

Terracotta frieze, castle of Schalaburg, Lower Austria, (Wiener Bauhütte).

4. Intarsia frieze, from the same castle.

5—6. Borders of robes, tombs in Niederstetten and Lensiedel, 16th century, (Musterornamente).

7. Renascence, manuscript ornament.

8—9. German Renascence, (Hirth, Formenschatz).

10. Archivolt of door, Otto-Heinrich building Heidelberg castle, German Renascence.

11. French, Renascence.

PLATE 96. THE UNDULATE BAND, &C.

1. Border, picture by Domenico Zampieri, 16th century, (Muster-ornamente).

2. Border, half-columns, Sta. Trinità, Florence, Italian Re-nascence.

3. Intarsia frieze, stalls, San Domenico, Bologna, Italian Re-nascence.

4. Wrought-iron trellis of balcony, Milan, (Gewerbehalle).

5. Frieze, Italian Renascence.

6. Modern, (César Daly).

7. Modern.

8—9. Laurel and oak borders, (Gewerbehalle).

10—11. Modern Borders, (Gewerbehalle).

THE EVOLUTE-SPIRAL BAND. (Plate 97.)

The wave of the sea has been suggested as the motive of this "wave" pattern; but its origin is purely geometrical. The line of the Evolute-spiral pattern divides the surface of the border into two parts, which in flat ornament are coloured differently. In plastic work, for which the pattern is also suitable, the lower part projects. In wrought-iron-work: the curved line runs freely between two bars. This pattern is adapted for borders of robes, shields, and plates; for use on vessels, friezes, cornices, and tablets in architecture; and also as borders, for tapestries, and mural-paintings.

A rosette is often placed at the volute-centres (Plate 97. 2 and 4); the interstices between the lines are sometimes decorated with leaves and flower-buds (Plate 97. 9—12). This occurs chiefly in the Renascence period, when the Antique seemed too simple. How

far this may be carried, in some cases, in shown by fig. 14, in w
the evolute-spiral line is nothing more than the skeleton of the c
ment. The Middle Ages did not use this form at all.

Angles, and centres are arranged as shown on figs. 4—7. T
band is excellently adapted for the framing round circular panels.

PLATE 97.   THE EVOLUTE-SPIRAL.

1—4.   Paintings, antique vessels.
5—6.   Angles.
7.   Central junction.
8.   Pattern round a circular panel.
9.   Painting of a stove tile, German Renascence, Germanisches
        Museum, Nuremberg.
10.   Modern borders.
11.   Border, by Sebastian Serlio, 16th century.
12.   Frieze, Otto-Heinrich building of Heidelberg castle.
13.   Wrought-iron trellis, temple of Apollo in the garden of the
        castle at Schwetzingen.
14.   Painting, Palazzo ducale, Mantua, Italian Renascence.

THE ENRICHMENT OF THE BEAD MOULDING. (Plate 98.)

Bead, or Astragal, is the name given to those small half-round
Mouldings, which are often enriched by ornaments like Pearls, strung-
together, &c., or as turned bands and cords.   Generally they are
only used in plastic art, and as a rule not alone; but below the Egg-
and-leaf ornaments, and similar cornice profiles (Plate 100).   They
also occur as intermediate members between the shaft and the capital
of columns.

Beads are enriched with balls, discs, or ovals, in rather more
than half relief.   The simplest bead-enrichment is formed of round
pearls, either close together or permitting the representation of the
thread to show between them.   Disc and oval enrichments are seldom
used alone, but arranged alternately, as shown in figs. 1 to 7.

In addition to the simple examples of the Antique, the Renascence uses richer forms, the single members being again ornamented,
profiled and more arbitrarily fashioned (Plate 98. 8 and 12), or
finished-off with small leaf calices (Plate 98. 9 and 10).   Wood
carving avails itself of strung discs seen in perpective (Plate 98. 11).

The enrichments may also suggest torsion.   After the moulding
is made, it is set-out like a screw, as indicated by the auxiliary
constructions in figs. 13—17.   Leaves or pearls sometimes lie in the
hollows and follow the thread of the screw (Plate 98. 17).

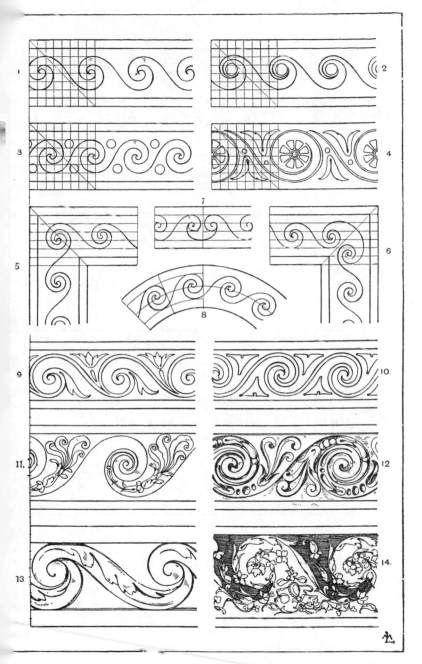

The Evolute-Spiral Band. Plate 97

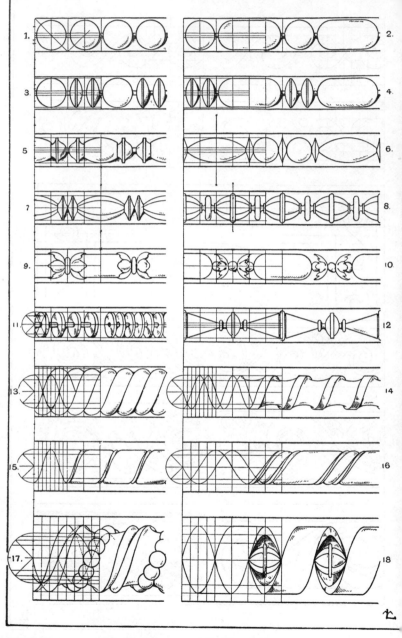

Plate 98. The Enrichment of the Bead Moulding.

Here also must be grouped those ribbons rolled spirally round ᵓds, such as we find in the art of the Middle Ages and the Re-ₗascence (fig. 18). Corners are generally covered with a small leaf.

THE ENRICHMENT OF THE TORUS MOULDING. (Plate 99.)

Torus is the name given to those larger mouldings of semi-circular or semi-elliptic section, such as are specially used in Architecture on the bases of columns and pilasters, on socles, on Mediaeval door and window arches, and on the ceiling mouldings of the Renascence and Modern times. While the smaller beads are ornamented with pearls and twisted cords, these more important mouldings are decorated by enrichments which resemble a bundle of rods round which ribbons are twisted at suitable places (figs. 1 and 2); by surrounding them with plaited or net work (figs. 3, 4, 7); by clothing them with foliage (figs. 6, 9, 10); or by combining the various systems (figs. 8 and 11). In modern times the Torus is enriched by bound clusters of fruit. Water-leaves, artificial leaves with serrated margins, laurel, oak, ivy, &c. are most in use for the leaf ornaments. As in the case of fruit clusters: ribbons are twined spirally at suitable placed round the fruit or foliage (figs. 5, 6 and 12).

All these examples are drawn by first marking-off the divisions on the profile, as indicated on the figures.

THE ENRICHMENT OF OTHER MOULDINGS. (Plate 100.)

The Egg-and-tongue enriches, in architecture, the ovolo moulding of capitals, and the lower members of cornices, &c.

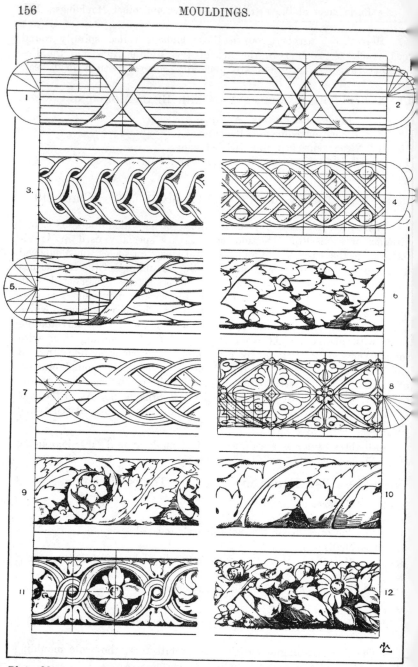

Plate 99. The Enrichment of the Torus Moulding.

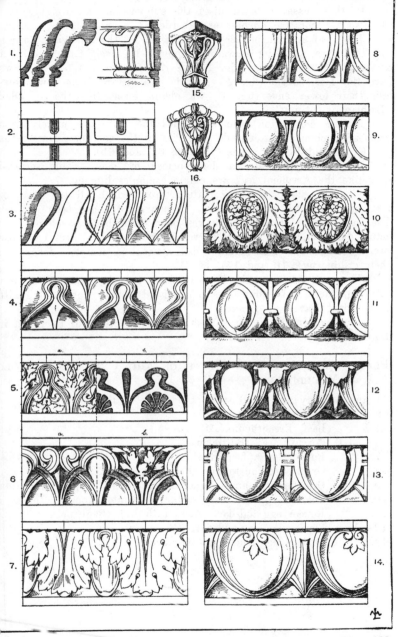

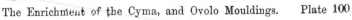

The Enrichment of the Cyma, and Ovolo Mouldings.　　Plate 100

In these cases it harmonises the support and the weight; and has also a decorative purpose as a bordering member.

The Leaf enrichment may be explained in the following way: a row of leaves, growing upwards, supports the weight, and is bent outwards by its pressure (fig. 1). If this only occurs partially, we have the Doric form (fig. 2). If the leaves are bent-down towards their lower ends (fig. 3), we obtain forms like the so-called "Lesbian cymatium."

A false conception, which regarded the leaf-shape merely as a geometrical element, afterwards gave rise to the corrupt forms of the late Greek and Roman styles (figs. 5a, 6a, and 6b).

If the simple waterleaf be replaced by more richly serrated ones like the Artificial leaf, we obtain examples like fig. 7.

Figure 8 shows the egg pattern, from which all the more or less misunderstood varieties have, in course of time, been derived. The dart-shaped intermediate leaves have often been developed into actual darts; and the eggs or curved surfaces of the leaves have also been covered with independent ornamentation, in complete defiance of their origin (figs. 10 and 14).

The corner is treated, either by freely carrying the pattern over into a palmette anthemion (figs. 15 and 16), or by covering it with independent leaves.

Further details on the subject of this chapter will be found in Bötticher's *Tektonik der Hellenen.*

PLATE 100.   THE ENRICHMENT OF THE CYMA AND OVOLO MOULDINGS.

1 and 3. Drawings to illustrate the origin of the pattern.
2.   Graeco-Doric, painted.
4.   Leaf, Erechtheum, Athens.
5 and 6. Corrupt leaf, (Bötticher).
7.   Roman leaf, (Jacobsthal).
8.   Greek egg-and-tongue, Erechtheum, Athens.
9.   Campana egg-and-tongue, Graeco-Italic, Campana collection
10.   Colossal egg-and-leaf, temple of Jupiter Tonans, Rome.
11.   Roman egg-and-dart, Arles cathedral, (Raguenet).
12—13. Renascence egg-and-dart, (Raguenet).
14.   Modern egg-and-dart, (Raguenet).

B.

FREE ORNAMENTS.

Those ornaments, which are applied to suggest the end or finish of an object, may be classed in a group which, following an expression already introduced, are termed "free ornaments", the word "free" implying not a severely-enclosed Band or Panel, but a freely-treated Edge-ornament.

The Edging may be arranged to grow in an upward, downward, or lateral direction; the character of the ornamentation will be dependent on these conditions. Endings with an upward direction are most numerous; and as plants, with their natural, upward growth, are adapted for this purpose, foliated ornament is the usual decoration of Akroters, Antefixes, Steles, Ridges, and Finials.

Crosses, Knobs, Rosettes, and Pendants, are independant Free-ornaments, which are generally geometrical in their treatment.

In Tassels and Fringes, which form endings in a downward direction, the organic plant motive is, of course, excluded; while Lace (woven, pillow, &c.) avails itself of both motives, either singly or combined.

Crockets are foliated excrescences which are popular in the Gothic style as an ornament of the edges, and ribs of buildings.

Gargoyles (as are termed the Rain-spouts which occur so frequently in the architecture of the Middle Ages and the Renascence) are also Free ornaments with a lateral direction; they have often the form of figures, less often those of decorated channels.

THE LINK BORDER. (Plates 101—102.)

Link Borders are so termed because the transversely-growing foliage is connected together by Scrolls which serve this purpose, like the "Links" of a chain. Of this class are much decoration of cornices, crestings in architecture, and fringes in textile art. Besides these, Link borders, which may be enlarged at will, and have a definite direction upwards or downwards, are used in a similiar manner as Borders as edgings for carpets, plates, and panels; as borders for walls, floors, and ceilings (in which case the edging almost invariably grows outwards); on the neck, body, and feet of vessels; and frequently in architectural friezes.

Palmette leaves, connected by circles or by links, are adapted for edgings. The typical form is found on Antique vessels and friezes; its forerunner is seen in the connected lily and pomegranate of the Assyrian style.

The Link-border is found in every subsequent style, both flat, and in relief.

It is generally composed of identical details, symmetrically repeated. Unsymmetrical and naturalistic forms are rarer, (Plate 101, 10).

PLATE 101. THE LINK BORDER.

1. Assyrian, painted bas-relief, Khorsabad.
2. External margin, Greek kylix, (Lau).
3. Greek hydria, (L'art pour tous).
4. Greek, cyma.
5. Mosaic ornament, San Marco, Venice, Byzantine, (Musterornamente).
6. Medieval, mural painting, Swedish church, (Racinet).
7. Old embroidery, Eisleben, (Vorbilder für Fabrikanten und Handwerker).
8. Painted, Cathedral, Brandenburg, (Vorbilder für Fabrikanten und Handwerker).
9. Illumination of a Koran, tomb of the Sultan El-Ghury, 16th century, (Prisse d'Avennes).
10. Majolica dish, Germanisches Museum, Nuremberg.
11. Majolica dish, 16th century, (Kunsthandwerk).
12. Modern, (Gewerbehalle).

PLATE 102. THE LINK BORDER.

1. Greek, carved frieze, Erechtheum, Athens.
2. Roman, frieze, (Fragments de l'architecture antique).
3. Romanesque, frieze, 13th century, (Musterornamente).

4. Arabic, mosque of the Sultan Hassan, Cairo, 14th century.
5. Italian Renascence, Marble frieze, tomb of the Conte Ugone, Badia, Florence, (Weissbach und Lottermoser).
6. Italian Renascence, Intarsia frieze, (Meurer).
7. Modern decoration, (Kolb und Högg, Vorbilder für das Ornamentenzeichnen).

THE LINK BORDER ON MOULDINGS. (Plate 103.)

The cyma in architecture is the topmost or concluding member of a cornice. It is frequently used as a gutter. The section is sometimes a concave or convex quadrant, but in most cases consists of two arcs curving inwards and outwards respectively, (fig. 3).

The ornamentation was merely painted in the earlier periods; but afterwards received a plastic form. It is chiefly composed of palmette leaves, either unconnected (fig. 1 and 2) or connected (figs. 3, 5 and 6), with Lily cups between. Artificial leaves, pointing upwards and lying close on the profile with calices or water-leaves peeping out between them (fig. 4) are also used.

The Middle Ages used both systems, especially the latter, with the latter, with the modifications required by the changed forms of the leaves, (figs. 7 and 8).

Both the Renascence and Modern art follow the tradition of the Antique; but give the Palmette ornament a richer form, (figs. 8—12).

PLATE 103. THE LINK-BORDER ENRICHMENT OF MOULDINGS.

1—4. Antique, (Bötticher).
5. Roman altar.
6. Graeco-Italic terracotta ornament, (Lièvre).
7. Romanesque cornice, house, Metz, 12th century, (Raguenet).
8. Cornice, Notre Dame, Paris, 13th century, (Musterornamente).
9—10. Cornice, Louvre, Paris, French Renascence.
11. Marble frieze, tomb in Sta. Maria sopra Minerva, Rome, Italian Renascence.
12. Modern, (Arch. Skizzenbuch).

THE CRESTING BORDER. (Plate 104.)

Crestings are intended to ornament the ridge or top of the roof. Such ornaments have been especially popular in France from Gothic

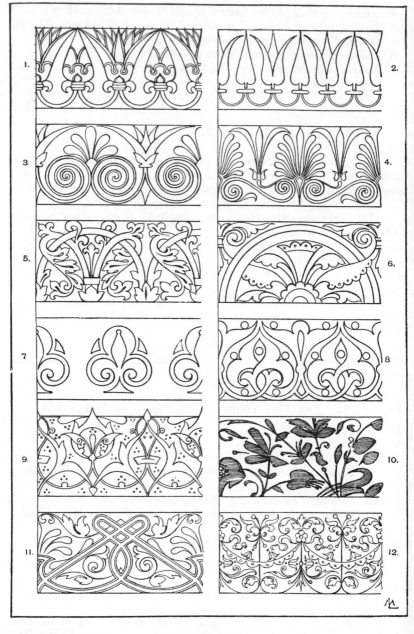

Plate 101.   The Link Border.

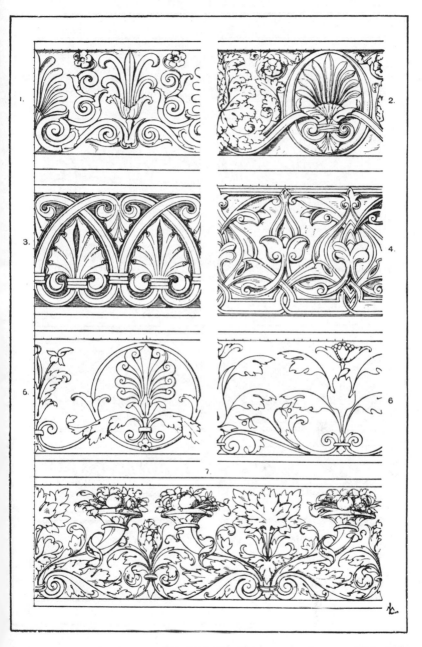

The Link Border. Plate 102.

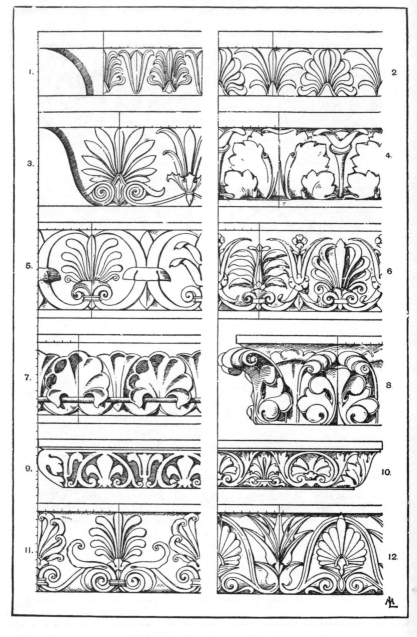

Plate 103.   The Link-border Enrichment of Mouldings.

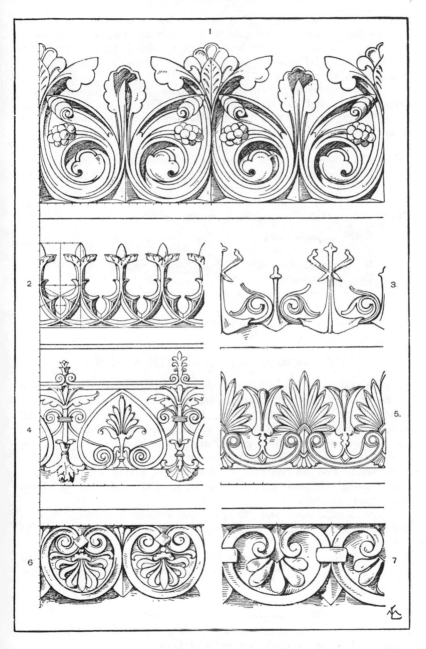

The Cresting Border.   Plate 104.

times to the present day. They are mostly of perforated work, and the top has usually a varied mass-shape. The materials used are stone, lead, wrought-iron, and, in modern times, zinc. Similar ornaments are also found as Finals of entablatures and attics, as well as on the Balaustrades of galleries.

Cresting ornaments appear on Gothic Altars, Shrines, Chimneypieces, &c., and in cast-iron on our modern Stoves, Railings, &c.

The Antique made no use of this form, although similar forms occur, as, for example, on the entablature of the well-known monument of Lysikrates. On the other hand, we must mention those Valence-like borders which are seen on the terracotta reliefs of the Campana collection, represented on figs. 6 and 7. In most cases, these latter ornaments, if reversed, may be used as crestings.

PLATE 104. THE CRESTING BORDER.

1. Gothic, (Jacobsthal).
2. Modern Gothic, cast-iron.
3. Modern French, castle of Pierrefonds, restored by Viollet-le-Duc, (Raguenet).
4. Modern French, Cour de Cassation, Paris, (Raguenet).
5. Modern German, by Gropius of Berlin, (Arch. Skizzenbuch).
6—7. Graeco-Italic borders, downward growth.

THE AKROTER, &c.   (Plates 105—106.)

The Akroter is the feature which serves as on ornamental finish to the apex of a gable. Antique temples bear this decoration in a great variety of materials: stone, terracotta, painted, plastic, and cast in metal. Groups of figures, griffins, &c., were sometimes used for this purpose; but the usual features were slabs of Marble, bearing a palmette ornament, the central decoration of which is sometimes a mask, (Plate 105. 5). Smaller ornaments of a similar kind are found ranged along the lower roof line, in front of the Imbrices; and these are termed Antefixes.

The Middle Ages and the Renascence make no general use of the Antefix, but it occurs on Modern monumental buildings in the Antique style.

The corner Akroter which isusually found at the lower ends of the gable lines, consists of half the motive of the central one, (Plate 105. 6).

PLATE 105. THE AKROTER, AND THE ANTEFIX.

1. Greek Akroter, painted, temple of Wingless Victory, Athens.
2. Greek Akroter, painted, Acropolis, Athens.

3.   Greek Antefix, Parthenon, Athens.
4.   Greek sepulchral Stele-crest, in the form of an Akroter.
5.   Graeco-Italic Akroter, terracotta, Museum, Perugia.
6—7. Front and side view of a corner Akroter, (Bötticher).

PLATE 106. THE AKROTER, &c.

1.   Greek Antefix, Propylaea, Athens, (Raguenet).
2.   Roman Antefix, temple of Jupiter Stator, Rome.
3.   Modern French Antefix, Théâtre des Celestines, Lyons, Architect Renaud, (Raguenet).
4.   Modern French Akroter, house in Paris, Architect Renaud, (Raguenet).
5.   Modern French Akroter, Orléans railway station, Paris, Architect Renaud, (Raguenet).
6—7. Akroter and Corner-akroter, fountain in the Certosa near Florence, Italian Renascence.

THE STELE CREST. (Plate 107.)

The Stele is the Greek tomb-stone. It usually takes the form of an upright tablet, sometimes tapering towards the top; and bears an inscription. It is sometimes decorated with rosettes, garlands and figures. At the top is a plain cornice,. on which an ornament, similar to the Akroter, forms the crowning finish. Although the Akroter and the Stele-crest often have a perfectly identical form (Plate 105. 4 shows a crest which might just as well have been an Antefix), still the style of the crest is as a rule more severe; and it is characteristic of a great number of Steles that they have not the striking palmette Centre, which the Akroter always possesses, (figs. 2 and 3). Very often, too, the crest is so designed that the sides are extended, to make a larger feature, (figs. 1 and 4).

These Monuments, dedicated to the memory of the dead, show better than almost anything else the special individuality and beauty of Greek ornament.

PLATE 107. THE STELE-CREST.

1. Stele-crest, (Stuart and Revett, Vulliamy, Jacobsthal).
2.   „   „   (Jacobsthal).
3.   „   „   ("L'art pour tous").
4.   „   „   (Lièvre).

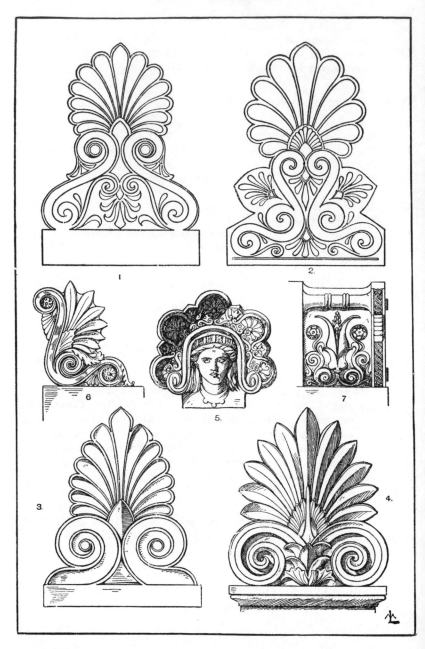

Plate 105.   The Akroter, and the Antefix.

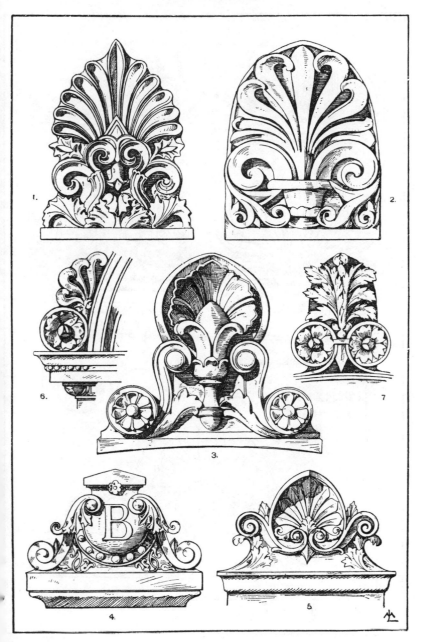

The Akroter, &c.   Plate 106.

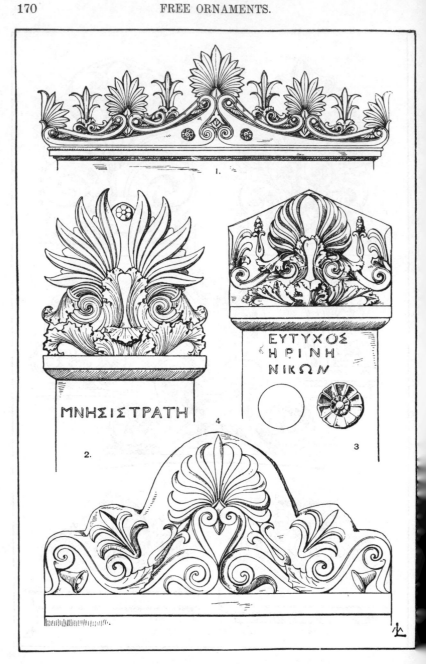

Plate 107.   The Stele Crest.

The Perforated Cresting. Plate 108.

THE PERFORATED CRESTING. (Plate 108.)

In modern wood buldings, the dressings, intended to form an ornamental finish to the construction, are often perforated.

The Gable is decorated by a Finial; smaller corner-ornaments are attached to the lower ends of the lines of the gable; the projecting ends of the gable-rafters are also provided with Barge-boards, both for decorative effect, and also, no doubt, to serve as a protection against the weather. The Finials are fashioned as Knobs of varied profile, with a direction downwards. The oblique lines of the Gable and the horizontal lines of the Roof are also covered with Barge-boards.

The material requires a special treatment; as the ornamentation must be large and broad, and have as many points of connection in itself as possible.

Wooden ornaments of this kind are found on Pavilions, watchmen's Huts, Farm-houses of richer construction, country Villas in the Swiss cottage style, &c.

Among architectural works which deal with wood buildings and especially with the decoration of them: we may mention the works of H. Bethke (Details für dekorativen Holzbau), from which the majority of the figures on Plate 108 have been taken.

PLATE 108. THE PERFORATED CRESTING.

1. Top ornament of a gable, by the architect Eisenlohr, of Carls-ruhe.
2—7. Various Barge-boards, (Bethke.

THE CROSS. (Plate 109.)

The Cross (Latin *crux*, French *croix*) is the most important symbol of Christian art. It symbolises the person of Christ, Christianity and Sacrifice. Its decorative applications are innumerable, and of great variety.

Various fundamental forms of the cross have been distinguished and are known by different names. The Greek (or St. George's) cross consists of two arms of equal length, bisecting each-other at right angles. In the Latin cross the lower limb is lengthened. These two forms are those most often used. In the St. Andrew's cross the arms cross each-other diagonally. St. Anthony's (the Egyptian or Old Testament Cross) is a Latin Cross without the upper limb.

Omitting from consideration the Crucifix, which represents the crucifixion of Christ, we shall find the Cross in the utmost variety

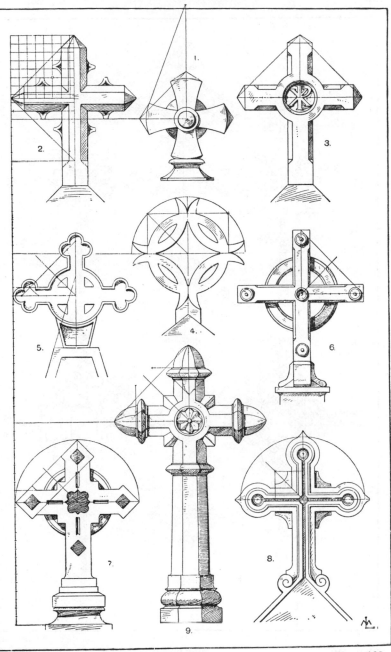

The Cross. Plate 109.

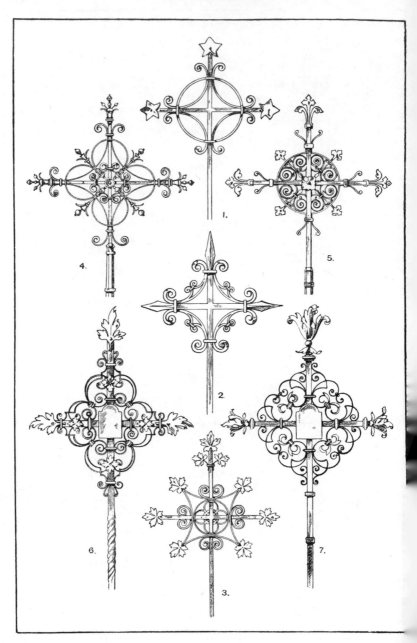

Plate 110.   The Cross.

of form on Utensils and Vessels, on Robes and Garments, on Carpets and Banners dedicated to religious uses; in Heraldry, and as a Free ornament to form the upper ornamental finial of Architecture. In Christian architecture: the Cross is used as a finial on Steeples and Gables, on Tombs, Pulpits, &c. Often it is employed alone, as a monument, (Tomb, wayside and votive crosses).

PLATE 109. THE CROSS: IN STONE.

1. Modern French, Charterhouse Glandier, (Raguenet).
2. Modern.
3. Modern French, with the Monogram of Christ, Genouilleux, (Raguenet).
4. Gable of a church, St. Urban's, Unterlimburg, Schwäbisch-Hall.
5. Tomb, churchyard, Baret, 11th century.
6. Modern French, Père-Lachaise, Paris, (Raguenet).
7. Steeple, St. Pierre, Montrouge, Paris, (Raguenet).
8. Tomb, St. Lazare, Montpellier, (Raguenet).
9. Granite, Tomb, Becon, (Raguenet).

THE CROSS IN METAL. (Plate 110.)

Wrought-iron, and, in late years, cast-iron and zinc, are sometimes used as a material for steeple and gable Crosses, as well as for monumental Crosses. The ductile nature of wrought-iron admits of a rich, delicate execution of these objects. The German Renascence, in particular, offers a wealth of forms in this respect.

The framework usually consists of strong bar-iron; the ornamental decoration is in flat or round iron, fastened to the frame by clamps or rivets. Hammered foliage is sometimes added. In many cases the point of the steeple Cross is decorated with a Cock as weather-vane.

The centre of monumental Crosses is often occupied by a plate of metal, to contain the Inscription.

PLATE 110. THE CROSS: IN METAL.

1—3. Mediaeval steeple Crosses, Franconia, (Gewerbehalle).
4. Modern steeple Cross, (Bad. Gewerbezeitung).
5. Steeple Cross, St. Ambroise, Paris, Architect Ballu, (Raguenet).
6—7. Wrought-iron tomb Crosses, Thiengen, 18th century.

THE FINIAL. (Plate 111.)

While the ordinary Cross rises as a Free-ornament in a vertical plane, the final makes a Cross, in plan. It extends its arms not only sideways, but also regularly to the front and back. Crocket-like additions (comp. plate 116) clothe the stem, which usually takes the form of an elongated four or eight-sided shaft. There may be one or more tiers of crockets.

The Finial serves to decorate Spires, Pinnacles, Baldachins, Tombs, &c., and is a specifically Gothic ornament. The most beautiful forms are furnished by French Gothic, from which most of the illustrations of our plate are taken.

PLATE 111.   THE FINIAL: IN STONE.

1.   Modern Gothic.
2.   Early Gothic, (Jacobsthal).
3.   French Gothic, (Viollet-le-Duc).
4.   Early Gothic, cathedral, Chartres, 13th century, (Musterornamente).
5—6. Modern, (Viollet-le-Duc).
7.   Modern, (Bosc).

THE FINIAL IN METAL.   (Plate 112.)

In the artistic wrought-iron work of the Middle Ages, the Renascence, and Modern times, we find charming Finials in the shape of idealised flowers. These decorations are found on the tops of Balaustrades, on the Gables over Doors, on Brackets and Chandeliers, on the supports of Rain-spouts, on Wall-anchors, &c.

Leaves, volute-like spirals, bell-flowers, and ears, are arranged round a central axis of iron; in many cases the centre is formed by spindle-shaped spirals of wire.

PLATE 112.   THE FINIAL: IN METAL.

1. Corner of a Mediaeval Grill, (Viollet-le-Duc).
2. Part of a Grill, Toulouse cathedral, 15th century, (Viollet-le-Duc).
3. Termination of a Fountain, Cluny museum, Paris, 15th century, (L'art pour tous).
4. Part of a Spanish Trellis Gate, 14th century, (L'art pour tous).
5. Part of a Chancel Screen, minster, Freiburg, 16th century, (Schauinsland).
6. Wrought-iron, 16th century, (Guichard).
7. Terminal, Bruges, 17th century, (Ysendyck, Documents classés de l'art).
8. Modern, wrought-iron, Ihne & Stegmüller, Berlin.
9. Modern, Post, by Ende & Boeckmann, Berlin, (Gewerbehalle).
10. Wrought-iron Coronal, Limburg on the Lahn, 17th century, (Kachel, Kunstgewerbliche Vorbilder).
11. Coronal, modern Gate, C. Zaar, Berlin.

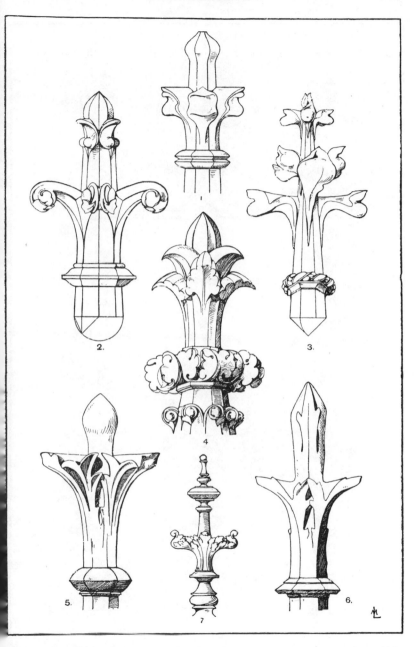

The Finial.   Plate 111.

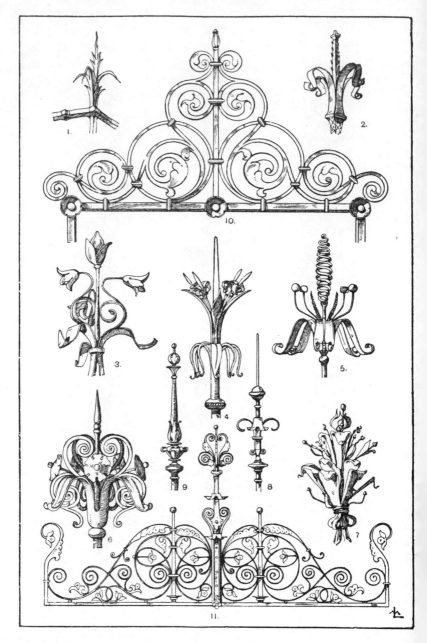

Plate 112. The Finial, &c.

THE FINIAL KNOB, AND VASE. (Plate 113.)

Knob is the term applied to ornamental terminations in the form of profiled bodies of revolution, naturalistic buds, fir-cones, &c.

Knobs are small features used as the terminations in architecture and furniture. They are also used on Flag-staffs, Bosses of Shields, Centre-pieces of rosettes, &c. The material, whether stone, wood, stucco, metal, &c., depends on the use to which they are to be applied.

Vases form another class of Finials. They are preferentially used on Tombs, Doorposts, in the centre of divided Pediments, on the Attics of ornamental Architecture, and instead of Antefixes.

PLATE 113. THE FINIAL KNOB, AND VASE.

1—2. Stone, Milan Cathedral, Italian Gothic, (Raguenet).
3.   Modern.
4.   Modern Fir-cone.
5.   Modern Vase, (Bosc).
6.   Modern French, Ministry of War, Paris, (Raguenet).
7—8. Modern French, house in the Park Monceau, Architect Tronquois, (Raguenet).
9.   Lower end of a Flag-staff or Lightning-rod, (Liénard).

THE PENDANT KNOB. (Plate 114.)

Pendants are hanging terminations; reversed Knobs, so to speak. In some cases, but not in all, the former may replace the latter. These Pendants are more or less elongated bodies of revolution. The decoration is produced by the addition of leaves, scales, beadings, nulls, &c. These being specially suitable to convex profiles, while the channelled treatment is better adapted to concave profiles.

Pendants, in stone, wood, stucco, or metal, are used as Brackets for lamps (hence their French name: *cul-de-lampe*); and as the lower terminations of Oriel-windows, Pulpits, &c. In the latter case the Pendants are generally only in half or three-quarter relief from the wall.

PLATE 114. THE PENDANT KNOB.

1—2. Part of Tripod, (Jacobsthal).
3.   Part of Lantern, Dijon, French Renascence, (L'art pour tous).
4.   Lower end of a Chandelier, 17th century, (L'art pour tous).
5.   Bracket under a Piscina, French, 16th century, Church, Moret, (L'art pour tous).
6.   Modern, stucco-work.
7.   Modern, wood.

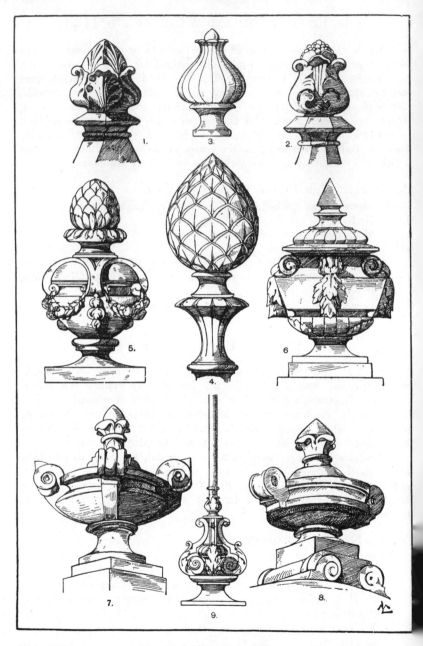

Plate 113.   The Finial Knob, and Vase.

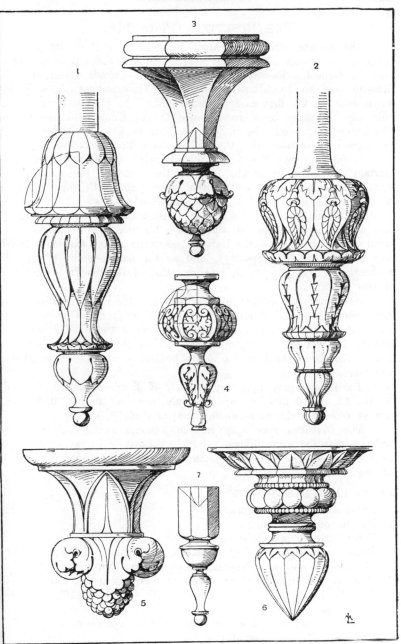

The Pendant Knob.   Plate 114.

THE ROSETTE. (Plate 115.)

The Rosette, strictly so called, is an artificial Rose. In a wider sense any ornament of a circular shape, which radiates from a centre, may be termed a Rosette. According to its execution and use: the Rosette may be considered either as a Free-ornament, or a Panel-ornament. In the first case, it must always be plastic, project prominently and have some resemblance to the Knob or Pendant. In the latter case, it may be in low relief or be a flat ornament. Here we have only to deal with the Rosette as a Free-ornament.

Considering the Rosette from this point of view: its most important application is as the Boss in the centre of Romanesque and Gothic ribbed Vaultings; and as the centre-piece of Ceilings, of which we find numerous examples in the temples of the Antique, the palaces of the Italian Renascence, and the vaulted Cupolas of ecclesiastical and secular architecture. Besides this, Rosettes are found on Furniture, Gates and Doors (the Italian Renascence makes the most lavish use of them in this capacity), and as the centre-pieces of modern Ceilings, &c. In these cases, however, their quality as Free-ornaments is less prominent.

As regards the formal plan of Rosettes: the Flower motive is the commonest; geometrical motives are rarer, and motives from figures rarer still. The arrangement is usually in a series of zones; the growth is from the centre, outwards; and in the majority of cases is radial, that is at right angles to the bordering circle; but sometimes the leaves are curved.

The Rosette may have any number of divisions; but 3, 4, 5, 6, 8, 10, 12, or 16 divisions are the rule; divisions into 7, 9, 11, &c., are as rare as divisions exceeding the number 16.

The Divisions may vary in the separate zones; but generally only so that the same divisions interlock, that is to say, the points of the leaves of one zone fall on the intervals between the leaves of the next.

PLATE 115. THE ROSETTE.

1. Antique, of four divisions.
2. Roman, of five divisions.
3. Naturalistic, of six divisions.
4. Romanesque Boss, of four divisions, chapter-hall of the monastery of Heiligenkreuz near Vienna, 13th century, (Musterornamente).
5. Early Gothic Boss, of three divisions, Sainte-Chapelle, Paris, 1240.
6. French, of four divisions, Louis XIII, (1610—1643), (Musterornamente).
7. Italian, of five divisions, the door of the baptistery, Parma, Renascence, (Musterornamente).
8. Modern French, ceiling-flower, stucco.

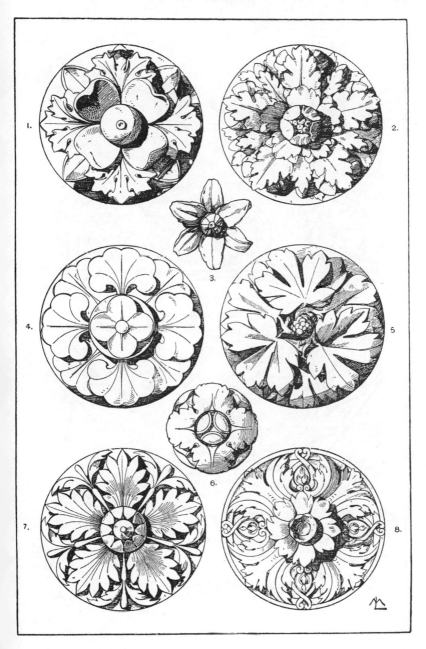

The Rosette. Plate 115.

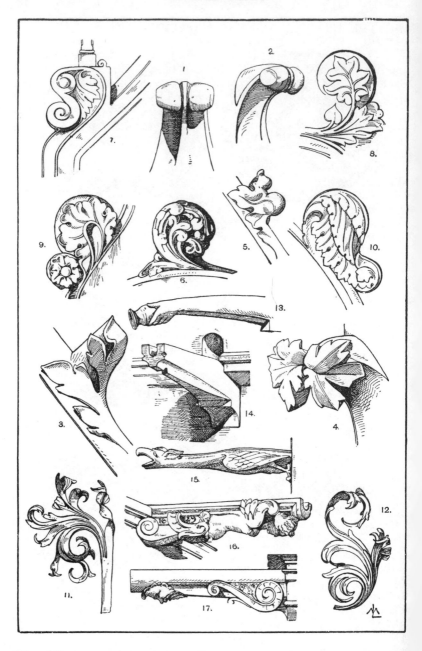

Plate 116.   The Crocket, and the Gargoyle.

THE CROCKET, AND THE GARGOYLE. (Plate 116).

Crocket is the designation applied to those excrescences which appear on the edges of Spires, and Pinnacles, and on the raking lines of Gables, in the richer Gothic styles. Occurring at regular intervals, they form an ornamental interruption to the bald architectonic lines.

At first of a rather naturalistic character (figs. 3 and 4), they evolved during the decay of the style a more artificial character, assuming bulbous forms (fig. 5), which have their own special peculiarities in England, France, and Germany.

Crocket - ornamentation has more or less been copied from stone Architecture in Furniture, Choir-stalls, &c. The arms of the latter (figs. 6—10), and the miserere-seats, are often foliated like a Crocket.

Metal, and particularly wrought-iron work, frequently makes use of Crockets, in forms suited to the nature of the material, (figs. 11—12).

Contrary to the modern method, by which the water that collects on the roofs of buildings is conveyed to earth through Pipes, the builders of the Middle Ages and the Renascence discharged the rain, clear of the wall, by means of long projecting Spouts. The spout was used in the Antique style in the form of lion heads, &c. In the ecclesiastical and monumental architecture of the Middle Ages they are termed Gargoyles; and are mostly of stone. In dwelling houses they are of sheet-metal; and they are either architectonically decorated (fig. 14), or human, animal, or fantastic figures, treated in a comic manner, the water flowing through the mouth or other orifices of the body.

Copious material on the subject of crockets and gargoyles will be found in Raguenet's "Materiaux et Documents de l'Architecture".

PLATE 116. THE CROCKET, AND THE GARGOYLE.

1—2. Front and side view of a plain Gothic Crocket, Amiens cathedral, restored by Viollet-le-Duc, (Raguenet).
3. Gothic Crocket, 14th century.
4. Modern Gothic Crocket, Paris, (Raguenet).
5. Gothic Crocket Milan cathedral, (Raguenet).
6. Arm of a Stall, Salisbury cathedral, (Raguenet).
7—10. Arms of Stalls, monastery, Maulbronn.
11—12. Wrought-iron, Gothic, Augsburg.
13. Gargoyle, Viollet-le-Duc, Eglise d'Eu, (Raguenet).
14. Gargoyle, bell-tower, St. Sernin, Toulouse, restored by Viollet-le-Duc, (Raguenet).
15. Gargoyle, Meaux cathedral, (Raguenet).
16—17. Gargoyle, St. Eustache, Paris, (Raguenet).

THE DECORATED HINGE, &c. (Plate 117.)

The Middle Ages, and after them the Renascence, brought the developement of wrought metal-work to the highest state of perfection. Here we have to consider the different kinds of bands, technically known, according to their shape, as Hinge, Strap, &c.

Although these bands were originally intended only to bind-to-gether the underlying wood construction of gates, doors, caskets, chests, &c., the bald, practical form was soon made decorative; and this the more readily that the Gothic principle of wood construction, with its narrow stave-like or matched strips of wood, offered only scanty opportunities of artistic decoration.

Delicate series of lines, designed as Free-ornaments, start from the Hinge and terminate as leaves and flowers. The heads of the necessary rivets and screws, themselves shaped as rosettes in the richer examples, give a pleasing relief. Gothic usually applies the extended Strap-hinge (figs. 7—8); while the Renascence, in accordance with its principle of bordering in wood constructions, prefers the shorter Butt-hinge (figs. 11—12). In the latter epoch the surface of the metal received further decoration trough the arts of etching, engraving, niello-work, &c. Book-mounts, in particular, offered a wide field for the application of these arts.

Modern times have with justice devoted increased attention to these objects; and have restored them to the domain of art from which various causes had excluded them for almost a century.

The plate gives a small selection from the copious material to be found in museums and publications.

PLATE 117. THE DECORATED HINGE, &c.

1. Gothic hinge, church-door, Viersen near Cologne, 15th century.
2—3. Plain terminations of hinges, Hefner-Alteneck collection, 16th century.
4—5. Terminations of hinges, Town-hall, Münster.
6. Termination of hinge, Prie-dieu, Gelnhausen, 15th century, (Musterornamente).
7. Gothic hinge, Door of a cabinet, Town-hall, Zwolle.
8. Gothic hinge.
9. Renascence hinge, old Kaufhaus, on the Limmat, Zürich, 1618.
10. Renascence hinge, Town-hall, Augsburg, 17th century, (Musterornamente).
11. Renascence hinge, Door in Ettlingen, United collections, Carlsruhe.
12. Door-hinge, German, 1580, Free imitation by Prof. Storck, (Zeichenvorlagen).

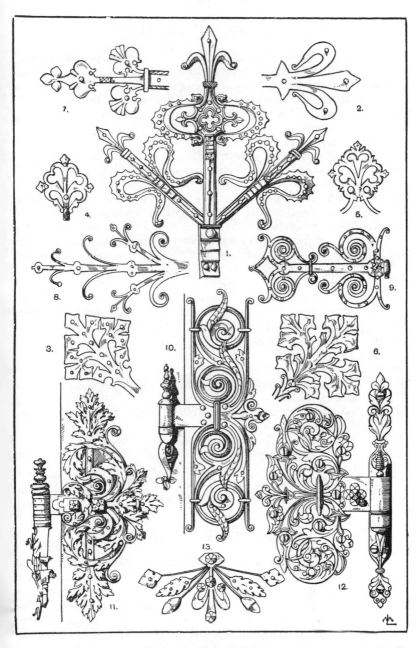

The Decorated Hinge, &c. Plate 117.

THE TASSEL. (Plate 118.)

The chief contributions of textile art to the group of Free-ornaments are Tassels, Fringes, and Laces. The two latter are current edgings, the first, on the contrary, are the termination of the lower end of cords or of shaped draperies. Thus we find Tassels used on Girdles, Bell-pulls, and Curtain-holders; as pendants from Flags, Standards, Valences, Cushions, Table-covers, Palls, and Tent-covers; also on Pouches, Hoods, Caps, Harness, &c.

The Tassel consists of a tuft of threads or cords, hanging straight down from a core of wood, turned in various profiles, and decorated with twisted threads. The original may be assumed to have been the cord with a simple knot, the knot being intended to keep the cord from ravelling-out. The Tassel is undoubtedly of great antiquity. The reliefs found in Khorsabad, Niniveh, and elsewhere, show that the Assyrians were great admirers of such kinds of trimming. And, although such a lavish use does not occur again; there would probably be little difficulty in finding examples of tassels from all periods of Art.

Not only form but also colour contributes to the effect of Tassels, so that the examples in our plate really only give half the effect. An exhaustive study of Trimmings, by Jacob Falke, will be found in Teirich's "Blätter für Kunstgewerbe" 1875.

PLATE 118.   THE TASSEL.

1.   French lady's girdle, 12th century, (Viollet-le-Duc).
2—3.   Tassels, Holbein, (Teirich).
4.   Tassels, Turkish harness, 17th century, United collections, Carlsruhe.
5.   Tassel, old standard, United collections, Carlsruhe.
6.   Tassel, Tunisian pistol, United collections, Carlsruhe.
7.   Leather tassel, lady's bag, German Renascence.
8—10. Modern tassels, by Aug. Töpfer, (Gewerbehalle).
11.   Modern tassel, by A. Seder, Munich.

THE FRINGE, AND THE VALENCE. (Plate 119.)

If, at the end of a piece of material, the weft-threads (parallel to the end) be drawn-out, the remaining warp-threads will form a simple Fringe. If we give the end greater security, by knotting or tieing the threads together in tufts, we get the ordinary Fringe. The Fringe, however, is not always made of the material; it is often manufactured independently, and sewed-on to the edge of the material. In this case the Fringe is combined with a woven heading-band (gimp).

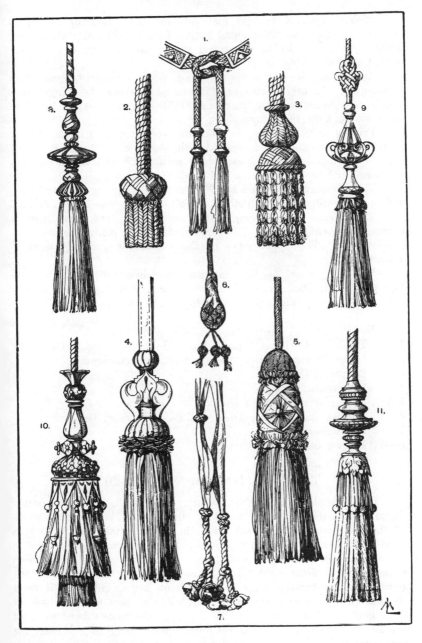

The Tassel. Plate 118.

Richer types of Fringes may be produced either by variety of the edge, so that tufts of unequal lengths form rhythmically alternating groups (fig. 2), or by using several thicknesses of Fringe, lying one behind the other, (fig. 4).

The Fringe is always applied long, when a pendant termination is required. In other cases as, for example, where the fringed material is to lie horizontally, like small Table-covers, Napkins, &c., it is advisable to keep the fringe short.

Fringes have been in use from the very earliest periods; but it is again the Orientals, and especially the Assyrians, who show a preference for this form. Fringes occur perpetually in various national costumes, and in the toilet of our modern ladies.

The Renascence adopted the Fringe as a trimming for furniture, and specially for chairs; although not always with true artistic feeling.

The Valence is a hanging textile termination; the lower edge is ornamentally cut, and is often ornamented with cords, tassels, embroidery, &c. The upper edge of the Valence is generally fixed to a moulding.

Valences occur as the interior furnishing of Windows, on four-post Beds, Baldachins, Canopies, Tents, Marquees, &c.; of late years, they have been used on Awnings, and Outside-blinds.

PLATE 119. THE VALENCE.

1.   Tomb of the Incas, Ancon, Peru, United collections, Carlsruhe.
2.   Indian-Mexican pouch, United collections, Carlsruhe.
3.   Egyptian, (Ebers).
4.   Renascence, (Storck).
5.   Mediaeval maniple, (Teirich).
6.   Turkish saddle-cloth, 1690, United collections, Carlsruhe.
7.   Renascence, silver.
8—9. Modern designs, by Prignot.

THE LACE BORDER. (Plate 120.)

Of all products of the textile art, Lace is the most interesting. There is something poetical about it, like flowers. The combination of the conventional treatment with those accidental features which hand-work confers upon the delicate, light material, gives them a peculiar charm. Who invented lace manufacture, and in what year, cannot now be determined. Lace is one of those things which the Renascence has handed down to us without having inherited it from the Antique. The stimulus, to the invention of lace and the basis of its manufacture, is probably to be found in the textile hand-work of the Middle Ages, such as was practised, particularly in convents, for ecclesiastical purposes.

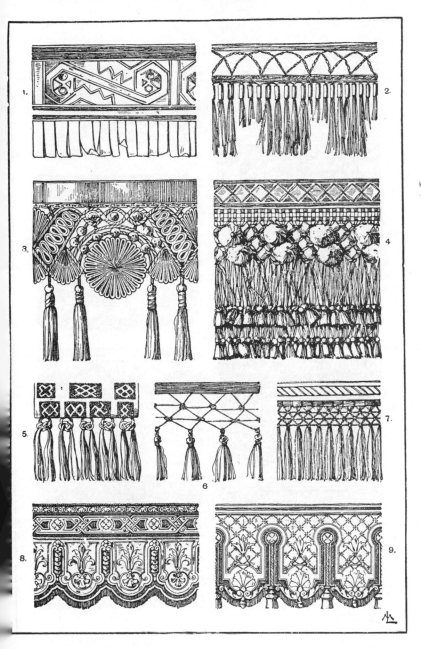

The Fringe, and the Valence. Plate 119.

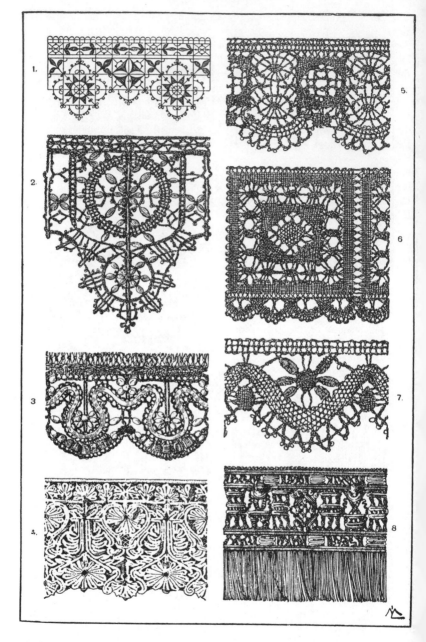

Plate 120. The Lace Border.

Lace belongs in most cases to the Free-ornaments. More rarely it is manufactured as an Insertion, with the character of a ribbon, or for independent use as a Shawl or Wrap. Compared with Fringe, the applications of Lace are freer and more varied, and by no means confined to the character of a pendant termination. The reader may be assumed to be acquainted with the various uses of lace.

If we exclude the allied Crochet-work as not strictly belonging to this section, we shall find that the manufacture of Lace may be divided into two groups: (1) sewed or Point lace; and (2) bobbin or Pillow lace. The former method has chiefly been practised in Italy, Spain, Ireland, and France; the latter in England, France, the Netherlands, Schleswig, Switzerland, and Saxony. The chief centres of the lace industry were and to some extent still are: Venice, Genoa, Milan, Ragusa, Devonshire, Buckinghamshire, Ireland, Alençon, Valenciennes, Brussels, Mechlin, Binche, Tondern, Annaberg, &c.

As in other branches, the cheap Machine-made article has nowadays reduced the manufacture of the dearer but far more valuable Hand-made lace to very modest limits. See Reports on Lace, by Alan S. Cole (Department of Science and Art).

Among the numerous kinds of Lace for which no generally recognised terminology as yet exists, we have selected some, principally of older date, among which the best patterns are to be found:

Point coupé (punto tagliato). The linen ground is cut-out and the edges worked with the needle.

Point tiré (punto a maglia quadra). Single compartments of a quadrangular knotted or woven net are filled-up.

Point tiré (punto tirato). The threads of the linen fabric are partially pulled-out, the others connected together and sewed round.

Point coupé (punto a reticella). Groups of threads stretched lengthwise and crosswise like a net, are spun round and connected.

Point noué (punto a groppo). Produced by plaiting and knotting the threads.

Point lace. The threads are sewed together, following the pattern, and joined together by "brides". This is almost the only kind of lace which can now be found on ladies' work-tables.

PLATE 120. THE LACE BORDER.

1. Venetian guipure, old pattern-book.
2. Point noué, end of the 15th century.
3—4. Old, point.
5—8. Modern, pillow, old patterns.
9. Modern, knotted, with fringe, (Macramo lace).

C.

SUPPORTS.

All those elements of ornamental art which express the idea of supporting or bearing, are here gathered into a special group to which is given the name "Supports".

Supports, in the strict sense of the word, are piers or columns. But it does not fall within the scope of this work to treat these forms from the architectural point of view, or to enter into the details and proportions of the so-called "Orders of Architecture". All that is required on this point may be gained from the works of architectural specialists: Bötticher, *Tektonik der Hellenen;* Mauch and Lohde, *Die Architektonischen Ordnungen;* R. Phené Spiers, *The Orders of Architecture*; Vignola; Durm and others. We will therefore disregard the undecorated forms, and discuss only the decorative details of these supports.

Like a tree which consists of root, trunk, and crown, Piers and Columns necessarily have a base, a shaft, and a capital. (The Doric Column is an exception as it has no base.) The natural model for the Pier and the Column is the trunk of a tree hewn into a cylindrical or prismatic form. The motive of the channellings and flutings of the shaft of a support is to be found in the channels and flutings of Endogeneous Plants.

Supports which, like piers and columns, are intended to bear a considerable weight, usually have a strong cylindrical or prismatic structure, generally tapering towards the top; the fundamental forms of the Candelabrum, which is meant to bear only an inconsiderable weight, like Lamps, &c., are freer, have more variety, and offer a wider field for decoration than the forms of the former group. The Candelabrum is also divided into foot, shaft, and crown. The shaft, again, is frequently composed of several distinct parts. The candelabrum as a whole will receive a more detailed consideration in Division III, (Utensils).

Small Pillars, shaped like a pier, column, or candelabrum, are also used for the construction of balaustrades; in which case they have to support only a Rail.

The small Pillars have thick, compact forms; Balausters, on the contrary, are slender bodies of revolution, with great variety in the profile.

Very peculiar forms of support are the antique Trapezophors or table-legs; the Legs of modern furniture bear more resemblance to balauster pillars.

Terminus is the name given to supports which widen out in an upward direction like an inverted Obelisk, and terminate in a bust or capital.

Beside the geometrical and plant elements, the human form is also used as a motive of supports. Male forms thus used are termed Atlantes; and female forms Caryatids.

The various forms of Consoles are included in the group of Supports.

THE FOLIATED SHAFT. (Plate 121.)

We have already mentioned that the Plant-world furnishes the motive for the forms of Supports. Reeds, Canes, Tree-trunks with knots, &c., were copied in the Antique.

The mural paintings of Pompeii show lofty airy constructions with extremely slender, foliated supports. The bronze Candelabra and Lampadaria, intended to hold lamps, are often direct imitations of plant stems, while the Roman State-Candelabra are often decorated with Artificial foliage. Later epochs have made little change in this respect; it may be said in general that, as regards delicacy of feeling, and moderation in the application of natural forms, they have seldom reached and still more seldom surpassed the Antique models.

PLATE 121. THE FOLIATED SHAFT.

1. Finial of the choragic monument of Lysikrates, Athens, (intended for the reception of a bronze tripod), Greek.
2. Part of the shaft of a Roman State-candelabrum, marble, Vatican museum, Rome.
3—4. Supports, mural paintings, Pompeii, (Jacobsthal).
5. Graeco-Italic, Lamp-stand, bronze.
6. Upper part of shaft, Graeco-Italic candelabrum, Bröndsted collection, (Vulliamy).

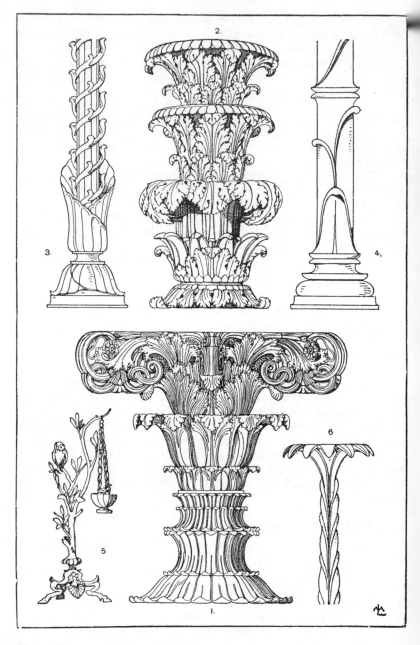

Plate 121.   The Foliated Shaft.

The Fluted Shaft. (Plate 122.)

Columns, Piers, Candelabra, and similar Supports frequently have annellings or flutings. The object of these is to give animation to the smooth shaft, and to emphasize the expression of the principle of weight-bearing. This latter is specially true of the channellings.

In the Doric style the Flutings are shallow without any interval, only divided from each other by a sharp edge, (figs. 1 and 2). The Ionic and Corinthian shafts, have deeper flutings (figs. 3 and 4), separated from each other by fillets formed of the untouched surface of the shaft. The channellings terminate upwards like small niches, with semicircular or elliptical heads, (fig. 5). Leaf-like terminations, like that on fig. 13 are rarer. The termination downwards is similar to those shown on figs. 6—8.

The number of channellings on a shaft varies from 18 to 24. On smaller constructions, such as Furniture, Balausters, &c., the number is reduced; but seldom less than 8. The Channellings taper proportionately with the shaft. Pilasters are also channelled to match the Columns. In strict Architecture, rich and composite channellings and flutings are rather injurious than otherwise (figs. 7—11); but on Candelabra, and Mouldings they often produce a good effect. When applied to the Torus and the Cavetto: the former (convex) should be decorated by Nurls; and the latter (concave) should have Flutes.

PLATE 122. The Fluted Shaft.

1 — 2. Sections of Doric Fluting.
3 — 4. Sections of Ionic and Corinthian Fluting.
5 — 6. Construction of the terminations of Fluting on cylindrical shafts.
7—11. Composite Fluting, with sections, and terminations.
12.   Part of an Antique Candelabrum, with tapered Fluting.
13.   Termination of the Fluting, monument of Lysikrates, Athens.

(The construction is clearly indicated on the drawings.)

The Base. (Plate 123—124.)

It is unquestionably more beautiful when something in the shape of a Base is interposed between the shaft of a column and the substructure on which it rests, than when, as in the Doric style, the column rises without any such base. Bases suggested by the radical leaves of plants, are common in Oriental styles. Plate 124, fig. 1 gives an Egyptian example of this kind. Decorations of this sort are, however, oftener applied to the lower end of the shaft than

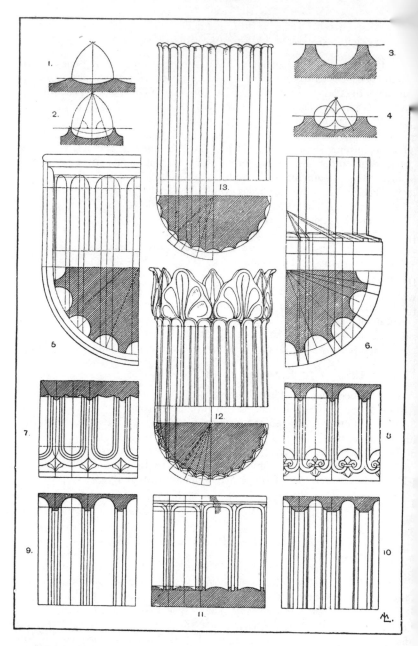

Plate 122.   The Fluted Shaft.

,o the Base itself. This natural method of decoration is also met-with on richly decorated examples of Roman style, where a row of Artificial leaves encircle the shaft, (Plate 123. 3). Antique Bases are composed of a square foundation slab (the plinth); and some mouldings which follow the circular plan of the shaft. The well-known and oft-used Attic Base, consists, beginning from below, of a plinth, a great torus, fillet, scotia, fillet, upper torus, fillet and apophyge. The last, as a quarter-hollow forms the transition between fillet and shaft. When the plinth is decorated, which is the case only in very rich examples, the motive is either a band or a scroll. The tori are decorated with braided work, as shown on Plate 99, the hollow or "scotia" is sometimes decorated with leaves, the smaller tori may be treated as astragals; and so on. Plate 123 shows three rich Roman examples. Others will be found in Bötticher's *Tektonik der Hellenen*.

The Byzantine and Romanesque periods follow the Antique in the treatment of Bases. The spaces which remain on the upper surface of the square plinth are, however, filled up with ornament (Plate 124. 3, 7, 8, 10), or with small animal figures, (Plate 124. 9). In the later Gothic style the torus overlaps the sides of the plinth, which reduces these spaces; the corners of the plinth are also sometimes finished as shown on Plate 124. 6.

The Gothic period prefers geometrical to organic form; and secures good effects by a variety of profiles placed high up on composite clustered columns, (plate 124. 11) gives an example of this. Remark the similarity with the Chinese example, fig. 2, which would seem to have been suggested by a cluster of juxtaposed shafts.

The Renascence and modern styles resort to direct copying from the Antique; but, as a rule, do not use ornamented mouldings.

The treatment of the Bases of piers and pilasters is usually identical with that of columns; so that there is no necessity for dealing with these separately.

PLATE 123. THE BASE: ROMAN.

1. Capitoline Museum, Rome, (De Vico).
2. Temple of Concord, Rome, (De Vico).
3. Baptistery of Constantine, Rome, (Vorbilder für Fabrikanten und Handwerker).

PLATE 124. THE BASE: ROMANESQUE, &c.

1. Egyptian, Temple of Tutmes III, Karnak, (Raguenet).
2. Chinese, (Raguenet).
3. Romanesque, coupled, Schwarzach.
4—6. Mediaeval.
. Romanesque.

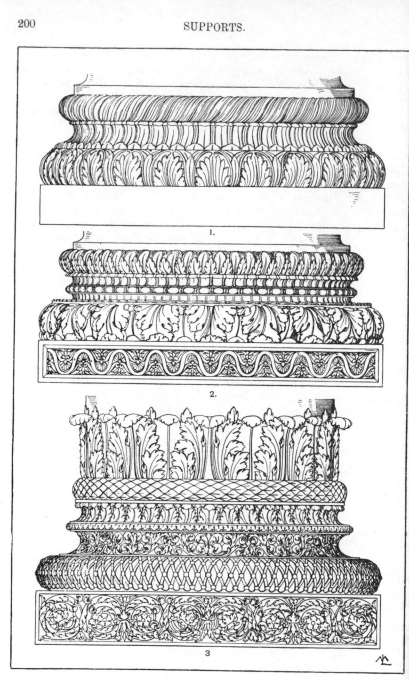

1.

2.

3.

Plate 123. The Base.

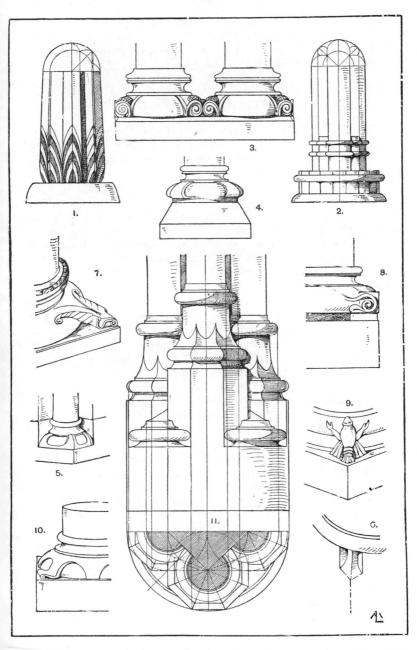

The Base.   Plate 124.

8. Romanesque, St. Remy, Reims, (Raguenet).
9. Romanesque, Cistercian monastery, Maulbronn.
10. Romanesque, Abbey "des Dames", Caen, (Raguenet).
11. Gothic, church, Brou-Asn, (Raguenet).

THE ORNAMENTED SHAFT. (Plates 125—126.)

The simplest, most natural and perhaps the most beautiful decoration of a Shaft is fluting, beyond which the Antique very seldom goes. Where it does: it clothes the stem in naturalistic fashion with plant-forms, (Plate 125. 4).

In the Byzantine, Romanesque, and Scandinavian styles: we often find the shaft covered with a geometrical network, and ornamented in a corresponding style, (Plate 125. 2—3). The Gothic style prefers to leave the slender shafts smooth.

The Renascence is not satisfied with the simple flute especially on small architectural work like Altars, Monuments, &c. The craving to give the Column a decoration commensurate with that of the other parts of the architecture became irresistible. It is raised on a pedestal; the shaft is banded, being divided into parts by projecting Cinctures, generally two, the lower at about one-third, the upper at about two-thirds of the height. On the lower part are suspended festoons, weapons, trophies, cartouches, &c., the upper part is channelled or decorated with Artificial foliage (Plate 125. 1); finally, festoons of fruit or drapery are suspended from the capital.

Where the Columns are not large, especially in Furniture, the cylindrical shaft is replaced by the richer profiling of a more candelabrum-like form, (Plate 126. 5). Flat ornamentation is also used, as well as plastic decoration, by means of painting, incrustation, or inlaying, (Plate 125. 5).

All these methods of application are more or less in agreement with the object and principle of construction of the Column, but the same cannot be said of the Renascence and the following styles of the Decadence, which build up their Columns of large and small drums, alternately ornamented and plain, or even give the Shaft a spiral twist and decorate it with spiral flutings.

PLATE 125. THE DECORATED SHAFT.

1. Italian Renascence, Tomb in Sta. Maria del Popolo, Rome, by Sansovino.
2. Romanesque.
3. Shaft, church, Tournus, (Raguenet).
4. Roman, marble.
5. Column, with intarsia decoration, German Renascence, (Hirth).

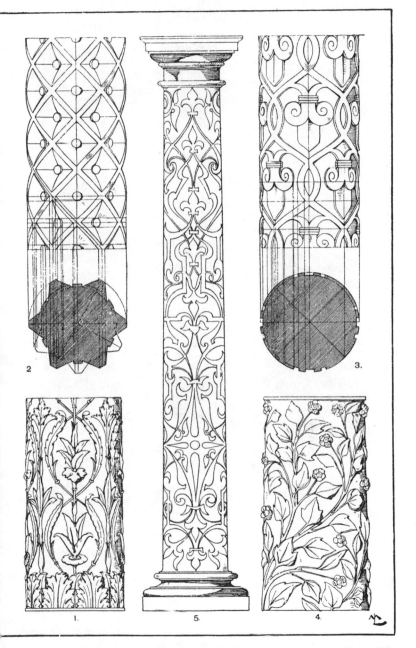

The Decorated Shaft.   Plate 125.

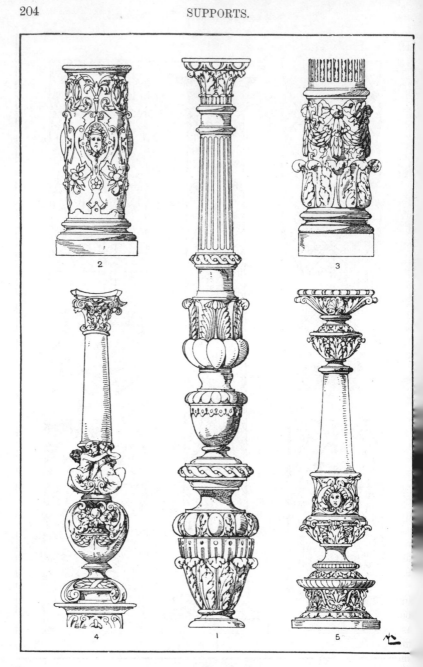

Plate 126.   The Profiled Shaft.

PLATE 126. THE PROFILED SHAFT.

1. Candelabrum-like column, tester-bed, French Renascence.
2. Lower part of a column, Mayence cathedral.
3. Lower part of column, Palais du Commerce, Lyons, (Raguenet).
4. Column, diploma, Modern.
5. Column, Modern, (Gerlach).

THE CAPITAL. (Plates 127—130.)

The upper termination of the column is the Capital. The Capital forms the transition from the supporting Shaft to the superincumbent Weight. This transition may assume either geometrical or organic forms. Very frequently both systems are combined; so that, strictly speaking, we can only say that one system or the other predominates.

The Egyptian capital is suggested by the cinctured bundle of Papyrus stems with buds (Plate 127. 4, 5), or with opened Papyrus or Lotus flowers, (Plate 127. 2, 3).

Abnormal capitals are found in the Old Persian style. Plate 127. 1, gives an example from Persepolis, composed of the fore-parts of Bulls.

As examples of Oriental forms: two Moorish capitals from the Alhambra in Granada are given on figs. 6 and 7 of the same plate.

Antique art adopts three general types of Capitals: Doric, Ionic and Corinthian.

The Doric Capital consists of the abacus, which is square in plan, and the echinos, which is circular. The transition to the shaft is effected by hollow mouldings and astragals. The Graeco-Doric Capital was painted. Where the sides of the abacus are decorated: a Fret pattern is employed (Plate 127. 8). The echinos is a member of conflict, and is ornamented accordingly. In the Roman and Renascence styles plastic ornamentation takes the place of painting. The band of leaves becomes an egg-and-dart ornament (Plate 127. 10). Leaves pointing upward are sometimes used (Plate 127. 9). At the top of the abacus a small moulding is used. A necking, generally decorated with rosettes, is interposed between Capital and Shaft. Similar rosettes decorate the spaces on the under side of the abacus (Plate 127. 9—10).

The Ionic Capital replaces the square abacus by a scroll rolled-in on both sides, in great volutes. The intervals, between the egg band and the scroll, are marked by palmettes. A neck may be added as in the Doric Capital, and it is frequently decorated with a palmette ornament (Plate 128. 4—5). The side view of the scroll shows plain profilings as on Plate 128. 1, decorated with leaves or scales in the richer examples. The Ionic Capital has two faces, and two sides. For this reason it is of only limited application, as, when the capital is applied to the corner column of two adjacent sides of a building, it is impossible to avoid a bad effect from the two reentering volutes on the inner faces.

The fundamental form of the Corinthian Capital is the calix. The decoration may be designed on two methods. Firstly a row of leaves, or two rows arranged alternately one above the other, clothe the lower cylindrical part of the capital, and plain broad waterleaves form the transition to the square abacus. To this class belongs the capital of the Tower of the Winds in Athens, and a capital found on the island of Melos, which is shown on Plate 128. 7. Or, secondly: volutes rise from the rows of leaves and unite in pairs under the corners of the abacus, which are then extended, so that the sides are rendered concave in plan. The centre of each sides of the abacus is decorated with a palmette or rosette (Plate 128. 8—9).

The fusion of the Ionic and Corinthian capitals produced the Composite capital; whose appearance is more interesting than beautiful (Plate 128. 10).

Early Christian, and, to a certain extent, Byzantine and Romanesque art, models the forms of capital on those of the Antique. The Corinthian Capital is the one mostly followed. The details are made correspondingly simpler and ruder (Plate 129. 6—11). But along side of these reminiscences of the Antique, new and independent forms appear. The antagonism between the cylindrical under part and the square upper termination is adjusted by geometrical constructions. Thus originated the Cushion and the Trapeziform Capital. The Cushion capital is specifically Romanesque. A half sphere is cut by planes below and on the four sides. Its simplest form is given on Plate 129. 1. The decoration is sometimes geometrical (Plate 129. 2 and 12), and sometimes contains foliage and figures (Plate 129. 5). The Double-cushion Capital is a variant of the Cushion capital (Plate 129. 4). The Trapeziform capital is specifically Byzantine. In this style: the cylindrical shaft is continued to the square abacus, which causes each side of the Capital to assume a Trapeziform shape (Plate 129. 3). Very often these Capitals are richly decorated with figures.

The arrangement of clustered-shafts, so popular in the Middle Ages, led to the Coupled-capital, which appears sometimes as conjoined capitals (Plate 129. 10), and sometimes as the juxtaposition of two ordinary capitals with a conjoined abacus.

In the Gothic style, particularly in its later period, the abacus becomes octagonal. Crocket-like knots of leaves are loosely attached to the calix-formed core. The vigourous projections of these leaf ornaments give the Capital the appearance of an inverted bell (bell capitals, Plate 129. 13—14).

The Renascence adopts the Doric and Ionic Capitals, and more usually the Corinthian Capital directly borrowed from the Antique; but the forms become freer and more varied; and, compared with the overcharged Roman examples, simpler. The volutes at the corners develope into independent forms, and are often replaced by dolphins, cornucopias, and other fantastic forms, scattered instances of which may, however, be found even in the Antique. Modern architecture, like the Renascence, also follows these traditions.

PLATE 127. THE CAPITAL.

1. Ancient Persian, Persepolis.
2. Egyptian, Kôm-Ombo.
3.   „   Philae.
4.   „   Memnonium Thebes.
5.   „   Luxor, (Owen Jones).
6—7. Moorish capitals, Alhambra, Hall of the two sisters, (Raguenet).
8. Graeco-Doric.
9. Roman-Doric, thermae of Diocletian, (Mauch and Lohde).
10. Doric, Italian Renascence, by Barozzi da Vignola.

PLATE 128. THE CAPITAL.

1. Graeco-Ionic, (Jacobsthal).
2. Ionic, Bassae, (Cockerell).
3. Ionic, Pompeii.
4. Roman-Ionic, (Musterornamente).
5. Graeco-Ionic, Erechtheum, Athens.
6. Ionic, Louvre, Paris.
7. Antique Corinthian, found in Melos, (Vorbilder für Fabrikanten und Handwerker).
8. Greek-Corinthian, monument of Lysikrates, Athens.
9. Roman-Corinthian, palaces of the emperors Rome.
10. Roman Composite, Louvre, Paris.

PLATE 129. THE CAPITAL.

1. Romanesque Cushion-capital, St. Gereon, Cologne, (Otte).
2.   „   „   „ the abbey church, Laach, (Otte).
3. Byzantine, Sta. Sofia, Constantinople.
4. Romanesque Double-cushion-capital, Rosheim church, XI. century.
5. Romanesque Double-cushion-capital.
6. Romanesque Cushion-capital, Freiburg.
7—9. Romanesque, former cloisters of the church, Schwarzach.
10. Romanesque Coupled-capital.
11. Romanesque.

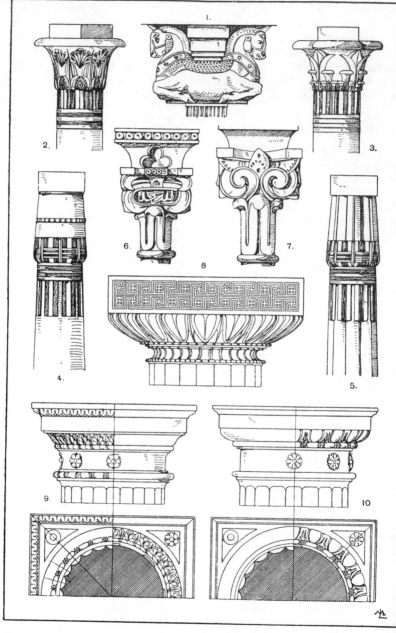

Plate 127.   The Capital.

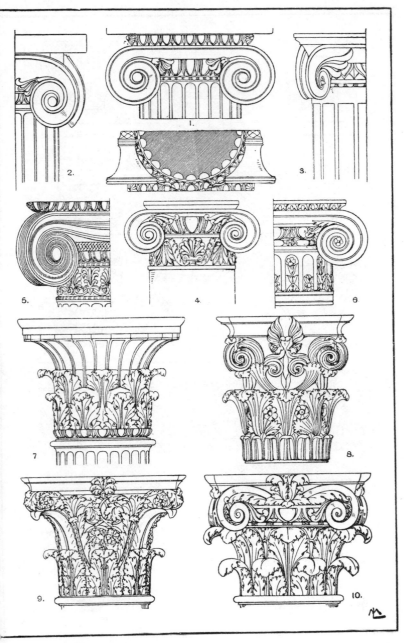

The Capital.   Plate 128.

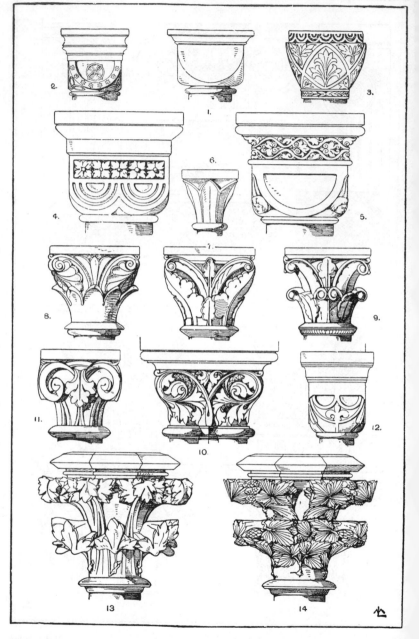

Plate 129.   The Capital.

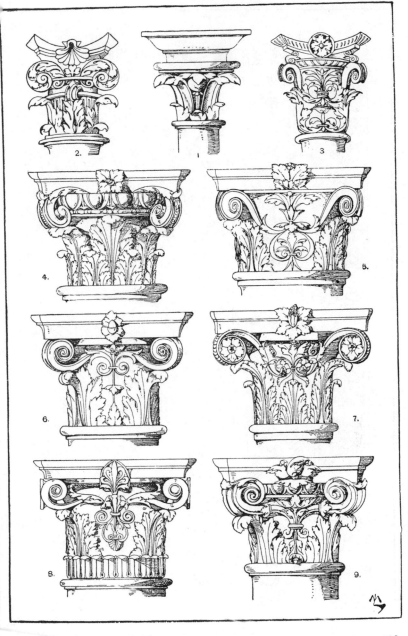

The Capital.

Plate 130.

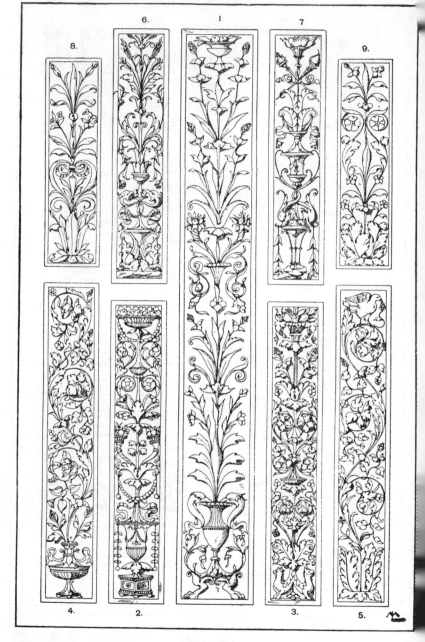

Plate 131. The Pilaster Panel.

:2.   Romanesque Cushion-capital, monastery, Lippoldsberg.
13—14. Late Gothic, triforium of the choir, minster Freiburg.

PLATE 130. THE CAPITAL.

1.   Renascence, drawing by Holbein, (Guichard).
2—3. Renascence, designs by Heinrich Voigtherr, (Hirth).
4.   Composite, Italian.
5.   Renascence, Palazzo Scrofa, Ferrara, Italian.
6.   Renascence, Tomb in Sta. Maria del Popolo, Rome, by San·
      sovino.
7.   Renascence, Italian, Palazzo Zorzi, Venice.
8.   Modern, municipal baths, Carlsruhe, Architect Durm.
9.   Modern French, Vaudeville theatre, Paris, Architect Magne.

THE PILASTER PANEL. (Plate 131.)

In many cases the Pilaster or wall-pier shaft is devoid of ornament. Unlike the column, the Pilaster does not, as a rule, taper upwards; and if the Pilaster is ornamented with fluting the tapering
is never permissible. The Pilaster frequently has cinctures, generally
two, the lower at $^1/_3$, the upper at $^2/_3$ of its height. The ornamental
decoration, when present, takes the form of an elongated, sunk panel
bordered by a moulding. The ornamentation may be of three kinds:
firstly: an ascending plant motive may be used, rising symmetrically
or in the form of a wavy line from calices, vases, &c., animal and
human figures being not infrequent accessories; secondly, the decoration may consist of festoons of flowers, fruits, trophies, shields, &c.,
varied by knots and ribbons, the points of suspension being rosettes,
rings, lion heads, &c.; thirdly, the panel may be decorated with flat
strapwork, as in the Elizabethan manner.

Of these three kinds of decoration the first is the most used;
and the most suitable. Few Antique examples have come down to
us; the Middle Ages make scarcely any use of the Pilaster; but
the Renascence is much richer in such examples. Stalls, Altars,
Sepulchral-monuments are scarcely to be found without Pilasters.
Plate 131 offers a small selection from the copious material; all the
panels show the first of the three kinds of decoration.

PLATE 131. THE PILASTER PANEL.

1.   Italian Renascence.
2—5. Italian Renascence, Sta. Maria dei Miracoli, Venice.
6 7. Italian Renascence, by Benedetto da Majano.
8—9. Modern Panels, in the style of the Italian Renascence.

THE PILASTER CAPITAL. (Plates 132—134.)

Generally speaking, the structure of the Capital of the pilaster follows that of the Column; and, to a certain extent, translates the forms of the latter from the round to the flat. This observation is true in the Renascence period; but not in the Antique.

In Pilaster-capitals in the Doric style one or more leaf or egg-and-dart mouldings run under the abacus, and are covered at the corners with palmettes or leaves. Beneath this proper part of the Capital a neck more or less high is usually found, decorated with rosettes or with other ornaments (Plate 132. 1). On modern Capitals of this class the neck may even be fluted (Plate 134. 7); not infrequently the centre of the Capital is still further decorated by the addition of masks, symbols, &c. (Plate 134. 7 and 8).

While the Renascence adopted the form of the Ionic Capital with scarcely any change for its pilasters (Plate 134. 4), the Antique possessed a special form of pilaster Capital of this order (Plate 132. 2).

The most numerous, varied and beautiful Capitals of pilasters are in the Corinthian order. The profile and general arrangement are the same as with the columns; generally, however, the pilaster is broader in proportion to its height. The lower part is encircled by Artificial leaves which sometimes dwindle to the two corner leaves supporting the volutes. The volutes are of the most varied descriptions, sometimes replaced by cornucopias, dolphins, chimeras, and other figures (Plates 132. 8 and 133. 5). Leaf-ornaments, vases, garlands, calices of flowers, &c., are arranged at the centres (Plate 132. 4—8), also masks (Plate 133, 4, 5 and 8). Neckings are rare on Corinthian capitals (Plate 133. 7). The egg-and-dart mouldings, which run along the bottom of Antique examples (Plate 132. 4—5), are reminiscences of the Doric style, so that these forms may also be regarded as a kind of transition Capital.

PLATE 132. THE PILASTER CAPITAL.

1.   Greek-Doric anta, Erechtheum, Athens.
2.   Greek-Ionic anta.
3.   Greek-Corinthian.
4—6. Roman-Corinthian, (Bötticher).
7.   Roman-Corinthian, Pantheon, Rome.
8.   Roman-Corinthian, Temple of Mars Ultor, Rome, (De Vico).

PLATE 133. THE PILASTER CAPITAL.

1.   Corinthian, Italian Renascence, Court of the Scala dei Giganti, Venice, (Wiener Bauhütte).

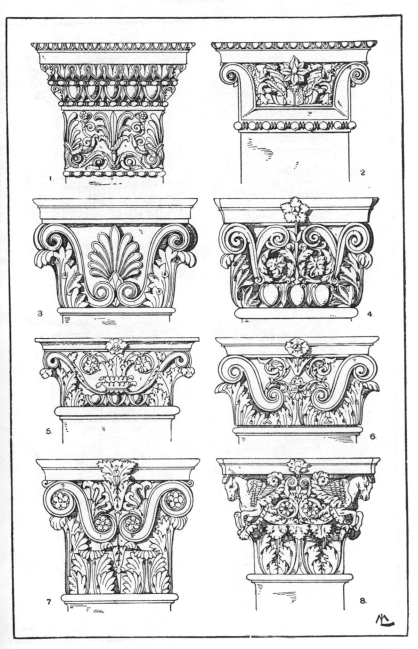

The Pilaster Capital. Plate 132.

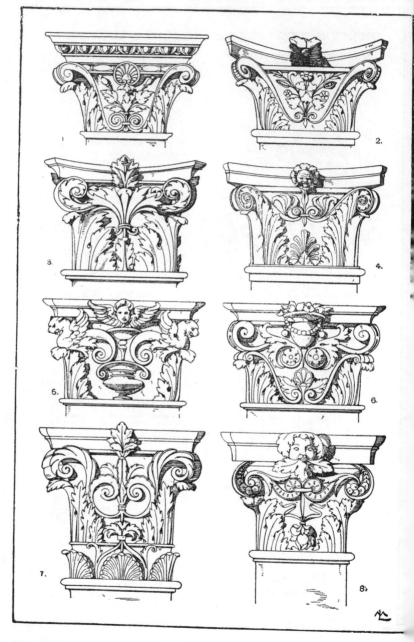

Plate 133.   The Pilaster Capital.

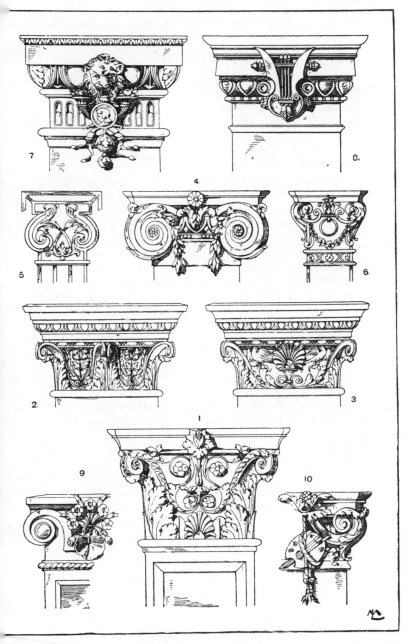

The Pilaster Capital.   Plate 134.

2. Corinthian, Italian Renascence, Sta. Maria dei Miracoli, Venice.
3. Corinthian, Italian Renascence, Certosa, Florence.
4. Corinthian, Italian Renascence, Scuola di San Marco, Venice,
    by Pietro Lombardo.
5—6. Corinthian, Italian Renascence, Chapel of the Palazzo Vecchio,
    Florence, (Musterornamente).
7. Corinthian, Italian Renascence.
8. Corinthian, French Renascence, Tomb of Louis XII, St. Denis.

PLATE 134. THE PILASTER CAPITAL.

1.   Corinthian, Italian Renascence, Portal of San Michele, Venice.
2—3. Corinthian, Italian Renascence, Palace of the Doges, Venice.
4.   Ionic, French Renascence, (Lièvre).
5.   Wrought-iron, castle at Athis-Mons, French, 17th century.
6.   Wrought-iron, by Jean Berain, French, 17th century, (Raguenet).
7.   Modern Doric, Architects Kayser and v. Grossheim.
8.   Modern Doric, new Opera House, Paris, Architect Garnier.
9.   Modern Ionic, Rue Dieu, Paris, Architect Sedille.
10. Modern Corinthian, atelier of a painter, Paris, Sculptor Bloche.

THE CANDELABRUM FOOT.   (Plate 135.)

For lighting, the Candelabrum played an important part in the
domestic and religious life of the Ancients. In the House, they
mostly employed slender, delicate bronze Candelebra; and for Religion,
the great State-candelabra of marble. The Candelabrum, like the
column, consists of three parts: the base, the shaft, and the capital.

To afford the necessary steadiness, the base of the Candelabrum
is planned on a comparatively large scale, and divided into three legs,
which stretch-out, towards the points of an equilateral triangle. For
the foot, the claw of an animal, and in particular the claw of the
Lion, is used. Not infrequently the claws rest on balls or discs
(Plate 135. 6). The transition to the shaft is designed with a double
calix, the upper leaves of which rise and encircle the shaft, and the
lower leaves descend and mask the junction of the three legs
(Plate 135. 1 and 5). A delicate anthemion may be perceived
between each pair of feet on richer examples (Plate 135. 2 and 3).
In exceptional cases the leg appears to grow from the mouth of an
animal (Plate 135. 6). Occasionally a circular, profiled and decorated
disc is used instead of the double calyx and anthemion. Sometimes,
too, the shaft is prolonged downwards beneath the disc in the form
of a knob, but does not touch the ground.

It is obvious that the delicate forms and the division into legs, which was so suitable for a material like bronze, could not be transferred directly to the construction in marble; but reminiscences of it may be seen in the retention of the triangular ground-plan, the reduced claws, the double calyx, &c. (Plate 135. 8).

PLATE 135. THE CANDELABRUM BASE.

1. Antique, bronze, Museum, Naples, (Bötticher).
2.   „   „   (Bötticher).
3.   „   „   Studj publici, Florence, (Weissbach and Lottermoser).
4—5. Antique, bronze, Museum, Naples.
6—7. Legs from antique candelabra: the former found in the ruins of Paestum; the other in the Museum, Naples.
8. Roman, State-candelabrum.
9. Renascence candelabrum, Collection of drawings, Uffizi, Florence.

THE CANDELABRUM SHAFT. (Plate 136.)

The decoration of the Shaft of the antique bronze domestic Candelabrum is simple; and consists of flutings or channellings, sometimes of naturalistic buds and leaves.

Far richer is the ornamentation of the Antique State-candelabrum. It is divided into zones (Plate 136. 2), or the shaft swells and diminishes alternately, giving a richer profile (Plate 136. 1). Smooth and fluted parts with contrast with foliage and figure; and the ascending decoration is varied by trophies and festoons. The effect depends on the propriety of the division. The repetition of similar masses or similar forms becomes tedious.

The Antique and also the Renascence, particularly in Italy, has transmitted to us a number of standard forms of Candelabra; of which a few examples are reproduced Plate 136.

PLATE 136. THE CANDELABRUM SHAFT.

1. Roman, marble.
2. Roman, marble.
3. Antique, (Bötticher).
4. Mast-socket, Piazza of S. Mark, Venice, bronze, Italian Renascence.
5. Candelabrum-like foot of a holy water-stoup, Pisa cathedral, Italian Renascence.
6. Italian Renascence, Badia near Florence.

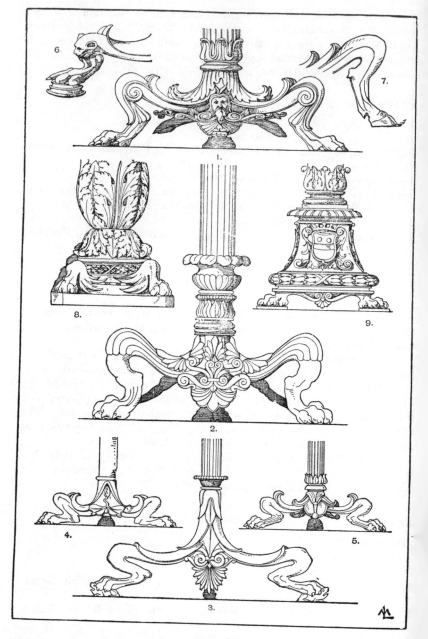

Plate 135.   The Candelabrum Base.

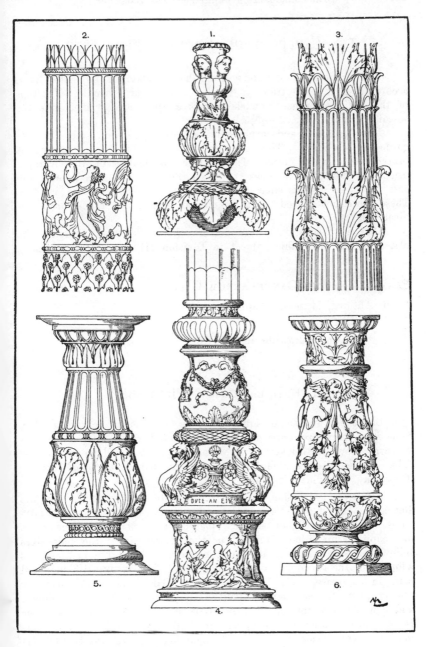

The Candelabrum Shaft.   Plate 136.

The Candelabrum Capital. (Plate 137.)

The Capital of a Candelabrum has a plate or cup-like form, according as it is destined to receive a lamp, or a candle. The tops of the Antique bronze Candelabra, as a rule, are profiled like the so-called Krater (figs. 1—5).

The profiles, and ornamentation already given, may be regarded as standards. The insertion of real capitals, or of figures, as bearers (fig. 6) is rarer. The marble Candelabra of the Antique usually terminate in a plate or table (fig. 7); and this is also the case with the Renascence Candelabra intended to receive candles. These were not placed in a cylindrical socket but stuck on a conical pricket.

On the decoration of Candelabra the reader may compare the plates dealing with this subject in Division III, (Group of Utensils).

Plate 137. The Candelabrum Capital.

1—6. Antique, Museum, Naples.

7.   Roman.

8.   Renascence, drawing in the Uffizi, Florence.

The Balauster. (Plate 138.)

Balausters are small squat columns of circular or square plan. Sometimes they are only symmetrical around their axis, sometimes however they are also symmetrical in an upward and downward direction. In most cases their construction is that of the candelabrum. They may be divided into base, shaft, and capital.

Ranged side-by-side in a row, balausters are employed by the Renascence and modern art in Parapets, Balconies, Attics, and Staircases. When the Balausters are placed on a Stair-case: the bases and capitals are either slanting, or the horizontals of the Balausters follow the slanting lines of the stair-case. The latter method was adopted in the Decadence of the Renascence, but is unjustifiable; and can, in any case, only be adopted with Balausters of a square or oblong plan. A rich variety may be obtained by the use of square and cylindrical forms in the same Balauster (fig. 5). The Balauster is occasionally used as a support for Stalls, and on Furniture. Raguenet's "Documents et Materiaux" contains a large number of Balausters; from which we have selected some examples.

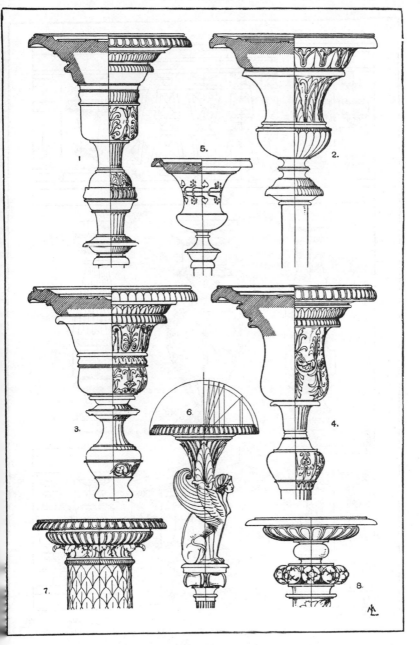

The Candelabrum Capital.   Plate 137.

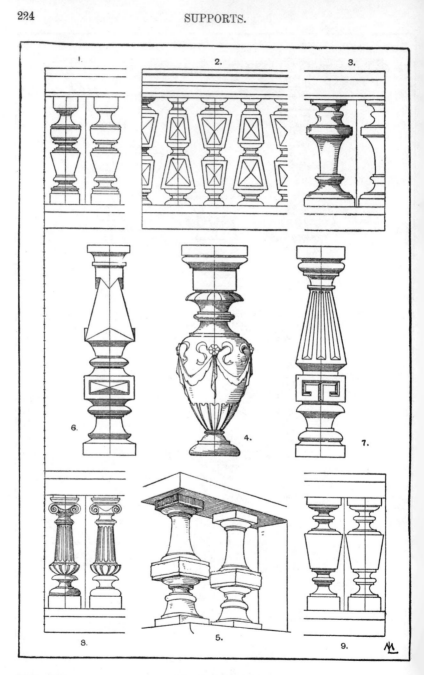

Plate 138.

The Balauster.

PLATE 138. THE BALAUSTER.

1. Square plan, Italian Renascence, Sta. Maria della Salute, Venice.
2. A system of square Balausters, Palazzo Pesaro, Venice.
3. Circular plan, Modern Italian.
4. Wood, Italian Renascence, stalls in Sta. Maria Novella, Florence.
5. Modern French, Architect Roux, Paris.
6—7. Square wooden, (Bethke: "Der decorative Holzbauer").
8—9. Modern, terracotta.

THE TERMINUS. (Plate 139.)

The Terminus is a pilaster-like support, the fundamental form of which is characterized by tapering downwards in a manner recalling an inverted Obelisk. The name is derived from the fact that similiar constructions were used in the Antique as milestones and to mark the Terminations of fields, &c. The Terminus consists of the profiled base, not infrequently supported on a special pedestal (figs. 3 and 7); the shaft tapering downwards and usually ornamented with festoons (figs. 3, 4, 5, 10); and the capital, which is often replaced by a bust or half-figure (figs. 4, 5, 9). In this latter case, it assumes the appearance of a caryatid; and, as the bust is that of Hermes (the God of letters), this application is often termed a "Hermes". Standing isolated, it serves as a Pedestal for busts and lamps, as a Post for railings, and in gardens and terraces. The last was exceedingly popular in the Rococo period. Joined to the wall, the Terminus often takes the place of the pilaster. This is especially true of the furniture and small architectural constructions of the Renascence period. It is also not uncommon on Utensils, e. g. tripods, handles of pokers, seals, &c.

PLATE 139. THE TERMINUS.

1. Upper part, antique, silver treasure of Hildesheim, Berlin Museum, (obviously from a Roman tripod).
2. Stone Terminus bust, Italian Renascence, Villa Massimi, Rome, (Raguenet).
3. Stone Terminus bust, German Renascence, mantel-piece, town-hall, Lübeck.
4. Stone Terminus bust, German Renascence, Otto Heinrich building, Heidelberg Castle.
5. Stone Terminus bust, German Renascence, monument, church of the castle, Pforzheim.

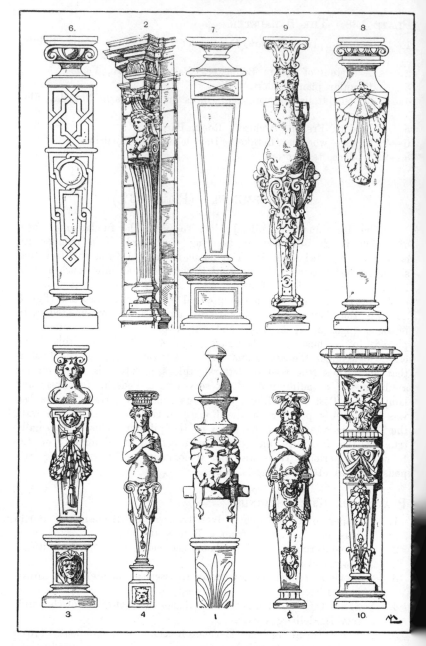

Plate 139. The Terminus.

6—8. Wooden Terminus, Renascence.
9.   Small Terminus figure, German Renascence, National Museum, Munich.
10.   Terminus with mask, modern chimney-piece, (Gewerbehalle).

THE PARAPET. (Plate 140.)

Besides the Parapets which are formed by rows of balausters, there are others which are arrangements of pierced or perforated tsone or wood, and cast or wrought iron. The Gothic style prefers Tracery, the Renascence prefers Scrolls for stone parapets (figs. 1 and 3). Parapets of perforated wood, which are typical of Swiss architecture, are composed of strips of boards, with shapes more or less rich, care being taken that the intervening spaces also form pleasing shapes.

To construct Parapets in the form of bi-axial trellises, was a popular custom of the Renascence; and it has continued so to the present day. But the function of the supports is only fully shown when the pattern has an upward direction. This, however, does not exclude the use of other treatments, e. g. panels. Raguenet has numerous examples.

PLATE 140. THE PARAPET.

1.   Modern Gothic, stone, Viollet-le-Duc, (Raguenet).
2.   Modern Gothic, stone, Viollet-le-Duc, Castle of Pierrefonds, (Raguenet).
3.   Stone, German Renascence, Dagobert tower, new Castle, Baden-Baden.
4—5. Trellis, Schinkel, (Vorb. f. Fabr. u. Handw).
6.   Modern French, Hôtel Mirabeau, Paris, Architect Magne, (Raguenet).
7.   Trellis, Barocco, wrought-iron, French.

RAILING POST. (Plate 141.)

Staircase railings, are formed of rows of upright Posts. These are of slender, delicate form; and take the place of the stouter balauster.

The usual materials for balausters are stone, terracotta, and wood; the Railings, on the other hand, are of metal, or, in their simpler forms, of wood. In the last decades, cast-iron was the ma-

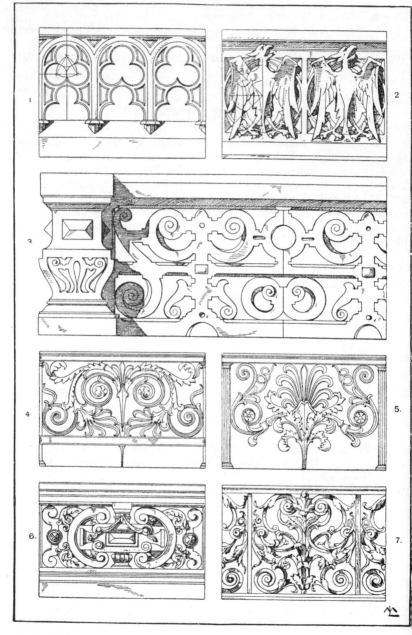

Plate 140.   The Parapet.

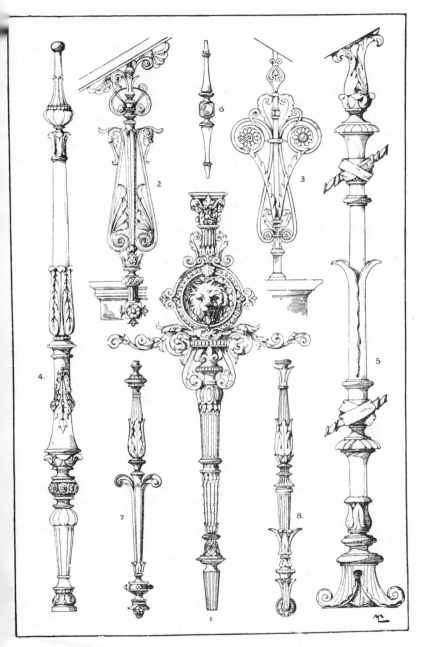

The Railing Post.   Plate 141.

terial most often used; but lately a return has been made to the more plastic wrought-iron. The ornamentation depends on the material selected. Wrought-iron Posts are decorated with scrolls and tendrils, while cast-iron uprights are decorated in bas-relief.

If the Railing-post has to stand on a horizontal plane, it is advisable to construct the foot in the manner shown in figs. 3, 4, and 5; if it is to be affixed to the sides of the treads of a staircase, arrangements similar to those in figs. 2, 7, and 8, are necessary. Where the upper end has to support the hand-rail, independent terminations, like figs. 2 and 5, may be adopted. Spherical heads may be applied to all angles (fig. 4).

PLATE 141. THE RAILING POST.

1. Modern Post, cast-metal, Architect v. Leins, Stuttgart, (Gewerbehalle).
2. Modern Post, cast-metal, Architect v. Hoven, Frankfurt, (Gewerbehalle).
3. Modern Post, wrought-iron, (Gewerbehalle).
4.   ,,   ,,   cast-metal.
5.   ,,   ,,   architects Gropius and Schmieden.
6. Plain wooden Post.
7—8. Modern Posts, cast-metal, Architect v. Hoven, Frankfurt.

THE FURNITURE LEG. (Plate 142.)

The Legs of wood furniture may be divided into two classes according to their height. Tables and chairs have high Legs; low Legs or Feet serve as supports for all kinds of cabinet and box-like articles.

The general plan is that of a balauster-like body of revolution as turned on the lathe. Angular forms, however, are also used.

High Legs are frequently decorated with carved ornaments; low Legs are usually left plain; and this would seem to be in accordance with their character.

Metal Feet are sometimes used for small pieces of furniture like caskets.

Where the Legs have to stand on the floor: it is advisable to taper them downwards (figs. 5—10); where they have to stand on raised platforms and seldom require to be moved: it is better to furnish them with a pedestal (fig. 1). It has lately become fashionable to apply metal casters to pianos, heavy chairs, couches, &c.

PLATE 142. THE FURNITURE LEG.

1.   Modern.
2.   Modern.
3.   Modern.
4.   Modern.
5—10. Various old designs.

THE TRAPEZOPHORON. (Plates 143—144.)

"Trapezophoron" is the name given to the support of the Antique table. They were usually of marble, the top itself was of wood or stone, sometimes ornamented with mosaic.

We may distinguish two principal classes of Antique tables: the circular table with three legs (compare Plate 143. 1); and the oblong table, resting on two end-supports (compare 143. 2 and 144. 6). The lower part, of the support of the round table, consists of a great leg which generally passes into a foliated calyx with a small head of a lion, lynx, panther, or other animal growing out of it (143. 5—10). The heads are sometimes human (144. 5) or human half-figures, such as the genius bearing a bowl on Plate 144. 2—3. In the early period of Antique art we find forms of more architectonic character like Plate 144, fig. 1. The end-support for the oblong table is a symmetrical duplication of the motive of the single leg already mentioned, with the addition of wings, and with the space between the animal forms filled either by figures or ornaments (Plate 143. 2—4 and 144. 6). Very striking in both classes of support is the difference in scale of the various elements (a phenomenon which also appears elsewhere in Roman art).

On Antique table-legs the reader may also consult Division III, (Furniture).

PLATE 143. THE TRAPEZOPHORON.

1.   Three-legged table, Roman, Legs of marble, table-top of mosaic.
2—3. Front and side view of the Support of a Roman table, found in the atrium of the house of Cornelius Rufus in Pompeii, (Fragments de l'architecture).
4.   Support of antique table.
5—6. Marble support of Roman table, Lynx head and claw, Museum, Naples.
7—8. Marble support of Roman table, Panther head and claw, British Museum.
9—10. Marble support of Roman table, Lion head and claw, Vatican, Rome.

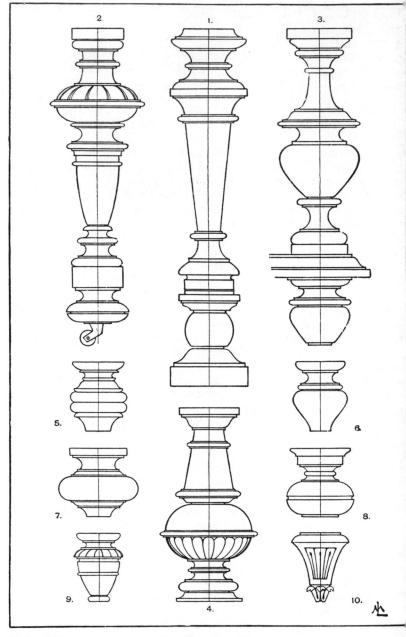

Plate 142.   The Furniture Leg.

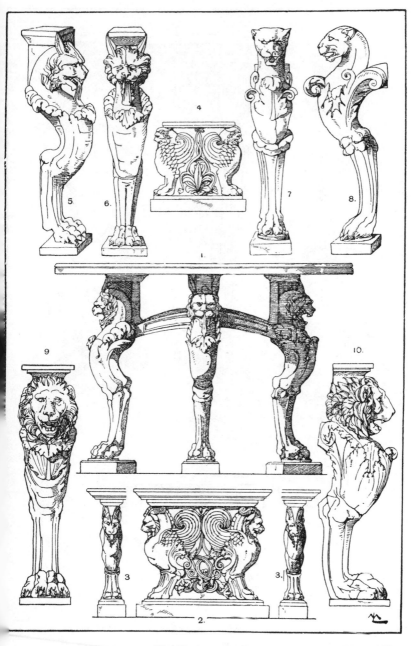

The Trapezophoron. Plate 143.

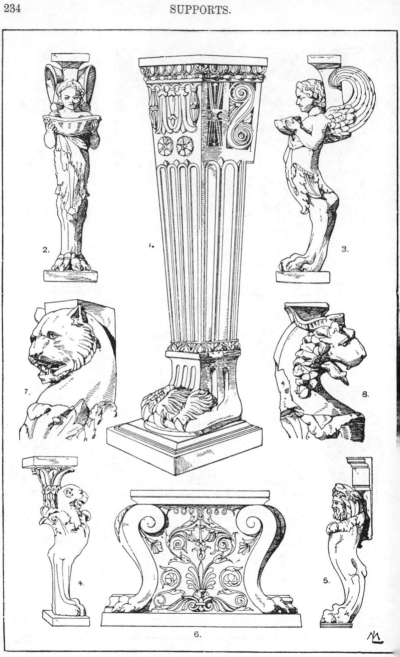

Plate 144. The Trapezophoron.

PLATE 144. THE TRAPEZOPHORON.

1. Marble support of antique table, Museum, Naples (judging from the symbolism of the ornamentation, the leg is probably from a table sacred to Zeus), (L'art pour tous).

2—3. Front and side view of a small Roman table-support, marble, Naples Museum, Panther claw, Eros garbed with the nebris.

4. Roman table-support, marble, British Museum.

5. „   „   „   , Head of Hercules and lion claw, Vatican.

6. Antique Support, marble, (Vulliamy).

THE CONSOLE. (Plates 145—147.)

The form of the Console is extremely varied; as are its uses and applications. It is determined by the function, and the material of which it is made, as well as by the style of the period.

Architectural members of the character of Consoles are early found in the Chinese and Indian, as also in the Assyrian style; but in the Egyptian style they are wanting.

Volute Consoles, very beautifully developed, are found sporadically in the Greek style; but the Roman style was the first to make an extensive use of these forms.

The decorated ends of Beams are probably to be regarded as the original model for Consoles. The **S**-shaped double volute, with a large and a small spiral, is the standard form. In this Console, the line of construction and the space for the actual decoration are given in the side-view, while the front, which is subordinate, is ornamented by scale motives, and leaves, which adapt themselves in graceful curves to the standard forms.

When the Console is used in the Console-band of a Cornice, or as the bracket of a Balcony, its attitude is recumbent. When it supports the Cornices of doors and windows, its attitude is erect. No other application is known in the Antique. A beautiful example occurs on the North door of the Erechtheum at Athens (Plate 145. 1—2). Some examples of recumbent Consoles, of Roman style, are given in figs. 3—8, of the same plate. The example 3—4, of the Late Roman epoch, shows decorative accessories of Swans. The bend of the curve of the volute here departs from the normal example, and approaches a more convex curve, which is demanded by the static calculation for these supports.

The Early Christian and Romanesque art adopted coarse copies of the Antique, and also created new ones suited to the new requirements. Thus early, we find those modillion forms which become typical for the wooden architecture of the Middle ages, being chiefly used beneath mouldings, and in corners of doors between the jambs and the lintel. The example on Plate 146. 11 may be taken as representative of this kind of support. Another class of Supports exhibits a central core, tapered downwards, like Pendants with a polygonal or round plan (Plate 147. 1 and 2). This latter form is also used in Gothic art as a Bracket for the Statues of the saints, which were applied to piers and the arches of portals.

The Renascense remodels the last-named console in its own way, but recurs by preference to the Antique form (Plate 146. 3), sometimes reversing the volutes (Plate 146. 1—2), and giving the front a richer and more independent ornamentation (Plate 146. 6). The combination of several smaller consoles to form a Composite - console, is shown on Plate 146. fig. 5. Just as the Pendant-consoles of the Gothic style imitate the calyx capital, so too does the Renascense remodel the Doric, Ionic, and Corinthian capitals for Consoles (Plate 147. 4—6). In wood architecture, we meet with Consoles which have the form of richly-decorated struts (Plate 146. 4).

The Barocco style, which followed the Renascence, also made essential additions to the richness of the forms. The strict line of the volute is abandoned and frequently broken by straight lines (Plate 146. 7—10). The Console is shaped in front-view like a pendant Triangle, or typographical Tail-piece (Plate 147. 3 and 8). Another invention of this period is the Triglyph-console (Plate 147. 7).

The Rococo period abandons the traditional standards, and sacrifices construction to picturesque license. Shell-work, and unsymmetrical scrolls, serve as supports.

Modern art recasts the elements of former styles, without adding anything essentially new, unless we regard as a novelty the custom of placing busts, clocks, and knicknacks, on independent Consoles which are used as Brackets.

Finally: we may mention that in almost every style, Consoles in the various forms have been used as the Keystones of door and window lintels, in which case they are, generally speaking, not Supports, as they have nothing to support.

It should be considered inadmissible to apply distorted Consoles i. e those which have vertical sides though they are on the raking sofits of pediments, as was done in the Late Roman period, and in imitation thereof by the Renascence in some examples.

Examples, of all periods, will be found in Raguenet's work; and an exhaustive essay on the Console by Dr. P. F. Krell in the *Gewerbehalle,* 1870, No. 10.

PLATE 145. THE CONSOLE.

1—2. Front and side view, Greek, North door, Erechtheum, Athen.
3—4. Front and side view, Roman, Vatican.

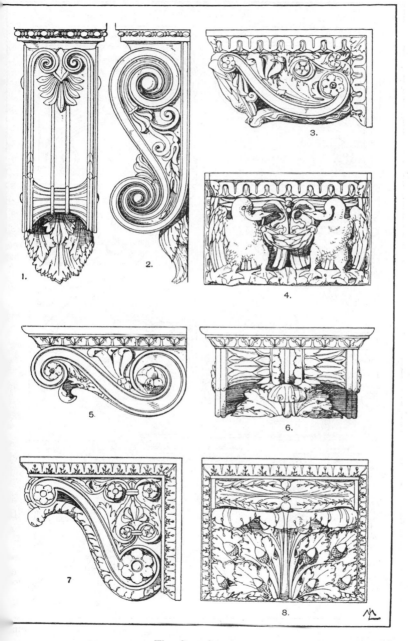

The Console.   Plate 145.

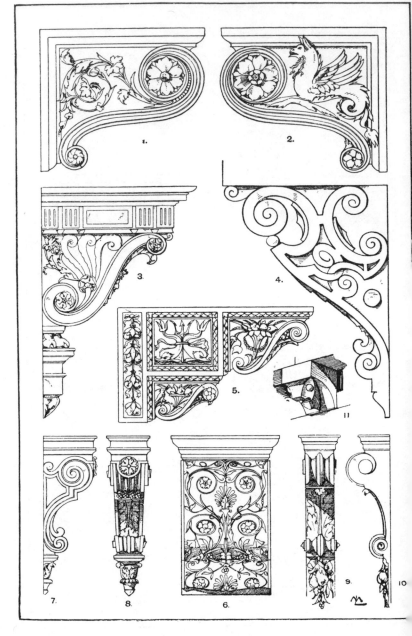

Plate 146.

The Console.

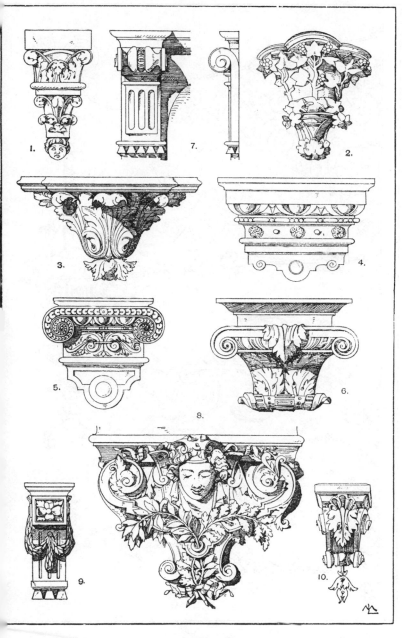

The Console. Plate 147.

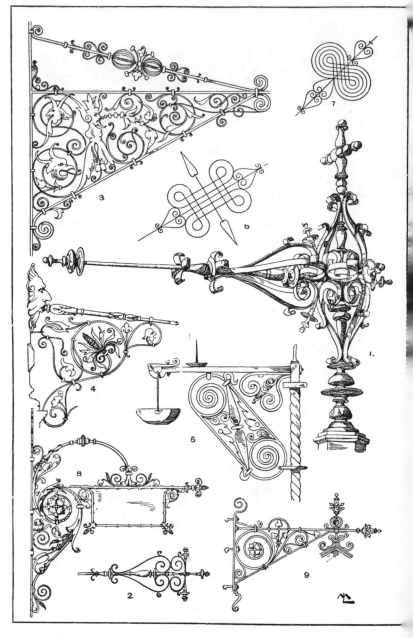

Plate 148.   The Bracket.

5—6. Roman, Front and side view, temple of Jupiter Stator, Rome, Vatican.
7—8. Roman, Front and side view, Vatican.

PLATE 146. THE CONSOLE.

1—2. Renascence, Side views, Vatican.
3.   Renascence, Hôtel d'Assezat, Toulouse, (Raguenet).
4.   Renascence, Wooden, French, Hôtel d'Assezet, Toulouse, (Raguenet).
5.   Renascence, Istrian limestone, Venetian, Hamburg, Museum.
6.   Renascence, Marble, Italian, Sta. Maria de' Miracoli, Venice, (Gropius).
7—8. Modern, French, Architect Roux, Paris.
9—10.   ,,   ,,   ,,   ,,   ,,
11.   Mediaeval, church, Athis, France.

PLATE 147. THE CONSOLE.

1.   Romanesque, Noyon cathedral, 12th century, (Raguenet).
2.   Gothic, St. Pierre sous Vezélay, (Gewerbehalle).
3.   Renascence, French, castle, Blois.
4.—5. Renascence, German, new Castle, Baden-Baden, (Gmelin).
6.   Renascence, German, Heidelberg castle.
7.   Renascence, Triglyph-console, Late French.
8.   Modern, French, library, Louvre, Architect Lefuel, (Raguenet).
9.   Modern, French, (Raguenet).
10.   Modern, French, New casino, Lyons, Architect Porte, (Raguenet).

THE BRACKET. (Plate 148.)

A special class of Supports is formed by those wrought-iron bearers which the Middle Ages, the Renascence, and Modern times, have produced in the shape of Brackets. The uses of Brackets are very various, e. g. in supporting Shop-signs, Conduit-pipes, Gargoyles, Candles, Lamps, Hats, Coats, &c.

In form, they vary with the style and richness of the workmanship. Square, flat and round iron, enriched by chasing and other methods of decoration, are used. They are frequently fastened to the wall by the aid of ribbon-like strips of metal, which may themselves be decorated with scrolls and curls.

The plate shows a number of such supports, of ancient and modern date, destined for a variety of purposes.

PLATE 148. THE BRACKET.

1—2. Part of Reading-desk, S. Benedetto, near Mantua, Italian Re-
       nascence, (Gewerbehalle).
3.   Wrought-iron, Sign, Regensburg, German Renascence, (Muster-
       ornamente).
4.   Wrought-iron bearer of conduit-pipe, Kloster Lichtenthal near
       Baden, German Renascence, (Gmelin).
5.   Wrought-iron bearer of water-stoup, sepulchral cross in ceme-
       tery, Kirchzarten, German Renascence, (Schauinsland).
6—7. Wrought-iron supports, for Gargoyles, German Renascence.
8.   Wrought-iron, Sign, Modern, Architect Crecelius, Mainz.
9.   Modern wrought-iron bracket, (Badische Gewerbezeitung).

THE CARYATID, AND THE ATLANTE.   (Plates 149 and 150.)

The freest and the richest motive for supports, is the Human
figure.   As early as Egyptian and Persian architecture, we find human
figures as bearers of beams and roofs.

The Greek and Roman styles also make use of this motive.   The
modern names for such supports are derived from the Antique.   According to Greek mythology, Atlas supports the vault of heaven at the
ends of the earth.   Hence is derived the name "Atlantes" for these
male supporters.   They are also sometimes termed "Telamons".   The
name "Caryatids", for female supporting figures, is derived from the
town of Caryæ in the Peloponnesus.   According to another version the
Caryatids are imitations of the virgins who danced in the temple at
Caryæ at the feast of Diana.   According to Vitruvius, their introduction into architecture is owing to the fact that ladies of Caryæ,
as a punishment for the support they rendered to the Persians, were
carried into captivity and compelled to serve as carriers of burdens.
The Caryatids are termed "Canephoræ" (basket bearers), when capitals
in shape like a basket are interposed between their heads and the
superincumbent burden.   Among well-known examples in the Antique
are the Atlantes in the temple of Jupiter at Agrigentum, and the
Caryatids of the Erechtheum at Athens.

The Middle Ages made little use of Atlantes and Caryatids; the
Renascence and the following styles, on the contrary, used them freely.

Atlantes and Caryatids occur isolated, and connected with walls;
and in both high and bas-relief.   Sometimes the whole length of the
figure is employed, sometimes only the upper half in conjunction with
a Console (Plate 149. 4—7), or with terminus-like bases (Plate 150.
4—5).   Composite bearers in the form of double Caryatids are also
a popular motive, as shown by the example on Plate 150, from the
Louvre at Paris.

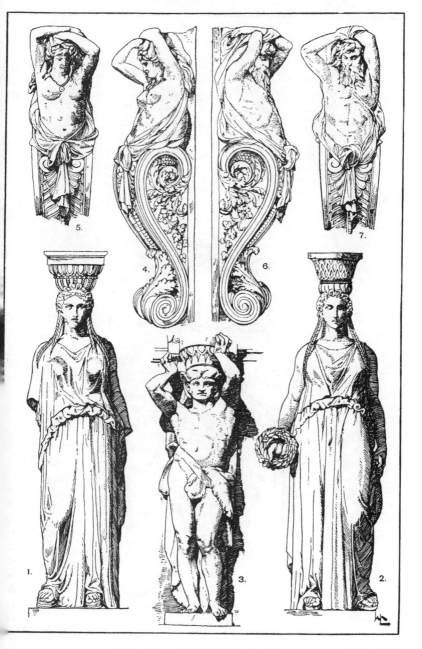

The Caryatid, the Atlante, &c. Plate 149.

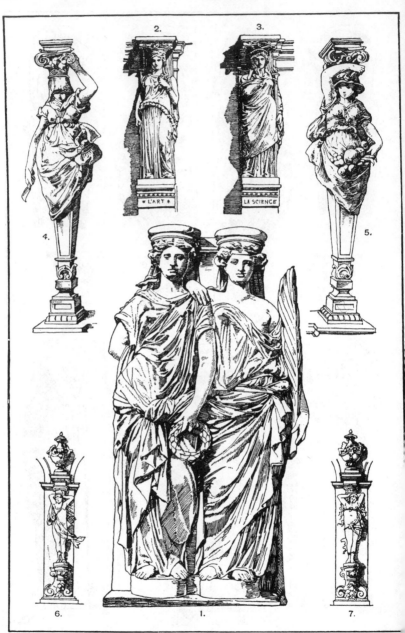

Plate 150.   The Caryatid, &c.

PLATE 149. THE CARYATID, THE ATLANTE, &c.

1. Greek Caryatid, Erechtheum, Athens, (Vorbilder für Fabrikanten und Handwerker).
2. Antique Caryatid, Villa Mattei, after Piranesi, (Vorbilder für Fabrikanten und Handwerker).
3. Modern French Atlante, house in Paris, Sculptor Caillé, (Raguenet).
4—7. Modern, Front and side views of Half-figure Consoles, Ziegler and Weber, Carlsruhe.

PLATE 150. THE CARYATID, &c.

1. Modern, Double Caryatid, Louvre, Paris, (Baldus).
2—3. Modern, Caryatids, Conservatoire des arts et métiers, Paris, Sculptor E. Robert, (Raguenet).
4—5. Modern, Caryatids, Director C. Hammer, Nuremberg.
6— 7. Modern, Caryatids, Director C. Hammer, Nuremberg.

D.

ENCLOSED ORNAMENT.

(PANELS.)

That Method of treatment, which has for its object to decorate a plane surface, and to cover it with ornament, &c., by means of painting, inlaying, engraving, etching, &c., we term flat decoration.

This falls into two classes. Firstly the ornament may be designed for a definite, bounded space, such as an oblong, according to artistic rules, so that it fits exactly into this space alone: in which case it is a discontinuous or "Panel" ornament. Or, secondly, the ornament may extend itself in every direction, repeating its details without regard to any definite boundary: in which case it is a continuous or "Diaper" ornament, such as a wall-paper.

Turning our attention first to discontinuous or Panel-ornament: we shall find, in addition to objects whose boundaries are arbitrary and to be fixed at will, that we have principally to consider the following shapes: the Square, the other regular polygons, the Circle, the Oblong, the Ellipse, the Lunette, the various forms of the Spanrail, the Lozenge and the Triangle.

Geometrical, natural, and artificial elements, either singly or combined, are used. The character of the ornament may be Naturalistic, or it may be Artificial, and adapted to some pre-arranged leading-lines of the Shape. This book does not treat of examples of the former character. Those of the latter character, i. e. Artificial ornament, will depend on the attitude of the Panel with regard to the Horizon.

When the panel is mon-axial, i. e. it is symmetrical on both sides of one axis: then the panel-ornament is suitable to a vertical surface. When it is developed regularly in all directions from the centre of the figure, and is symmetrical to two or more axes: then the panel-ornament is suitable to a horizontal surface. The central feature of a horizontal panel is not infrequently emphasized by a rosette ornament, while the decoration of the remaining surface is kept in low-relief. Trifling variations, from absolute symmetry and regularity, are often met-with; but they are confined to the details, the impression of symmetry and regularity being preserved in the general effect.

These remarks, as well as some further relations arising out of the nature of the subject, we now proceed to illustrate in detail in the following chapters and plates. For the most part we shall confine ourselves to the best known and most frequent figures; and shall only offer some few examples of abnormal panels.

THE SQUARE PANEL. (Plates 151—155.)

The lines, on which the decoration of the Square may naturally be based, are the two Diagonals, and the two Diameters which join the centre of the opposite sides. These lines cut each-other in a common point, the centre of the shape; and form an eight-rayed star with rays of alternately unequal lengths. They divide the figure into 8 equal spaces, which are usually decorated with repeated ornament, and are therefore suitable to the horizontal attitude, (compare Plate 151, figs. 2—6 and others). Numerically this mode of decoration is predominant. Rarer are the cases in which the angle is once more bisected and the square consequently divided into 16 triangles, (compare Plate 154, fig. 7). The simplest decoration is the many-rayed star, which is termed the Uraniscus, in the coffers or Greek ceilings (comp. Plate 151, fig. 1). The centre of the figure is generally accentuated by the addition of a rosette, and the direction of growth, like plant-motives, is from the centre outwards (Plate 151, fig. 2, 3, 5, 6 and others); or alternately from the centre outwards and inwards (comp. Plate 151. 4). Slight variations from strict symmetry and regularity are partly caused by the use of the geometrical interlaced band (Plate 153. 3 and 4), and are partly the deliberate result of artistic freedom of conception (Plate 152. 2. and 151. 7). The latter example is highly remarkable in this respect; and its originality may serve as a model. The example is also one of the rare cases in which the ornamentation is symmetrical to the Diagonals, and not to the Diameters.

Another kind of Square decoration is that in which it is sub-divided into separate spaces, each of which receives an independent ornamentation. Plates 9 and 10 of the Handbook give a number of such divisions of Squares; a similar mode of decoration will be found on Plate 151, fig. 8, Plate 153, figs. 6 and 7, and elsewhere. The decoration of the Square in an upright attitude, with symmetry to one axis, belongs to the same category as the Oblong; and we may therefore refer to what will be said below with reference to this latter figure.

Square panel are to be found in all styles; we have taken some striking examples from the coffer-ceilings of the Antique and the Renascence, from the pavement-tiles of the Middle Ages, and from the metal-work of the Renascence and Modern times.

PLATE 151. THE SQUARE PANEL.

1. Greek, Uraniscus, coffer of ceiling, Propylaea, Athens.
2. Roman, bas-relief, found during the rectification of the Tiber near the Farnesina, Rome, in 1879, Museo Tiberino.
3. Assyrian pavement, Kouyunjik, (Owen Jones).
4—5. Greek, Coffers of ceilings, Propylaea, Athens.
6. „   „   „   „   , Athens.
7. „   „   „   „   , Parthenon.
8. Roman, mosaic pavement, Pompeii, (Owen Jones).
9. Byzantine, bas-relief, San Marco, Venice, (Owen Jones).

PLATE 152. THE SQUARE PANEL.

1. Decoration, of a book, 10th century, Library of the Duke of Devonshire, (Racinet).
2. Scandinavian bas-relief, Celtic stone cross, churchyard, Meigle, Angus, (Owen Jones).
3. Bas-relief, tomb of "Pierre le Vénérable", Cluny museum, 12th century, (L'art pour tous).
4—7. Mediaeval, tiles, (Owen Jones, Racinet &c.).
8. Tiles, Cistercian monastery, Bebenhausen.
9. Moorish Tiles.
10. Gothic, tiles, Bloxham church, England, 15th century.

PLATE 153. THE SQUARE PANEL.

1 and 3. Inlaid work, 14th or 15th century, Sauvageot collection, (Racinet).
2. Arabian mosaic, (Prisse d'Avennes).
4. Moorish, Alhambra, 14th century.
5. Arabian, wood door, 16th century, (L'art pour tous).

6.   Renascence, Intarsia, German (Hirth, Formenschatz).
7.   Modern.
8 — 9. Renascence, Intarsia, Sta. Maria gloriosa ai Frari, Venice,
        15th century, (Musterornamento).

PLATE 154. THE SQUARE PANEL.

1.   Renascence, Motive from a Robe in the Sacristy, Sta. Croce,
        Florence, Italian.
2.   Renascence, Tiles, Collection of the Count d'Yvon, (Racinet).
3.   Renascence, Motive after Peter Flötner, German.
4.   Renascence, Mosaic flooring, cathedral, Spoleto, (Jacobsthal;
        the centre altered).
5.   Renascence, Intarsia, stalls, Certosa near Pavia, Italian.
6.   Renascence, Majolica Tiles, Sta. Caterina, Siena, Italian.
7.   Renascence, Intarsia, door of the Cambio, Perugia, by Antonio
        Mercatello, 1500, Italian.
8—10.   Renascence, Door of the Madonna di Galliera, Bologna, Italian,
        (Musterornamente).

PLATE 155. THE SQUARE PANEL.

1 and 3.   Wrought-iron, French, 17th century, (L'art pour tous).
2 and 4.   Wrought-iron, German Renascence, (Hirth, Formenschatz).
5.   Wrought-iron, Oxford, 1713, (L'art pour tous).
6 — 7.   Wrought-iron, Modern.
8 and 10.   Wrought-iron, Modern, cemetery, Carlsruhe.
9.   Wrought-iron, by Georg Klain, Salzburg, 17th century.

THE STAR - SHAPE PANEL.   (Plate 156.)

The decoration of polygonal Stars is generally based on radiating axes. Exceptions, in favor of symmetry to one or two axes, are
comparatively scarce (fig. 3).

Where there is no Sub-division into independent panels, according to Plates 11 and 12 of the Handbook (fig. 7): the ornament
follows the natural lines of division furnished by the diagonals. In
this case the number of the single, similar triangles of division
depends on the number of sides (fig. 6).

Decorated Star-shaped panels are extremely common in the Arabian
and Moorish styles, where the ornament is often of such a character
that it would very well suit a simple polygon, and only fills out
accidentally (so to speak) the star angles (figs. 4, and 5).

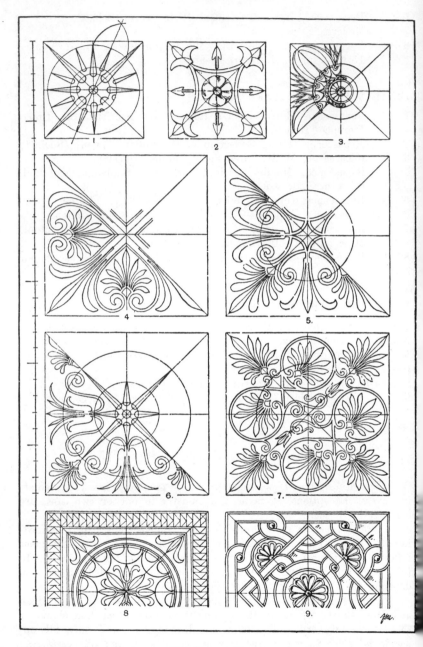

Plate 151. The Square Panel.

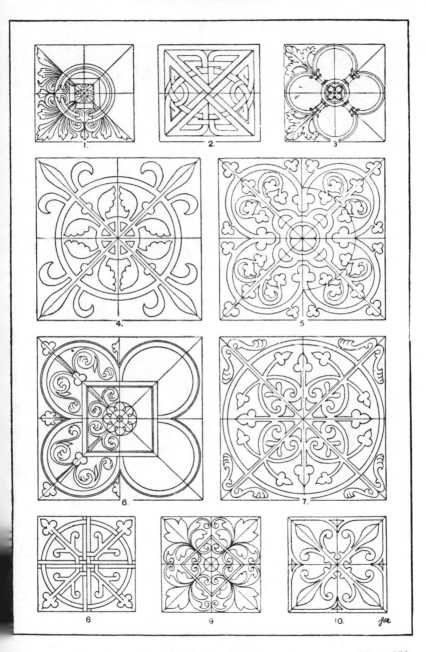

The Square Panel.   Plate 152.

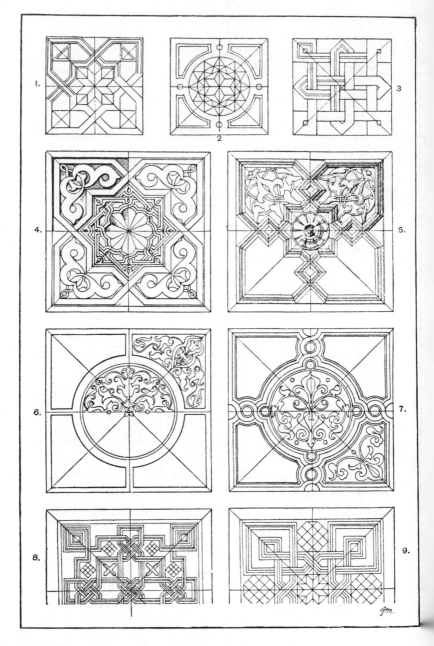

Plate 153. The Square Panel.

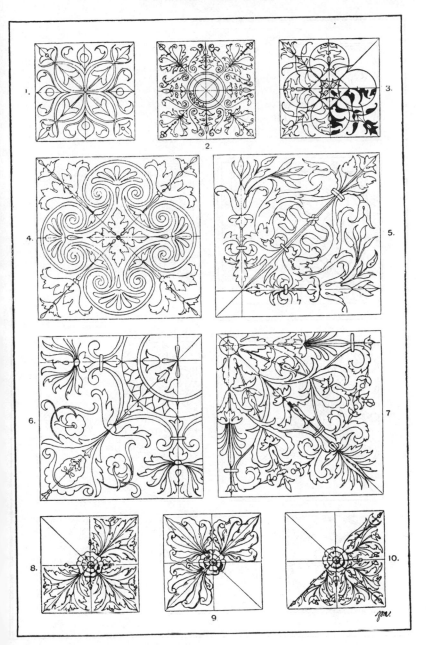

The Square Panel.   Plate 154.

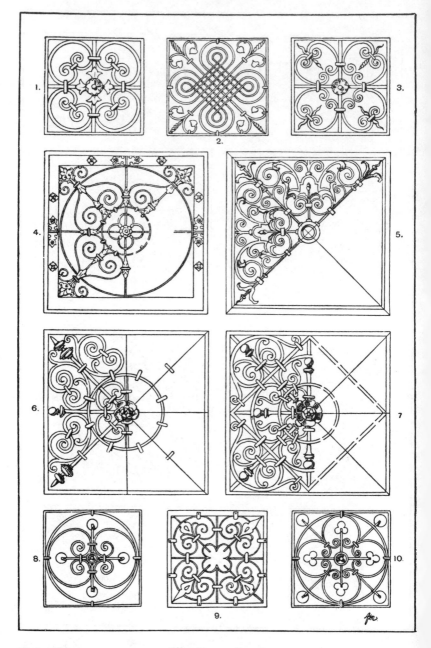

Plate 155. The Square Panel.

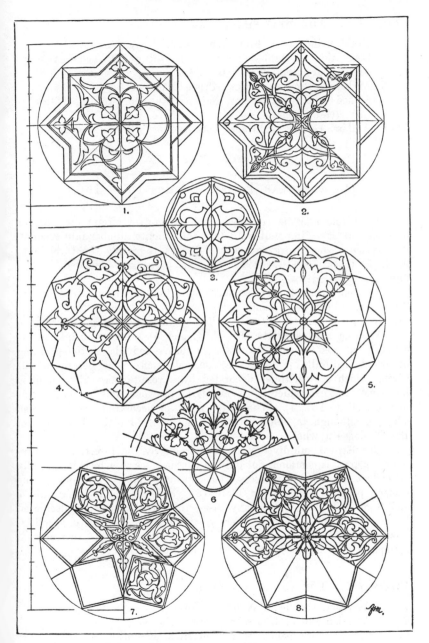

The Star-shape Panel.   Plate 156.

PLATE 156. THE STAR-SHAPE PANEL.

1.   Mural painting, S. Francesco, Assisi, (Hessemer).
2.   Decoration of Arabic koran, 17th century, (Prisse d'Avennes).
3.   Arabian architecture, (Prisse d'Avennes).
4—5. Arabian ceiling paintings, (Prisse d'Avennes).
6.   Etched ornament, armour, National Museum, Munich, 16th century, (Gewerbehalle).
7—8. Arabian ceiling paintings, 18th century, (Prisse d'Avennes).

THE CIRCULAR PANEL. (Plates 157—160.)

The Circle may be regarded as a polygon of an infinite number of sides. As it is impossible to take this infinite number into account, it is usual, when working on radial axes to divide the Circle into 3, 4, 5, 6, 8, 10, 12, or 16, similar parts, as indicated in the figures.

Another principle of frequent application is that of division into Zones; each ring-like band being ornamented independently. This principle predominates in the so-called archaic styles, e. g. on Etruscan and Assyrian shields (Plate 157. 2, 4, and 5). This principle is excellently adapted to the decoration of dishes and plates, the profiling of which naturally points to a zonal division. The centre of the Circle, which is sometimes decorated by a rosette, may also be filled by some feature which is symmetrical to one axis or is unsymmetrical (Plate 157. 4). The latter mode of decoration has also been adopted, although in comparatively rarer cases, for the decoration of the Circle as a whole.

Geometrical sub-division of the circle, by the insertion of polygons, or arcs, is common, not only in Gothic tracery, which is specially dependent on these processes, but in every other style (comp. the tracery panels 7 and 8 on Plate 158, and the niello ornaments 7 and 8 on Plate 159). In many cases, the circular panel is decorated by an ornament which is merely an enlarged Rosette or Cieling-flower, so that no clear line can be drawn between the two classes, (compare what has been said of the Rosette on p. 191)

PLATE 157. THE CIRCULAR PANEL.

1.   Assyrian, pavement, Nimrud, (Owen Jones).
2.   Assyrian shield, Khorsabad, (Owen Jones).
3.   Old Frankish panel, Sacramentarium, Rheims.
4—5. Greek, paintings on Vases, (Lau).

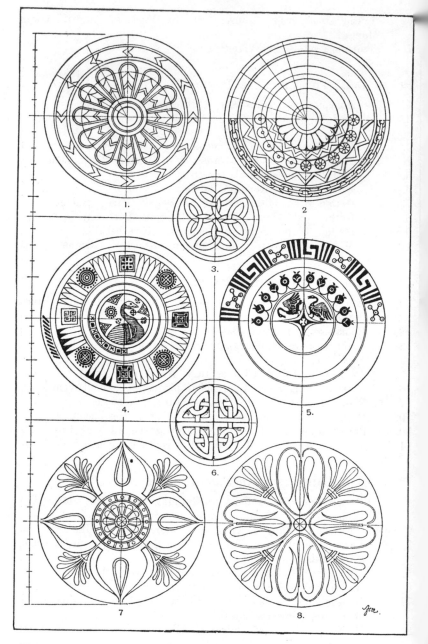

Plate 157.　　　　　The Circular Panel.

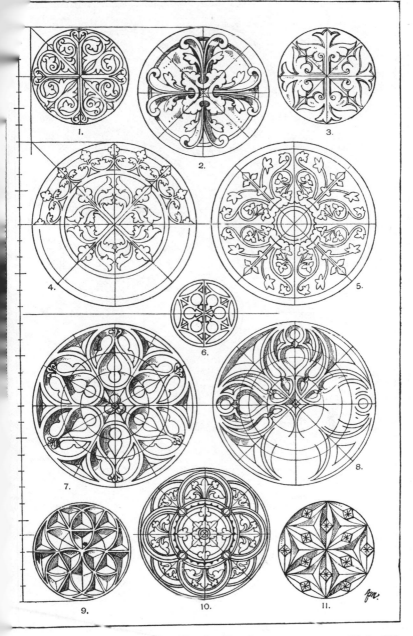

The Circular Panel.

Plate 158.

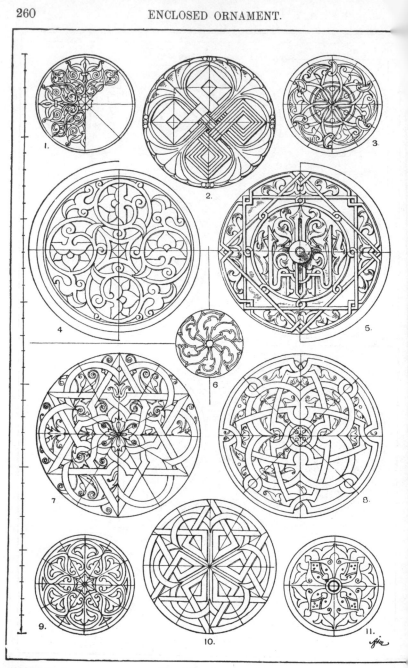

Plate 159.

The Circular Panel.

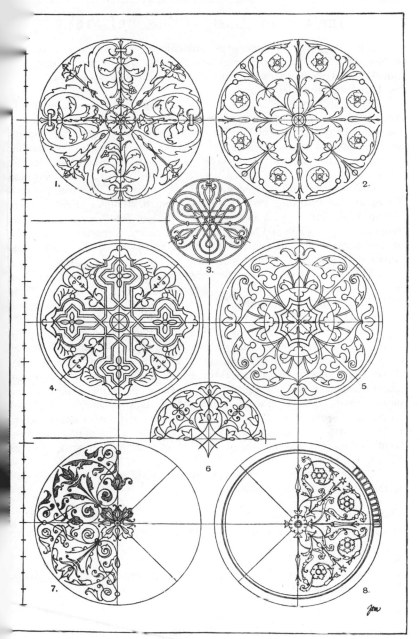

The Circular Panel. Plate 160.

THE OBLONG PANEL. (Plates 161—164.)

The shape of the Oblong is particularly adapted to receive b
a bi-axial and a mon-axial treatment; and as it is by far the most f.
quently-used shape: numerous examples of the two treatments are
be found in all styles.

When the Oblong is not sub-divided (as shown on Plates 13 t
16.), the natural axes, around which the ornament is grouped are,
for the bi-axial treatment, the two diameters, which join the centres
of the opposite sides. These lines divide the figure into 4 smaller
oblongs, each of which receives an identical decoration (comp.
Plate 161, figs. 1—3, and Plate 162, figs. 1—5). To use the
diagonals as lines of symmetry, as is the rule with the square, produces an unfavourable effect; because the 8 triangles thus formed,
although similar to each other, do not present the same angle to the
centre (comp. Plate 161. 4). This panel differs from the usual rule,
as the organic growth of the ornament is not from the centre outwards, but from the 4 angles inwards.

The strict Greek palmette ornamentation, which has such an
excellent effect in the Square, is less suitable for the Oblong (Plate
161, figs. 1 and 2) than the freer decorations of the Roman period
(Plate 161. 3) and the Renascence (Plate 162. 1—5).

On vertical surfaces: the attitude of the Oblong panel may be
either "figure-wise", or "landscape-wise". Examples of the former
attitude are figs. 2 and 3; and of the latter are, figs. 1 and 5 on
Plate 164. The vertical line through the centre is the axis of these.
The ornament is seldom geometrical; organic or artificial motives are
mostly used. The mon-axial treatment is most properly employed
where it is applied in a really vertical plane, e. g. on Pilasters (comp.
p. 225, shafts of pilasters), on Walls, Doors, &c. The poly-axial treatment is best adapted for the decoration of horizontal planes, such as
Floors, Ceilings, &c.

Copious material is furnished by the inlaid-work, bas-reliefs, and
metal-work, of the Renascence.

PLATE 161. THE OBLONG PANEL.

1—2. Greek, Painted coffers of ceilings, Propylaea, Athens, (Owen
      Jones).
3.   Roman.
4.   Roman, under-side of the architrave, Temple of Vesparian, Rome.
5.   Renascence, Church, Kamenz, German, (Gewerbehalle).

PLATE 162. THE OBLONG PANEL.

1. Renascence, Intarsia, Cabinet, Perugia, Italian, (Jacobsthal).
2. Renascence, Palazzo vecchio, Mantua, Italian, (Jacobsthal).

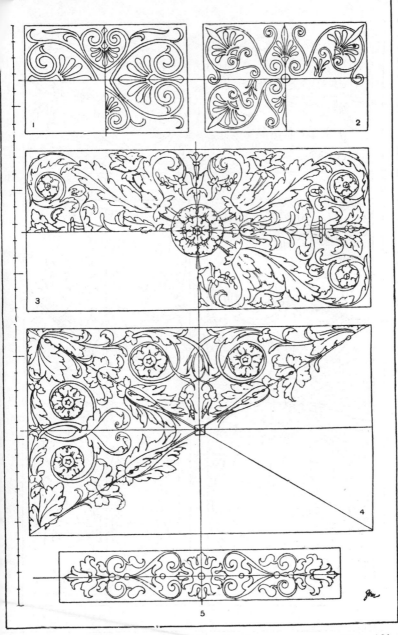

The Oblong Panel.   Plate 161.

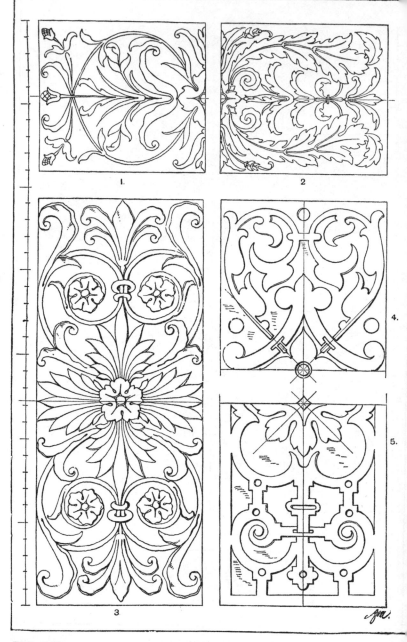

Plate 162.   The Oblong Panel.

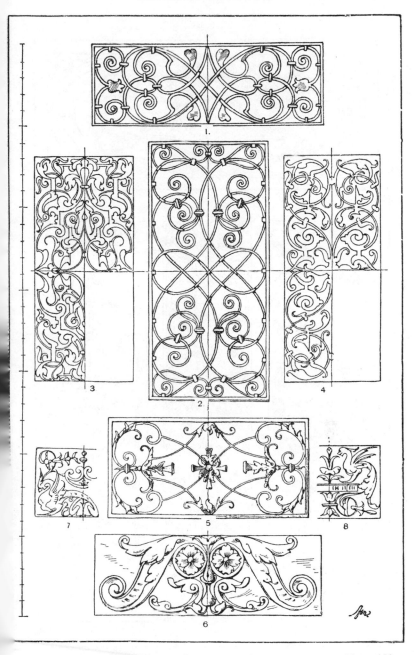

The Oblong Panel.   Plate 163.

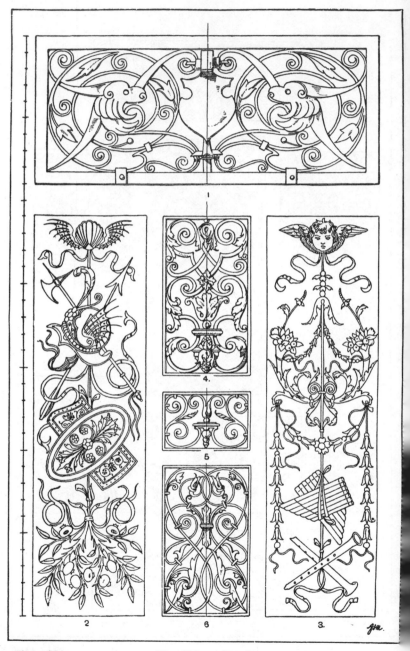

Plate 164.　　　　　　The Oblong Panel.

3. Renascence, Marzuppini tomb, Sta. Croce, Florence, (Jacobsthal).
4. Renascence, Tomb, Stiftskirche, Stuttgart, German, (Musterornamente).
5. Renascence, S. Michael's, Schwäbisch-Hall, German, (Musterorna-
    mente).

PLATE 163. THE OBLONG PANEL.

1. Renascence, Wrought-iron Grill, Italian, (Gewerbehalle).
2. Wrought-iron Grill, Choir of S. Blasius, Mühlhausen, Thuringia,
    17th century, (Musterornamente).
3—4. Ivory inlays, by Hans Schieferstein, 16th century, Museum,
    Dresden.
5. Wrought-iron, house, Freiburg, Switzerland, 17th century,
    (L'art pour tous).
6. Ornament, over picture of saint, by Barthel Beham, Carlsruhe,
    German Renascence.
7—8. Stalls of the Laurentian Library, Florence, Italian Renascence.

PLATE 164. THE OBLONG PANEL.

1. Grill, Schlettstadt, 1649, (Gewerbehalle).
2—3. Intarsia, S. Petronio, Bologna, 1495, (Musterornamente).
4. Wrought-iron balaustrade, 18th century.
5. Wrought-iron, French, 18th century.
6. Wrought-iron, Stift Strahov, Prague, German, Renascence.

THE ELLIPTIC PANEL. (Plate 165.)

As regards the principle of decoration, the Ellipse bears the same
relation to the Circle that the Oblong does to the Square. When not
sub-divided (see Plate 20, fig. 15), it is treated either mon-axially,
with the ornament symmetrical to one of the axes (fig. 1); or it is
treated bi-axially, with the ornament symmetrical to both (figs. 2
o 8).

The Elliptic panel was not often used in decoration during the
best periods. In the 17th and 18th centuries, it was used as the form
for snuff-boxes, sweet-boxes, &c., the decoration being carried-out in
niello, and similar metal work. It was also in use during the same
period in centre-ornaments for the covers of books. From such examples,
most of the figures on the Plate have been taken.

PLATE 165. THE ELLIPTIC PANEL.

—2. Renascence, German, (Formenschatz).
3. Centre of a book-cover, gold blocking on vellum, German
    16th century, (Storck).

4—7. Renascence, Book-cover blocks, Germanisches Museum, Nurem-
       berg. German, (Musterornamente).
8.   Renascence, Pavement, tomb of Princess Johanna Elisabeth,
       Stiftskirche, Stuttgart.

THE LUNETTE, AND THE SPANRAIL PANELS.
(Plates 166—167.)

The Semicircle scarcely admits of any entirely satisfactory subdivision. The best method is to describe a circle in the semicircle
so that the circle touches the centre of the semicircle above and the
centre of its chord below; this arrangement is especially useful when
a medallion or a clock is to be placed in it. There are two methods
of decorating the Lunette: either an upright panel-ornament is designed symmetrical to one axis, an arrangement which is the best, as
the semicircle, in the majority of cases, is used on vertical planes
(Plate 167. 1 and 3); or the Semicircle is divided, like a fan, into a
number of sectors, which receive an identical decoration, an arrangement which is chiefly adopted for Door-heads (Plate 166. 2). In
such cases a central semicircle is usually inserted; and the small
panel, thus formed, is decorated independently. The object of this
is to obviate the inelegant and difficult accumulation of radii at the
centre.

In consequence of an optical illusion, the semicircle gives the
impression of being really less than the half of the whole circle; and
for this reason it is sometimes "stilted", that is the centre of the arc
does not lie on the springing-line, but is shifted a little higher.

The name "spanrail" is given to the spaces of various shape
which remain after circular shapes are taken-away from quadrangular
ones. The commonest figure of this kind is the Trianguloid, which
is formed on either side of a semicircle when this latter is described
in an oblong Frame. The same shape results when a circle is inscribed
in a square, which frequently occurs in the decoration of ceilings. Sometimes the decoration of the Trianguloid consists of a rosette in its
centre; or laurel, palm, and oak sprays, circular wreaths, and waving
ribbons, trophies, figures in relief, and similar motives, in a more or less
naturalistic style, are employed. In severer decoration, the axis of
symmetry is the line of bisection of the right angle. The motives are
sometimes geometrical (Plate 166. 5—6); but more frequently organic
(Plate 167. 4—5); and, among artificial forms, varieties of strapwork
are used (Plate 167. 6—9).

When a series of arcs has a common bounding straight line, the
spanrail is shaped as shown by fig. 4, Plate 166. This figure is the

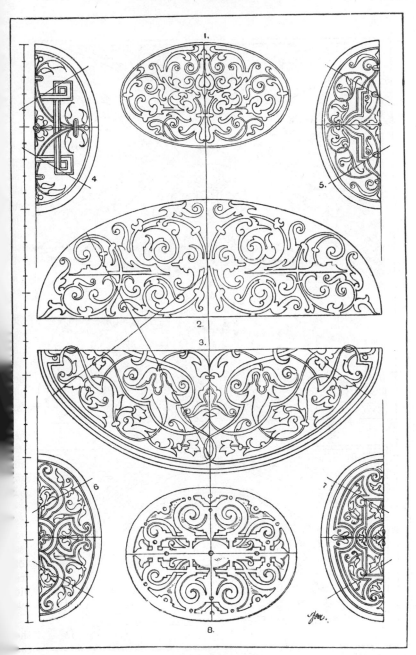

The Elliptic Panel. Plate 165.

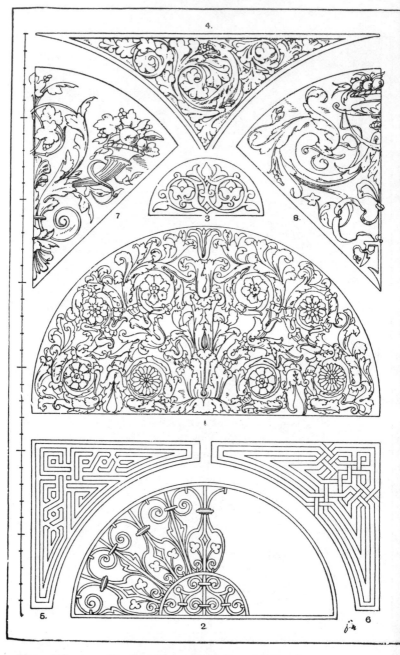

Plate 166. The Lunette, and the Spanrail Panels.

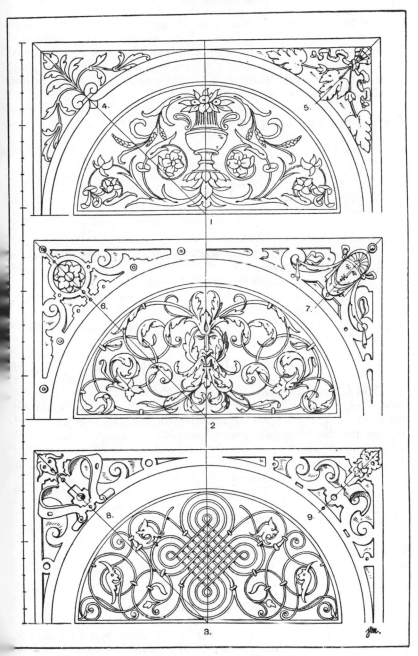

The Lunette, and the Spanrail Panels.   Plate 167.

same as two conjoined Trianguloids. It has a vertical central axis.

Another well-known shape results when two smaller semicircles are taken-away from a larger, as when, for instance, two round-headed window lights are enclosed by a common arch. Finally we may mention the Quadrant, which is not infrequently used in the angles of ceilings (figures 7 and 8 of Plate 166).

PLATE 166. THE LUNETTE, AND THE SPANRAIL PANELS.
1.   Roman, (Vulliamy).
2.   Italian Renascence, (Gewerbehalle).
3.   Arabian, (Prisse d'Avennes).
4.   Early Gothic Spanrail, Stone Church, England.
5—6. Arabian, mosaic Spanrail, (Prisse d'Avennes).
7—8. Modern.

PLATE 167. THE LUNETTE, AND THE SPANRAIL PANEL.
1.   Renascence, intarsia, Sta. Maria in Organo, Verona, Italian.
2.   Wrought-iron Grill.
3.   Renascence, Wrougth-iron Grill, German.
4.   Renascence, plinth of a column, St. Antonio, Padua, (Meurer).
5.   Modern, Vaudeville theatre, Paris, (Raguenet).
6—9. Renascence, by Vredeman de Vries.

THE LOZENGE PANEL. (Plate 168.)

The Lozenge in decorative art includes the · Rhombus, and the Square when one of its diagonals is vertical. The Lozenge is treated either as an upright panel, symmetrical to one axis (figs. 2, 4, and 5); or the two diagonals are the axes of symmetry for a bi-axial pattern (figs. 1, and 3). In the former case, the ornament consists of two; and in the latter case of four, similar parts. The Lozenge is not often employed. Occasionally it finds a place as a panel in Lattices, Doors, Dadoes, Ceilings, &c.

PLATE 168. THE LOZENGE PANEL.
1.   Door, Nördlingen church, 17th century.
2—3. Grill, Townhall, Würzburg, German Renascence.
4—5. Modern decorative painting.

VARIOUS PANELS. (Plates 169—170.)

Plate 169 and 170 give a number of incidental Panel-shapes, of which there is a great variety. The principle of decoration must

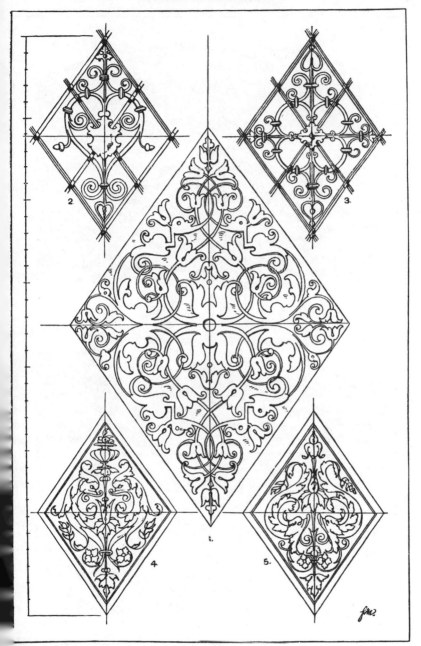

The Lozenge Panel. Plate 168.

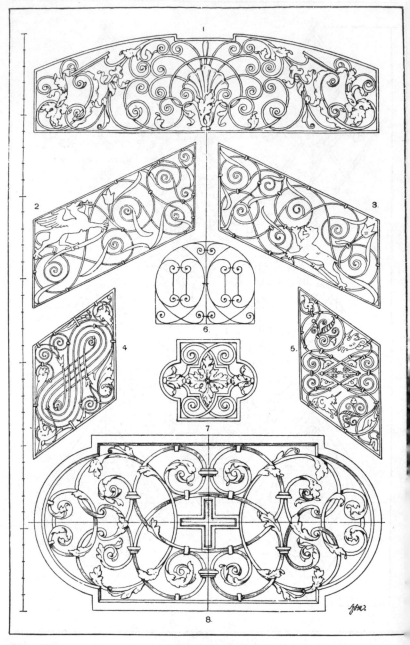

Plate 169.   Various Panels.

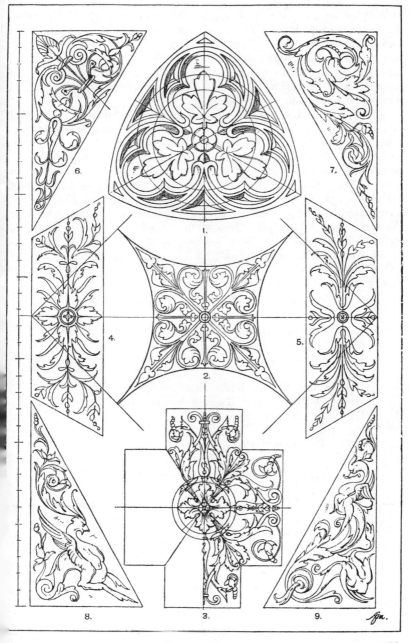

Various Panels.

Plate 170.

be adapted to each case; and should follow the analogy of the principles enunciated above. Thus, for example, regular polygons with convex or concave sides (Plate 170. 1 and 2); are treated similarly to polygons with straight sides.

Figures like those on Plate 169. 7 and 8, are decorated in the manner of an Oblong or an Ellipse. The ornament of Plate 169. 1, recalls the decoration of the Lunette.

The Trapezoid is treated either as an upright panel, the central axis being perpendicular to the two parallels; or the ornamentation approaches that of a bi-axial Oblong panel; but it will be somewhat modified, to fit the angles (Plate 170. 4 and 5). This latter circumstance has also to be taken into consideration in the case of a right-angled Triangle of unequal sides, when the line of bisection of the right-angle is used as the axis of symmetry (Plate 170. 6); an unsymmetrical arrangement is best in this case, see figures 7 to 9 on the same plate. This latter free style of design, which is not bound by axial lines, may also be recommended for the Raking Parallelograms which occur on staircases.

PLATE 169. VARIOUS PANELS.

1.   Wrought-iron Grill, Townhall, Villingen, late German Renascence.
2—3. Balaustrade of staircase, Frankfort on the Main, German 16th century, (Gewerbehalle).
4—5. Grill, Pulpit-steps, Thann, German 16th century, (Gewerbehalle).
6.   Grill, Padua, Italian Renascence.
7.   Detail of Lattice, late German Renascence.
8.   Grill, late German Renascence.

PLATE 170. VARIOUS PANELS.

1.   Trefoil tracery, Gothic, (Jacobsthal).
2.   Mural painting, Swedish, Romanesque, (Racinet).
3.   Louvre, Paris.
4—5. Marble inlaid-work, Pulpit, Cathedral, Savona, Italian Renascence, (Meurer).
6—9. Triangular panels, Stalls of the Laurentian Library, Florence, ascribed to Michel Angelo.

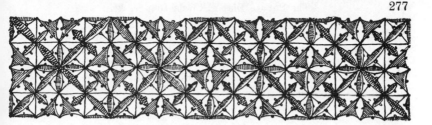

E.

REPEATING ORNAMENT.

(DIAPERS.)

It is the essence, of repeated ornament, that it may be extended on all sides at discretion, the component parts of the design (i. e. the pattern) admitting of uninterrupted repetition. The elements are either geometrical, organic, or, as in the majority of cases, geometrical are combined with organic elements, sometimes with the addition of figures and artificial accessories. Diaper ornament has either a poly-axial or a bi-axial character. In the former case, the decoration expands regularly on all sides; the basis is a system of intersecting axes of symmetry, as shown in the square or triangular Nets on Plate 1. In the second case, the decoration consists of growth in an upward direction, the repetition on each side being secured by "turning the pattern over" symmetrically, or by juxtaposition (in the usual sense of the word). Here, also, combination frequently occurs to this extent that many patterns have a poly-axial basis while single panels and medallions have upright decoration.

Growth in a downward direction, or in an oblique upward direction, &c., must be classed as exceptions to the rule.

When Diaper patterns are applied to circumscribed surfaces, e. g. on Walls: they are either cut-off abruptly, as in Wall-papers, or are stopped-short of the limits, and a Border is applied. There is seldom much difficulty in the case of geometrical patterns; but with organic designs the sides of the upright patterns usually terminate at the axis of symmetry.

Diaper ornament is applied to many purposes. Mosaic, Parquetry, Marquetry, using geometrical patterns; the Textile, Wall-paper, and

Wall-painting crafts using the organic elements; and Floor-coverings, Glass-painting, Inlaying, and similar Metal-decorations, using both. The treatment of large Grills sometimes demands a repeated pattern, that may be expanded at will; so that we may add this branch to the others.

THE SQUARE DIAPER. (PARQUETRY.) (Plate 171.)

Parquetry is the term applied to the overlaying of flooring with mosaic of hard woods. The patterns are almost exclusively geometrical; the basis is the quadrangular or triangular Net. The single parts are first put together to form square or regular hexagonal figures, which are then tongued and grooved, and fixed to the boards. The Plate shows a number of modern Parquet-patterns: figures 2, 8, 9 and 10 being based on the triangular; and the others on the quadrangular Net. Parquet-patterns which are so designed that the floor has the effect of projections and hollows, are inadmissible because they are unsuited to a Floor, which is intended to be walked on, and should, therefore, be flat in design as well as in reality.

PLATE 171. THE SQUARE DIAPER, &c.

1—10. Modern Parquet-patterns.

THE CIRCLE DIAPER. (MOSAIC.) (Plate 172.)

Mosaic *(opus musivum)* is, in its wider sense, the designing and inlaying of pieces of stone, wood, glass, leather, straw, &c., to make a picture or pattern. More strictly: Mosaic means pictures and patterns composed of pieces of stone, pottery, pearl, and glass, the last being coloured or underlaid with metal-foil.

There are two principal classes of such Mosaic. The *opus tesselatum* is composed of small pieces, mostly cubes, held together by being inlaid in a kind of cement. The *opus sectile* is composed of little slabs, varying in shape according to the object to be represented. Mosaic work is very ancient; and is mentioned as early as the Book of Esther. A large number of Roman mosaic pavements, in opus tesselatum, have been preserved to us. Early Christian art also decorated walls and piers with geometrical mosaic *(opus Grecanicum)*, numerous examples of which are to be found in Ravenna, Palermo, Venice, and elsewhere. All kinds of mosaic have been practised in Italy down to the present day, less, it is true, for the decoration of walls and pavements than for Ornaments, Pictures, Table-tops, &c.

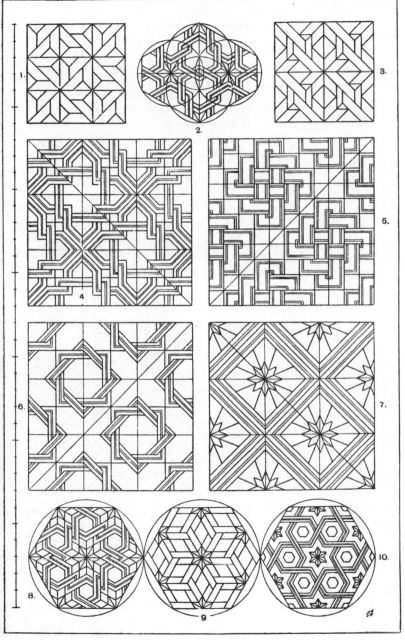

The Square Diaper, &c.   Plate 171.

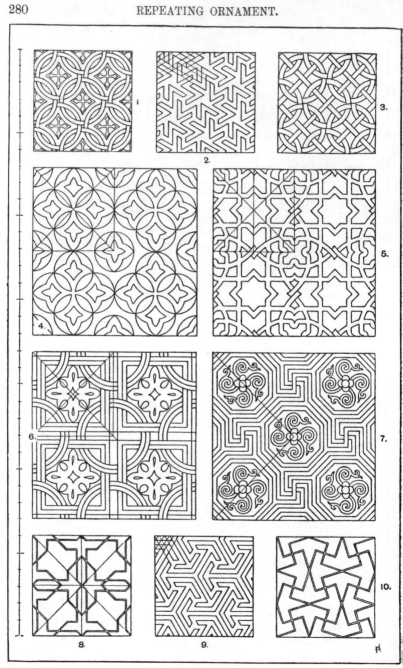

Plate 172.   The Circle Diaper, &c.

In the Arabian and the Moorish styles, incrustations of Mosaics in stone and glazed terracotta were a popular method of wall-decoration. The art of mosaic has never acquired a firm footing in northern countries.

PLATE 172. THE CIRCLE DIAPER, &c.

1. Mosaic, cathedral, Monreale, Sicily.
2. Arabian mosaic, stucco on stone, (Prisse d'Avennes).
3. Roman mosaic.
4. Marble mosaic, windows, cathedral, Florence, (Hessemer).
5. Geometrical pattern, Sta. Croce, Florence.
6. Marble mosaic, San Vitale, Ravenna, (Hessemer).
7. Modern tesselated mosaic, Sorrento.
8 and 10. Moorish mosaic, Ambassadors' Hall, Alhambra, Granada, (Owen Jones).
9. Arabian mosaic, stucco on stone, (Prisse d'Avennes).

THE SCALE DIAPER, &c. (ENAMEL.) (Plate 173.)

Where the surfaces of metal utensils and vessels are to receive a flat decoration this is usually effected by engraving, etching, damaskeening, enamel, or niello work. In the process of Engraving, the decoration is engraved by means of the graving-tool, and the hollows in some cases filled up with coloured lacquer, &c. In Etching, the metallic surface is protected against the action of the etching-fluid by being coated with a film, so that the design is sunk where the protecting film is removed by the Artist. In Damaskeening, the precious metals are fastened on iron and steel, by being hammered into engraved hollows which have been undercut with a roughened ground. The processes of Enamelling are very various. In the cloison process: bent bands or fillets of metal (cloisons) are soldered-on to the metal ground, and the hollows or cells thus formed are filled with pulverised glass paste (glass coloured with metallic oxides) which are then vitrified by heat. In the sunk or "champ-levé" process: the hollows in the metallic ground are produced by the graver, or by casting and subsequent chasing, and are then filled with enamel. Niello resembles black enamel: the enamel paste being replaced by a composition of metal and sulphur.

Enamel work (sunk-work) was known in Antique times. The Cologne enamel was celebrated in the Middle Ages. Cloison enamel has been practised in the East, in China, and in Japan, from the earliest times. The so-called Limoges "enamel" is painted on a plain metal ground, without any previous cloisons or any sunk-fields for

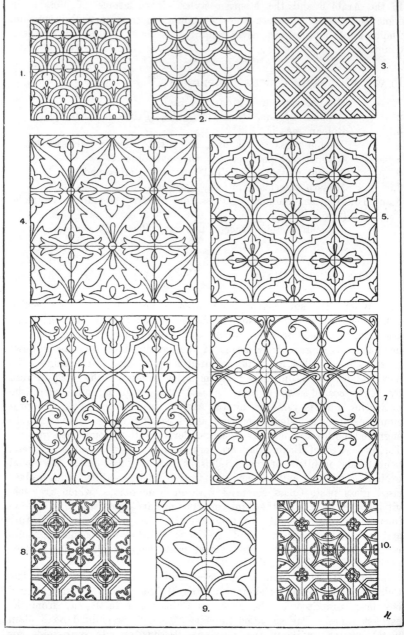

Plate 173.   The Scale Diaper, &c.

the pigments. Damaskeened objects are found in German and Old Frankish tombs. This art, however, disappeared in the West only to be pursued more energetically in the East, where it still flourishes, e. g. in Persia, and India. Niello, Engraved, and Etched work were most fashionable at the time of the Renascence.

PLATE 173. THE SCALE DIAPER, &c.

1—3.	Chinese and Japanese.
4, 5 and 9.	Indian and Persian.
6 and 7.	Renascence.
8 and 10.	Mediaeval, (Cologne enamel).

THE CIRCLE DIAPER, &c. (TILES.) (Plate 174.)

The decoration of walls and pavements, with glazed clay Tiles, dates back as early as Assyrian times.

The Middle Ages made a most extensive use of pavement tiles. The individual tiles are mostly of a square shape; and vary in size from 3 ins. to 6 ins. The pattern is generally in intaglio; and frequently filled-in with clay of another color. The designs of these tiles are usually excellent. The tile contains either the whole of the repeating ornament; or only a part of it so that 4 tiles form the unit of design. These tiles are common in England, France, and Germany.

Majolica tiles are used in Italy; and are generally adopted for the Wall-decoration so popular in England.

PLATE 174. THE CIRCLE DIAPER, &c.

1—10.	Various mediaeval tiles, after Owen Jones, Racinet, and others.
1.	Fontenay, Côte d'Or.
4 and 7.	Rouen Museum.
5.	Cathedral, St. Omer.
6.	Troyes, Archives de l'Aube.

THE CIRCLE DIAPER, &c. (STAINED GLASS.) (Plate 175.)

Window-glazing is an introduction of the Middle Ages, and was unknown to the Antique. Coloured windows were first used for Churches. The oldest process consisted in fitting-together pieces of coloured glass in the mosaic style. About the year 1000, the principal place of manufacture was Kloster Tegernsee. In the 11th and

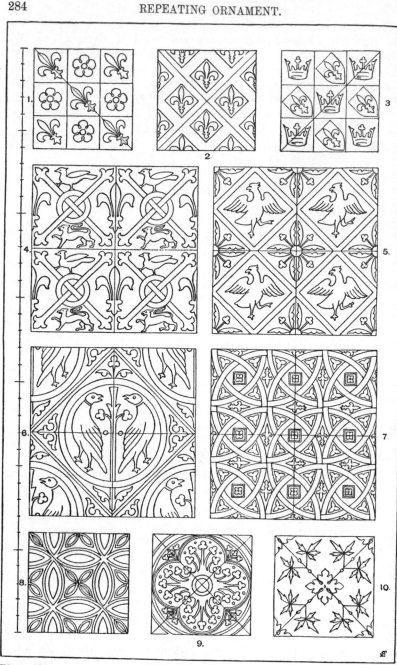

Plate 174.   The Circle Diaper, &c.

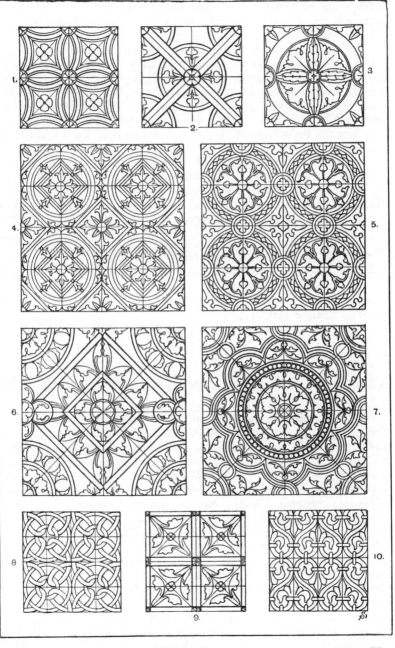

The Circle Diaper, &c. Plate 175.

12th centuries, painting begins, followed by Glass-painting strictly so-called, the design being outlined in brown paint; flashed glass, &c. followed later.

After passing through a period of decadence; and almost vanishing during the last two centuries; Glass-painting has, of late years, again become the object of great attention, and especially that branch which, leaving strict painting on one side, produces its most striking effects with coloured glass and leaden cames. The vigorous outlines, produced by the lead-setting, enhance the brilliancy of the colours, and prevent the unpleasant optical effect produced by the blending of contiguous tints.

We have here to deal only with the ornamental decoration of snrfaces by painting or mosaic. The best examples are to be found in the transition period from the Romanesque to the Gothic style in the churches of Germany, France, and England, the three countries which may be regarded as the true home of stained glass.

PLATE 175. THE CIRCLE DIAPER, &c.

1—10. Various patterns, Romanesque and Early Gothic (Owen Jones, Racinet, and others).
1 and 9. Chartres cathedral.
2 and 3. Bourges cathedral.
6.   Soissons cathedral.

VARIOUS DIAPERS. (MURAL PAINTING.) (Plates 176—177.)

The models and precursors of Mural-decoration are to be looked-for in hangings of carpets and textiles. The Egyptian style offers the earlist known examples of the decoration of surfaces by means of wall-painting. The scheme is generally a Meander or similar pattern, varied by rosettes, &c. (Plate 177. 1 and 2). The Pompejan artists used figures and architectural representations in perspective instead of Diaper patterns. Early Christian art used mosaics, which were gradually driven-out by wall-painting during the Romanesque, and Gothic periods. Churches and public buildings are again the first edifices whose interiors were decorated by "tapestry paintings", as we may term this style of decoration in view of the mutual relation between it and textile art. With respect of the principles of design: we may refer the reader to the general introduction, page 277, and to the plates 176—177. The use of Wall-papers in Modern times has greatly narrowed the sphere of Mural painting: its principal task being now confined to the decoration of Public Buildings.

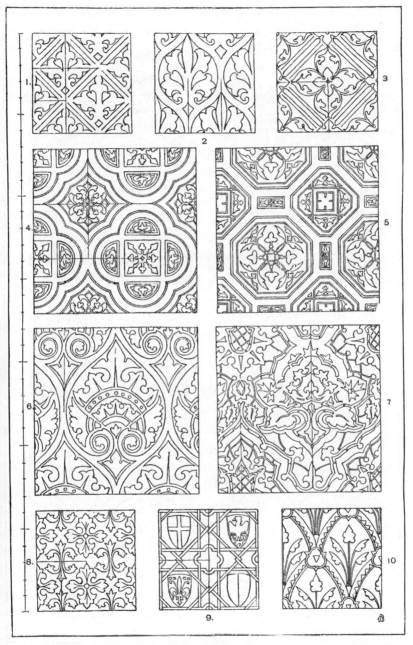

Various Diapers.

Plate 176.

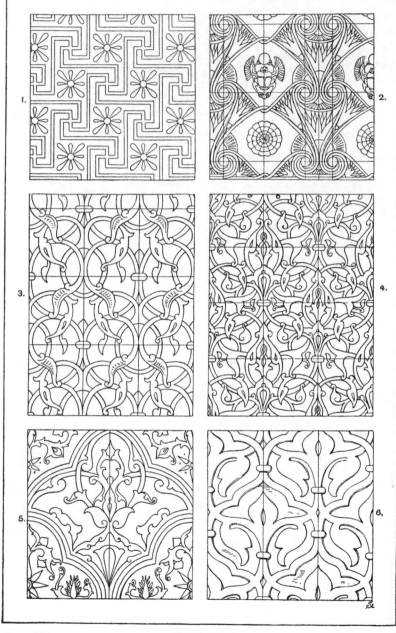

Plate 177.   Various Diapers.

PLATE 176. VARIOUS DIAPERS.

1—2.   Painting, old cabinet, Brandenburg, beginning of the 15th century, (Musterornamente).
3.   Painting, Sta. Croce, Florence, Italian Renascence.
4—5.   Painting, consistory church, Assisi, 13th century, (Hessemer).
6 and 10. Modern French, church painting.
7.   Painting, castle of Trausnitz, Landshut, end of 16th century, (Gewerbehalle).
9.   Painting, Palazzo del Podestà, Florence, 14th century, (Musterornamente).

PLATE 177. VARIOUS DIAPERS.

1.   Ancient Egyptian, meander.
2.   Ancient Egytian, ceiling painting, (Racinet).
3—5. Arabian paintings, Kaitbey mosque, (Prisse d'Avennes).
6.   Arabian mural painting, mosque of Ibrahim Aga, Cairo, (Hessemer).

VARIOUS DIAPERS. (WEAVING.) (Plates 178—179.)

The artistic decoration of Textile fabrics goes back to the very earliest times; and is of a most varied character. After the decoration of animal Skins, by sewing and embroidering, came the creation of patterns in plaited Mats by the use of material of various colours; and this again was followed by the different products of Weaving, variegated by the use of coloured yarns, by Embroidery, by Printing, &c. It is due to the perishability of the material that scarcely any products of the loom of the older epochs are to be found in our museums; and that we can only infer their patterns from descriptions and pictures. All the richer, on the other hand, is the choice offered by the Renascence, the Middle Ages, and the East.

It would go beyond the scope of this book to give a detailed historical and technical description of Textile industry; and we refer the reader to the special works and monographs on this subject*. Usually the mode of decoration depends on the object, and varies with the artistic conceptions of the different styles. By the side of purely geometrical patterns (Plate 179. 1 and 3), we find organic elements in a geometrical framing (Plate 178. 1 and 2, Plate 179, 4). By the side of poly-axial arrangements (Plate 179. 1, 2 and 3), there are others with mon-axial features (Plate 178. 1 and 2). By the side of symmetrical "turn-over" patterns (Plate 178. 3), we have others unsymmetrical (Plate 178. 4). By the side of Artificial flowers and rosettes powdered

---

* Otto v. Schorn, "Die Textilkunst". Leipzig.

over the ground (Plate 179. 9), there occur natural elements like the curious Japanese design on Plate 179, fig. 7; and so on. The great principle of style, in the standard examples of all periods, is the avoidance of representations of relief, or of perspective views of architecture, which contradict the nature of the flat surface. Important is also the proper distribution of the masses, so that distracting lines or empty spaces may be avoided. Of equal importance with the design is the Colour, but the plan of this work compels us to leave it out of consideration.

Next to the fabrication of Textiles for ecclesiastical vestments and secular garments: the most important manufacture is that of Carpets, and of Tapestries for use on walls, as curtains, portières, &c. Of the introduction of the latter into painting, we have already spoken, on Plate 176. Here we will only refer to the tapestried backgrounds, common in pictures of the 14th to the 16th century, examples of which are to be seen in figs. 3 and 4 of Plate 178. Woollen and silk tapestry were followed by sheets of Stamped-leather, an Arabian invention, which in its turn was followed by the modern Wall-paper, at first in painted single Sheets, and afterwards in the printed Rolls now so common. That we do not devote a special chapter of our work to this important product of modern art, is due to the fact that a difference between Mural painting and Textile patterns really only exists in the mode of manufacture, there being no essential distinction in respect of Design. Modern Wall-papers have, on the average, a breadth of 21 ins., on which the pattern is arranged once or oftener, according to the size of the design. The repeating of the pattern in an upward direction is partly due to technical considerations. In printing by hand from a wooden block, the length of the repeating pattern varies from 21 ins. to 30 ins.

PLATE 178. VARIOUS DIAPERS.

1 and 5. Mediaeval textile, (Gewerbehalle).
2.   Textile, 12th century, original in silk and gold; found in a tomb in the Abbey of St. Germain des Prés, Paris, (Racinet).
3.   Patterned gold ground of altar shrine, monastery of Heilbronn, end of 15th century, (Gewerbehalle).
4.   Patterned gold ground of altar shrine, church of St. Egidius, Barthfeld, (Gewerbehalle).
5.   French silk tapestry, 15th century, (L'art pour tous).

PLATE 179. VARIOUS DIAPERS.

1. Bishop's robe, Sacristy, Sta. Croce, Florence.
2. Pillow pattern, tomb, St. George's, Tübingen, German Renascence. (Gewerbehalle).

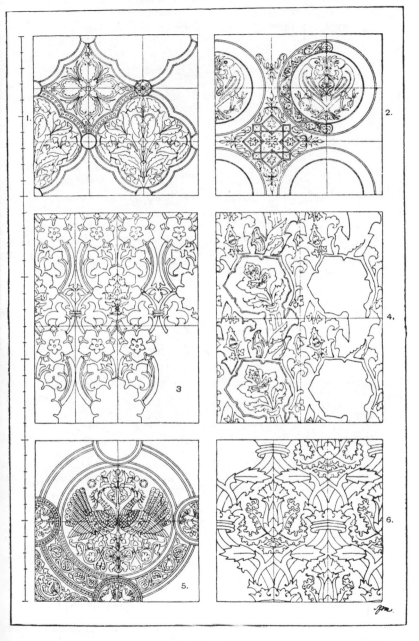

Various Diapers. Plate 178.

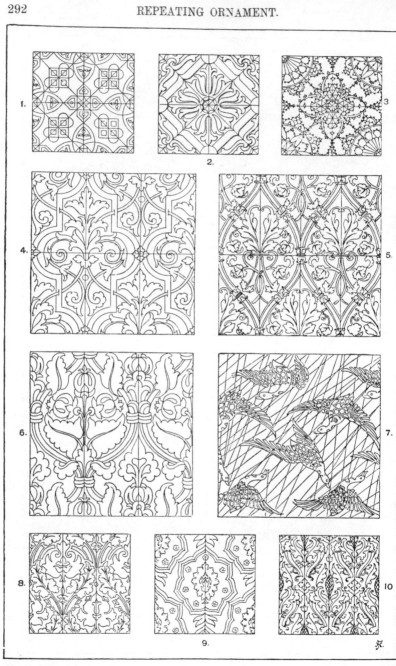

Plate 179.   Various Diapers.

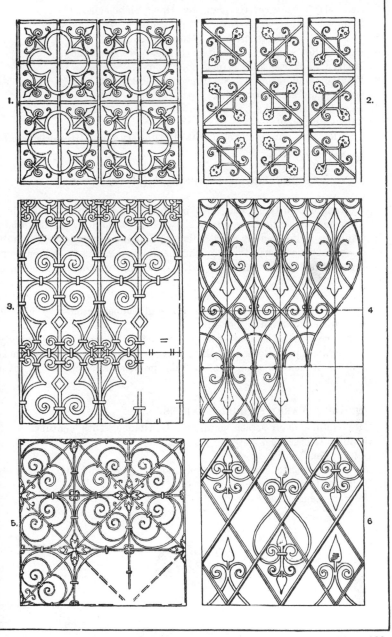

Various Grill Diapers.   Plate 180.

3. Lace, 16th century, German, by Hans Siebmacher.
4. Stamped-leather, book-cover, 17th century, (Gewerbehalle).
5. Textile, German Renascence, (Musterornamente).
6. Carpet, Rottweil, German Renascence, (Gewerbehalle).
7. Modern Japanese silk, (L'art pour tous).
8. Painted gold ground, St. Lorenzo, Rottweil, end of the 15th century, (Musterornamente).
9. Carpet, Stiftskirche, Comburg, beginning of the 17th century, (Musterornamente).
10. Textile, Venetian picture, 1560, Berlin Museum, (Gewerbehalle).

VARIOUS GRILL DIAPERS.　(Plate 180.)

Wrought-iron Grills may also be treated as Diapers; and Railings and Gratings are often treated as shown by the figures in the Plate. The skeleton is formed by bars interlaced on the basis of the quadrangular or lozenge Net; the compartments being filled, either continuously, or at regular intervals, with recurring ornamental accessories (figs. 1, 2, 5 and 6).

Another system places a repeating scroll-like ornament between parallel bars (fig. 3). The straight lines of the skeleton may also be replaced by curved bars (fig. 4).

The material is square, round, and flat iron bars; either singly, or in combination. Both the Middle Ages and the Renascence have transmitted numerous examples in this branch; a selection is given in the Plate.

PLATE 180.　VARIOUS GRILL DIAPERS.

1. Late Gothic, choir-screen, minister, Constance, 15th century.
2. German Renascence.
3. Italian Renascence.
4. Modern, by Ende and Böckmann, Berlin, (Gewerbehalle).
5. German, 17th century.
6. German Renascence.

DIVISION III.

DECORATED
OBJECTS.

A.   Vases, &c.
B.   Metal Objects.
C.   Furniture.
D.   Frames, &c.
E.   Jewelry.
F.   Heraldry.
G.   Writing, Printing, &c.

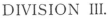

PREFATORY REMARKS.

The third division of the Handbook is entitled "Decorated Objects". It is intended, firstly, to show in what manner and on what principles Decoration is applied to objects, (thus complementing the work of the second division); and secondly, it will pass a little beyond the strict limits of Aisthetics, and enter on the sphere of Tectonics, in order to present a view of the construction, profiling and general plan of objects of art, e. g. Vases, Utensils, Furniture, &c.

These considerations, and the wish to be as comprehensive as possible, have necessitated the inclusion of some objects which are not *decorated*. This inclusion will increase the bulk of the Book; but the selection of objects will be restricted, as much as possible, to those which illustrate the Principles of Decoration.

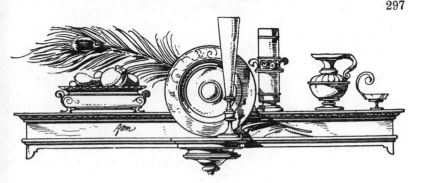

A.

VASES.

Vases, with which this division opens, are one of the most interesting and important of its groups. Gottfried Semper, who has treated Keramics brilliantly in his epoch-making work "Der Stil", says in the introduction to the chapter on this subject: "The products of Keramic art were held in unusually high esteem by all peoples and in all periods. They had attained a religious symbolical significance long before the times of monumental edifices, which latter, indeed, were greatly influenced by the former; directly, in that Keramic works served for the construction and ornamentation of the monuments; indirectly, because architecture took up principles of beauty and style and even finished forms which had already been developed in Keramic work, and had first been fixed by the art potters of pre-architectural times".... "They are the oldest and most eloquent documents of history. Show us the pottery which a nation has produced, and we can in general tell what manner of nation it was and what height of culture it had attained!" Professor Gmelin, who, in his essay: "Die Urformen und Gestaltungsprinzipien der Töpferei" and in his work: "Die Elemente der Gefässbildnerei", has attempted with much success to popularise Semper's theories, says: "A bit of Darwinism is here unfolded in the sphere of industry: the way in which the development of man has been influenced by climate, the character of the soil, food, &c., finds its parallel in Keramics in the formation of vessels as conditioned by the joint causes of aim, material, and technique".

How far Pottery goes back to prehistoric times, is proved by the calculations made from the alluvial deposits of the Nile valley, and the geological conditions on the coasts of Scandinavia, which give us the respectable age of 10 000 to 12 000 years for the pottery discovered in those spots. The circumstance that, besides satisfying the needs of daily life, Pottery was used in religious and funeral rites, more especially the custom of placing vessels in the grave of the departed, of enclosing the ashes of the dead in urns before committing them to the earth, has at any rate preserved to us certain kinds of pottery, of which, otherwise, only sherds and fragments had remained.

By Keramics we understand not only earthen-ware, but the design and making of vessels in general. Next to the various clays, glass, and metals, which have the first claim on our attention, stone, wood, and ivory, along with other less common materials, are the substances generally used. Each of these Materials imparts its own character to the vessels made of it; the corresponding technique will limit or modify the Form. A metal vessel requires form and decoration different from one of glass or porcelain; the profile of a clay vase cannot be made in marble without much modification. On the other hand the Purpose, for which the vessel is intended, will influence the choice of the Material; so that a reciprocal interaction arises, which stimulates to the study of Keramics, and makes it charming and instructive.

That the majority of the examples in this group of pottery have been taken from the Antique, is due to the fact that this epoch offers a general picture complete in itself; and that it is chiefly in the Greek style that the above-mentioned reciprocal interaction, regularity of form, and tectonic principle are, on the average, most clearly expressed. That, on the other hand, we have brought the constructions of other countries and periods into suitable connexion with the Antique, arises from our wish to meet the wants and requirements of our time in a greater degree than can be done by monographs of Greek Keramics alone, such as we possess in a large number of special wocks*.

In view, of the immense importance of Antique Keramics and of Clay as a material in general: it may be well to offer here a few general remarks on this subject, reserving our observations on other materials and styles till the elucidation of the plates in question. Pottery is generally made on the potter's wheel. In Egypt, India, and

---

* Among such works whose size, get-up, and text render them suitable for school and educational purposes, we may mention:

Th. Lau: *die griechischen Vasen, ihr Formen- und Decorationssystem.* 44 Tafeln mit einer historischen Einleitung und erläuterndem Text von Dr. Brunn und Dr. Krell. Leipzig: E. A. Seemann.

A. Genick: *griechische Keramik.* 40 Tafeln mit Einleitung und Beschreibung von Adolf Furtwängler. Berlin: Ernst Wasmuth.

Mesopotamia, the use of this important implement of civilisation goes back to the very earliest times. The mural paintings of Beni Hassan, which have been referred to the 19th century B. C., show that pottery was then already known; while Germany did not use pottery before the Roman period; and America, previous to the arrival of Europeans, was only acquainted with the formation of pots by hand, in spite of the great achievements of the Peruvians. The formation of pottery by hand, is still in use in many countries. To this class belongs the building-up with zonal or spiral strips, and the moulding over plaited moulds or gourds which are then destroyed in the firing. Wooden and stone moulds were used in early times; and also in modern times in connection with the wheel. At the outset, people contented themselves with drying the clay; afterwards drying was followed by firing. An intermediate stage is to fire beneath a covering of cow-dung, the air being excluded; when the smoke penetrates into the clay, and colours it gray or black. Originally only smoothed and polished, the vessels were afterwards rendered more impervious to liquids by being painted with a Varnish, such as is seen on Greek vases; and by the discovery of the tin and lead Glazes, such as are found on the so-called "majolica ware". The porosity, of many oriental vessels, is intentional, in order that the contents may be kept cool by the process of evaporation on the surface of the vessel. Of the chemical composition of these ancient Varnishes, we are not so well informed as we could wish.

Antique pottery is found in all places where ancient civilisation penetrated; but the principal sources are: Greece, Sicily, and Italy, particularly Campania and Etruria. To this latter circumstance is ascribed the erroneous use of the name "Etruscan", in the last century, as a collective name for antique pottery in general. Athens, Corinth, and Chalcis, were the chief factories of pottery in Greece; and Tarentum and Cumae in Italy, where pottery established itself after the decay of Greek art. Apart from prehistoric products, it can be proved that Greek vase-painting begins historically in the 7th century B. C.; attained its golden age about 400 B. C.; and decayed with the invasion by the Romans about 200 B. C. According to peculiarities of form and finish, we distinguish different periods, the leading characteristics of which are as follows: —

1. *The geometrical style:* clay natural colour, yellowish-grey, rough; decoration brown, in bands, rings, zigzag lines, checks and other simple patterns, borrowed from the technique of weaving and wood carving, sometimes in connection with representations of domestic animals, teams, &c., in rhythmic sequence, (compare Plate 194. 2 and 3).

2. *The Asiatic style:* clay natural color, yellowish, impregnated and smoothed; decoration dark brown, dark red, and white,

with fantastic winged creatures, lions, panthers, geese, sphinxes, mostly arranged in zones. The intervening spaces, between the animals, are filled with rosettes, flowers, &c. The Zonal decoration is often replaced by Scales, (compare Plate 194. 4).

3. *The Black Figure style:* clay reddish-yellow, coloured with oxide of iron; decoration black, pure white being used for the carnations of female figures, horses, &c. The conception of the figures is frequently archaic, drawn in uncoloured compartments bordered by ornamental bands. The lines of drapery, &c. are scratched through the black colour, to the clay.

4. *The Red Figure style:* clay red, very smooth: the entire vessel, with the exception of the ornaments and figures, coated black; the black sometimes having a greenish shimmer. White only occasionally found, for grey hair and the like. The tendency to simplification is predominant in respect of both ornament and figures; usually with only one figure or with simple groups of figures; outlines are painted-in with the pencil.

5. *The Painted style:* clay as in No. 4; the vessels frequently of colossal size (they are then not intended for practical use, as may be inferred from their having no bottom); the numerous red figures on the black ground are placed one over the other, with the addition of architectural decoration: technically the decoration is executed in a careless manner; dark red, white, yellow, and gold are also used; luxuriant brushwork ornament, patterns in perspective, and painted reliefs, are common.

The succession of these styles, in time, is generally that of the above order; but they often blend with each other without any definite demarcation, forming composite styles and varieties. We find, for instance, certain drug-pots which have polychrome painting on a white background, and so on.

FUNDAMENTAL VASE-FORMS.   (Plate 181.)

Vases, as a rule, are composed of a number of simple forms or parts. These are usually the foot, the body, and the neck; to which a handle, a lid, and a spout, may also be added. The most important part is the Body. In the majority of cases it determines the fundamental form of the vessel. The natural models for vessels are the hollow hand, the egg, the husks of fruits (gourds, nuts), the horns of animals, the skins of animals, and similar objects. These have, as a matter of fact, been used in all ages as models, for more r less direct imitation; and were undoubtedly used by mankind in the lowest stages of civilisation, instead of artificial vessels. Certain stereotyped forms recur again and again: first among them (due to the use of the potter's wheel) the form of the so-called body of revolution. An attempt is made, on Plate 181, to give a general view of the commonest fundamental forms, with their names. The Sphere, the Cylinder, and the Hyperboloid, are the simplest of these. The Sphere is altered, by equally flattening or extending, to the Spheroid, or the Ellipsoid. If these bodies be cut-away at both ends: we have the erect, and the recumbent vessel. Unequal flattening and extending produce forms which we may term Echinus, Cake, Egg, and Top forms; or, if the length much exceeds the breadth: Wedge, Spindle, and Drop forms. If only the top be cut-into: we have either the Dish, or the Cup form. Conical, Bag, and Canopus forms may be derived from the Cylinder. In a similar way the Hyperboloid also leads to new forms. If the height of the vessel be a high multiple of the diameter, we get slender, tapering forms: in the reverse case, we have dishes and plates.

The Egg is the commonest form in Pottery. Cylindrical and Conical forms, i. e. such bodies as have a developible surface, are best adapted for Sheet-metal work.

Mathematical curves, e. g. arcs of circles, are not strictly adhered-to in the profiles. Vessels, which are not made on the wheel, often exhibit arbitrary forms which cannot be grouped in the scheme of the Plate. In the Chinese and Japanese styles, for example, prismatic forms are very common (compare Plate 187. 1); human and animal shapes are found in the Antique, as forms of vessels, (compare Plate 194. 12).

The Various junctions, of the Body with the Neck, or the Foot, will produce a series of new forms. The use of Double-curvature in the profile will also produce new forms, the simplest of which are the Bell, and the Pear. The so-called "Gourd-pots", the Pilgrim-bottles, &c., also form special and rarer groups of forms. Here too, may be mentioned duplex vessels formed by the juxtaposition of two vessels on a common foot, or by uniting them with a common handle. These forms are found sporadically in Prehistoric and all subsequent periods.

As regards the Feet of vessels: we have first to remark that in the earliest times footless and three-footed vessels are by no means rare. The former were sunk in the earth, the latter would stand on an uneven surface. The usual form of foot presupposes a level standing surface and therefore some degree of civilisation. Intermediate, between the absence of a foot and the high foot, is the Ring-foot, a torus or profiled circular ring, forming the lower end of the vessel. It evidently arose from the early custom of placing footless vessels in hyperboloid Rings, which were afterwards incorporated with the vessel itself. The decoration of the foot is generally subordinate to that of the body; and consists of simple motives, channellings, &c.

The Neck receives a cylindrical, conical, or hyperboloid form, according to the object of the vessel. As experience showed that pouring-out is best done through a narrow opening, and filling through a wide one: funnel-shaped necks, intended to meet both requirements, arose. A good decoration of the neck is to surround it at its narrowest part with a neutral band, from which the motive of decoration may be developed upwards and downwards.

The upper margin or Mouth is either bent outwards or inwards, or is straight; the latter especially when the vessel was intended to be closed by a Stopper. Pouring-out is facilitated if the vessel be provided with a Spout, or curved Lip, as is the case with some mugs and cans. The decoration of the Mouth, when round, is usually a beading or row of leaves curving downwards and outwards. The curved Lip depends for its effect on the line of its curve, or, like the Spout, is decorated by masks, scallops, &c.

The Lid generally fits into, on-to, or over, the upper margin. It may be raised by means of a knob, hoop, or ring; and if it does not lie loose on the mouth, is fastened by a hinge, or by cords and chains (Censer). Antique lids have sometimes the form of little vessels, or dishes.

The Handle varies in size, position, and number, according to the use and size of the vessel. The points of attachment of the vertical handle lie in a vertical plane; those of the horizontal handle are in a horizontal plane side by side; and those of the hoop handle are opposite each other in a vertical plane. The *vertical* handle is most used. The *horizontal* handle is specially intended for lifting; the vertical for tilting the vessel when pouring-out. Vertical handles are most suitable for tall vessels; and horizontal handles for flat ones. Other forms are produced by combination, as when a vertical handle is added to the centre of a horizontal one. As a rope was originally used instead of a handle, the latter frequently takes that form, (compare Plate 182. 4). If the vessel be intended for pouring-out: the handle should be so attached that the pouring-out may be done with equal ease whether the vessel be full or nearly empty.

––––––––––

Attempts have often been made to classify vessels according to their uses; but definite divisions cannot be made, as many vessels may serve for a number of purposes, which gives rise to combinations and intermediate groups. We mainly follow Semper's classification when we divide vessels into the following groups:

1. *Holders;* their chief object being storage and preservation.

     To this group belong: the Amphora, Urn, Krater, dish and salver, the Ampulla, the Alabastron, and similar small vessels, flower-vase, salt-cellar, ink-pot, snuff-box, holy-water stoup, &c.

2. *Dippers;* chiefly used for drawing and filling into other vessels.

     To this group belong: the Hydria, bucket, spoon, and Patera.

3. *Pourers;* for pouring-out.

     To these belong: the Prochoüs, Olpe, Oinoché, Lekythos, mug, can, and bottle.

4. *Drinking vessels.*

     The principal representatives of this class are: the antique drinking vessels of the forms Kylix, Kantharos, Kyathos, &c.; the drinking horn or Rhyton, beaker, bowl, goblet, Rummer, Tumbler, and all the various forms of our modern drinking-glasses.

The various vessels will be treated in this order.

In many cases: one half of the cut shows the geometrical view; and the other shows the vertical section. Decorative figures are frequently omitted, particularly on Antique vases; the decoration has sometimes been omitted, when that was required by the minuteness of the scale; and sometimes it has been only partially drawn or indicated, in order to avoid unneccessary work.

a. Holders.

THE AMPHORA. (Plate 182.)

The Amphora is of frequent occurrence in the Antique. It was intended to receive water, oil, and wine. Originally serving for practical purposes, it was afterwards employed merely as a show, or state vessel. The form was often revived in later styles; and has the following characteristics: erect, extended body, like an inverted egg (Plate 182. 9), a spindle (Plate 182. 7), a bag (Plate 182. 6), more rarely conical (Plate 182. 11), hyperboloid (Plate 182. 10), or cylindrical Plate 182. 14). The neck is narrow, more or less extended, with shoulder (Plate 182. 6), or without (Plate 182. 5), thickened at the he rim. Two vertical handles, diametrically opposite each other. At first without a foot (Plate 182. 3—7), afterwards with a round or

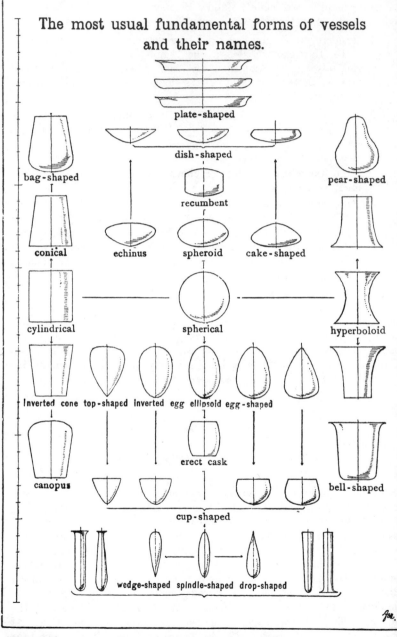

The most usual fundamental forms of vessels and their names.

plate-shaped

dish-shaped

bag-shaped   pear-shaped

recumbent

conical   echinus   spheroid   cake-shaped

cylindrical   spherical   hyperboloid

Inverted cone top-shaped Inverted egg ellipsoid egg-shaped

erect cask

canopus   bell-shaped

cup-shaped

wedge-shaped spindle-shaped drop-shaped

Plate 181.   Chart of Fundamental Vase Forms.

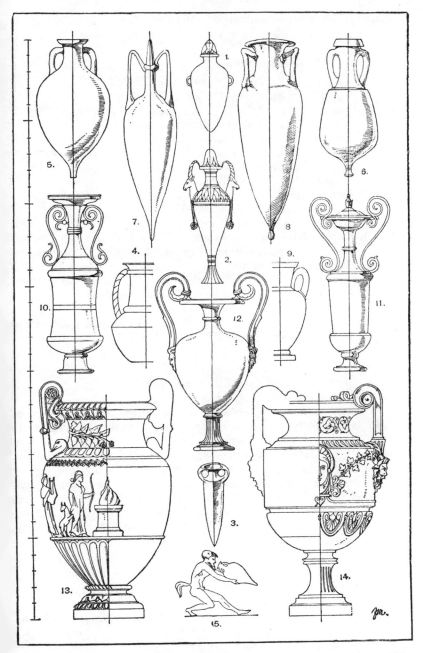

The Amphora. Plate 182.

high foot. With or without cover. Material: clay, more rarely glass, or other materials. Size: very variable, according to use.

PLATE 182. THE AMPHORA.

1   Egyptian, with cover, Thebes, Thutmes III.
2.   Egyptian, with cover, Thebes, XX dynasty.
3.   Small four-sided, with Latin inscription, found in Egypt, unpainted clay, United collections, Carlsruhe.
4.   Assyrian, with rope handle, clay.
5.   Roman, unpainted red clay, United collections, Carlsruhe.
6.   Roman, unpainted yellow clay, found near Aquileia in 1877, United collections, Carlsruhe.
7.   Roman, glass, with stopper, Rouen, Museum, (Deville).
8.   Roman, iridescent glass, found at Pompeii.
9.   Ancient, Attic, painted clay (so-called Diota), Munich, (Lau).
10—11. Clay, painted in polychrome, with band-shaped handles, so-called Alexandrian style, (Lau and Jacobsthal).
12.   Antique, black painted clay, (Gropius).
13.   Antique state amphora, white marble, with swan handles, "Vase of the Athenian Sosibios", Louvre, Paris.
14.   Modern French, state amphora, by Liénard.
15.   Faun with amphora, from the painted neck oi an Antique Drinking-horn, (compare Plate 202. 5—6).

THE URN. (Plate 183.)

The Urn is met-with, not only in the Antique and all subsequent styles, but in early times everywhere and specially in Prehistoric styles. Apart from other purposes, the Urn was frequently used in funeral rites, as a repository for the ashes of the dead, as a coffin, and so on. It has an erect body, profiled like an inverted egg or spindle. The neck is comparatively wide and low, the mouth straight or curved outwards, usually closed by a cover. Either without feet, or with a low round foot. Without handles, or with two small horizontal handles, attached to the greatest prominence of the body. Material: clay. Generally of considerable size.

PLATE 183. THE URN.

1.   Egyptian, rubbing an Urn, (Ménard et Sauvageot).
2.   Prehistoric, Gallic, (Bosc).
3.   Grey clay, ornamentation in relief, United collections, Carlsruhe.
4—5. Greek, painted clay, Munich.
6.   Majolica, 15th century, Italian.

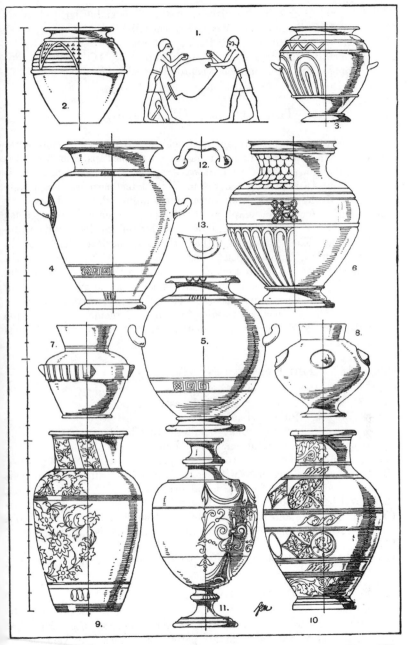

The Urn.   Plate 183.

7—8. Slavic, found in the district of the Elbe and Oder.
9.   Modern Faience, Bombay, (Gewerbehalle).
10.   Majolica, 16th century, Italian, (Storck).
11.   German, cut crystal, small with high foot, 16th century, National Museum, Munich, (Kunsthandwerk).

THE KRATER. (Plate 184.)

The Krater is an Antique vase, chiefly used for mixing water and wine (wine was not drunk unmixed); and perhaps also for ablutions. Although we meet with it as early as Egyptian times, it is not found in Antique Keramic art until its later periods. As a state vessel, the Krater has probably been more highly developed than any other form. Modern art employs the Krater preferentially as a garden vase for plants. A characteristic of the Krater is its great width at the top. The body is either a hemispherical dish (fig. 9), or has a wide, cup-shaped neck, (figs. 7 and 8). Where the junction is formed without a shoulder: we have the bell-shaped Krater (figs. 3 and 4). The Foot is frequently small; and so arranged that it stands on an independent base (fig. 10). Two, sometimes four, or more, horizontal or vertical handles, or hints of them. The principal materials were clay, marble, and metal. Kraters are usually of considerable size.

PLATE 184. THE KRATER.

1.   Egyptian, with lotus cups.
2.   Egyptian, Thebes, XVIII dynasty.
3—4. Greek, Munich, (Lau).
5.   Greek, with columnar handles, Munich, (Lau).
6.   Greek, with volute handles, (Lau).
7.   Antique, Uffizi, Florence, (Gropius).
8.   Antique, marble, with four handles, found at Ostia, evidently copied from a metal original.
9.   Ditto, found at Tivoli, England.
10.   Antique, state Vase, marble, the decoration of the neck, consisting of figures or rich scroll ornament, is omitted.
11.   Assyrian.
12—13. Antique, for ladies' toilet, Greek vase-paintings.

THE BASIN, AND DISH. (Plate 185.)

Basins, and Dishes, are vessels of such common use, that they are found everywhere, and in all periods in which the Keramic art

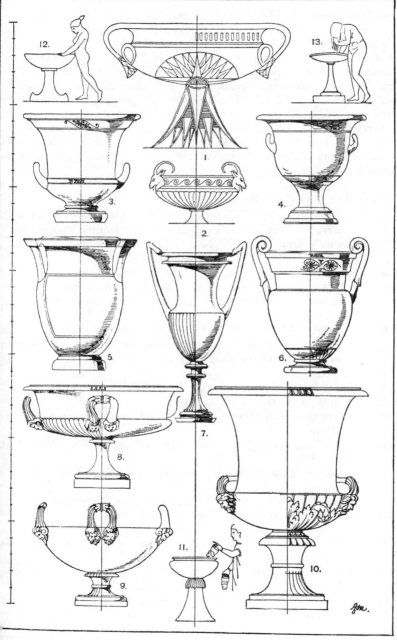

The Krater.   Plate 184.

has been practised. Their uses are manifold; their form is indicated
by their names: Dishes are the *deeper*, Plates the *shallower* vessels.
They occur without foot, and with a round or high foot. The last
was specially adopted for the Greek Kylix. Handles are wanting, or
occur singly, or in pairs, horizontal, vertical, as hoop handles, and so
on. Material, and size: various. The decoration of Dishes is generally
on the exterior; and of Plates is generally on the inner or upper
face. In the latter case: the border and the centre are ornamented
separately, being divided from each other by a neutral, undecorated
zone, (figs. 13—16). To paint the entire surface with figures, disregarding the division of border and centre, would be contrary to
correct Style.

PLATE 185. THE BASIN, AND THE DISH.

1. Egyptian Dish, with hoop handles, Metal, (Ménard et Sauvageot).
2. Egyptian Dish, with erect handles, Metal, (Ménard et Sauvageot).
3. Greek Dish, yellow clay, painted brown and red, Geometrical style, United collections, Carlsruhe.
4. View from above, of the handles of the above.
5. Greek Dish, yellow clay, ornamented with horn-like excrescences, painted red, Geometrical style, United collections,
Carlsruhe.
6. Greek Dish, with high foot (Kylix), yellow clay, decoration
brown, Geometrical style, Munich, the interior is decorated
with the ornament shown on Plate 157. 4.
7. Ditto.
8. Greek, flat Dish, with ring foot, Munich, (Lau).
9. Antique footless Dish, (Jacobsthal).
10. Antique, small Dish, with low foot, silver treasure, Hildesheim.
11. Antique, metal Dish, with high volute handles, (Ménard et
Sauvageot).
12. Roman, glass Dish, with pierced handle ring, Found in Normandy, (Deville).
13—14. Majolica Dish, view and section, Italian Renascence.
15—16. Modern glass Plates, with scalloped border.
17. Modern Soup-tureen, with cover.
18. Modern French metal Dish, with vertical handle and three
feet, (Julienne).
19. Modern Spanish, small Dish, of variegated glazed clay,
Malaga, United collections, Carlsruhe.
20. Modern Coffee-bowl, with horizontal handles.
21. Handle of No. 20, viewed from above.

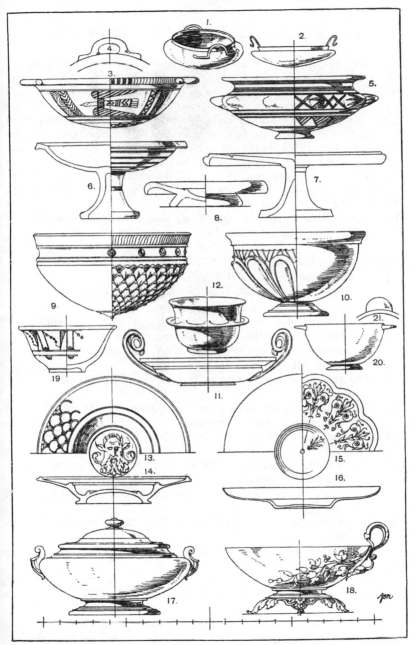

The Basin, and the Dish.   Plate 185.

THE AMPULLA, ALABASTRON, &c. (Plate 186.)

The Ampulla is a diminutive Amphora, often in black painted clay, adorned with impressed ornament (figs. 4—6). The Phiale is a slender vessel, without handles, with elongated body, and long narrow neck, of clay or glass (figs. 1—3). The Alabastron has a bag-like or cylindrical body, no foot, a very narrow neck with a shoulder, a large plate-like mouth, and little ear-shaped handles (figs. 13—14). This vessel was intended for the reception of oils and unguents; it was made of alabaster or striped glass, whence its name. The Lachrymatory, so-called from its tear-like profile, or from its purpose, is a glass vessel, of the forms shown in figs. 11 and 12. Not less frequent are little bag forms like the handleless vessels given in figs. 6, 9, and 10. Like those already named, they were intended for toilet or religious purposes.

PLATE 186. THE AMPULLA, ALABASTRON, &c.

1.	Egyptian Phiale, with cover, Thutmes III.
2.	Antique Phiale, painted clay, Munich, (Lau).
3.	Antique glass Phiale, (Stackelberg).
4.	Antique glass Ampulla, striped bright blue and yellow.
5.	Antique Ampulla, black painted clay with impressed ornaments, Athens, United collections, Carlsruhe.
6.	Ditto, Athens.
7—10.	Antique, Small Vessels, painted clay, United collections, Carlsruhe.
11—12.	Antique glass Lachrymatories, Museum, Nuremberg, and United collections, Carlsruhe.
11.	Antique Alabastron, veined glass, imitating oriental alabaster.
14.	Antique Alabastron, milk-white glass, with brown stripes, Campana collection, (L'art pour tous).
15.	Vase, white iridescent glass, Campana collection, (L'art pour tous).
16.	Modern Japanese, Small Vase, with mask handles, Landesgewerbehalle, Carlsruhe.
17.	Old German, Small stoneware Vase.

THE FLOWER-VASE, &c. (Plate 187.)

Flower-vase is the name given to vessels intended to receive and support bouquets of living or dried flowers. Various as the forms of these vessels may be in other respects, their purpose requires that they

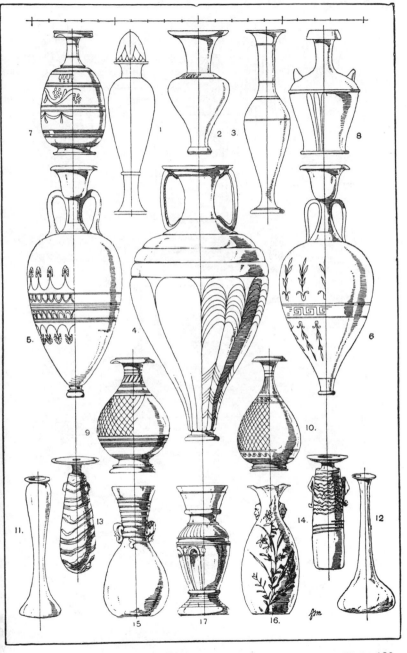

The Ampulla, the Alabastron, &c.   Plate 186.

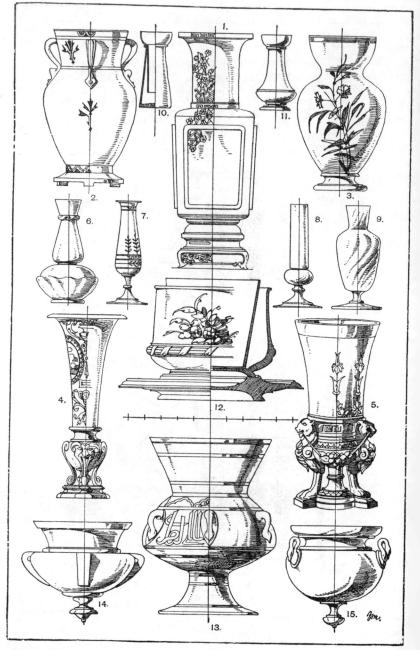

Plate 187.   The Flower-Vase, &c.

should have a funnel-shaped mouth. Japan and China, which have been especially prolific in this group, use cylindrical and prismatic forms. Such vessels do not possess a cover; handles, which are equally super-fluous, are also generally wanting; the decoration should avoid any attempt to imitate natural plant motives. Glass, clay, and porcelain are the predominant materials. A special example of these vessels is the so-called "Hyacinth-glass" intended for forcing bulbs in water. As it is desirable that the root should be visible, recourse must be had to some transparent material. Decoration is excluded in the case of the ordinary Flower-pot, which must admit air and moisture. This has led to the use of the Decorated Flower-pot, an example of which is given in fig. 12. The suspended Flower-vase, like suspended vases in general, must be furnished with three or more handles to which the cords and chains may be attached; but it need not have a foot unless it intended to stand also.

PLATE 187.   THE FLOWER-VASE, &c.

1.   Chinese, with cloison enamel, (Lièvre).
2.   Modern English, in oriental style, blue glazed clay, with black ornament, Landesgewerbehalle, Carlsruhe.
3.   Modern, glazed clay, with decoration in colours.
4.   Modern Italian majolica, Landesgewerbehalle, Carlsruhe.
5.   Modern, coloured stoneware, (Gewerbehalle).
6.   Glass, 17th century.
7—9.   Modern, glass.
10—11. Modern, Hyacinth-glasses, (No. 10 is patented: the upper part is made to lift out for greater convenience of pouring-in water).
12.   Modern, decorated Flower-pot, green glazed clay.
13.   Arabian suspended Lamp, enamelled glass, conventional form, (part of the ornamentation is omitted).
14—15. Modern suspended Flower-vases, of glazed clay.

VASE-FORMS FOR VARIOUS PURPOSES.   (Plate 188.)

This plate exhibits a number of receptacles for salt and other spices, vinegar, oil, ink, &c. The name "cellar" and "stand" have little connection with the form of these vessels, which may be very various. Receptacles for oil and vinegar are often called "Cruets" Vessels belonging to this group have not been preserved to us from the Antique; but we may not conclude, from this, that salt, oil, &c., were not preserved in vessels in those days: on the contrary, some small vessels in the silver treasure at Hildesheim, have been supposed to be Salt-cellars, though we have no definite evidence that this was so.

The Salt-cellar usually takes the form of a dish or bowl, sometimes of a little trough or tub. The material is glazed clay, glass, porcelain, metal, &c. The Renascence period created Salt-cellars of rich design: the most celebrated is the famous one by Cellini.

With the increased use of writing, the Inkstand has undergone an immense number of changes of form. The wooden Inkstand, with glass lining, was in use, for a long time, till it was rendered obsolete by vessels of clay and glass. What is required of a good Inkstand is: — it should not fall-over easily, and if it does should not spill; the evaporation must be reduced to a minimum; the height of the contents must be easy to regulate. To fulfil all these requirements numerous inventions have been made, some of which we will notice here. In fig. 10 the centre of gravity lies in the foot, and this, with the form of the glass, prevents falling-over, or spilling. In fig. 12 the level of the ink can be regulated by an India-rubber stopper. The funnel-shaped tube in which the ink rises is convenient for dipping the pen; and it reduces the evaporation. Fig. 13 shows an Inkstand with sloping bottom, and revolving cover, which may be adjusted to the varying level of the ink. The form of fig. 14 is intended to prevent falling-over, to reduce evaporation, and to maintain the level uniform for a long time; a result which is attained, notwithstanding the simplicity.

Oil and Vinegar Cruets are usually small bottles with a shoulder. They are generally placed in pairs, in a frame (fig. 7); a direct union of the two, as in fig. 6, is rare.

The Pepper-box has of late years taken the form of the pepper mill or grinder (fig. 8), otherwise it is associated with the Salt-cellar, and receives the same form. The Inkstand and the Sand-box were also often associated together; but Blotting-paper renders the latter unnecessary.

PLATE 188. VASE-FORMS FOR VARIOUS PURPOSES.

1. Salt-cellar, Renascence, (Formenschatz).
2. Salt-cellar, German, 16th century.
3. Majolica Salt-cellar, Italian Renascence, (Teirich).
4. Spice-frame, glass, 18th century.
5. Modern Cruet-frame.
6. Modern Cruets, coloured glass, Antique model.
7. Modern Cruet-frame.
8. Modern Peppermill.
9. Old Inkstand, wood.
10. Modern Inkstand.
11. Inkstand, Glazed clay.

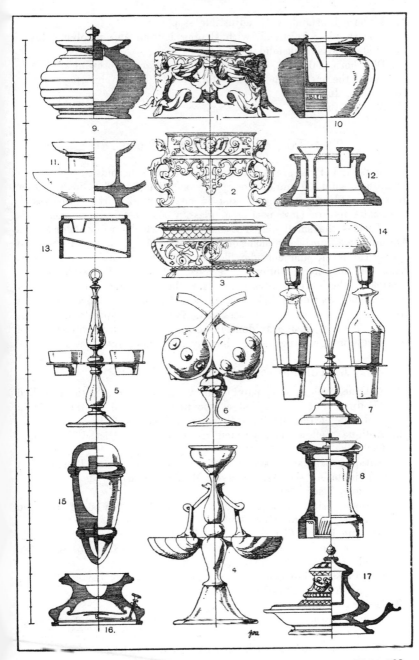

Vase-forms for Various Purposes.   Plate 188.

12. Modern Inkstand, with adjustible stopper.
13. Modern glass Inkstand, with sloping bottom and revolving cover.
14. Modern glass Inkstand.
15. Old horn Inkstand, for the pocket; after unscrewing the foot-piece, the metal pin may be forced into the Table-top.
16. Modern Inkstand.
17. Modern Inkstand.

THE JAR, THE CIST, &c. (Plate 189.)

Jars and Pots are small receptacles of spheroid or cylindrical form, for solid, granular, or pasty substances. The lid is either loose, or affixed by hinges; and is an essential part of the vessel. The materials are clay, porcelain, glass, wood, metal, ivory, &c.

Besides the small clay Pots and Boxes which are common in the Antique: we must also mention the Cist. This is a metal vessel of cylindrical form, and considerable size, which was used for religious rites, and for the reception of jewelry, rolls, &c. The style is conventional: there were three claws for the feet; and the exterior of the cylinder was decorated with incised figures, and furnished with rings to which chains were attached, for the transportation of the vessel. The lid is slightly domed; and the handle usually consists of two wrestlers grasping each other by the shoulders (fig. 6).

PLATE 189. THE JAR, THE CIST, &c.

1. Antique, yellow clay, painted brown and red, this is the so-called "Dodwell vase" celebrated as the first-discovered of the vases in imitation of the Asiatic style, dug-up near Corinth.
2. Antique, yellow clay, painted red and brown, United collections, Carlsruhe.
3. Antique, with small Kylix as lid, yellow clay, painted brown and red, imitating the Asiatic style, Munich, (Lau).
4. Antique, black clay.
5. Antique, painted clay, belongs to the later period of the red figure style, metal ring, Berlin, Museum.
6. Antique bronze Cist, Louvre, Paris, (L'art pour tous).
7. Modern Japanese, lacquered gold and black, the lid forms a dish, Landesgewerbehalle, Carlsruhe.
8. Old Persian, repoussé copper, the decoration is too small to be given, (Kunsthandwerk).
9. Modern Snuff-box, birch bark.
10. Modern Tobacco-jar, Norwegian, carved in wood, Landesgewerbehalle, Carlsruhe.
11. Metal box, with collapsible Drinking-cup, Modern.

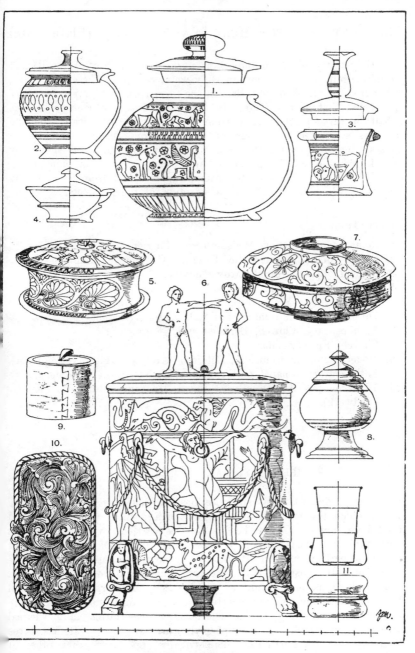

The Jar, the Cist, &c.

Plate 189.

THE FONT, AND THE HOLY-WATER STOUP. (Plate 190.)

Holy-water plays an important part in many rites of the Roman Catholic Church. It is kept in Holy-water Stoups. These are bowls, either free, or attached to walls. In the former case, the form generally approaches that of the Krater; in the latter case, the edge projects as a half or three-quarter circle from the surface of the wall; and the stoup is supported on a pilaster, column, or console. For use in houses: the Stoup takes the form of a suspended dish, as shown by fig. 11. The decoration is mostly symbolic, e. g. crosses, monograms, cherub-heads, &c. Most of the examples are taken from the work by Raguenet, which contains a large selection of these objects.

PLATE 190.

1. Romanesque, minster, Weissenburg, (Raguenet).
2. Romanesque, Church of the Crucifix, Compiègne, (Raguenet).
3. Romanesque, church, Picardy, (Raguenet).
4. Romanesque, church, Charleville, (Raguenet).
5. 12th century, (Viollet-le-Duc).
6. 16th century, Church, Mas d'Azil, Ariège, (Raguenet).
7. 17th century, Church, Cormontreuil, (Raguenet).
8. Church, Picardy, (Raguenet).
9. Modern, church, Couthuin, Belgium, Architect Halkin, (Raguenet).
10. 16th century, Chapel of the castle, Mello, France, (Raguenet).
11. 17th century, beaten silver, Royal Museum, Stuttgart, (Kunst-handwerk).

b. Dippers.

THE HYDRIA. (Plate 191.)

The Hydria, as its name implies, is the water-pot. It is the vessel which the maidens took to the spring; filled with water; and then bore home on their heads. It was carried, when empty in a horizontal; and when full, in a vertical attitude. Of all vases: it is the most perfect in form; its aim being so well expressed in its con-struction. It must be easy to carry, convenient to fill and empty, and to hold as much fluid as possible; it therefore has a vertical body of the shape of an inverted egg (this form places the centre of gravity at the top, which facilitates transportation in a vertical attitude); on which a funnel-shaped neck is placed. It has three handles: two are horizontal, diametrically opposite to each other at

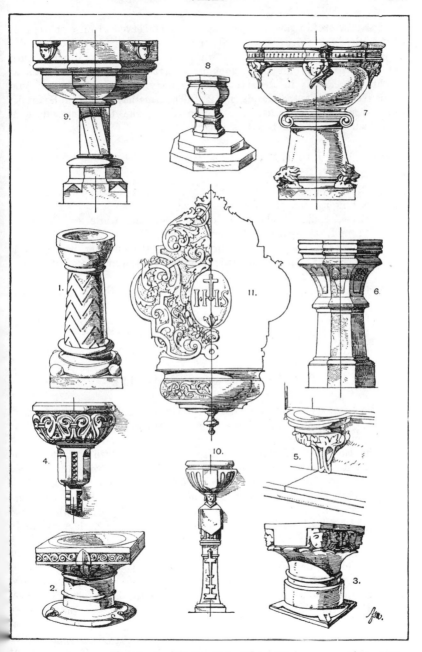

The Font, and the Holy-Water Stoup. Plate 190.

the greatest protuberance of the body, which served to raise the vessel
when full; the third is vertical, placed on one side of the neck,
which served to carry the vessel when empty, to steady it when full
and when pouring-out. The foot is always small. The neck has a
shoulder, or blends in a curve with the body. A special kind of the
latter treatment is the Kalpis (fig. 2). The smaller, slenderer Hydrias,
which were not intended to be carried on the head, are termed
Hand-hydrias. The material is clay.

PLATE 191. THE HYDRIA.

1.   Greek, (Jacobsthal).
2.   Greek, of the Kalpis form, body smooth, black, painted with
      red figures on the shoulder.
3.   Greek, painted black, reddish brown and white on the clay
      ground, Campana collection, Louvre, Paris, (L'art pour tous),
      the decoration is of the highest class, the shoulder is decorated
      by an ivy band, which is omitted in this figure, but given
      on Plate 32. 4.
4—5. Graeco-Italic Hand-hydrias, unpainted clay, United collections,
      Carlsruhe.
6—8. Greek Vase-paintings, showing the mode of carrying and using
      the Hydria.

THE BUCKET, &c. (Plate 192.)

We have seen that the Hydria gives beautiful expression to the
idea of pouring-out; the Bucket, on the other hand, is distincly a
dipper, and the Funnel a filler.

The Bucket is of specifically Egyptian origin; with it water was
drawn from the Nile; and hence the drop-like form, with the centre
of gravity low down. Two such Buckets were carried on a yoke.
The form serving to prevent spilling, (figs. 1—4). The Assyrian
Bucket generally terminates below in a lion mask, from which the
bag-shaped neck rises, (fig. 6). In the Graeco-Italic style, we find
footless Buckets resembling an inverted egg (fig. 10); others with a
ring foot are, however, not uncommon, (figs. 7, 8, 9 and 11). Instead
of one hoop handle there were sometimes two (figs. 7 and 9).

The ecclesiastical art of the Middle ages gave its portable Holy-
water Stoups the form of buckets, modifying the shape of the latter
to fit them for this purpose (figs. 13, 14). Sometimes the Bucket
is furnished with a spout, or a nozzle (fig. 15).

The Funnel, as a rule, takes the shape of an inverted cone, with
or without a tubular continuation; the handle is vertical (figs. 20, 21),

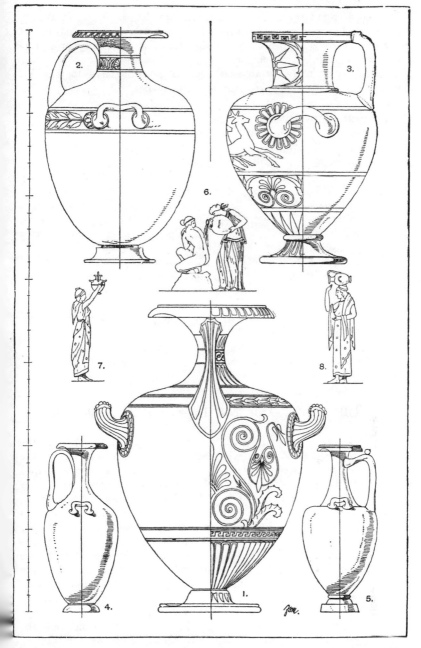

The Hydria. Plate 191

hoop-shaped (fig. 19), or two horizontal double (fig. 18). A Watering pot is shown in fig. 19: the hole at the top is intended to let
the water flow when opened, or to stop the flow by atmospheric pressure when closed by the finger.

Metal, as the more durable material, is generally used for Buckets
and Funnels: clay, glass, &c., are less common.

PLATE 192. THE BUCKET, &c.

1.	Egyptian, Thebes, Tutmes III.
2—4.	Egyptian, bronze.
5.	Egyptian Bucket-like Vessel, without handle.
6.	Assyrian, with cord handle.
7—11.	Graeco-Italic, bronze, of various forms.
12.	Antique, with hoop handle, red clay, painted black, United collections in Carlsruhe, the eye in the uppermost zone, which is found in Greek Keramics, has been explained as a protective against the "evil eye"
13—14.	Mediaeval, beaten copper, 15th century, (Viollet-le-Duc).
15.	Modern Italian, clay, with hoop-handle and nozzle, (Gropius).
16—17.	Modern Coal-vases, sheet-metal, square and round.
18.	Antique clay Funnel.
19.	Mediaeval Vessel, for watering the ground, clay, (Viollet-le-Duc).
20.	Modern Funnel, for watering the ground, sheet-metal.
21.	General form of the modern sheet-metal Funnel.

THE SPOON, AND THE LADLE. (Plate 193.)

Spoons and Pateræ form a special class of dippers. As the
Table-spoon, strictly so-called, will come up for discussion among the
utensils, we have here to consider only the larger spoon-shaped
vessels and the Pateræ (handled dishes) used for religious and other
purposes. The natural model of the Spoon is the hollow hand,
whence the spherical, elliptical, or oval dish-shape, with an attached
handle. The latter usually lies in the plane of the rim, but it may
also form an obtuse angle with it, or, as in the case of the antique
Simpulum (fig. 11), a right-angle. Egyptian Spoons, which are
richly decorated, often possess a cover rotating round a pin (compare
the projections on the dish, fig. 2), the spoon then becomes a kind
of pot or receptacle. A foot is of course superfluous on the ordinary
Spoon; but the Pateræ with handles not infrequently have a ring-
foot to enable them to stand (figs. 7—8). The Spoon and the
Pateræ may also be furnished with a special spout or lip (fig. 6).

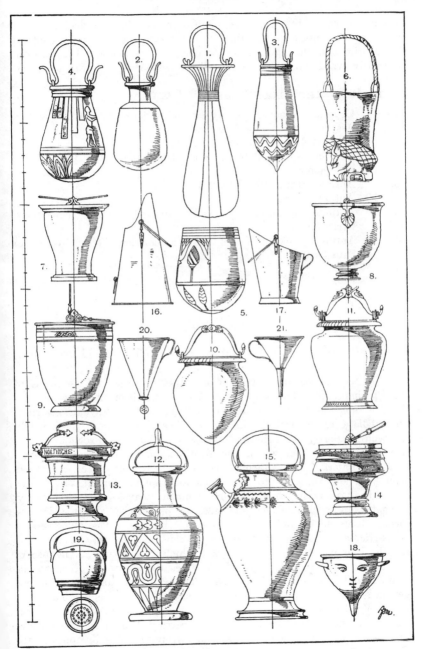

The Bucket, &c. Plate 192.

As a rule: the Dish is plain, or is slightly decorated by
engraving the interior, (fig. 6). The decoration is generally confined
to the rim and the handle, or its points of junction. The material
is usually wood, bone, or metal. The size varies with the use.

PLATE 193. THE SPOON, AND THE LADLE.

1—4. Egyptian Spoons, plainly or richly finished, partly painted.
5. Assyrian spoon-like Vessel.
6. Antique bronze Patera, with lip.
7, 9, 10. Antique bronze Pateræ, seen from the side, from above,
   and below.
8. Antique terracotta Patera.
11—12. Antique Simpula.
13. Antique spoon-like Vessel, bronze, United collections,
   Carlsruhe.
14. Antique cooking Vessel, like a handled dish, (Ménard et
   Sauvageot).

c. Pourers.

THE PROCHOÜS, THE OINOCHOË, THE OLPE, &c. (Plate 194.)

We commence the series of pourers with the antique forms of
the Prochoüs, Oinochoë, Olpe, &c. As the definition of these appella-
tions is not yet finally settled: it will be best to leave the various
intermediate forms entirely unnamed. The vessels were used partly
for secular, partly for religious purposes. Thus the Prochoüs is the
sacrificial vessel from which the libations of wine were poured-out,
into the Patera. The Oinochoë is believed to have been a secular
wine jug; and the Olpe to have been a receptacle for oil, &c.

All these vessels have this in common: that the mouth is wavy,
elongated to a channel on one side, or pinched-in at the sides, to
form a large spout and facilitate the pouring-out. The older vessels,
in particular, show great boldness in thus making the form of the
mouth different to the circular plan which is a result of the use of
the Potter's-wheel; but in the later times there was a return to the
simpler and more beautiful shape. The Prochoüs and the Oinochoë
generally have an upright body, in shape like an egg. The Olpe
invariably has a cake or bag-shaped body, a form which is occasionally found in the Prochoüs. The vertical handle is raised above
the vessel and is attached in a bold sweep to the side opposite the
lip. The foot is usually ring-shaped. Bronze and clay are employed

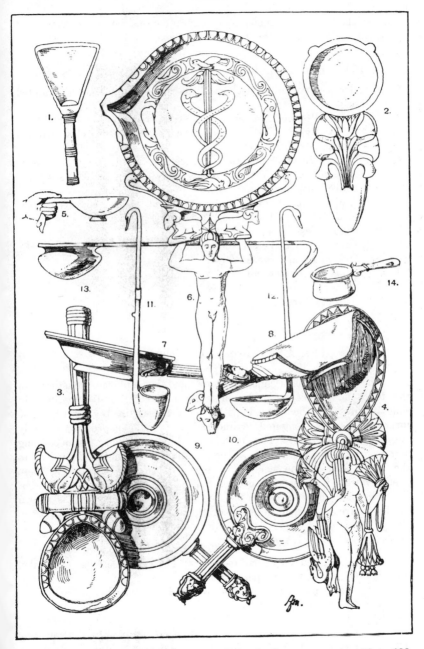

The Spoon, and the Ladle.   Plate 193.

as materials. The Prochoüs and Oinochoë are, generally, vessels of considerable size, while the Olpe is smaller.*

PLATE 194. THE PROCHOÜS, THE OINOCHOE, THE OLPE, &c.

1. Greek Prochoüs, archaic form and ornamentation, painted clay.
2. Greek Prochoüs, geometrical style, red clay, painted black.
3. Greek Cyprian Vessel, geometrical style, yellow clay, painted brown, Munich, (Lau).
4. Greek Oinochoë, Asiatic style, yellow, painted clay, (Semper).
5. Antique small Vessel, yellow clay, painted black, United collections, Carlsruhe.
6. Antique small Vessel, clay, painted black, engraved ornament, United collections, Carlsruhe.
7—9. Greek Vessels, painted clay.
10. Greek bronze Vessel, collection of Herr von Pulsky, Pesth.
11. Graeco-Italic bronze Vessel.
12. Prochoüs in the form of a female head, Museum, Rome.
13—14. Antique Olpe, painted clay.
15. Antique bronze Olpe, Museum Rome.

THE LEKYTHOS, &c. (Plate 195.)

The Lekythos is a small antique pourer, employed sometimes in the toilet as a receptacle for oils and unguents, and sometimes in funeral rites, to be placed with the deceased in the grave. The form is generally elongated, cylindrical or spindle-shaped, more rarely bag-like or spherical. The foot is a plain ring foot, the neck long and narrow with a shoulder. The handle rises from the body up to the upper end of the neck. As regards form and decoration, these pretty vessels form special groups. The slender forms are the older, the spherical and depressed the later. Upright palmettes, as shown in fig. 1, are a characteristic decoration. The material is clay.

PLATE 195. THE LEKYTHOS, &c.

1—3. Greek, red clay, painted black, United collections, Carlsruhe.
4—6. Greek, red clay, painted black.
7. Greek, painted black and white, later period.
8. Greek, Attic style.
9. Ditto.
10—12. Greek, red clay, painted black, United collections, Carlsruhe.
13. Greek, red clay, painted black and white, Munich, (Lau).

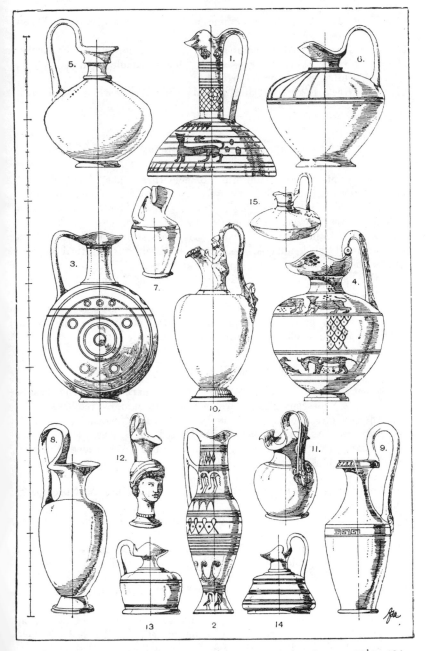

The Prochoüs, the Oinochoë, the Olpe, &c.   Plate 194.

14.   Greek Aryballos (perfume vase), United collections, Carlsruhe.
15.   Greek Aryballos, painted black, United collections, Carlsruhe.
16.   Greek, Perfume-vase, with hoop handle, painted black,
United collections, Carlsruhe.
17.   Greek Lekythos, later period, United collections, Carlsruhe.

THE LIP-SPOUT PITCHER.   (Plates 196—197.)

The want of some uniform nomenclature makes itself felt not
only in the case of antique vessels, but also with such colloquial
expressions as "pitcher", "jug", "pot", "can", "bottle", &c., which
include a great variety of forms, so that what one calls pitchers and
pots another calls jugs and cans.   To maintain at least some kind
of system in this handbook, we class all vessels with vertical handles,
(unless they belong to some special category), as "Pitchers" if they
have the usual mouth with a lip; and as "Pots" if they have a pipe-
like spout.

The material and size, of the Pitcher vary greatly, according to
its purpose and period.   The principal representatives are the ewers,
and jugs, of glass, clay, stoneware, and metal.

PLATE 196.   THE LIP-SPOUT PITCHER.

1. Egyptian, with saucer, recalling our modern ewers and basins.
2. Antique iridescent glass, Germanisches Museum, Nuremberg.
3. Antique glass, found in Trouville-la-Rivière, Normandy, (Deville).
4. Antique glass, found near Mainz, United collections, Carlsruhe.
5. Roman, glass, from a grave at Bingerbrück, Wiesbaden Museum.
6. Antique, blue glass, Louvre, (Deville).
7. Like No. 5.
8. Antique, yellowish green glass, Germanisches Museum, Nuremberg.
9. Like No. 4.
10. Antique, glass, found in Rouen, 3d century A. D., Rouen Museum,
(Deville).
11. Antique ring-shape, unpainted clay, United collections, Carlsruhe.
12. Roman-Alemannic, red clay, found in Käferthal near Mannheim,
United collections, Carlsruhe.
13. Antique (?) bronze, with cover, found at Saumur, (Ménard et
Sauvageot).
14. Ancient American, grey clay, time of the Incas, excavated at
Trujillo in Peru, (the round compartment of the body is fantastically adorned with figures), United collections, Carlsruhe.

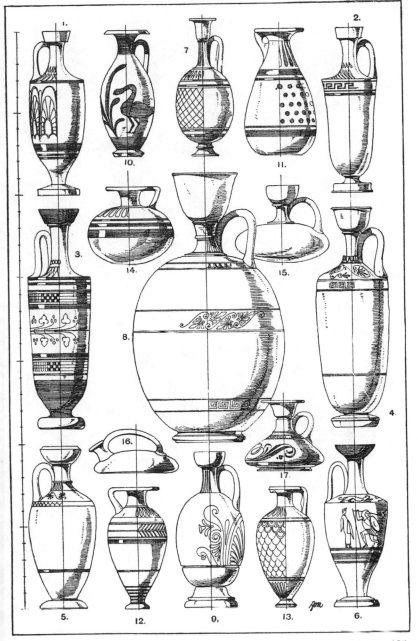

The Lekythos, &c.   Plate 195.

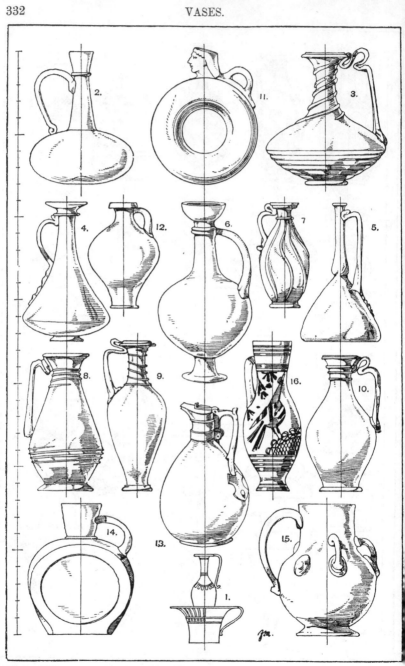

Plate 196.

The Lip-spout Pitcher.

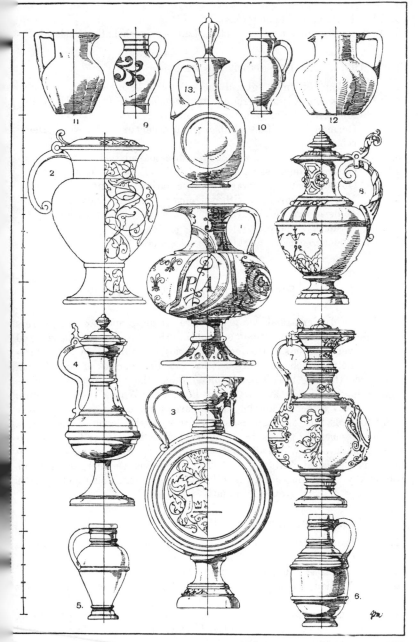

The Lip-spout Pitcher.   Plate 197.

15. Old German, Bohemian glass.
16. Modern Hungarian, glazed clay, Landesgewerbehalle, Carlsruhe.

PLATE 197. THE LIP-SPOUT PITCHER.

1.   Italian Faience, glazed in colours, 16th century, the blue
      lilies on a gold ground are the coat of Julius III., Cluny
      Museum, Paris, (L'art pour tous).
2.   German, by Hans Holbein, 16th century, (Hirth, Formen-
      schatz).
3.   Old German, stoneware, with disc-shaped body.
4.   German Renascence, pewter, (Hirth, Formenschatz).
5—6. Old German, stoneware, the decoration is omitted.
7.   Modern stoneware, with tin cover, by Dir. Kachel.
8.   Modern majolica, Carlsruhe.
9—10. Modern, stoneware.
11—12. Modern, green and blue glass.

THE PIPE-SPOUT POT. (Plate 198.)

As already remarked, we group here all those one-handled pourers
which possess a separate spout or mouth. Here too, material, size, and
form are very various. Distinct categories are formed by the State-
jugs of metal, such as were in use at the period of the Italian
Renascence (fig. 1), the Oriental metal Jugs, the Venetian small glass
Jugs, milk, coffee, tea and watering Pots, &c. Where a spout occurs:
it is generally attached at the lower part or middle of the body, more
rarely towards the top; and usually reaches to the level of the mouth.
The Spout generally tapers in an upward direction; its orifice is sometimes a mask or a widened mouth-piece; in the case of the Watering-
pot it is furnished with a rose. The handle is vertical, or a hoop.
Noteworthy is the long stump-handle of some modern Coffee-pots (fig. 9).
The vessels of this group frequently have a lid.

PLATE 198. THE PIPE-SPOUT POT.

1.   Italian Renascence, State-jug, metal, design by Polidoro
      Caravaggio, Uffizi, Florence.
2.   Japanese, enamelled metal, Louvre, (L'art pour tous).
3.   Arabian, metal, 16th century, Cluny Museum, Paris, (L'art
      pour tous).
4—5. Venetian glass, 16th century, (Hirth, and L'art pour tous).
6.   Modern Oriental, unglazed clay, from Jerusalem, United
      collections, Carlsruhe.

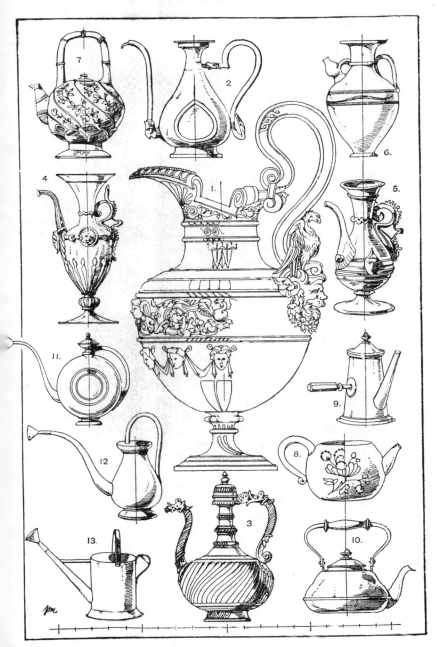

The Pipe spout Pot.   Plate 198

7.   Oriental Tea-pot, painted china.
8.   Milk-ewer, painted faience, 18th century, United collections, Carlsruhe.
9.   Modern Coffee-pot.
10.   Modern Tea-kettle, metal, hoop handle, with wooden guard.
11—13. Modern Watering-pots, sheet metal.

THE BOTTLE. (Plates 199—200.)

The Bottle has a spherical, elongated, or bag body; and an elongated, narrow neck, which usually expands like a funnel towards its upper extremity, and is sometimes closed by a stopper. Bottles have either a ring foot or no foot at all, high feet are exceptional. Handles are seldom attached; where this is done, they appear in pairs. In the case of Pocket-flasks, which are usually of a disc or watch shape, the handle serves to attach the flasks to a cord or belt. The material is chiefly glass; but clay and metal are also used. The Bottle form has been specially cultivated in the East, in Persia, China, Japan, &c. A natural model is frequently found in the Calabash, which is itself often used as a Vessel.

PLATE 199. THE BOTTLE.

1—2.   Egyptian, front and side view.
3.   Antique, small watch-shaped Perfume-bottle, blue and white glass, with handles for suspension, like a hunting-flask, Campana collection, (L'art pour tous).
4.   Antique, glass, with handles for suspension, (Deville).
5.   Antique, Perfume-bottle, transparent emerald green glass.
6.   Antique, Campana collection, (L'art pour tous).
7.   Antique, two-handled, iridescent glass, Campana collection, (L'art pour tous).
8.   Antique, iridescent glass, United collections, Carlsruhe.
9.   Antique, iridescent glass, United collections, Carlsruhe.
10.   Old German, glass, from the Spessart, (Friedrich, Die Altdeutschen Gläser).
11.   Modern, cut glass, Dresden, (Gewerbehalle).
12.   Modern, green glass, with ring stopper.
13.   Modern, yellowish green glass.
14.   Modern, "Florentine flask", covered with bast.

PLATE 200. THE BOTTLE.

1.   Egyptian, without foot, two rope handles for suspension.
2.   Antique, red, unpainted clay, United collections, Carlsruhe.

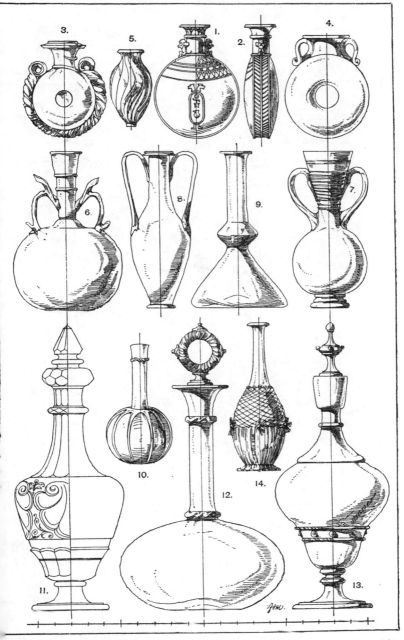

The Bottle. Plate 199.

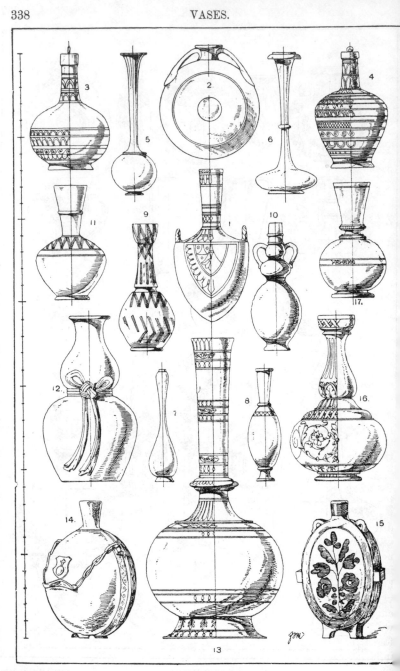

Plate 200.   The Bottle.

3. Antique, hammered bronze, with cover and ring, Castellani collection.

4. Ditto, United collections, Carlsruhe.

5—7. Japanese, bronze.

8. Persian, clay.

9—11. Modern, Egyptian, unglazed gray clay, United collections, Carlsruhe.

12. Chinese, blue porcelain, (Lièvre).

13. Persian, damaskeened metal, (L'art pour tous).

14. Wrought-iron military Flask, holding 44 pints, 15th century, Cluny Museum, Paris.

15. Modern Hungarian military Flask, colored glazed clay, Landesgewerbehalle, Carlsruhe.

16. Majolica, colored plastic ornamentation, Modern English, Landesgewerbehalle, Carlsruhe.

17. Modern, French, green glazed clay.

d. Drinking Vessels.

Plates 201—210 show drinking vessels. Drinking vessels are as ancient as drinking itself; and they are consequently found in every style. Their forms and kinds are infinitely various; especially in the Antique, the Middle Ages, and the Renascence. Semper says on this point: "Athenaeus gives us the names and descriptions of more than a hundred drinking vessels, although he confines himself to those of the precious metals, which, long before his time, had replaced earthenware drinking vessels among the Greeks. The same variety rules in the drinking vessels of the Middle Ages; and although, in this branch too, our poverty of invention is obvious, compared with the earlier fecundity; still, an enumeration of the different forms and kinds of drinking vessels now in common use would be fairly extensive; and would be all the more difficult inasmuch as our modern time does not adhere to typical forms; or, more correctly speaking, has lost all idea of what a type is. Nowhere is the influence of caprice, and heedless confusion of forms more conspicuous than in this class of vessels; so that any attempt to classify drinking vessels, and to enumerate the subdivisions which have existed and still exist, can meet with little success. But if we disregard "freaks" and those anomalous forms of drinking vessels, which have been evolved more by the influence of fashion, and caprice than by the intended use, we shall find that the distinctions which we found to be true for the forms of vessels in general, are applicable to drinking vessels in particular".

Notwithstanding this, we will attempt to classify the forms of drinking vessels. This will be done, partly according to style, placing the commonest antique forms on one Plate, specifically Old German forms on another, and the drinking vessels of our own time on a third. Partly, too, we will place, on other Plates, definite groups which have either an identical fundamental form or a common object, regardless of their belonging to the same or to different styles, e. g. Drinking-horns and Rhytons, Cups and Beakers, Chalices and Goblets, State-Cups, Rummers, Mugs, and Tankards.

The Kylix, the Kantharos, &c. (Plate 201.)

Drinking vessels of clay and the precious metals, played the chief, part in Antique times, while glass, which was employed for other purposes, was only occasionally used.

A very common form is the two-handled dish or Kylix, with a low or high foot. Both the form and the name of the later Calyx and our Chalice are derived from Kylix. When formed of clay, the Kylix is a plain shallow dish, ornamented on the under side, sometimes with figures on the inner side, and with two horizontal handles (figs. 1—2). In metal, the form becomes richer, the handles are elongated and bolder in curvature (figs. 3—4).

The fundamental form of the Kantharos is that of the deep dish or Krater, with two vertical handles. The decoration is only external; the simplicity in clay (fig. 5), passes into richness when metal is employed (figs. 6—7). Bacchic attributes, the vine, ivy, the thyrsos, masks, &c., from the decoration.

The Kyathos, a dipper and drinking vessel at once, is a dish with the handle elongated vertically and sometimes replaced by a straight handle, which gives the vessel somewhat of the appearance of a spoon (figs. 8, 9, 10).

The Skyphos is a dish with two horizontal handles (figs. 11); the Kothon (fig. 12), is the military drinking vessel, "a vessel with a broad rim bent inwards, out of which one could only drink by bending the neck right back; but it was convenient for dipping water from brooks, and the in-curved rim caught the impurities of the water so that they remained behind both in dipping and drinking", (Semper).

We might further adduce the Deinos, the drinking vessel of Hercules, the amphikypellon, a double beaker mentioned by Homer, the Kalathos, and others. But the examples selected above may suffice.

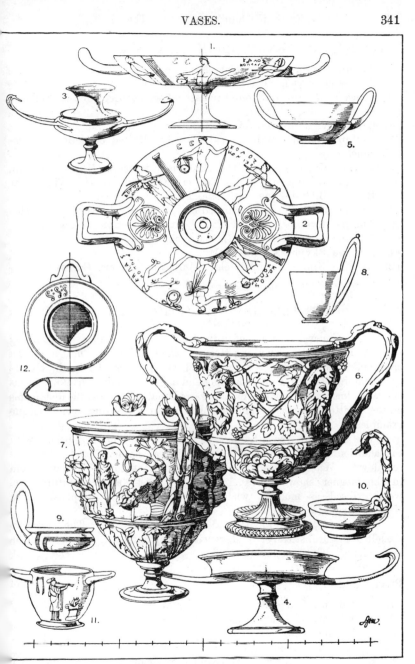

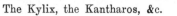

The Kylix, the Kantharos, &c.   Plate 201.

PLATE 201. THE KYLIX, THE KANTHAROS, &c.

1. Antique Kylix, painted clay, Museum, Naples.
2. The same vessel, viewed from below.
3. Greek Kylix, bronze, found in sarcophagus at Cephalonia, (Stackelberg).
4. Greek Kylix, bronze, found in Ithaca.
5. Antique Kantharos, black painted clay, United collections, Carlsruhe.
6. Antique Kylix, beaten silver, Hildesheim treasure, Museum, Berlin.
7. Antique Kantharos, beaten silver, found at Berthouville near Bernay, Bibliothèque Nationale, Paris.
8. Antique Kyathos, black painted clay, United collections, Carlsruhe.
9. Antique Kyathos, painted clay, United collections, Carlsruhe.
10. Antique Skyphos, metal, (Ménard et Sauvageot).
11. Antique Skyphos, painted clay.
12. Antique Kothon, painted clay, United collections, Carlsruhe.

THE RHYTON. (Plate 202.)

The primæval custom, of using the Horns of animals as drinking vessels, led to the Drinking-Horn. The Antique is not alone in creating, in the Rhyton, a special kind of these vessels: in the Middle ages and in Modern times, in England and Germany, Drinking-horns are well known. In view of the varied and often complicated forms of these latter, we shall confine ourselves to presenting some Antique examples.

The form of the Rhyton was that of an animal's head, with the addition of a handle. As a rule, it has no foot; and cannot be set down. When pierced at the lower end, it could be drunk-from in the manner shown in fig. 11. Stags, asses, swine, vultures, &c. were utilised as models, whence the special names Elaphos, Onos, Kapros, Gryps, &c.

Sometimes the human head was used, (fig. 2). The vessel is modelled naturalistically; and receives a painted decoration on the neck alone. The material is clay.

PLATE 202.

1.   Antique, (Tragelaphos) with a ram head.
2.   Antique, with a human head.
3.   Antique, (Kapros) with a swine head.
4.   Antique, (Elaphos) with a stag head, (Semper).
5—6. Antique, (Hippotragelaphos) on one side a ram, on the other an ass head.

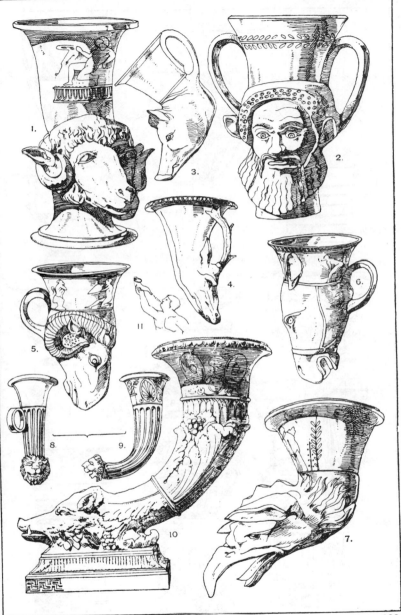

The Rhyton.

Plate 202.

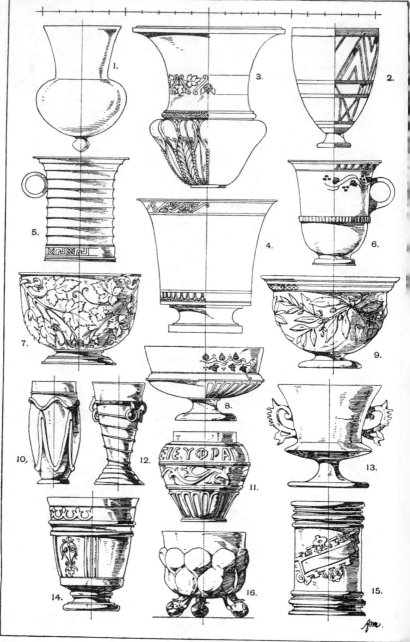

Plate 203.   The Cup, and the Beaker.

7.   Antique, (Gryps) with vulture head.
8—9. Antique drinking-horn, with lion mask as spout.
10.   Antique State Rhyton, marble, Vatican Museum, Rome.
11.   Picture from an Antique Vase, showing the manner of drink-
      ing from the Rhyton.

THE CUP, AND THE BEAKER. (Plate 203.)

Drinking vessels of these forms are of very general occurrence.
They may be hemi-spherical, cylindrical, like an inverted cone, or of
a mixed shape; without foot, with a ring foot, or supported on
balls; without a handle, or with one, two, or more handles. The
use of the Cup restricts it to a certain size; the material is metal,
glass, clay, stoneware, &c. Richly-decorated Cups have come down
to us from the Antique, and the Renascence.

PLATE 203. THE CUP, AND THE BEAKER.

1. Assyrian, from a relief.
2. Assyrian, painted clay.
3. Antique, silver, parcel gilt, found on Ithaca.
4. Antique Kalathos, found in Athens.
5. Antique, clay, painted black, United collections, Carlsruhe.
6. Antique, red clay, painted black, United collections, Carlsruhe.
7. Antique, beaten silver, found in Pompeii, now in Naples.
8. Antique, originally decorated in sunk enamel, Hildesheim treasure,
   Berlin, Museum.
9. Antique, beaten silver, Hildesheim treasure, Berlin, Museum.
10. Antique, green glass, found in Normandy, (Deville).
11. Antique, glass, (Deville).
12. Old German, glass.
13. Venetian, glass, British Museum.
14. Old German, stoneware.
15. Old German, stoneware.
16. German Renascence, Metal, with bosses and ball foot.

THE CHALICE, AND THE GOBLET. (Plate 204.)

These are deep vessels of the form of half an egg, without
handle, and with a high foot. The form was chiefly used in the Middle
Ages, and Renascence; for both secular and religious purposes. For
the former purpose, the material is glass or metal, and the size is

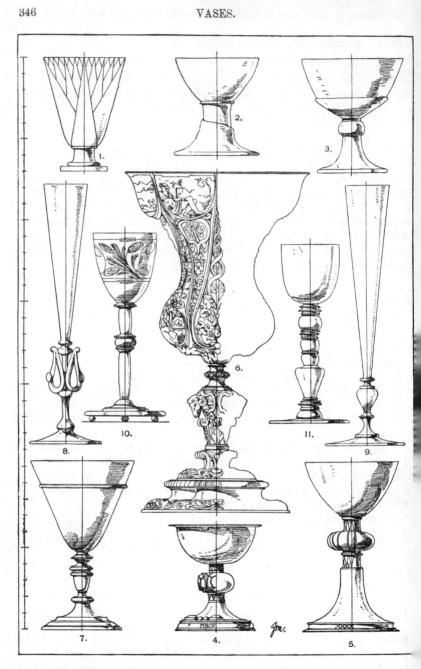

Plate 204.   The Chalice, and the Goblet.

various; for the latter purpose, the chalice is invariably of metal, mostly of silver chased and gilt, enamelled, set with jewels, &c. In the Romanesque style, the cup is hemispherical and shallow; in the Gothic style and the Renascence, it becomes deeper.

PLATE 204. THE CHALICE, AND THE GOBLET.

1. Egyptian, Thebes.
2. Antique, red clay, United collections, Carlsruhe.
3. Antique, clay, painted black.
4. Romanesque Chalice, chased silver set with jewels, Villingen church.
5. Gothic Chalice, chased silver, Wertheim church.
6. Silver State-Goblet, German, 16th century; this goblet, along with two others, is said to have been the model for the master-pieces of the goldsmiths; and is usually attributed to the Nuremberg goldsmith Jamnitzer, although this has lately been doubted; the bossed outline is copied from the flower of the columbine *(Aquilegia vulgaris)*, Municipal collection, Nuremberg.
7. Crystal Goblet, with cut ornaments, 17th century, National Museum, Munich,
8. Venetian glass Goblet, 17th century, British Museum, (L'art pour tous).
9. Modern Champagne-glass, Landesgewerbehalle, Carlsruhe.
10. Old German glass Goblet, 17th century.
11. Old German glass Goblet, 17th century.

THE HANAP. (Plate 205.)

The same blending of forms which the reader will have observed in the treatment of cups and goblets occurs in the case of Hanaps. Ordinary colloquial language makes no definite distinction between them. A State-cup presupposes a considerable richness of decoration, it is usually a cup or goblet-shaped product of the goldsmith's art, provided with a cover, or it may even be a richly finished glass of similar form.

PLATE 205. THE HANAP.

1. Design, by Hans Holbein, German, 16th century, (Formenschatz).
2. Design, German, 16th century, (Formenschatz).
3. Design, 2nd half of the 16th century, the cover makes an independent Cup, (Musterornamente).

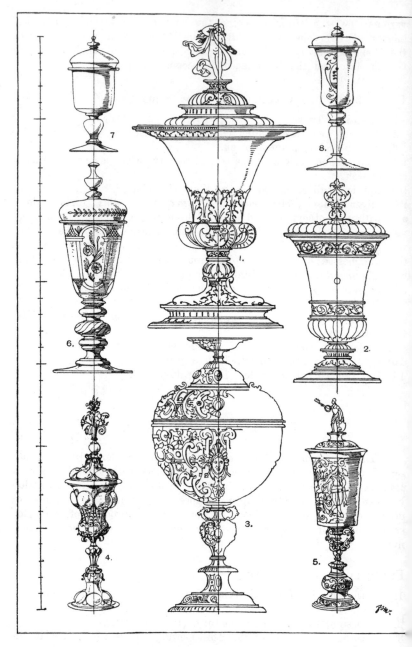

Plate 205. The Hanap.

4—5. German, 16th and 17th centuries, chased silver, treasure of Regensburg, (Musterornamente).

6—8. Old German, glass, 17th century.

The Römer or Rummer. (Plate 206.)

The Rummer, the glass *par excellence* for Rhenish wine, is the most important representative of the Old German drinking glasses, and is altogether one of the handsomest forms of vessels. C. Friedrich in his work *"Die Altdeutschen Gläser"*, the study of which we warmly recommend, states that the fragments of antique glass were worked-up again into fine glass-ware; and that this ware was called "Romanum vitrum" or "Romarium vitrum". That led to the designation "Romarii" which then became "Römer" and "Rummer". The original form of the Rummer is somewhat cylindrical (fig. 1); instead of a foot it has a ring at the bottom. At a later period a low foot was added, upon which the body began to be divided into members (figs. 2, and 3). The high foot eventually led to the goblet form (figs. 10, and 11). Rummers, in which the contents reach to the bottom, belong to the 2nd half of the 16th century; Rummers with spun foot, the wine reaching to the middle-piece, are to be ascribed to the 17th century; while Rummers with an independent middle-piece are the product of the 18th century. All three forms have been revived in late years. The colour of the Rummer is green or yellowish-brown; for æsthetic reasons, and not because it was impossible to manufacture clear glass. The middle-piece is often divided from the cup by a ribbed band and ornamented with bosses. In later times the cup was decorated with cut or painted ornament (figs. 5, and 6). Such modern examples, as Rummers with white feet and pink cups, are aberrations of taste. The Rummer is generally of moderate size; but examples of large size are sometimes met-with.

Plate 206. The Rummer.

1—4. Older forms, (Friedrich).
5—6. White and light-green, engraved ornaments, Bavarian Gewerbemuseum, Nuremberg, (Friedrich).
7—8. Modern copies.
9. Old form, without foot, (Friedrich).
10—11. Modern forms.
12. Wooden vessel resembling a Rummer, lacquered black, from Borneo, United collections, Carlsruhe.

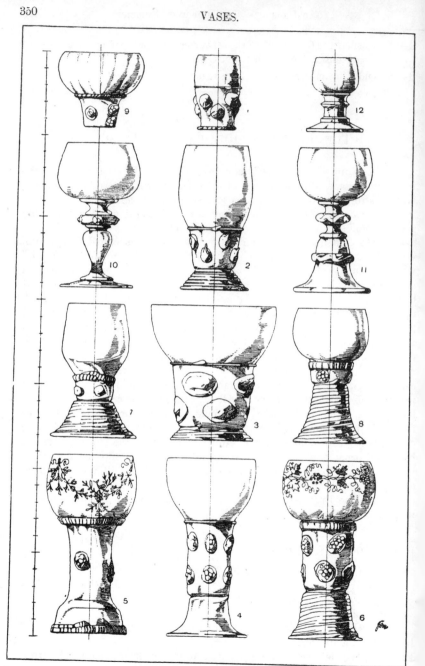

Plate 206.   The Römer or Rummer.

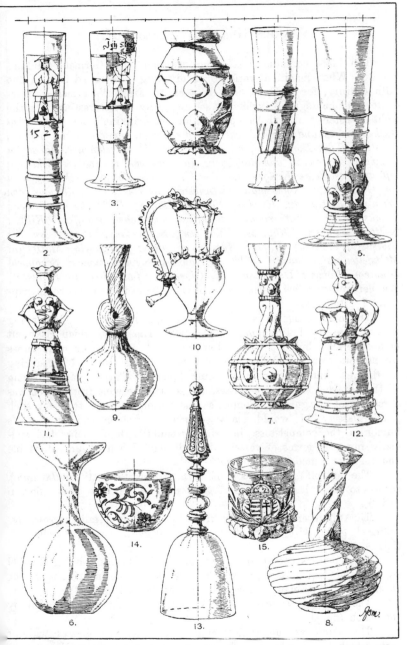

Various Drinking Vessels. Plate 207.

Various Glasses. (Plate 207.)

The Plate contains a selection of other Old German drinking vessels. What manifold varieties of drinking glasses existed, in the 16th century, for instance, may be seen in Fischart's romance "Gargantoa and Pantagruel", which is sociologically so interesting. In the eight chapter, entitled "a conversation on drinking", he says: "*Da stachen sie eynander die Pocal auff die Prust, da flogen die mühele, da stibeten die Römercken, da raumt man die dickelbächer, da soffen je zween und zween aus doppleten, die man von eynander bricht, ja soff aus gestifleten Krügen, da stürzt man die Pott, da schwang man den Gutruff, da trähet man den Angster, da riss und schält man den Wein aus Potten, aus Kelchen, Napffen, Gonen; Hoffbechern: Tassen: Trinkschalen: Pfaffenmasen: Stauffen von hohen stauffen: Kitten: Kälten: Kanuten: Köpffen: Knartgen: Schlauchen: Pipen: Nussen: Fiolen: Lampeten: Kufen: Nüsseln: Seydeln: Külkesseln, Mälterlin: Melkgelten, Spitzmasen, Zolcken, Kannen, Schnäulzenmas, Schoppenkännlein, Stotzen: Da klangen die Gläser, da funckelten die Krausen.*" We here offer a few forms, some of them named in the above description of Fischart's.

The name Angster is applied to a high narrow-necked drinking bottle (from the Latin *angustus,* narrow). The neck, which rises out of a spherical, bulbous body, often consisted of 2, 3, or more tubes wound round one another, frequently bent to one side and broadening at the top into a cup-like mouth (fig. 8). These glasses belong to the category of Puzzle-glasses, to extract the wine from which was a matter of "anguish". Semper's observation is very true for such puzzle-glasses: "it would really seem as if fashion and the toper's humor of the competitors, in drinking-bouts with obstacles, had specially invented forms of vessels which demanded a most uncomfortable and ingenious mode of drinking."

The Gutrolf (gutterer, kutrof, perhaps from the Latin *gutturnium*), seems to have been a similar glass with a straight neck (figs. 6 and 9).

The Spechter (presumably from Spessart) is a tall, narrow, cylindrical glass with a low foot, decorated with bosses, scrolls, &c. (figs. 4, 5).

The Passglas (peg-tankard) resembles the spechter, but is divided by rings into equal divisions which served as a scale in drinking bouts. It often bears painted figures, inscriptions &c., (figs. 2, 3).

The form of the cabbage-stalk glass in sufficiently indicated by the name (fig. 1).

The Tummler and Handtummler (tumbler) are glasses without feet, which totter when set down; and if laid on their side at once resume a vertical position (figs. 14, 15); as also glasses like that shown in fig. 13, which must first be drunk empty before they can be set down.

To those times also belonged: Puzzle-glasses from which the liquor had to be sucked-out at the end of the handle (fig. 10); vessels in the shape of ladies (figs. 11—12), and of fantastic animals.

It would carry us too far to enter upon the details of manufacture: we therefore refer the reader once more to C. Friedrich's *"Altdeutsche Gläser"*.

PLATE 207. VARIOUS DRINKING VESSELS.

1. Green cabbage-stalk Glass, Germanisches Museum, Nuremberg.
2—3. Old German Peg-tankards, painted.
4—5. Old German Spechters.
6. Kutrolf (Angster), 16th century, Bavarian Gewerbemuseum, Nuremberg.
7—8. Old German Augsters, No. 8 in the Bavarian Gewerbemuseum, Nuremberg.
9. Kutrolf (Angster) with winding neck.
10. Puzzle-mug, (Friedrich).
11—12. Old German Glasses, in the form of ladies, No. 12 in the Bavarian Gewerbemuseum, Nuremberg.
13. Large Tumbler, 18th century, with metal handle; in the original a figure of Mercury stands on the ball, Bavarian Gewerbemuseum, Nuremberg.
14. Painted glass Tumbler, (Friedrich).
14. Hungarian coronation Glass, painted.

THE MUG. (Plate 208.)

In accordance with its purpose, the form of the Mug is essentially different from that of other drinking vessels. The body usually has a cylindrical form, and is without a foot, or with only a ring foot. A movable lid of metal, mostly tin, is attached by a hinge to the vertical handle, in order to keep the liquid as fresh as possible, in view of the great surface of evaporation. For the same reason the material is preferably stoneware. That glass has of late years been preferred to stoneware, is due to the fact that the liquid is visible and more easily investigated in glass vessels; and that these are more easily cleaned. Compared with the wine-glass, the Mug will always have a greater circumference, and show a more robust treatment. The hinge must be so attached that when the lid is wide open, it forms an obtuse angle with the rim.

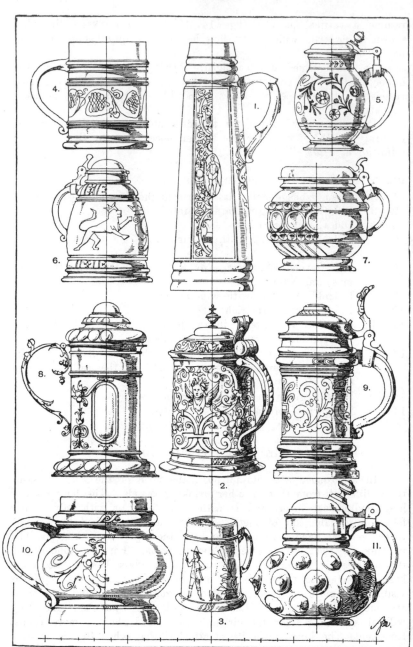

Plate 208.   The Mug.

PLATE 208. THE MUG.

1. Renascence Mug (schnelle), stoneware, German.
2. Renascence Mug, chased silver, Regensburg treasure, (Gewerbehalle).
3. Old German Beermug, brown glass, painted, Bavarian Gewerbemuseum, Nuremberg.
4, 6, 7. Old German stoneware Beermugs.
5. Old German glass beermug.
8. Renascence Mug, amber, mounted with silver, Grünes Gewölbe, Dresden.
9—10. Modern stoneware Beermugs, from old patterns.
11. Modern Beermug, brown glass, with green bosses.

THE TANKARD. (Plate 209.)

The Tankard is a drinking vessel, more or less coarse in shape like a cylinder or an inverted cone; and made of glass, stoneware, &c. The name is also given to vessels of more architectural pretensions, like that in fig. 9. The Tankard is less for individual than for social use; and is intended chiefly for beer, hence its size and robust form. Of special importance are the eagle, imperial, electoral, and guild Tankards of the Renascence period.

PLATE 209. THE TANKARD.

1. Roman Glass, of tankard form, found in Pompeii, (Deville).
2. Ditto, (Ditto).
3. Old German green glass Tankard, (compare this form with that of the Rummer on Plate 206).
4. Ditto.
5—6. Old German glass Tankards.
7. Old German armorial Tankard, (Friedrich).
8. Modern brown glass Tankard.
9. Modern brown glass Tankard, painted, (Keller-Leuzinger).

MODERN DRINKING GLASSES. (Plate 210.)

Great laxity is apparent in the forms of modern drinking vessels. Alongside coarse forms in transparent blown and cast glass: delicate glasses, cut and etched, appear in the market. Of late years old examples of coloured glass have been frequently copied, with

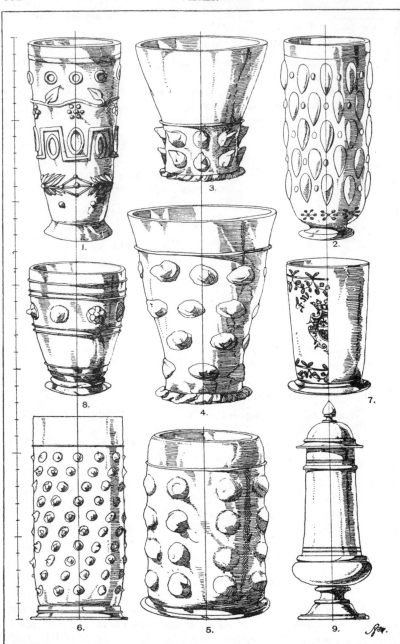

Plate 209. The Tankard.

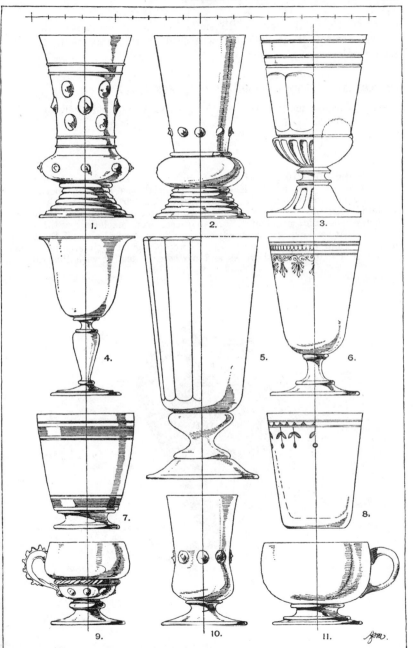

Modern Drinking Glasses.　　　　Plate 210.

more or less skill and intelligence. It is to be hoped that the
general revival of Applied Art will lead to the attainment of high-
class results in this branch also.

PLATE 210. MODERN DRINKING GLASSES.

1—11. Various modern Glasses for water, wine, and beer, of white
and coloured glass.

Plates 191—210 present some 50 different classes of vessels in nearly
500 specimens. But even this copious material was far from permitting
every form to be taken into consideration. The first place was accorded
to definite groups and to conventional, ever-recurring shapes; while the
arbitrary, sporadic, accidental, and barocco, were excluded. Still, it is
possible that we have not succeeded in giving a general view of the group
of pottery and vessels. Readers who desire to pursue their studies further
are referred to the special works and periodicals dealing with this subject.

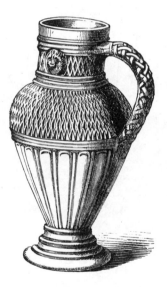

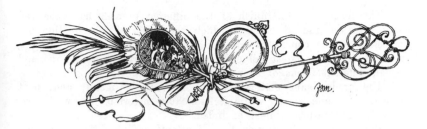

B.

METAL OBJECTS.

(UTENSILS.)

Utensils are very various; and an exhaustive treatment of them is quite impossible within the scope of this Handbook. Beside this, decoration is quite excluded in many cases. Still, definite divisions of this group have been created by the fact, that their representatives in certain periods have received artistic treatment; and hence they may be reduced to a system.

Although, on the one hand, a number of utensils have found no place on the Plates devoted to this group: we have, on the other hand, been able to form a number of subsidiary divisions, each complete in itself. Thus, for example: chapters 211—220 will deal with the interesting subject of utensils for Illumination, chapters 221—225 with the utensils of Ritual, chapters 226—230 with the utensils of War and Hunting, chapters 231—235 with those of the Table, and chapters 236—240 with a variety of Household and Toilet utensils, Tools, &c.

a. Utensils for Illumination.

Utensils of illumination, both for religious and household use, are extremely numerous. Great attention and artistic finish have been lavished upon them in all styles; and especially in the Antique. We need only mention the Candelabra of the Antique and the Renascence, Greek Lamps, the Chandeliers of the Middle Ages, &c.

The forms and the finish of the different utensils have changed along with the radical changes which the mode of illumination has undergone in the course of time. Oil, lamp-light, candle, torch-light, gas-light, and our latest achievement, the electric light, all demand special, different forms of bearers, and apparatus.

The predominant material would seem to be metal; and, next to this, clay, and glass; while imflammable materials like wood are, by their very nature, almost excluded.

Here, too, it is proper to call attention to a difference which must be borne in mind between Antique and Modern illuminating utensils. The difference is this: that whereas the Antique with all its artistic perfection, is very defective from a practical point of view; Modern apparatus, while surpassing the Antique in the matter of technical adaptation to its purpose, scarcely ever reaches the Antique beauty, and generally falls below it.

We will consider the Candelabrum, the Antique Lamp, the different kinds of Standard, Hand, and Bracket Candlesticks, Hanging Lamps, Lanterns, Chandeliers, and Modern Lamps; taking them in this order.

THE CANDELABRUM.   (Plates 211—212.)

The Candelabrum (from *candela* = candle) was, as its name indicates, originally intended to carry a candle. But as candle-light, like the illumination by means of torches and pitch-pans, gradually receded before the use of Lamps in Antique times, and was more and more reserved for the purposes of ritual; the Antique Candelabrum came to be employed as a Lampstand or Lampadarium. Hence it comes that the upper end of a Candelabrum is furnished sometimes with a bowl, sometimes with a pricket or socket to receive the candle, sometimes with a flat disc, and, sometimes with projecting clips and hooks to hold the lamp or to suspend it from. The last is the most frequent form. The great State-candelabra, for religious observances, have bowls; and are made of marble. The shaft of such a Roman Candelabrum of conventional form is given on Plate 121, fig. 2. Candelabra for household use were made of bronze. In height: they are of two different dimensions, according as they were meant to stand on the ground, or on a table. The former are of an extremely slender construction (Plate 211. 1), of an average height of 3 feet to 4 ft. 6 ins. The form of the latter class *(candelabrum humile)* is less slender (Plate 211. 5 and 6), and the extreme height is about 1 ft. 8 ins. The design of the Antique Candelabrum is either of architectonic character, or free and natura-

listic. We have already mentioned, in chapters 135—137, that in
the former case: the base, shaft and bowl, are generally decorated.
The second class includes standing and sitting figures, behind which
the shaft of the candelabrum rises, or by which it is borne (Plate 211.
2 and 3); or of bearers in the form of trees, beneath which figures
or groups are seated (Plate 211. 4). Occasionally examples are found
so arranged that they can be taken apart and adjusted to different
heights (Plate 211. 7). The majority of the Antique bronze Candelabra which have been preserved to us are of Etruscan origin.
Plate 211 shows seven different examples selected from the copious
material.

PLATE 211. THE ANTIQUE CANDELABRUM.

1. Antique, bronze stand from which to suspend lamps *(lychnucus,
   lampadarium)*, found in Pompeii, Berlin, Museum.
2. Etruscan, bronze, Bibliothèque National, Paris.
3. Antique, bronze, found in Chiusi, (Ménard et Sauvageot).
4. Antique, bronze, found in Herculaneum.
5. Antique, bronze, to hold a candle or torch, (Ménard et Sauvageot).
6. Antique, *(Candelabrum humile)*, bronze, Museum, Naples.
7. Antique, bronze, adjustable to different heights, found in Herculaneum.

The Candelabrum was revived at the time of the Renascence
along with the tradition of Antique art. It accepted the form; but
remodelled it in its own fashion. Since that time the Candelabrum
occurs in countless modifications, both for state and use, in religious
and secular buildings. It is no more a Lampstand, but bears a
candle in a pricket or, more rarely, in a socket. The Roman Catholic
ritual, in particular, the services of which require lighted candles,
has given an impetus to the new forms of Candelabra in metal, and
carved wood set-off by painting and gilding. The finest examples of
this kind are to be found in the churches and palaces of Italy.

PLATE 212. THE RENASCENCE CANDELABRUM.

1. Altar candlestick, church of the Benedictines, Villingen, wood,
   gilt and silvered, Late German Renascence, 3 ft. 9 ins. high.
2. Bronze, end of the 16th century, Italian.
3. Altar candlestick, Certosa near Pavia, 17th century, Italian,
   (Musterornamente).
4. Medicean chapel, San Lorenzo, Florence, Italian, Renascence.
5. Bronze, Italian, Renascence, Bargello, Florence.

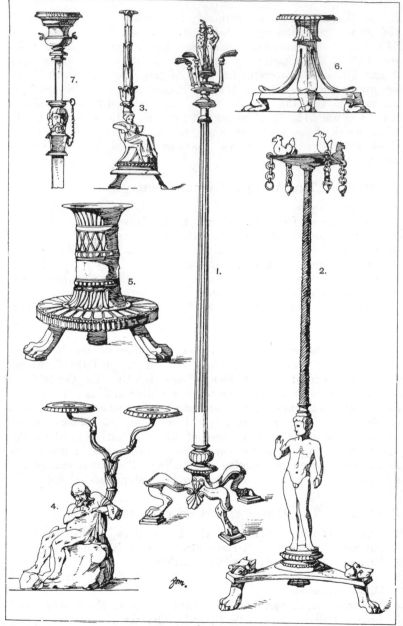

Plate 211. The Antique Candelabrum.

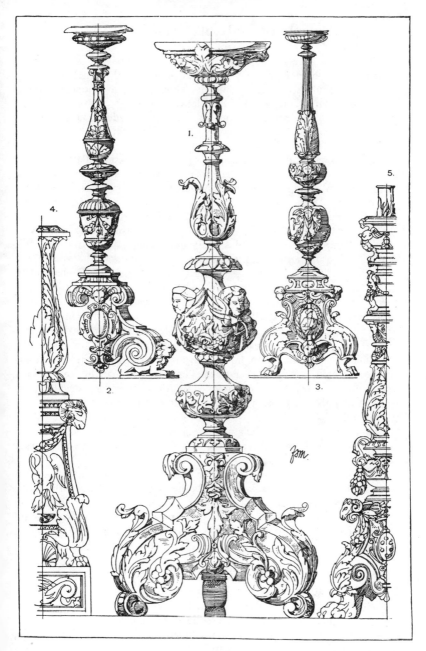

The Renascence Candelabrum. Plate 212.

The Antique Lamp. (Plate 213.)

The Antique Lamp (*lychnus*, *lucerna*) is, strictly speaking, a combination of holder and pourer; and might with equal propriety have been included in the group of Vases. The fundamental form, which was retained down to the latest times, is found in early Egyptian household utensils; and is created by adding a handle, a funnel for filling, and a spout with an opening for the wick, to a spheroid body, figures 1 and 2.

In Greek and Roman Lamps: the body becomes flattened, the funnel contracts to a simple orifice, and the round handle is either replaced by a straight one or combined with it, (figs. 4 and 9). Very frequently the lamp has several wick-openings (*dimyxos*, *trimyxos* &c.) instead of only one, (figs. 5, 10 and 11).

Clay and bronze are the materials almost exclusively employed. The clay Lamps are mostly plastically decorated, more rarely painted. The decoration is most conspicuous on the handle and the spout; the upper part of the body is often treated with figures in bas-relief, (fig. 4). Bronze Lamps are decorated with figures, with covers fastened by hinges, wick-trimmers, &c., (fig. 10). And it was the bronze Lamps which were especially arranged to be suspended from Lampadarii. Small Lampstands, in the form of low tripods, are also not scarce (figs. 8 and 9); occasionally Tripod and Lamp are combined, as in the example shown in fig. 7. By the side of examples tectonically constructed, we find freer forms, imitating human figures, animal shapes, human feet, &c. In some cases these may be considered as "happy thoughts"; in others they are simply an aberration of style (figs. 12 and 13).

The early days of Christendom show reminiscences of the Antique, e. g. the Lamp in fig. 13, which also bears the monogram of Christ.

In later periods: the decoration degenerates, although the fundamental form has been retained till the present time, in the East, for household lamps; the design of the modern lamp from Jerusalem (fig. 14) is of the simplest possible description. In the West: the old form is gradually dying-out, since the introduction of the glass cylinder, which enables the illuminating gases to be more thoroughly consumed.

Plate 213. `The Antique Lamp.

1—2. Egyptian, clay.
3. Antique, painted clay, (Ménard et Sauvageot).
4. Antique, red clay, United collections, Carlsruhe.
5. Antique, red clay, with two spouts and vertical ring handle, United collections, Carlsruhe.

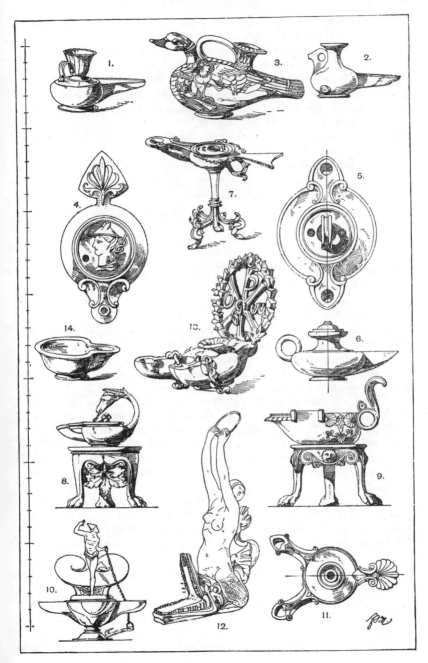

The Antique Lamp. Plate 213.

6.   Antique, with cover and ring handle, red clay, United
      collections, Carlsruhe.
7.   Antique, bronze, with high stand, the missing cover was
      evidently a human mask, Louvre, Paris.
8—9. Antique, bronze, on small tripods *(candelabrum humile)*.
10.   Antique, bronze, with three spouts, the figure serves as a
      handle for the cover, a wick-trimmer is attached to it by a
      chain, found in Herculaneum.
11.   Antique, bronze, with two spouts, found in Herculaneum,
      Museum, Naples, $^1/_6$ of original size.
12.   Antique, bronze, for suspension, (Formenschatz).
13.   Early Christian, bronze, with the monogram of Christ, for
      suspension, from the catacombs, Rome.
14.   Modern, Oriental, clay, from Jerusalem, United collections,
      Carlsruhe.

THE CANDLESTICK.   (Plates 214—215.)

The Candlestick is the candle-bearer of the Middle Ages, the
Renascence, and Modern times. It is distinguished from the Candelabrum, if a distinction can be made at all where the forms thus
blend with each other, by its smaller dimensions and simpler forms;
and it is chiefly used for secular purposes.

The principal materials beside brass, iron, copper, tin, &c., are
clay, porcelain, and glass.

In the Middle Ages; it was usual to stick the candle on a conical
pricket; our Modern times prefer the cylindrical socket. The design
includes base (often tripartite), shaft, and socket, as in the case of
the Candelabrum. The upper end is furnished with a saucer or bowl,
to catch the droppings. The saucer is sometimes loose, so that it
may easely be taken-off and cleansed, in which case it is termed a
"save-all".

Often the upper part is furnished with a number of arms to
receive several candles. As regards decorations: the principles laid
down for the Candelabrum, in the chapter on Supports, hold good.
The Seven-branched-candlestick, of the Temple at Jerusalem, is historically celebrated; fig. 1 of Plate 215 reproduces this from the representation of it on the triumphal arch of Titus. The fundamental
form of it has been retained, to this day, in Jewish ritual.

High Candlesticks, of simple form, made of wrought-iron, are not
rare in the Middle Ages (Plate 215. 2). Richly-finished examples,
in wrought-iron and bronze, were created in the Renascence, (Plate
214. 5, and 215. 3). The Japanese and Chinese bronze candlesticks

have a certain similarity to the Romanesque ecclesiastical candlesticks of the same material, (Plate 214. 1—4).

Modern productions in clay, glass and porcelain have scarcely any artistic importance; all the more must we praise modern art for recurring to the old models in metal work; and thus producing very gratifying results, (Plate 214. 6, 7, 8, and Plate 215. 4 and 5).

PLATE 214. THE CANDLESTICK.

1. Romanesque, bronze, 11th century, Dugué collection, (Viollet-le-Duc).
2. Romanesque, bronze, Cathedral, Hildesheim.
3. Romanesque, bronze.
4. Ancient Chinese, bronze.
5. Brass, 17th century.
6. Modern, bronze, (Gewerbehalle).
7. Modern, bronze, Gewerbehalle, Carlsruhe.
8. Modern, bronze, by Prof. Schick, Carlsruhe, (Gewerbehalle).

PLATE 215. THE CANDLESTICK.

1. The Seven-branched-candlestick of the Temple at Jerusalem, Arch of Titus, Rome.
2. Wrought-iron, S. Peter's, Tarrosa, Spain, 14th century, (L'art pour tous).
3. Wrought-iron, for 3 candles, 17th century.
4. Wrought-iron, Modern.
5. Wrought-iron, with several arms, by C. Zaar, (Gewerbehalle).

THE HAND-CANDLESTICK. (Plate 216.)

The term Hand-candlestick includes any kind of portable candlestick; and it assumes the existence of some kind of handle to hold and carry it. The Hand-candlestick is always of modest dimensions; and it is generally low in height, as in our flat candlesticks.

It may be constructed on an immense variety of plans, so that a number of different forms occur. Candlesticks frequently recur of the form shown in fig. 2, in which a screw thread enables the height of the socket to be adjusted. The Middle Ages and the Renascence exhibited great ingenuity in the invention of such arrangements (fig. 1).

As the Hand-candlestick is liable to gutter: the "save-all" has here undergone a special developement, so that in a certain class of

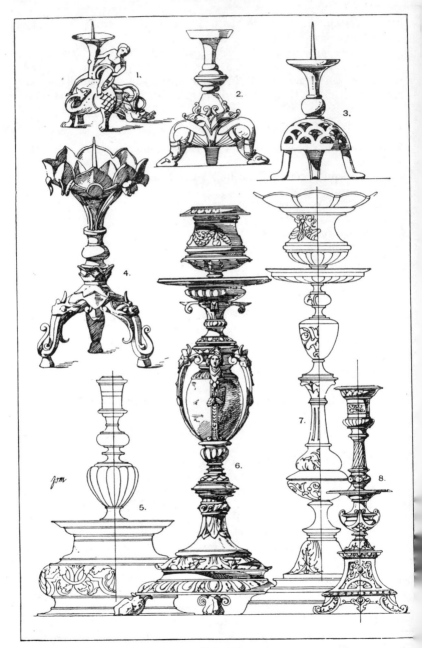

Plate 214. The Candlestick.

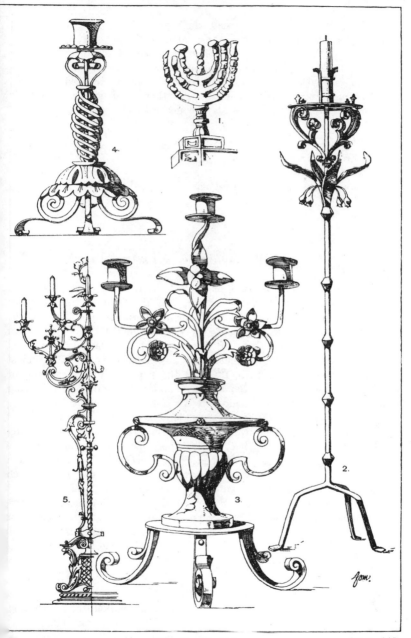

The Candlestick.   Plate 215.

candlestick it consists of a broad dish out of which rises a shaft
with a socket-bowl at the end (figs. 216. 6, 7, 8).

Often an Extinguisher is combinet with the Candlestick, especially
when the latter is of wrought-iron; as shown by the original example,
fig. 4; of late years Match-holders have also been included.

The material is the same as for other candlesticks. There is
nothing special to say as regards the decoration.

PATE 216. THE HAND-CANDLESTICK.

1—3. Wrought-iron, 17th century.
4—5. Modern, wrought iron.
6.   Modern, by P. Fauré of Paris, (Gewerbehalle).
7.   Modern, brass.
8.   Modern, brass.

THE CANDLE-BRACKET.   (Plate 217.)

Candle-Brackets are fixed or movable bearers attached to vertical
surfaces, e. g. columns, pilasters, &c. In the Middle Ages and the
Renascence they were chiefly used for Torches and Candles; at the
present time they are employed for Candles and Gas. Their form
naturally differs from that of the upright Candlestick. Curved
scroll-work and consoles of metal (for this material is the one almost
exclusively used) bear on their free end the prickets, or the sockets, or
the burners and globes, which last are employed to diffuse the glaring
light and soften the sharp shadows. A primitive method of connecting
the bracket with the wall is by hook and eye (fig. 1); in articles of
better finish this is done by means of rosettes or wall-plates and cartouches (figs. 6, 7, 8, 9). The Bracket may be used for one or more
lights. In the latter case: several prickets or sockets are placed on a
common disc (fig. 2); or, which is artistically better, the main branch
divides into a number of subsidiary arms (fig. 3). The Bracket
on a large scale, is used for Street-lighting, for Churches, Theatres,
Halls, Mansions, Palaces, Restaurants, &c.; and on a smaller scale, for
Pianofortes, &c. In designing Brackets for gas: care must be taken
to provide for the Gas-pipe. The modern adjustible Brackets, being
mostly without decoration, need not be considered.

PLATE 217. THE CANDLE-BRACKET.

1—2. German, Renascence, wrought-iron, National Museum, Munich
3.   Rococo, for 3 candles, bronze gilt, Milan Museum, (Raguenet)
4—5. Modern, by M. Weinholdt, Munich, (Gewerbehalle).
6—7. Wall-plates, to 4, and 5.

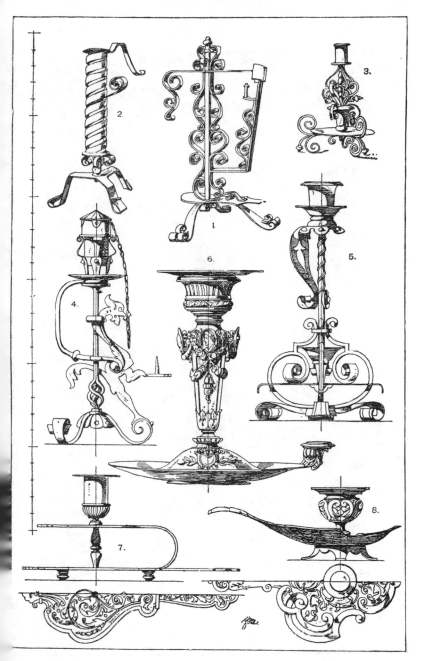

The Hand-Candlestick. Plate 216.

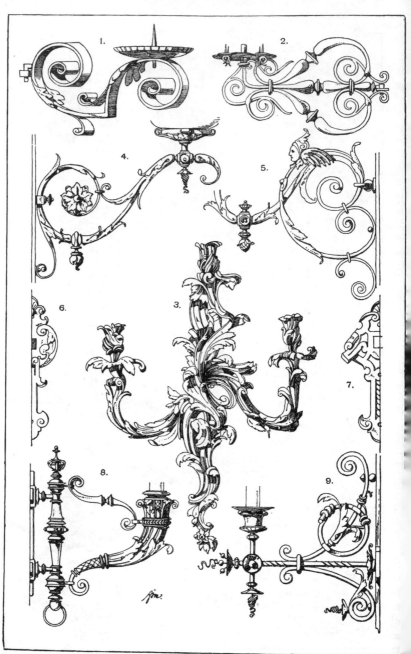

Plate 217. The Candle-Bracket.

8.   Modern, (Gewerbehalle).
9.   Modern, wrought-iron.

THE PENDANT-LAMP. (Plate 218.)

Both aesthetic reasons, and the danger of being knocked-over to which upright candlesticks are subject, led in early times to the construction of Pendant-lamps. In addition to the small bronze lamps, which could be used both standing or hanging, the Antique offers us Lamps which could be used only for suspension. The latter form is still common in the East (compare Plate 187. 13), and in the West in Christian and Jewish ritual. The introduction, of Paraffin, Gas, and the Electric light, has afforded plentiful opportunities of giving an artistic form to Hanging-lamps. The spherical globes of ground glass lend themselves especially to such treatment, (figs. 4, 5, 6). Box-shaped holders, either open or closed by panes of glass, are termed Lanterns. Modern lanterns, for illumination in the open air, are generally devoid of any really artistic decoration; but the Middle Ages and the Renascence created many objects of perfect form in this branch. The most suitable material for Lanterns is wrought-iron (figs. 2 and 3). It is self-evident that Lanterns must be so arranged that they can be opened for cleaning, &c.

PLATE 218. THE PENDANT-LAMP.

1.   Old Moorish, iron, United collections, Carlsruhe.
2.   Mediaeval, wrought-iron, for several candles, German, (Formenschatz).
3.   French, Hôtel Vogué, Dijon, 17th century, (L'art pour tous).
4.   Modern, for Electric glow-light, by Peter, of Esslingen, (Gewerbehalle).
5—6. Modern, (Gewerbehalle).

THE CHANDELIER. (Plate 219.)

The arrangement, of a considerable number of lights in circular form on a framework intended for suspension, led to the construction of the Chandelier. In the Middle Ages: the lights were all placed in the same plane so that they formed a ring (fig. 2); the Renascence secured greater richness and variety of design by a number of rings, an arrangement which has usually been retained in our modern Chandeliers (fig. 3 and 4). Further variety is attained by the alternation of the lights in the different rings. Wrought-iron

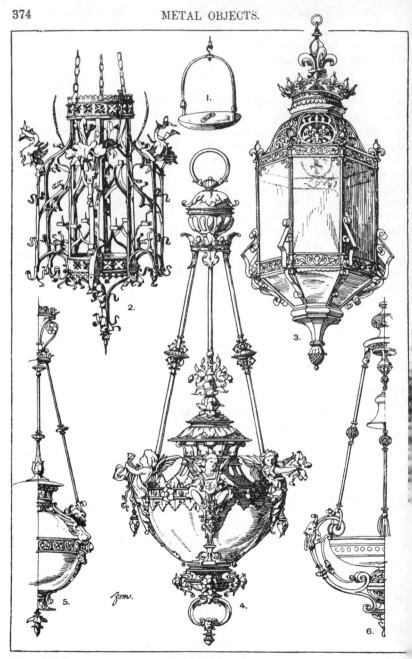

Plate 218.   The Pendant-Lamp.

and bronze, along with glass (Venetian chandeliers), and of late years cheap cast-iron, and zinc, are the chief materials. Original and unique in design is the mermaid chandelier consisting of female half-figures terminating in fish-tails, and furnished with antlers to carry the candles (fig. 1). The slender chains by which these mermaids, and other lamps and lanterns, were suspended, are replaced in modern chandeliers by a tube which also serves as a gas-pipe. In the former case the chain was carried over pulleys so that the light could be shifted higher or lower; in modern chandeliers the adjustment is effected by means of a stuffing-box with balance weights (fig. 7). Very frequently the lower end of the Chandelier terminates in a ring, to facilitate the change in height. In addition to the globes round the flames, guards are often placed over them, to protect the ceiling from heat and soot. Each burner must be connected with the main gas-pipe by means of a separate pipe. Where the Chandelier is intended for Electric lights; the latter may be bent downwards instead of upwards, so that the frames for the globes will cast no shadow. The Plate gives a number of ancient and modern Chandeliers, partly in half profile, the foreshortened arms, which interfere with the drawing, having been omitted. A regular arrangement, of 4, 5 or 6 arms, is the rule: more or fewer arms occur more rarely. In the case of Chandeliers with a great number of lights: each arm is arranged after the fashion of a bracket with several candles.

PLATE 219. THE CHANDELIER.

1. Modern, style of the German Renascence.
2. German, Renascence, Hemispherical, for 8 candles.
3—6. Modern, bronze and wrought-iron.
7. Modern, French, by the sculptor Villeminot, (L'art pour tous).

THE MODERN LAMP. (Plate 220.)

The principal value, of the modern Lamp, lies in the technical completeness, and adaptation to its purpose. There is, it is true, no such wealth of artistic fancy as is shown by Antique Lamps; but still some good examples may be found among the two or three fundamental forms of the Paraffin-lamp, with which we have mostly to do. Metal, glass, porcelain, and majolica, again appear as materials. As a general rule we have a profiled foot, on which the oil-receiver rests, from which latter the burner, chimney, and globe rise, (figs. 1 and 2).

More richly finished examples have a masked receiver, the latter being enclosed by a vase (figs. 3, and 4). Attempts have lately been

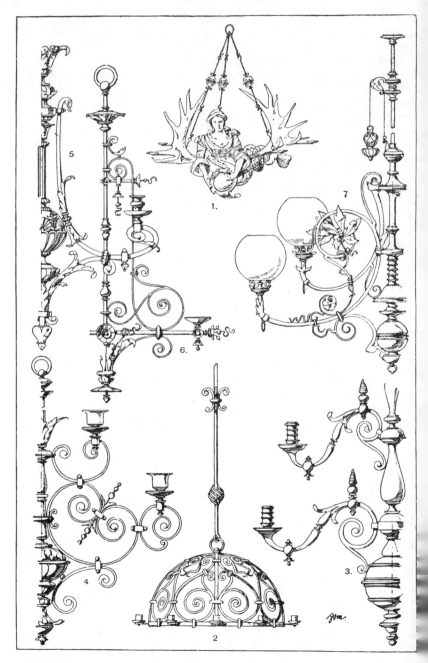

Plate 219.

The Chandelier.

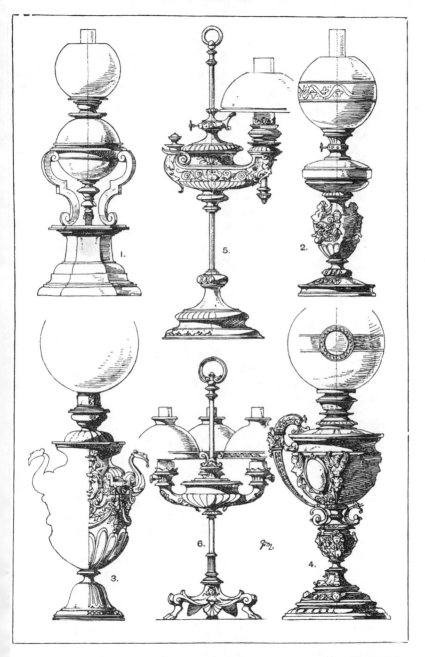

The Modern Lamp. Plate 220.

made to replace these conventional forms by more original designs. An example of this is the "vestal lamp" (fig. 5), which must be admitted to be successful. This form admits of adjustment of height; can be easily filled and cleaned; and allows of a combination of several burners (fig. 6).

PLATE 220. THE MODERN LAMP.

1—2. Paraffin lamps, with visible oil receiver.

3.   Oil Lamp, with concealed receiver, by the sculptor Piat of Paris, (L'art pour tous).

4.   Paraffin Lamp, with concealed receiver, by Paul Stotz, of Stuttgart, Bronze, (Gewerbehalle).

5.   Paraffin Lamp, "Vestal lamp", Berlin.

6.   Paraffin Lamp, with 3 burners, by the architect Böhringer, of Stuttgart, (Gewerbehalle).

b. Religious Utensils.

Notwithstanding the varied character of Religious Utensils: we devote only five Plates to them, principally because many have been already dealt-with in other groups. We cannot attempt to give a complete view of the apparatus of ritual; but must confine our selection to objects taken, partly from Heathen, and partly from Christian examples.

THE ALTAR. (Plate 221.)

The original form of the Altar (from *alta ara*) was no doubt extremely simple. Blocks of rock and stones, piled-up beneath the blue sky or under trees, were probably the earliest. With the evolution of art, and especially of architecture, the Altar entered into the service of the Temple; and received a more artistic finish. The plan of the Antique Altar is usually triangular, quadrangular, or circular. The material is generally marble. Its top is a table-like Slab, generally with a hollow to contain the sacrificial fire. The decoration was of symbolic character. Skulls of animals, Festoons of fruit, votive Wreaths, Figures of the Gods, Genii, and similar creations, were used almost always. The triangular Altar was often used as the base of the Antique State-candelabrum; e. g. the altar represented on fig. 5, which is the base of a Candelabrum.

The so-called "Altars" of the Christian religion have nothing in common with those of the Antique; and they do not fall within the scope of our work.

PLATE 221. THE ALTAR.

1. Assyrian, triangular sacrificial stone.
2. Assyrian, round sacrificial stone.
3. Assyrian, sacrificial slab, from a relief in the British Museum.
4. Roman, three-sided Altar, like a number of examples, differing little from one-another, in the museums in London, Paris, &c.
5. Roman, three-sided Altar, used as the base of a Candelabrum.
6—9. Roman, various altars, fig. 9 with the masks of 12 Deities, and the signs of the Zodiac, (Ménard et Sauvageot).

THE TRIPOD. (Plate 222.)

The name Tripod is applied to any three-legged support, whatever the use to which it may be put. More accurately, the Tripod is a construction in three parts: the top part being a bowl, dish, or slab. The Antique Tripod played an important part both in religious rites and in daily life. Originally an article of practical use, for cooking, &c., its form is simple; when it was elevated to an utensil of Religion, to bear the sacrificial pans and the consecrated offerings for the Deities, or to be the Prize of Victory in the games: it assumed conventional forms, and received an artistic finish. The material was generally bronze, except for the great, monumental State-tripods, which were of marble. The Greek, Roman, and Etruscan Tripods differ characteristically from each-other, in their detail; but have this in common, that they are supported by three smooth, rod-like legs, which are terminated at their lower end in animals' claws; and are connected together by rings (fig. 3), or struts (figs. 1 and 2); and at the top are either connected directly with the dish (figs. 1 and 2), or with a ring intended for the reception of a loose dish (fig. 3). For the sake of greater convenience, handles are sometimes attached to the dish (fig. 1); the legs may be adjusted to different heights (figs. 1 and 2); or the Tripod may be so arranged that it can be taken to pieces. These antique Tripods, of which some of the simpler examples are given on the Plate, afford us, better than anything else, an insight into the Antique art of bronze-working.

The Middle Ages and the Renascence have also transmitted to us numerous Tripods. Their principal, use is in households as stands for washing-basins, &c.; and they are generally of wrought-iron (figs. 4, 5, 6). After the art of working in wrought-iron had been revived in modern times, we find them as Stands for washing upparatus, Trays for visiting-cards, Stands for wine-coolers, (fig. 7), &c.

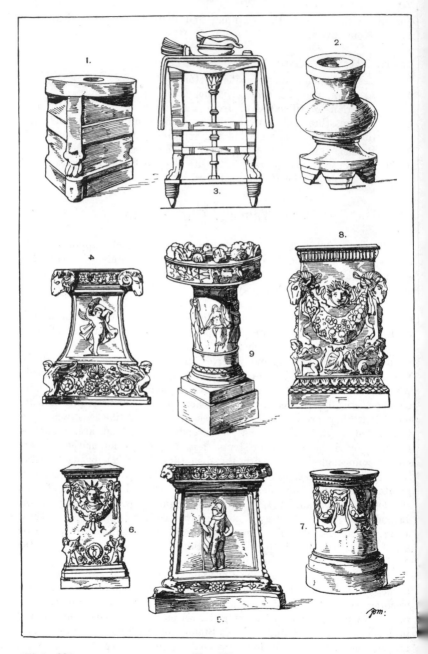

Plate 221.

The Altar.

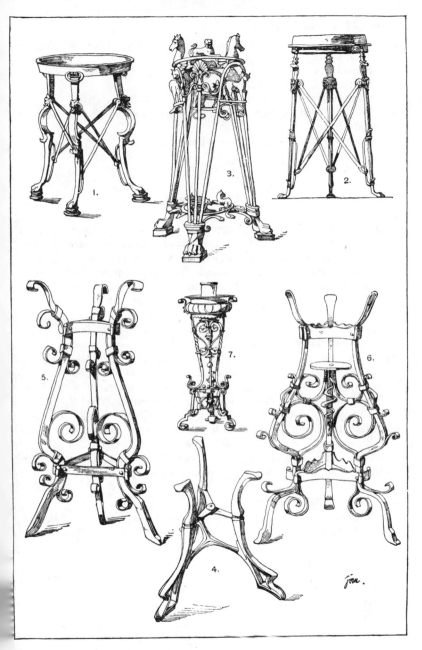

The Tripod.

Plate 222.

PLATE 222. THE TRIPOD.

1. Antique, bronze, found in Pompeii, about Museum, Naples. 28 ins. high.
2. Romanesque, bronze, (Ménard et Sauvageot).
3. Etruscan, bronze, Berlin Museum.
4. Mediaeval, bronze, Pierrefonds castle, (Viollet-le-Duc).
5—6. Italian, 17th century, wrought-iron, about 4 ft. high, (L'art pour tous).
7. Modern, wrought-iron, for wine-cooler, by the architect Zaar, (Gewerbehalle).

THE CENSER. (Plate 223.)

One of the oldest ecclesiastical utensils is the Censer or Thurible, in the use of which the rising clouds of incense are a symbolical representation of prayer ascending to heaven. The material is silver, bronze, iron, copper, or brass. The lower part consists of a dish with foot, containing the fire-pan. The pierced cover is kept in its place by means of the three chains which pass through the three holes made for the purpose. These three chains hang from a small plate with a ring. The cover is fastened to a fourth chain, which also terminates in a chain and may be drawn up through a hole in the plate (fig. 7). The decoration is frequently symbolic, and Inscriptions are also used. The Romanesque and Gothic Censers often exhibit an architectonic design of domes and towers (figs. 2, 4, 6). The Renascence prefers the strict form of a vessel (figs. 8, and 9). Modern art avails itself of Ancient models, without having anything independent to show. An appendage of the Censer, in a certain sense, is the Censer-boat, or incense-holder, usually an elliptical dish with a partition and two hinged covers. The incense is conveyed from the Incense-boat to the Censer by means of a Spoon.

PLATE 223. THE CENSER.

1—2. Romanesque, bronze, 6th and 12th centuries, each $7\frac{1}{2}$ ins. high, Collection of antiquities, Grand-ducal Court, Mannheim.
3. Romanesque, bronze, French, beginning of the 13th century, $5\frac{3}{4}$ ins. high, (Viollet-le-Duc).
4—5. Gothic, from stone statues, Cathedral, Chartres, 13th century, (L'art pour tous).
6. Gothic, with tower shaped cover.
7—8. Renascence.
9. Renascence, South Kensington Museum, London.

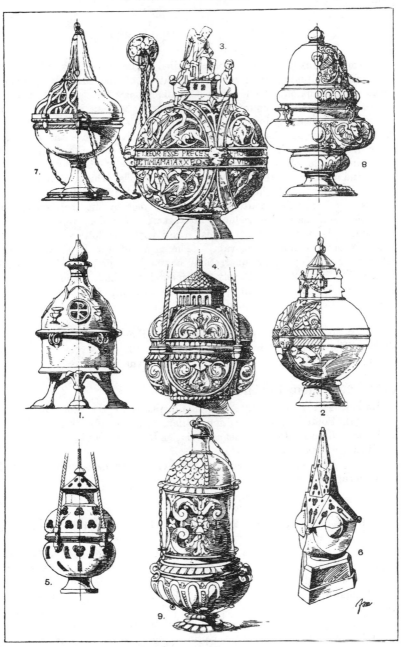

The Censer.   Plate 223.

THE CRUCIFIX. (Plate 224.)

The Crucifix (from *crucifixus* = nailed to the cross) does not appear in Christian ritual until after the abolition of the shameful punishment of Crucifixion. The oldest Crucifixes may be dated about the 6th century. In the course of the following styles: it underwent a variety of transformations. The older examples often represent the crucified Christ as clothed (fig. 3), while in later times the body is more frequently nude, with the clothing restricted to the cloth round the loins. The older renderings of Christ show a straight stiff attitude, and a calm expression; while later periods exhibit a more lifelike conception, and the expression of pain. At first: each foot is pierced by a separate nail, later the two feet by one nail only; so that the four nails are reduced to three. A nimbus appears above or behind the head; and over this a roll with the letters I. N. R. I. (Iesus Nazarenus Rex Iudaeorum). The arms of the Latin Cross are often terminated in four quatrefoils containing symbols of the four Evangelists (figs. 2, 3). Purely ornamental terminations of the arms and decorations at their intersections are also not uncommon (fig. 1). When the Crucifix is intended to stand upright on the Communion-table: it is furnished with a candelabrum-like base (figs. 1, 2, 3). The bases are generally of similar style to the accompanying Candlesticks. The materials are chiefly metals, wood, and ivory, the body of Christ and the Cross being often of different materials.

PLATE 224. THE CRUCIFIX.

1. Italian, 1511, silver gilt, the inlaid plates of the cross are rock crystal, Poldi Pezzoli collection, Milan, (Kunsthandwerk).
2. Italian, bronze, Certosa near Pavia, 4 ft. 4 ins. high, Renascence, (Musterornamente).
3. Italian, Bronze, Renascence, evidently of earlier date than the base.
4. Modern, Carved wood.

THE CROZIER, AND THE MONSTRANCE. (Plate 225.)

The Crozier or Pastoral-staff has been the badge of episcopal dignity since the earliest period of the Middle Ages. In the West: it had the shape of a crutch up to the 12th century; and it has retained this form in the East up the present day (fig. 1). Afterwards the upper end was curved spirally. The curved end and the staff itself are separated by a knob. In the Middle Ages: the curve is decorated with crockets and inscriptions; and its centre bears figures. In many cases the war of the Church against the Evil One is sym-

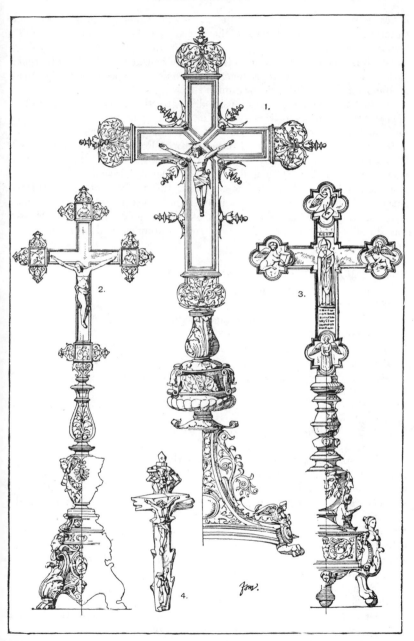

The Crucifix.   Plate 224.

bolically represented by the fight with the dragon (fig. 4). In the Gothic period the knob below the curve is developed into an architectonic lantern. The length of the Crozier is 5 to 6 ft. The material is wood, ivory, and metal, usually contrasting in the different parts. The Plate only reproduces the upper ends; as these alone are of importance by their decoration.

The Monstrance is a utensil allied to the Ciborium and Reliquary. It is an expository vessel in which, since the institution of the feast of Corpus Christi by Urban IV in 1264, the consecrated wafer is shown and carried in processions in Roman Catholic churches. It possesses great varieties both of style and size, the height varying from 1 ft. to 5 ft. It usually has a slender hexagonal or octagonal foot, and a knob. From the foot rises a tower-like receptacle (turricula), or a "Glory" with a disc-shaped glass box in which the wafer rests on the so-called eye. The material is gold, silver, or brass. The Plate gives one of the numerous examples which have been preserved.

PLATE 225. THE CROZIER, AND THE MONSTRANCE.

1.   Romanesque, Bishop Gerard of Limoges, † 1022.
2—3. Romanesque.
4.   Transition period from Romanesque to Gothic, French, (L'art pour tous).
5. Gothic, Martin Schongauer, end of 15th century, (Wessely).
6. Rococo, ivory.
7. Monstrance, gilt brass, 23 ins. high, Hotzendorf.

c. Utensils of War and Hunting; Weapons.

Utensils of war and hunting, in their most primitive forms at least, are as old as mankind itself. Savages of the earliest as well as of modern times, show great skill, and a certain originality in the decoration of these utensils, as we may see in our ethnological collections. So long as these utensils continued to be made of horn, bone, and such materials: and also so long as they belong to the so-called "Stone age", they are comparatively simple. They do not assume a richer form and finish till the introduction of bronze and iron. The great revolution which ensued on the transition from the "Stone" to the "Bronze age" finds a not less imposing parallel in the revolution wrought by the invention of Gunpowder.

Utensils of War and Hunting may be divided into two great sections: weapons of Defense and weapons of Offense. To the former belong Shields, Helmets and Armour. The kinds and number of

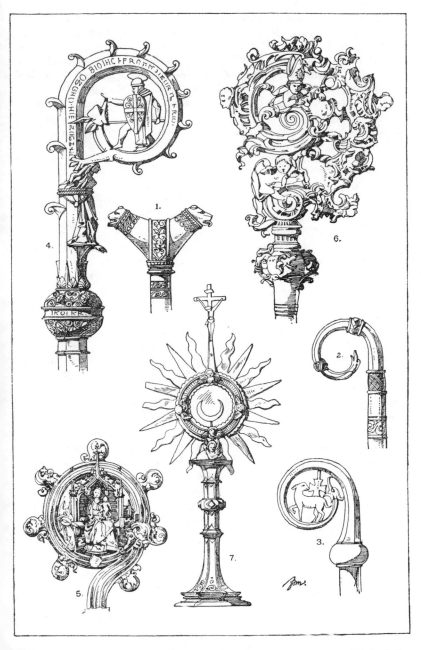

The Crozier, and the Monstrance.   Plate 225.

weapons of offense are far more manifold. Swords, Daggers, Spears, Pikes, Lances, Axes, Maces, Arrows, Rifles, and Pistols, are the principal. It is unfortunately impossible, in this work, to give due consideration to every single form; still the chief representatives have been included, with the exception of Firearms and Armour, in which only the engraved or chased details are of decorative importance.

The most striking examples, in our Armouries and Museums, have lately been published, in numerous works; so that it is not difficult to obtain a general view of this section; monographs on Weapons have also been published, among which we may specially mention Boeheim's *Waffenkunde* (E. A. Seemann, Leipzig).

THE SHIELD. (Plate 226.)

The Shield, which from the earliest times has been the usual weapon of defense against blows and thrusts, is generally a domed disc, the form of which has varied considerably. Circular, elliptical, semi-circular, and kite-shapes, are found alongside others of richer outline. The materials are wood, plaited osiers, leather, metal, and combinations of these. The Shield is held in the left hand by a handle, or slung on the arm by a strap. The size varies from 20 ins. to 5 ft. The Antique Shield was circular; and frequently ornamented with a boss in the centre. Among the ancient Teutons, the form was large and square; in the Middle Ages, it was triangular. The Standing-shields or Pavises, of the 14th and 15th centuries, were very large, and provided with feet, so that they would stand upon the ground, without being held. The Tilting-shield had a hole cut away in which the lance was laid. With the introductions of fire-arms the Shield became worthless, and disappears as an article of practical use; but it has continued to be employed for State-purposes down to the present time; and, from a decorative standpoint, these State-shields are of high interest. They offer to metal-workers an exceptionally favourable field for the display of their art. The simple zonal divisions of the Antique Shield have given place to freer divisions and a richer decoration with figures and ornaments.

PLATE 226. THE SHIELD.

1. Roman, with boss, bronze partly-silvered, found near Mainz, Wiesbaden, Museum.
2. Etruscan, bronze, Campana collection, (L'art pour tous).
3. Mediaeval, time of the Crusades, (Viollet-le-Duc).
4. Renascence, time of Henry II of France, hammered metal.

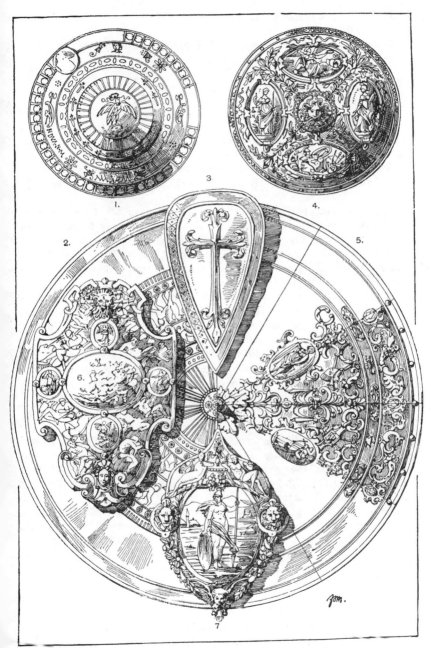

The Shield.   Plate 226.

5. Renascence, decorated in the centre with a rosette and pointed knob, Turin.
6. Renascence, with rich decoration of figures, in hammered metal.
7. Renascence, hammered silver, by P. van Vianen.

THE HELMET. (Plate 227.)

The armour for the defense of the head is the Helmet. It was probably originally made of leather; at a later date it was of metal; and in Modern times it again consists of leather with metal accessories. Its form has suffered many transformations in the course of the centuries, arising sometimes from practical, sometimes from æsthetic reasons.

The greatest perfection of form is found in the Greek helmet, which, like Antique armour in general, fits very closely to the human body. We need only remind the reader of the plain but beautiful Helmets in which Pallas Athene is shown on Antique gems. The Medusa head and Sphinxes are popular motives of decoration. The decoration is most prominent on the front, and on the moveable cheek-pieces. Fig. 1 shows a Greek Helmet with a crest which is similar to the form of the Phrygian cap. The Etruscan Helmet (fig. 2) is similar to the Greek. The Roman Helmet is simpler. Helmets were often decorated with plumes of feathers or horse-hair; and were provided with sockets for fixing these accessories. The Roman gladiators' helmets, with their rich, florid, often overdone decoration, and their large face-guard and heavy crest, have something awkward, without becoming ugly.

Very manifold, although of no great importance decoratively, are the Helmets of the Middle Ages. Leaving out of account the less important transitional forms, we will here give the names of the principal classes in order of historical succession. They are the Heaume (fig. 8), the Salade or sallet (fig. 7), the Tilting-helmet (fig. 9), the Armet (fig. 10), and the Helmet with barred Vizor (fig. 11). The section on Heraldry may also be consulted.

The Helmets of the Renascence, especially the State-helmets, are richly, sometimes too richly, decorated. To the forms received, from the Middle ages, were added the Burganet (fig. 13), and the Morion (fig. 12). Some of these State-helmets are also copied from the Antique, as may be seen in fig. 14. The Modern creations in this section are of no artistic importance.

PLATE 227. THE HELMET.

1.   Greek, bronze, Campana collection, (L'art pour tous).
2.   Etruscan, bronze, Campana collection, (L'art pour tous).

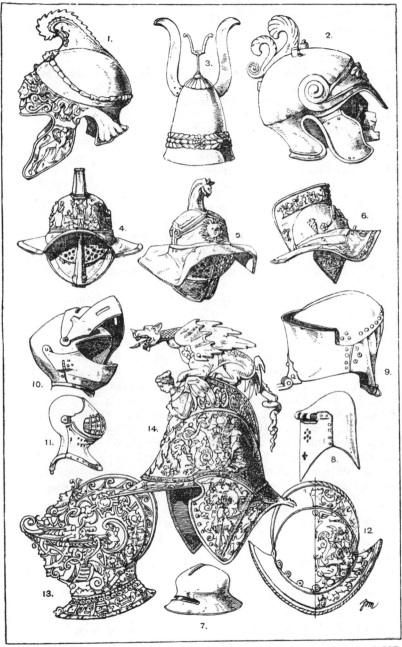

The Helmet.

Plate 227.

3.   Roman, bronze, Louvre, Paris, (Ménard et Sauvageot).

4—6.   Roman, bronze, for gladiators, different views, (Ménard et Sauvageot).

7.   Mediaeval Salade, iron.

8.   Mediaeval Heaume, iron, the chain was hooked into the cross-shaped slit.

9.   Mediaeval Tilting-helmet, iron.

10.   Mediaeval Armet, iron.

11.   Mediaeval, iron, with barred vizor.

12.   Renascence, Morion, etched iron.

13.   Renascence Burganet, German.

14.   State-helmet, 16th century, (L'art pour tous).

THE SWORD. (Plate 228.)

The Sword is the most universally used of the offensive weapons. Much as these weapons for cutting and thrusting differ from each other in size and finish; they generally consist of three principal parts: the Blade, single or double-edged, tapering more or less towards the point, generally straight, but sometimes curved or waved, also sometimes fluted to save weight, only decorated by means of engraving, etching, damaskeening, &c.; the Handle, with or without pommel, cup, or basket; and the Scabbard or sheath, with or without a hanger. The two latter, the handle and scabbard, offer the most scope for decoration. The material of these is, in addition to iron, the other metals and alloys, wood, bone, leather, coloured stones, &c. Here, also, from an artistic point of view, we have to consider less the practical than the State-swords, on which the Renascence, the following styles, and Modern art, have found ample opportunity to exercise their artistic skill. Plate 228 offers a small selection from the copious material in our armouries and collections of weapons.

PLATE 228. THE SWORD, AND ITS SCABBARD.

1—3.   Assyrian, from reliefs.

4 and 6. Egyptian.

5.   Prehistoric, bronze, found in Switzerland.

7—9.   Mediaeval, and Renascence.

10—12.   Renascence.

13—15.   Renascence, Pommel, guard, and chape, by Hans Holbein the Younger, (Formenschatz).

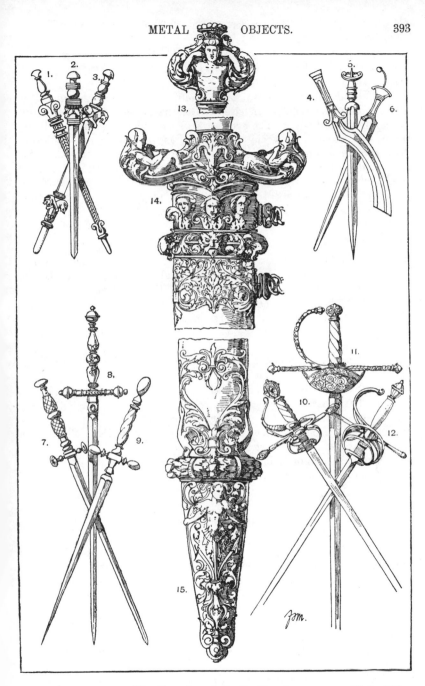

The Sword, and its Scabbard.   Plate 228.

THE DAGGER. (Plate 229.)

The Dagger is a Sword in miniature, in which the guard is either omitted or reduced in size. What has been said of the Sword will apply to the Dagger. The greatest artists of the Renascence: Holbein, Dürer, Cellini, and others, did not disdain, as the plate shows, to devote their artistic genius to this weapon, which was often worn more for fashion than for practical purposes. The "Dance of Death" (fig. 5) is a very popular motive in the decoration of the scabbards of Daggers. Considering the object of the weapon, a more pregnant and appropriate decoration can scarcely be imagined.

PLATE 229. THE DAGGER, AND ITS SCABBARD.

1.   Egyptian, blade of white bronze, handle of cedar wood, plated with gold and silver, tomb of Queen Aah - Hotep, Qurnah near Thebes (1800 B. C.), Bulak, Museum.
2.   Egyptian, blade of gold, handle of cedar wood plated with gold and incrusted with red and blue enamel, (as No. 1).
3.   Renascence, handle, end of 15th century, Basel, (Kunst im Hause).
4.   Renascence, handle, end of 15th century, Basel, (Viollet-le-Duc).
5.   Renascence, German, Basel, (Kunst im Hause).
6—8.   Designs, by Hans Holbein the Younger, (1497—1543), (Formenschatz).
9.   Designs, by Albrecht Dürer, (Formenschatz).
10.   Renascence, German, blackened iron parcel-gilt, Collection of Napoleon III, (L'art pour tous).
11.   Creese, from Sumatra, wooden handle and sheath, United collections, Carlsruhe.

THE HALBERD. (Plate 230.)

Among the multifarious utensils of war of the Middle Ages and the Renascence: we may specially mention the following: —

The Lance and the Pike, wooden shafts with a leaf or awl-shaped iron spike. (Fig. 11 shows a Pike-head of complicate shape). A small flag was often attached to the Lance just below the head.

The Partizan is a Pike with a flat blade and symmetrical lateral points (figs. 1, 4, and 5).

War - scythes and War-forks: the shapes of which are indicated by their names (figs. 3, and 7).

The Battle-axe, and Martel, are axe and hammer-shaped weapons,

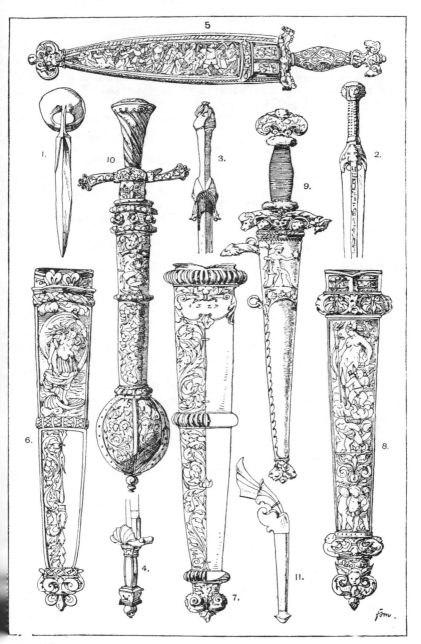

The Dagger, and its Scabbard.   Plate 229.

with one side terminating in an axe or a hammer, and the other in a point (fig. 9).

The Halberd is a combination of the Pike or Partizan with the Battle-axe (figs. 2 and 8).

The Mace is a handle with a knob of various forms; when it is set with spikes, it is called a "Morning-star", and when set with radiating blades, it is termed a Quadrelle (fig. 10).

The War-flail is distinguished from the Mace by the knob being fastened to the handle by a chain.

And so on, in endless variety.

So far as decoration is concerned: the first place is due to Halberds and Partizans; not only because the shape of the blade is frequently very varied and handsome, but also because the union with the shaft, by means of bands, nails, tassels, &c., gives an opportunity for rich colour. The blades, also, are often decorated by damaskeening, engraving, gilding, etc.

PLATE 230. THE HALBERD, &c.

1.   Partizan, richly-etched, German, 16th century, Historical Museum, Dresden, (Kunsthandwerk).
2.   Halberd, richly-etched, German, 1613, Artillery Museum, Paris, (L'art pour tous).
3.   Fauchard, richly-etched, German, 1580, Artillery Museum, Paris, (L'art pour tous).
4.   Partizan, richly-etched, German, 17th century, Artillery Museum, Paris, (L'art pour tous).
5.   Partizan, richly-etched, German, 1712, Royal Armoury, Berlin, (Kunsthandwerk).
6 and 8. Halberds.
7.   Combination of War-scythe and War-fork.
9.   Battle-axe, Hindu, United collections, Carlsruhe.
10.   Mace, so-called quadrelle, (Viollet-le-Duc).
11.   Pike.
            (The shafts have been omitted, or only partially indicated).

c. Table Utensils.

THE SPOON. (Plate 231.)

The Spoon is, strictly speaking, a dipper; and has already been alluded-to in the discussion of the group of Vessels (comp. Plate 193). It is here treated in the group of Utensils. As a table utensil the

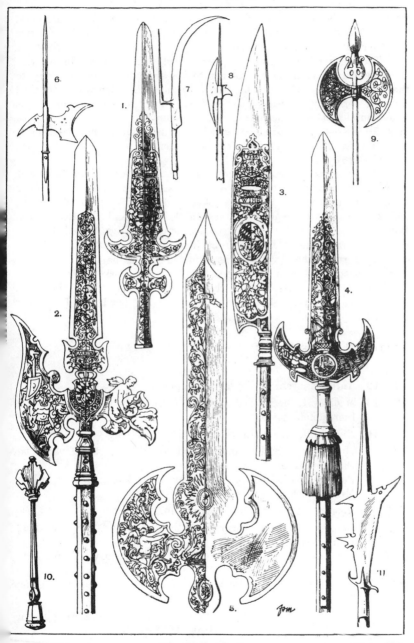

The Halberd, &c. Plate 230.

Spoon has been in use from the earliest times; its fundamental form has undergone very little alteration; although its style and size have varied in different periods.

The form of the Bowl is spherical, elliptic, or oval (in the last case the handle is usually attached to the broad end, more rarely to the narrow one). The Handle has a cylindrical, prismatic or conical tapering form, or is spatulate. Spatulate handles broaden out at the free end; and are decorated with cartouches or pierced work (figs. 26, 28—30). Prismatic, cylindrical, and conical, handles usually terminate in knobs, busts, or little whole-length figures (figs. 13—17, and 19—23).

The handles of small Antique spoons for eating shellfish, &c., often taper to a point to serve as openers. Double-spoons, as shown in fig. 24, are rare. Folding Pocket-spoons, as in figs. 18, 19, 21 and 22, are not infrequent in the Middle Ages, and the Renascence. Bowl and handle either lie in the same plane (figs. 3 and 16), or they form an angle at the point of junction (figs. 8, 10 and 11).

As a rule: the decoration is confined to the handle; where the bowl is decorated, it is with some kind of flat work (engraving, or enamelling). The materials are the precious metals, alloys, tin, bone, horn, wood, &c.; very often, the handle and the bowl are of different materials.

PLATE 231. THE SPOON.

1. Egyptian.

2—12. Antique, bronze, (ligulae), Pompeii.

13—14. Mediaeval, hammered copper, 13th century, $6\,^1/_4$ ins. long, Pierrefonds castle.

15—16. Mediaeval, tin, 12th century, $6\,^3/_4$ ins. long.

17. Mediaeval, chased and hammered brass, $5\,^1/_8$ ins. long, Pierrefonds castle.

18. Folding Pocket-spoon, 15th century, $4\,^7/_8$ ins. long, Cluny Museum, Paris, (Viollet-le-Duc).

19. Renascence, South Kensington Museum, London.

20. Renascence, silver, terminating in a Madonna, $6\,^3/_4$ ins. long, Cluny Museum, Paris.

21. German, folding Pocket-spoon, 16th century, 7 ins. long, Dziatinska collection.

22. Renascence, folding Pocket-spoon silver, $5\,^7/_8$ ins. long, Cluny Museum, Paris.

23. Renascence, bowl of agate, handle of copper gilt, $5\,^1/_8$ ins., Cluny Museum, Paris. (L'art pour tous).

24. Double-spoon, bronze, Germanisches Museum, Nuremberg.

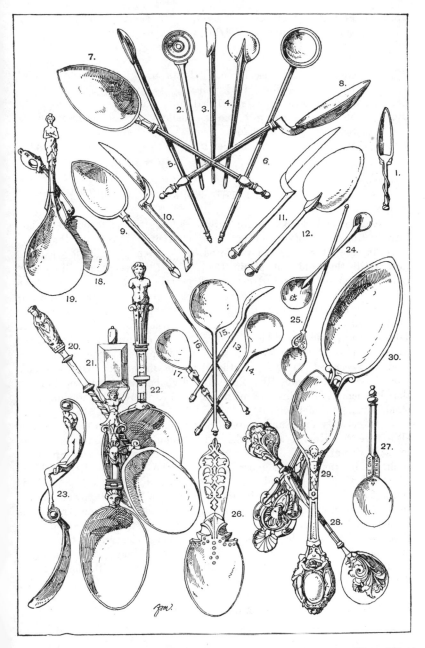

The Spoon. Plate 231.

25.   Persian, from an inkstand, 17th century, $4\,^3/_4$ ins. long,
        Duhousset collection, (L'art pour tous).
26.   Persian, 17th century, $4\,^1/_4$ ins. long, Duhousset collection,
        (L'art pour tous).
27.   German, tin, inscription: "Trink und is, Gott nit vergis",
        United collections, Carlsruhe.
28.   Modern, French, (Gewerbehalle).
29.   Modern, silver gilt and enamelled, by the architect F. O.
        Schulze, (Gewerbehalle).
30.   Modern, silver, by F. Seitz.

The Knife and the Fork. (Plate 232.)

Knives and Forks, unlike Spoons, are of comparatively late
introduction as table utensils. Although it is probable that they
were in use at a very early period as kitchen utensils for carving
food, still they did not attain the rank of a recognised dinner set
until the art of eating had reached a certain refinement. It has been
maintained that Knives and Forks appeared on dinner tables towards
the close of the Roman Empire. In our own country it can be
proved that they did not come into general use until the 15th or
16th century. This may be explained by the circumstance that in the
earlier period of the Middle ages, as at the present time in the East,
food was carried to the mouth with the fingers or with a spoon,
after having undergone the necessary division into small portions in
the kitchen. Cleanliness was ensured by frequently washing the
hands during dinner.

As regards form and material: what has been said of Spoons, is
also true for Knives and Forks. The handles are similarly shaped,
to secure uniformity in the whole set; the bowl of the Spoon is
replaced by the two, or more prongs of the Fork, or by the blade
of the Knife. The Handle is made of wood, ivory, &c., and it is
comparatively stronger as it must possess a greater power of re-
sistance because the tang or prolongation of the blade, which is
always made of steel, must be let-into it. As the Plate shows, the
shape of the blade has passed through many changes in the course
of time. To cut the "consecrated bread" the Middle Ages employed
peculiar knives, the blades of which were engraved with mottoes and
musical scales.

Plate 232. The Knife, and the Fork.

1—2.   Mediaeval, (13th—15th century), wooden handle inlaid with
        silver.

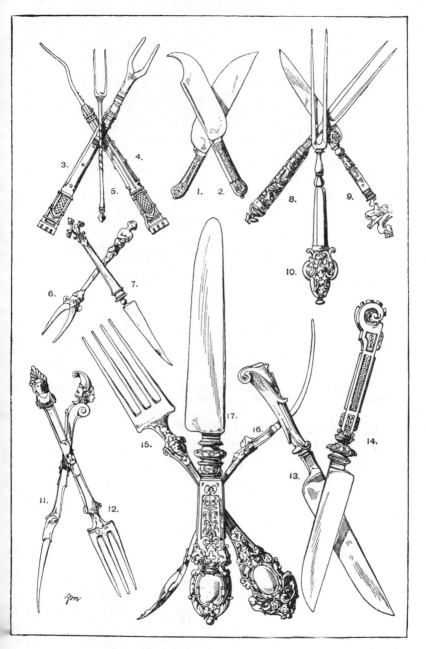

The Knife, and the Fork. Plate 232.

3—4.   Gothic, 14th century, the prongs of alloy, the handle of ivory mounted with silver, 7 $^1/_2$ ins. long, Garneray collection.

5.   Mediaeval, copper gilt, 4 $^1/_4$ ins. long, Garneray collection.

6.   Renascence, ivory, Leon Bach collection, (L'art pour tous).

7.   Renascence, South Kensington Museum, London.

8.   Renascence, Bach collection, (L'art pour tous).

9.   Renascence, Bach collection, (L'art pour tous).

10.   Barocco period, South Kensington Museum, London.

11—12. Renascence, Dresden, (Musterornamente).

13—14. Ditto.

15—16. Modern, silver gilt and enamelled, by F. O. Schulze, (Gewerbehalle).

17.   Modern, silver gilt and enamelled, by F. O. Schulze, (Gewerbehalle).

THE PAPER - KNIFE.   (Plate 233.)

Paper - knives are an invention of Modern times. As the name implies, they are used for cutting paper, the edges of books, newspapers, and letters; and they find a place on every desk.

The form is usually that of a one or two-edged Knife. As the blade does not require to be very sharp, it is generally made of the same material as the handle, and in most cases of ivory, wood, or brass.

The decoration is generally confined to the handle; the blade is at most decorated with flat enrichment.

PLATE 233.   THE PAPER - KNIFE.

1.   Modern, brass.

2 — 3. Modern, ivory or wood, by Dir. G. Kachel, (Gewerbehalle).

4—6. Modern, wood carving, by J. Eberhardt, Heilbronn.

7.   Modern, pierced metal.

THE SCISSORS.   (Plate 234.)

Scissors, intended primarily for use in ladies' work, and afterwards applied to a variety of other purposes, are mostly met-with in two different fundamental forms. The earlier form (French: *forces*), which held its ground up to the end of the Middle Ages, has a spring hoop which unites the two blades (fig. 1). The later form (French: *ciseaux*), which begins to appear sporadically as early as the 10th century, has two separate blades moveable round a central

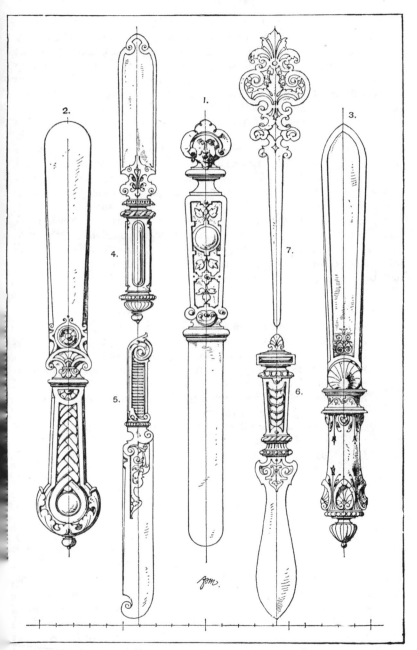

Tho Paper-Knife. Plate 233.

pivot, and terminating at one end in the blades and at the other in handles with ring-shaped eyelets to receive the fingers (figs. 2, 3, 5, 6). The shape is usually symmetrical. Variations, like fig. 4, are rare. Not infrequently, the scissors are provided with a chain by means of which they may be suspended, either alone or with other articles, from a Chatelaine. The points are sometimes protected by a guard (fig. 10). The decoration is generally confined to the handles, and frequently consists of pierced work; the blades are plain, or decorated by inlaying, &c. Where handle and blades are not of the same metal, which in this case can only be steel, the handles are often of brass or silver. Between these two extremes are gilt, silvered, and nickelled handles. The Renascence gratified its luxurious taste to the full, in the matter of Scissors; in Modern times, the plainer and simpler forms are preferred. The length of the blades varies, according to the purpose; but the size of the handles remains the same, being governed by that of the human hand; hence the proportions between the two are very various. Among Scissors which are intended for special purposes, and depart from the usual form: may be mentioned Snuffers, and "Lazy-tongs" (fig. 9).

PLATE 234.   THE SCISSORS.

1.   Renascence, Sonth Kensington Museum, London.
2.   Renascence, blades etched, handles gilt, August I of Saxony, Royal Historical Museum, Dresden, (Kunsthandwerk).
3—4. Persian, 17th century, $7\,{}^{1}/_{8}$ ins. and $6\,{}^{1}/_{4}$ ins. long, Duhousset collection, (L'art pour tous).
5.   Renascence, South Kensington Museum, London.
6.   Renascence, German, Dresden, (Musterornamente).
7.   Renascence, handles silver gilt, German (Kunsthandwerk).
8.   Snuffers, in bird form.
9.   Lazy-tongs, United collections, Carlsruhe.

THE HAND-BELL.   (Plate 235.)

In those utensils of which it may be said that as a rule they are artistically decorated beyond what is wanted for practical purposes, we may reckon the Hand-bell. During the Middle Ages and the Renascence: the Hand-bell seems to have been chiefly used in an official capacity in Council-chambers and for ecclesiastical purposes; and its introduction into ordinary households, to summon the attendants did not take place till later. In our own times, so prolific of Parliamentary and other Meetings: the Hand-bell is indispensable. The necessary parts are: the resonant Cup, the Clapper suspended in the

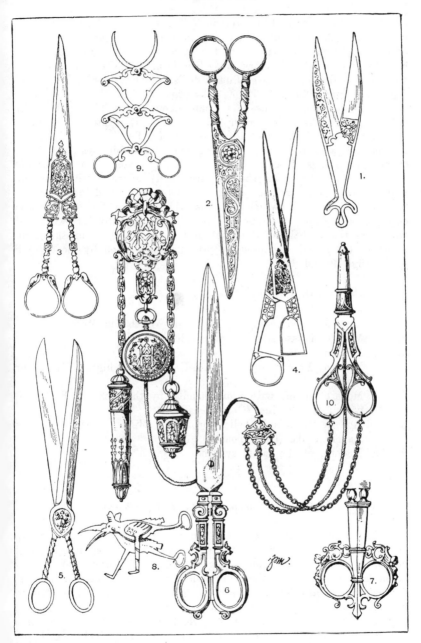

The Scissors. Plate 234.

interior of the cup, and the Handle. The two former are always of metal; the cup of an alloy, or sometimes of silver; and the clapper of iron. The handle may be of the same material as the cup, or it may be made of wood, ivory, &c. The form of the cup is generally the same as that of the large Church-bells, which is based on practical experience (figs. 2, 3). Forms like figs. 1, 5 and 6, are rarer. Hand-bells for domestic use are small (about 4 ins. high); those for official purposes are larger (up to 12 ins). The latter class often have a non-essential adjunct in the shape of a Pedestal (figs. 7 and 8). The handle takes the form of a long extended knob (figs. 2, 3, 7, 8), or of a hoop (figs. 1 and 6). The decoration extends to the handle and the cup of the bell, which is frequently adorned with heraldic bearings, and zones of inscriptions. Sometimes we find Hand-bells in the form of ladies, in which case the wide skirt of the dress is the cup (fig. 4). Cups of open-work are also occasionally met-with. Of late years the traditional Hand-bell has yielded place to another form in which the sound is caused by pressure on a knob by means of a spring (figs. 9 and 10).

PLATE 235. THE HAND-BELL.

1.   Modern, brass, from an old model.
2—3.   Renascence, bronze, $4^3/_4$ ins. high, Wiesbaden Museum.
4.   Modern, brass, after an old model.
5.   Modern, brass.
6.   Modern, French, by D. Rénard, $4^3/_4$ ins. high, (L'art pour tous).
7.   Modern, silver, with ivory handle, by the architect F. Schulz, with foot $7^7/_8$ ins. (Gewerbehalle).
8.   Modern President's bell, Town-Hall, Milan, by the architect Angelo Colla, (Gewerbehalle).
9—10. Modern, of the latest systems.

e. Various Domestic and Toilet Utensils.

The promise, which was made in the introduction to the group of utensils, to devote some plates to Domestic and Toilet utensils must not be construed as an undertaking to exhaust the whole field. Very much has already come under discussion: the utensils of Illumination, for instance, are also for the most part, domestic utensils. The following five plates will therefore, to a certain extent, bring-together from the remaining domestic utensils those which in the first place deserve consideration from the point of view of decoration, including Door-knockers, Keys, Mirrors, Fans, Tools, and Instruments. As regards

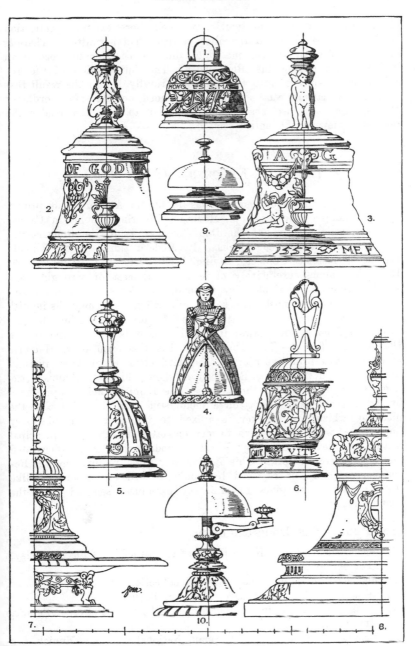

The Hand-Bell. Plate 235.

these latter objects in particular, a much more extensive collection might have been made if the allotted space had permitted. There is scarcely a Tool or Instrument which did not occasionally receive an artistic finish during the Renascence. The introduction of the so-called "master-pieces" into the Guilds, naturally led to the result that unnecessary labour was sometimes expended on the most ordinary things. But still we shall offer sufficient to give the reader the necessary view of the entire section.

THE DOOR-KNOCKER. (Plate 236.)

Although the Door-knocker was in use in Antiquity, as proved by an example (the head of Medusa with ring) found in Capua: still the strict period of the Door-knocker is in the Romanesque, Gothic, and Renascence epochs. In Modern times: it has already become a historical object, having been ousted by Bellpulls, &c. It is made almost exclusively of bronze, and cast or wrought iron. Its dimensions are variable, like those of the doors and gates themselves, to which it must bear some proportion. We may distinguish three principal classes. The first has the form of a Ring, usually suspended from a lion's jaws; in which case it is at the same time a Door-handle (figs. 1—7). The second has the form of a Hammer moveable on a primitive hinge. The third class, which arose in Italy in the best days of the Renascence, shows Figures, Animals, &c. (figs. 9 and 11). In all three classes the requisite noise is produced by the moveable part falling on a metal stud. In the third class the plate by which the knocker is affixed to the door is of subsidiary importance, while in the two former classes it is often the principal feature of the design. The Gothic period devised richly-decorated plates of pierced-work. This motive was often retained by the Renascence (fig. 4), or replaced by double-headed eagles and the like (fig. 5). The Plate gives 11 different examples, selected from the copious material.

PLATE 236. THE DOOR-KNOCKER.

1. Romanesque, bronze, North portal of the cathedral of Puy-en-Velay, 11th century.
2. Mediaeval, $7\,^7/_8$ ins. square, Soyter collection, Augsburg.
3. Renascence, $2\,^3/_4$ ins. square, Museum, Berlin.
4. Transition from Gothic to Renascence, $5\,^1/_2$ ins. square, S. Peter's, Strassburg.
5. Renascence, wrought-iron, German, National Museum, Munich.
6. Renascence, (Guichard).

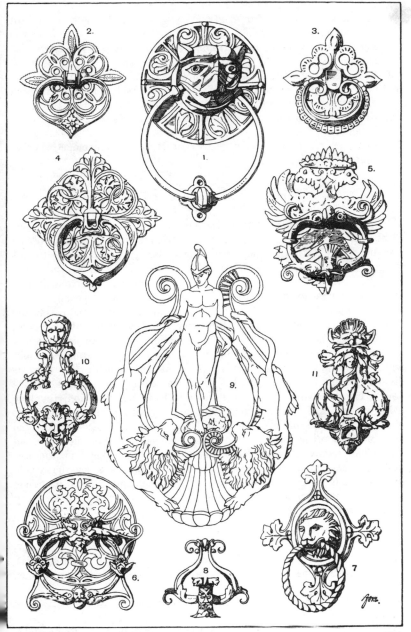

The Door-Knocker. Plate 236.

7. Mediaeval, bronze, 15th century, $8^{1}/_{2}$ ins. high, East portal of the cathedral of Noyon.
8. Renascence, wrought-iron, Dutch, $14^{1}/_{8}$ ins. high, Vermerch collection.
9. Renascence, bronze, Italian, $13^{1}/_{2}$ ins. high, David with the head of Goliath, house in Ferrara, (Vorbilder für Fabrikanten und Handwerker).
10. Renascence, bronze, Italian, 1560, South Kensington Museum, London.
11. Renascence, bronze, Italian, Austrian Museum, Vienna, (Gewerbehalle).

THE KEY. (Plate 237.)

It is not the task of this Handbook to follow the developement of the Lock through its various stages from the Antique up to the present day. It would also carry us too far if we were to attempt to go into the decorative details of the case of the lock; one plate, however shall be devoted to the Key; while the escutcheon will find its place in the group of Frames. Apart from such special designs as that shown by fig. 2, the Key usually consists of three parts: the Bow, the Stem, and the Bit. Keys may be divided into two classes, according as the stem is tubular, or is solid. The stem is generally cylindrical, or profiled; more rarely angular, or prismatic. The bit, which projects as a rectangular plate at the end of the key, is divided by notches into wards. The decoration is applied to the bow. The Pompeian key, shown in fig. 1, is an exception, the bow being smooth and the bit and stem prettily ornamented. Keys are made of iron and bronze, the stem being frequently of iron, and the bow of some other metal; the bow, and indeed the whole key, is often gilt. The palmy days of Keys were the Middle Ages and the Renascence; compared with these, our Modern keys are on the whole smaller, simpler, and, if less beautiful, are certainly more practical. Finally we may mention those colossal examples which were formerly made to serve as Signs; and are even now met-with.

PLATE 237. THE KEY.

1. Antique, Pompeii, (Blümner: Das Kunstgewerbe im Alterthum).
2. Roman, bronze, found on the Hohenkrähen, United collections, Carlsruhe.
3. Romanesque, bronze, United collections, Carlsruhe.
4—5. Renascence, (Kunst und Gewerbe).
6—8. Renascence, Museo Medio Evo e Rinascimento, Rome, (Gewerbehalle).

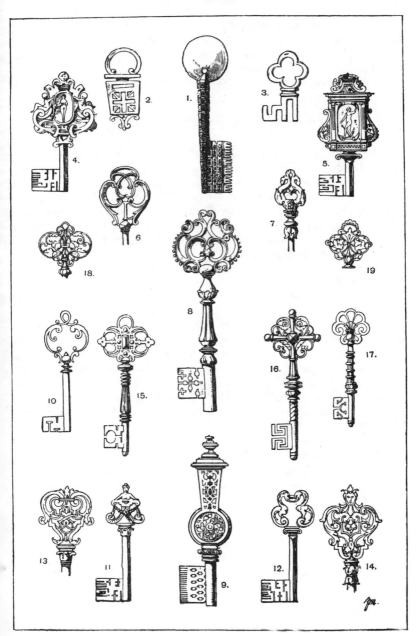

The Key.

Plate 237.

THE HAND-MIRROR. (Plate 238.)

The first place in the series of ladies' toilet requisites belongs to the Hand-mirror. Its history falls into two periods. In Antiquity and in the earlier years of the Middle Ages: mirrors were made of polished metal, either bronze or silver. About the 13th century, glass begins to be used, the reflecting surface being backed with metal foil. The Antique, and particulary the Etruscan mirrors, of which a large number have been preserved to us, show engraved ornaments and figures from mythology and daily life, mostly of primitive, but sometimes of excellent, workmanship. Glass mirrors are, generally, flat. The fundamental shape of the Antique mirror is circular or spatulate (figs. 1—6); and that of the glass mirror is circular or elliptical (figs. 8 and 9). The plastic decoration of Antique mirrors is confined to the handle, and the frame. The handle and frame may be of a great variety of materials, wood, ivory, or metal. Here, too, it is the Renascence which shows the richest decoration. Where the decoration consists of figures, these are in keeping with the object; and show Amorini and Aphroditic personages. With the increasing use of wall or plate-glass mirrors, the Hand-mirror has lost much of its former importance; so that modern art no longer devotes much attention to it.

PLATE 238.   THE HAND-MIRROR.

1.   Egyptian, bronze, United collections, Carlsruhe.
2.   Egyptian, bronze, handle of carved wood, British Museum, London.
3—4. Greek, bronze.
5.   Pompeian.
6—7. Etruscan, engraved figures, handles lost.
8.   Renascence, (Kunst und Gewerbe).
9.   Renascence, by Etienne de Laulne (1549 to 1583), (Wessely).

THE FAN. (Plate 239.)

The Fan is undoubtedly the most interesting of all toilet requisites. Its history can be traced back uninterruptedly for 3000 years, although

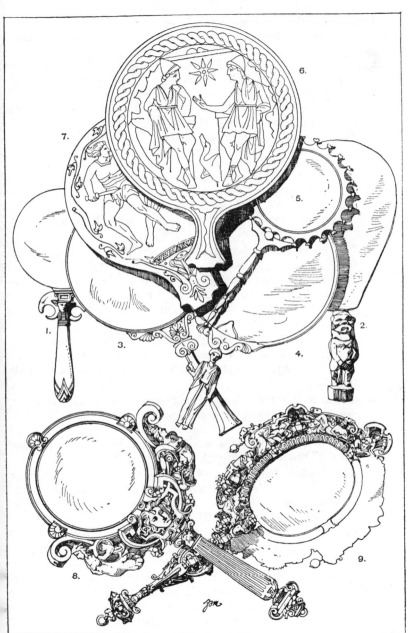

The Hand-Mirror. Plate 238.

it did not enjoy the same measure of popularity in every period. It alone would almost suffice to furnish a historical picture of the artistic and technical developement of industrial art through all periods. The object of the Fan is twofold. Firstly, it is used to direct a current of cool air to the face; and secondly, to keep off flies and other insects. From its first use it derives its Latin name of *"flabellum"* (from *flare* = to blow, French *"éventail"*); from its second use its Latin name *"muscarium"* (from *musca* = a fly, French *"esmouchoir"*). Fans of this latter class are usually called "Fly-flappers". Occasionally, the fan is used to blow the fire (as in ancient Persia, where the blowing of the fire with the lips was forbidden for religious reasons); and as a Symbol of dignity in ecclesiastical and court ceremonies. A consideration of its purpose renders it obvious that it is chiefly employed in the hotter countries of the globe.

The manifold forms of the fan may be reduced to 5 different principal types:

1. The Fixed Fan: a leaf immovably attached to a handle (figs. 6—9).

2. The Pennon Fan: attached to the side of the handle, and movable round it in a horizontal direction (figs. 10 and 11). The forms and materials of the fixed and the pennon fan are of the utmost variety.

3. The Radial Fan: a rectangle of paper, silk or some other material, fastened to a handle in such a manner that it may be folded together and spread out in the form of a circle (fig. 12).

4. The Lamellar fan: pieces of stiff material e. g. slips of ivory, are connected together at one end by a pin, which serves as the axis. They are collapsible into a narrow shape, and may be opened-out to a semi-circle. They are held-together by a ribbon drawn through them (fig. 13).

5. The Folding fan: distinguished from the preceding by the lamellæ being covered by a sheet of paper, silk, &c., which is folded-together or spread-out by the opening of the sticks which compose the frame (fig. 14).

It appears from this that the Fixed, the Pennon, and the Radial fans have handles, while the Lamellar and the Folding fans have not. The Radial fan, being a folding fan with a handle, is a kind of intermediate form. The size of the fan varies according to fashion and the purpose for which it is intended, regard being usually paid to convenience of handling; as a general rule, it may be said that the firmer, stiffer and more impervious to air the fan is: the smaller it may be. Fans for cooling should have a short, broad form, Fly-flappers require a longer, narrower shape.

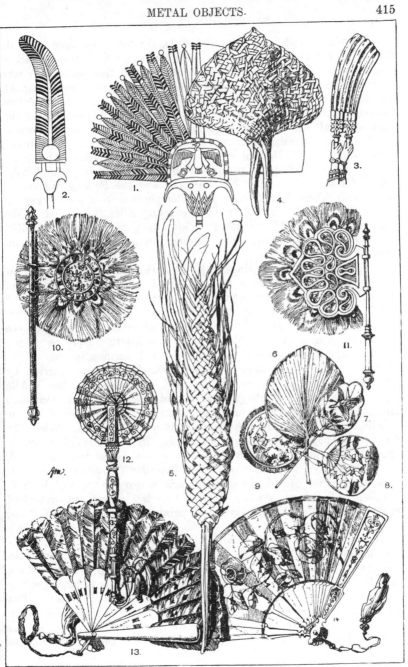

The Fan.

Plate 239.

On the subject of history and style, the following may be said: The Fixed fan is the oldest and most primitive. Its natural model is a leaf on a stalk, just as savages at the present time make their fans of dried palm-leaves or of plaited work in the form of leaves (fig. 4). The feather may also be regarded as a natural model, and hence its frequent application to fans of every kind. The Pennon fan is the least practical, its domain is the Middle Ages and the early Renascence, together with certain parts of the East (India, Turkey, Morocco, Tunis, &c.). The Radial fan was also in use in the Middle ages (with a long handle), and down to the present time in certain parts of Italy, Persia, China, and Japan. The Lamellar and the Folding fan are of later date. Their introduction is contemporaneous with the general use of the fan in Europe (15th century). After the period of the lamellar fan in the 17th century, follows the golden age of the folding fan in the Rococo period. The Folding fan is also the predominant form in Modern times.

Egyptian mural paintings and Assyrian reliefs frequently show Fan‑bearers, with larger or smaller Fly‑flappers, in the retinue of the kings. The most common Egyptian forms are given in figs. 1 and 2, the Assyrian in fig. 3. Scarcely any vestige has been preserved of Antique Fans. Judging by the pictures on vases, &c., the Greek Fan consisted of a leaf, cut to a palmette‑shape, on a long handle. The Roman ladies were somewhat luxurious in the matter of fans, which they either managed themselves or had carried by slaves; and under the Emperors the men were also. In the Middle Ages, the fan entered into the service of the church; deacons and ministrans kept-off flies from the consecrated host by means of the flabella, which often took the form of six-winged seraphs. When the fan became popular for secular purposes, its use was given up in churches. As already observed, the Renascence passed from the Fixed, to the Lamellar and Folding fan. The Lamellar fan offered numerous opportunities for carved and pierced work in ivory, horn, tortoiseshell, filigree, and enamel work. The Folding fan offered an unlimited field for decoration by painting; and painters, like Boucher, Watteau, and others, devoted themselves to fan‑painting (pastoral scenes &c.). During this period the "Puzzle-fan" was invented, which shows different pictures according to the way it is folded. Lace fans, fans with mirrors, monograms, and autographs, and the bespangled Empire-fans, complete the category. The Modern ball-room fan is a large Folding fan generally decorated with naturalistic paintings of flowers. But all possible forms ara occasionally used. France, China, and Japan supply the fan market. Heinrich Frauberger, who has written a most valuable monograph on the Fan*, maintains that the latter countries

---

* *H. Frauberger:* "Die Geschichte des Fächers." *Leipzig: K. Scholtze.*

alone manufacture between them about $^3/_4$ of the 400 million fans which are annually made on the globe.

Finally we may briefly enumerate the materials which are principally used in the manufacture of fans. They are: bamboo, palm-leaves, wood, bone, horn, ivory, tortoise-shell, mother-of-pearl, metal, paper, straw and other plaited material, silk, lace, gelatine, mica, leather, feathers, &c.

PLATE 239. THE FAN.

1. Egyptian, Fly-flapper, feathers, handle omitted.
2. Egyptian, feather-fan.
3. Assyrian, Fly-flapper, from a relief, British Museum.
4. Modern, Fly-flapper, plaited palm-leaves, South Caroline Islands, (Frauberger).
5. Modern, Fly-flapper, plaited palm-leaves, United collections, Carlsruhe.
6. Modern, palm-leaf, cut and bound at the edge.
7—8. Modern, Japanese, bamboo and paper.
9. Modern, printed paper with silk fringe and gilt wooden handle.
10. Modern, Siamese, handle of whipped wood, centre of pasteboard, decorated with rosettes and bordered with peacock feathers, United collections, Carlsruhe.
11. Modern, Hindu, handle of wood, centre of pasteboard covered with silk, braid, and butterfly wings, bordered with peacock feathers, (Frauberger).
12. Mediaeval, Radial-fan, French, (Viollet-le-Duc).
13. Modern, Folding-fan, wood and grouse feathers.
14. Modern, Folding-fan, wood, painted silk, and gold.

VARIOUS TOOLS. (Plate 240.)

Among the Tools and Instruments which only occasionally or accidentally receive an artistic finish we may mention: Hammers, Tongs, Compasses, Cocks, Pestles, Hour-glasses, and Clocks, along with many other things. No attempt can be made here to treat these articles in detail. But it may be said that, in general, the highly-decorated examples have been specially made for State-occasions, e. g. the Hammer (fig. 1), with which Pope Julius III inaugurated the Jubilee year (1550) by knocking three times on the walled-up main-portal of S. Peter's, as a sign that it should be opened.

Plate 240 exhibits a number of such objects.

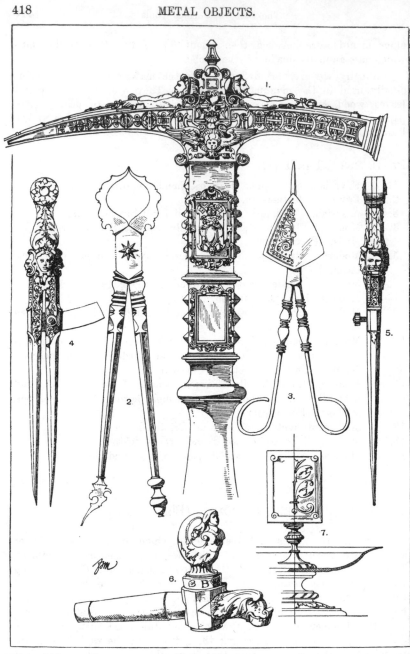

Plate 240.   Various Tools.

PLATE 240. VARIOUS TOOLS.

1. Ceremonial-Hammer, silver gilt, Italian, 16th century, presented by Gregory XIII to Duke Ernest of Bavaria, beneath the enamelled armorial bearings is the inscription: "Julius III Pont. Max. Jubilaeum VIII condidit feliciter MCCCCCL.; the relief on the reverse shows Moses striking water from the rock, with the words: Percussit petram et fluxerunt aquae", National Museum, Munich; (Kunsthandwerk).

2. Tongs, iron, German, Germanisches Museum, Nuremberg.

3. Snuffers, brass, German, Renascence, Germanisches Museum, Nuremberg.

4—5. Compasses, bronze, chased, engraved, and gilt, German, 16th century, half the size of the original.

6. Cock, brass, cast and chased, German, 16th century, $11^{3}/_{4}$ ins. long, (Vorbilder für die Kleinkunst in Bronze).

7. Match-holder, bronze, Modern.

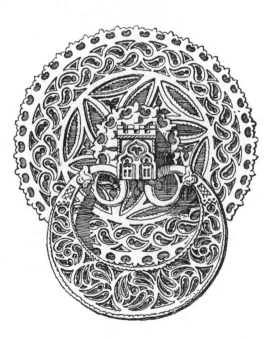

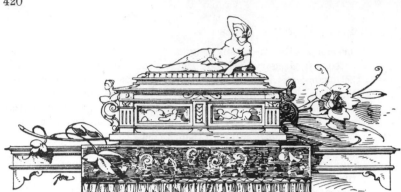

C.

FURNITURE.

Furniture, in its broader sense, is a collective name for all kinds of household goods and chattels. It is more strictly confined to such objects as Chairs, Tables, Wardrobes, &c. But even in this narrower sense the examples of Furniture are so numerous that it is not possible to give a detailed description and discussion of each individual article on the 20 Plates which are devoted to this group. And it is the less necessary to do this as our object is only to give a view of the application of decoration to furniture in general. We show a series of the more important articles, while others, such as Pianos, and Wardrobes, have been omitted. They have been so grouped that Plates 241 to 250 contain the different varieties of Chairs, while the following 10 Plates are devoted to Tables, Cabinets, Bedsteads, Cradles, &c.

The examples have been chiefly taken from the Antique, the Renascence, and Modern times; while the Middle Ages, the Barocco and Rococo periods have only occasionally been taken into account. That particular attention has been paid to the German Renascence, is based on the fact, that this period is specially distinguished for its achievements in the field of richly-decorated furniture.

This chapter might seem to offer an inducement to give a historical account of the development of tectonic form in the different periods of art. But to do this, with any thoroughness, would also require us to abandon the conciseness we have hitherto maintained; and we will therefore only refer the reader to the details in Semper: *"Der Stil"*, and to the highly-interesting work by Georg Hirth: *"Das Deutsche Zimmer der Gothik und Renaissance, des Barock-, Rokoko-, und Zopfstils"* (G. Hirth, Munich and Leipzig). The necessary information about the furniture of the Egyptians, Assyrians, Greeks, and Romans will be found in Ménard et Sauvageot: *"La Vie Privée des Anciens";* and about the Middle ages in Viollet-le-Duc: *"Dictionnaire Raisonné du Mobilier Français";* from both of which works we have taken numerous examples for our Plates. Besides these, there is such a number of cyclopaedic works on this subject that it is impossible even to name them all here.

a. Seats.

As regards Seats: the fundamental form has generally been dependent on the special purpose, and on the ever-varying mode of life; while the details have been influenced by the artistic taste of the time, and by the material used. Definite fundamental types often recur by the side of new and arbitrary special forms; and we have attempted a classification according to these fundamental forms.

The simplest and most primitive form, although for many purposes the least comfortable, is that of the Taboret or Ottoman, which is without a back. The Chair is more comfortable because of the addition of the back; and it becomes still more so, when arms are added. To this group belongs the Throne, which in view of its purpose is more monumental in form, and richer in material. Revolving, folding, and rocking Chairs meet the demand for special purposes. The Stall, and the "Prie-dieu" also have peculiar accessories, due to their being used for other purposes than sitting. The Bench and the Couch offer a seat or repose for several persons simultaneously.

In spite of the variety of forms, one feature is common to nearly all, namely, the height of the seat. In order to sit comfortably, the feet should just reach the ground, and the height of the seat is therefore from 15 ins. to 18 ins. The depth of the seat shows greater variations, from 12 ins. to 24 ins. The height of the back varies from 30 ins. and more; the fact having to be taken into consideration that the head, when it is leant back, should have a proper support. The upper surface of the arms should be about 12 ins. above that of the seat. Straight, upright backs are less comfortable than curved lines adapted to the vertebral curve. Similarly: flat, horizontal seats are not so suitable as those which slope downwards towards the back.

The principal materials are wood, cane, and metal; stone, terracotta, &c., are rarer. As it is unpleasant to rest against a hard

material for any length of time, recourse is had to cane, or flexible
seats, skins, cushions, and upholstering. In course of time, chairs
have become more comfortable with the progress of comfort in general.
It may be specially emphasized that the handsomest and most richly-
decorated seats are not usually the most practical; further remarks
are reserved for the discussion of the different forms.

THE CHAIR   (Plates 241—243.)

The Chair is a stool with a back to it. The most usual form
has four legs. Sometimes the legs are connected-together by braces
or ties, which are called Foot-rails. The seat generally has the shape
of an oblong, a square, or a trapezium. Circular and polygonal seats
are less common. Hexagonal and octagonal Seats, with a corresponding
number of legs, begin to appear in the 13th century; and certain
wooden chairs of the Renascence have seats in the form of regular
or semi-regular polygons (Plate 242. 3, 5, 6). The legs are prismatic
or turned, frequently with claw feet, while the top of the back
terminates in knobs, animal-heads, or masks (Plates 241. 1; 242. 1;
243. 4, 5, 6). Instead of legs, the seats of the wooden chairs of the
Renascence are sometimes supported by perforated and carved boards,
either at the two sides or in front and behind (Plate 242. 3, 5, 6).
Where the back is carved out of a single piece, as is the case with
many Renascence and Modern chairs, the two hinder legs have the
same form and height as the front legs (Plates 242. 7, 8; 243. 1).
Very often the back is treated as a frame (Plate 241. 5, 8, 10),
or is bent into a cylindrical plan, as in the Greek "klismos" (Plate 241.
6, 7), and its imitation, the Empire chair (Plate 241. 11). Openings
for the hand are made in carved wooden backs for convenience in
moving (Plate 242. 7, 8, 9). Where the top of the back is horizontal, it is often crowned with a cornice or an ornament (Plates 242. 6;
243. 9). Where the seat, alone or in conjunction with the back, is
of woven cane-work or padded, the Chair is termed a "cane" or an
"upholstered" chair. Sometimes not only the padding but also the
entire structure of the chair is upholstered in some material, just as,
on the other hand, chairs may be made entirely of cane or rushes.
The seats and backs of upholstered chairs are covered with leather, or
textiles (Plate 243. 6). The overlaying of wood with metal occurs in
the Assyrian style, and occasionally in later periods; the State-
chairs of the Middle Ages, especially the Byzantine, are not infrequently decorated with coloured stones; a similar treatment may be
observed in the Renascence example (Plate 242 figs. 5, and 6). In
addition to the decoration by carving (which will always be the chief

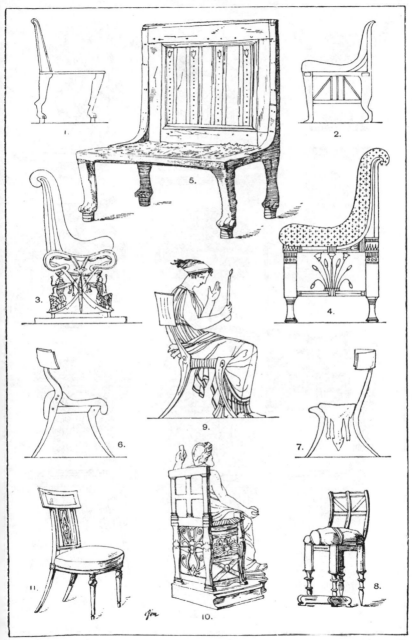

The Chair.

Plate 241.

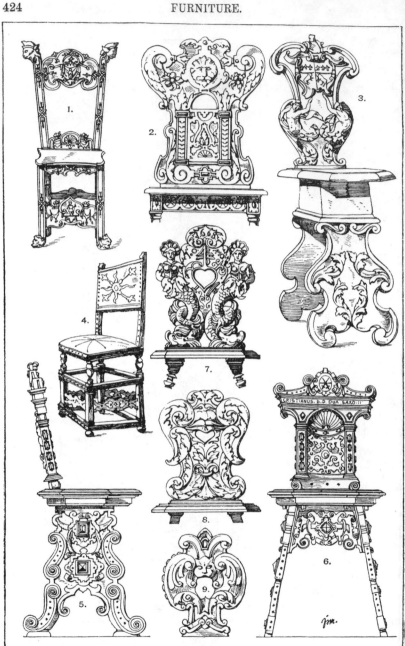

Plate 242. The Chair.

material of common frames), we find inlays of bone, (the socalled "Certosina work" of the 15 th century), metal, &c.

PLATE 241. THE CHAIR.

1—2. Egyptian, (Ménard et Sauvageot).
3.   Egyptian, mural painting, tomb of Ramses III, Thebes, (Ménard et Sauvageot).
4.   Egyptian, upholstered with patterned material, British Museum.
5.   Egyptian, British Museum.
6—7. Greek, draped with skin, "Klismos" form, (Ménard et Sauvageot).
8.   Antique, with cushions and foot-stool, Pompeian, (Ménard et Sauvageot).
9.   Greek, vase, painting.
10.   Antique, with statue of Jupiter, (Ménard et Sauvageot).
11.   French Empire period, (Gallien).

PLATE 242. THE CHAIR.

1.   German, Renascence, wood, Moreau collection, (L'art pour tous).
2.   Flemish, wood, 17th century, (L'art pour tous).
3.   Italian, wood, 16th century, (L'art pour tous).
4.   Dutch, upholstered in leather, (Crispin van den Passe, 1642).
5—6. German, decorated with stones, Renascence, Museum, Dresden.
7—8. German, 17th century, (Gewerbehalle).
9.   German, 17th century, Germanisches Museum, Nuremberg.

PLATE 243. THE CHAIR.

1.   Modern, "Inn-chair", by Dir. Kachel, (Gewerbehalle).
2—3. Modern, cane, (Gewerbehalle).
4—7. Modern, (Gewerbehalle).
8.   Renascence, (Raguenet).
9.   Modern, (Gewerbehalle).

THE THRONE, AND THE ARM-CHAIR.   (Plates 244—245.)

Thrones and Arm-chairs have been grouped-together, because the former almost always have the same form as the latter, and there is no essential difference since the time of the Renascence. The Throne, being the Seat-of-honour, has naturally, from the earliest periods, received more attention and decoration. It is planned on a larger and more monumental scale than the ordinary Chair. For this reason, and also because it does not require to be so often moved as common

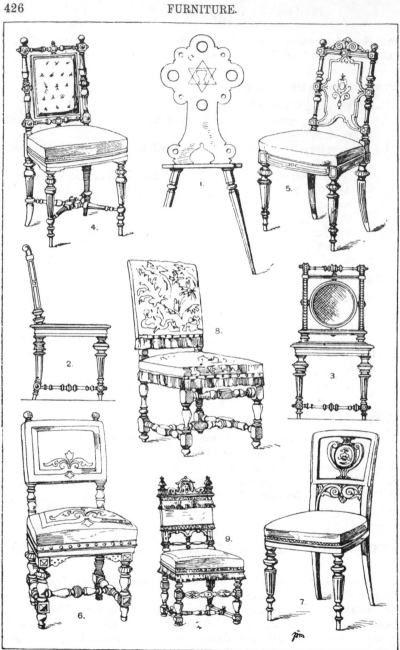

Plate 243. The Chair.

Chairs, it is often made of marble, metal, &c. Very often it is raised on a Dais, with steps, or a Foot-stool is placed in front of it; not infrequently it is covered by a Baldacchino or canopy, with Hangings, or a Cornice. This is especially the case with those for royal personages and bishops in the Middle Ages. As regards the decoration: figures and symbols may be added to the other decorations of the frame.

The Arm-chair, in its simplest form, is distinguished from the ordinary Chair by the addition of arms, which are generally supported from the fore-legs, and connected with the back, whereas in the case of the throne, when the material is stone, the arms are made in one solid piece with the whole. Compared with the ordinary Chair, the Arm-chair is larger, and more conducive to repose. Where it is intended to serve as the Seat-of-honour for the head of the family, or a chairman, it corresponds in style to other Chairs of the set, and only differs from them in its size and its richer finish. The furniture of our modern drawing-rooms generally consists of 4 or 6 chairs, with 2 easy-chairs, &c.

In addition to the Egyptian and Assyrian thrones, and the Roman State-chair, the "Sella Curulis": we may mention as belonging to this group. the Norwegian stall of the 12th century (Plate 245, 1), and the polygonal chair enclosed by a lattice, as shown by fig. 5 of the same Plate.

PLATE 244   THE THRONE, AND THE ARM-CHAIR.

1. Egyptian Throne, with lotus ornament, the arms formed by the wings of the sacred hawk, (Teirich).
2. Ancient Persian Throne, bas-relief, Persepolis, the decoration represents a king sitting on his throne borne-up by slaves, (Ménard et Sauvageot).
3. Assyrian Throne, relief, (Ménard et Sauvageot).
4. Greek Priest's-chair, marble, by the door of the temple of Themis, Athens, (Raguenet).
5. Greek Judge's-chair (proëdra), marble, found on the site of the Prytaneum, Athens.
6. Antique Bath-chair, (sella balnearis), the openings served to admit the vapour, (Ménard et Sauvageot).
7. Greek Arm-chair, relief of a tomb, representing the deceased on the thronos.
8. Greek Throne, Harpy Monument, from Xanthos in Lycia, British Museum.
9. Roman Arm-chair, with decoration symbolic of Ceres, (Ménard et Sauvageot).

10. Roman Arm-chair, found in Herculaneum, Museum at Portici, (Raguenet).
11. Antique terracotta, representing an Arm-chair in the form of the hollowed-out body of a sphinx, (L'art pour tous).
12. Chair of S. Peter, wood with ivory reliefs iilustrating the story of Hercules, S. Peter's at Rome, (Ménard et Sauvageot).

PLATE 245.   THE THRONE, AND THE ARM-CHAIR.

1. Norwegian Stall, 12th century, from Bö, Telemark.
2. Mediaeval Arm-chair, with foot-stool and draped back, (Viollet-le-Duc).
3. King David's Arm-chair, 13th century, from relief, portal of cathedral, Auxerre, (Viollet-le-Duc).
4. Frame of Mediaeval arm-chair, iron, the drapery omitted, (Viollet-le-Duc).
5. Mediaeval polygonal chair, painting, chapel in Toulouse, (Viollet-le-Duc).
6. Mediaeval Arm-chair, metal, the drapery omitted, 13th century, (Viollet-le-Duc).
7. Mediaeval Arm-chair, decorated with fringe, end of the 15th century, bas-relief, stalls, Amiens, (Viollet-le-Duc).
8. English Arm-chair, 16th century, wood, upholstered.
9. Arm-chair, Louis XVI style, wood carved and gilded, (Williamson).
10. Modern Arm-chair.
11. Modern Arm-chair.   (Raguenet).

THE STALL.   (Plate 246.)

The rows of seats along the north, west, and south sides of the Choir in chapels, &c., are termed Stalls. They have a peculiar construction corresponding to their special use. In the earliest period of the Middle Ages the single seats to the right and left of the bishop's chair were built into the wall of the chancel, at a later period they were replaced by moveable seats; and these again, from about the 13th century onwards, were replaced by Stalls, strictly so-called; the seats being united in a continuous row, with an architectonic character and construction. There are generally two rows, one behind the other, and the hinder row is a little elevated. Partitions divide the seats from one another; and serve as arms. Between the partitions are the seats. These are either fixed or arranged to fold back. In the latter case a console-like projection is attached to the underside of the seat, to serve as a kind of rest when the seat is folded-back; thus, out of *pity* for the aged monks, rendering it possible to rest

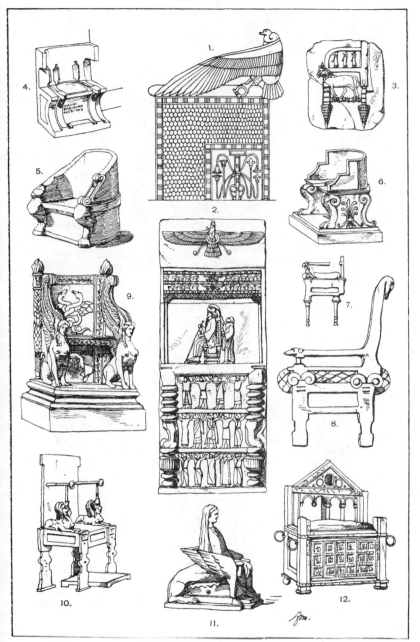

The Throne, and the Arm-chair.

Plate 244.

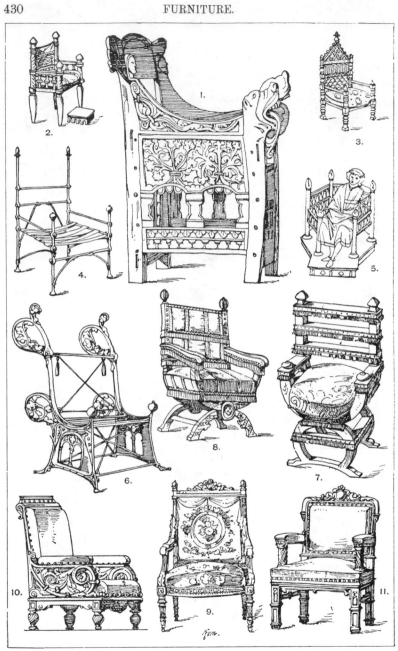

Plate 245.   The Throne, and the Arm-chair.

while appearing to stand; hence the significant name of these supports, "miserere". The backs of the hinder row of seats form a Screen; and are usually decorated with carving, intarsia, &c.; and are furnished with a canopy. In front of the seat, there is generally a kneeling-stool. Where there are several rows of seats, the prayer-desks of the one row serve at the same time as the backs of the next lower row. When the front rows are interrupted by passages leading to the hinder rows, the Stall-ends are richly decorated.

A large number of magnificent Stalls of the Gothic, and still more of the Renascence period, have been preserved in England, Germany, France, Italy, and elsewhere, To enumerate them all would take too long. Enormous pains have frequently been lavished on these works. Rich ornamental and architectural motives alternate with representations from Bible history and the legends of the saints; secular and satirical compositions are also no rarity; so that Stalls are altogether of high importance for the history of art as well as of civilisation. To exemplify what has been said, the Plate gives a few examples, which are far from being among the most sumptuous.

PLATE 246. THE STALL.

1. Sta. Maria Novella, Florence, decorated with intarsias, by Baccio d'Agnolo, end of the 15th century, (Teirich).

2. Side-view, and section of above.

3. Laurentian Library, Florence, beginning of the 16th century, said to be by Michelangelo, (Gewerbehalle).

4. Side-view, and section of the central row, great church, Dortrecht, Dutch Renascence.

5. Modern French, Convent of Elisabeth, Fourvières near Lyons, Artect Leo, (Raguenet).

THE STOOL. (Plate 247.)

The simplest seat is the Taboret or Stool, which is the chair without a back. As our Plate shows, it has been in use from the earliest times. The most primitive, and at the same time the most stable, is probably the round seat with three legs; the Egyptian example, (fig. 2), may be regarded as the prototype of the modern Cobbler's-stool. The Plasterer's-stool, which has only one leg, is indeed still simpler; and bears some resemblance to our modern Walking-stick Camp-stools. The four-legged Taboret is generally square, and possesses the same features as the lower part of a Chair. It is made with or without upholstery, and with or without foot-rails. Here,

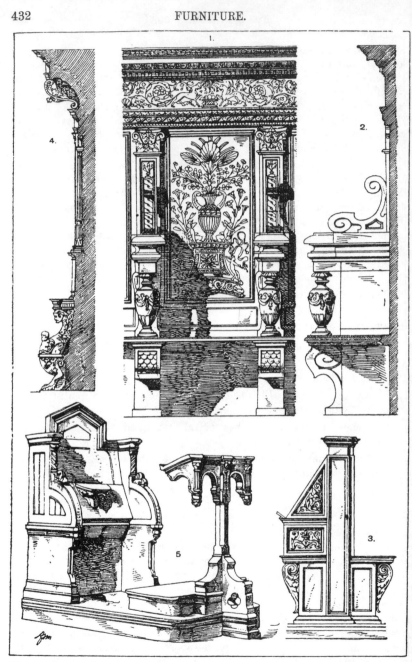

Plate 246. The Stall.

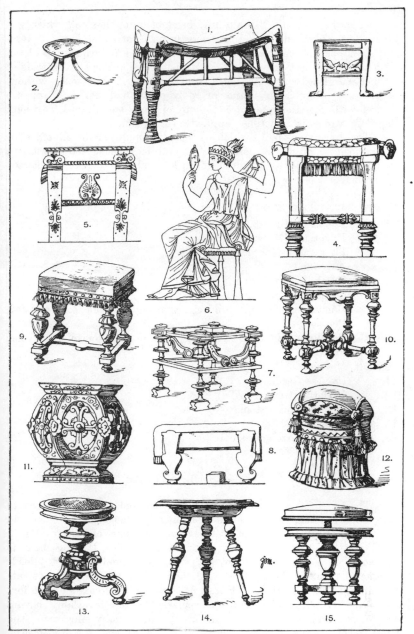

The Stool.   Plate 247.

too, we may group, the "Bisellium", or Roman double-stool, which was granted as a distinction, and was mostly made of metal (fig. 7). Box-stools, supported on boards instead of legs, are furnished with an opening in the seat to enable them to be moved. The Garden-seats of burned and glazed clay, introduced from China (fig. 11) are made without backs; and, from their round or polygonal ¡fundamental plan, are classed with the Taborets; also the upholstered and draped treatment (fig. 12), which is sometimes applied to a commode.

The Revolving-stool, which is chiefly employed in an office or for performers of music, permits of lateral movement, and adjustment to different heights as required (figs. 13 and 15). This is effected by means of a screw.

PLATE 247. THE STOOL.

1.   Egyptian, British Museum.
2.   Egyptian, (Ménard et Sauvageot).
3.   Etruscan, (Ménard et Sauvageot).
4.   Assyrian.
5.   Greek, vase-painting.
6.   Greek, vase-painting.
7.   Roman Bisellium, bronze, covering of the seat omitted, Pompeii.
8.   Bisellium of L. M. Faustus, tomb of Naevoleia Tyche, Pompeii.
9—10. Modern.
11.   Chinese Garden-seat.
12.   Modern, (Gewerbehalle).
13.   Modern Music-stool.
14.   Modern.
15.   Modern Revolving-stool.

THE FOLDING-CHAIR.   (Plate 248.)

The idea of a Chair which could be folded-together so as to take up less room, and be more conveniently transported, is an old one. The principle is found as early as the time of Ramses III in the Egyptian chair shown on Plate 241. 3. The Folding-chair is common in the Antique, either with four legs combined and joined-together like a saw-horse (figs. 1, 2, and 4), or with crossing struts combined to form a ribbed chair. Antique Folding-chairs of the for-mer kind (Diphros okladias) are remarkable for invariably having claw feet, sometimes turned outwards, but usually inwards. The ribbed chair, which recurs in the Middle Ages and the Renascence, scarcely admits of decoration, and is, therefore, mostly plain.

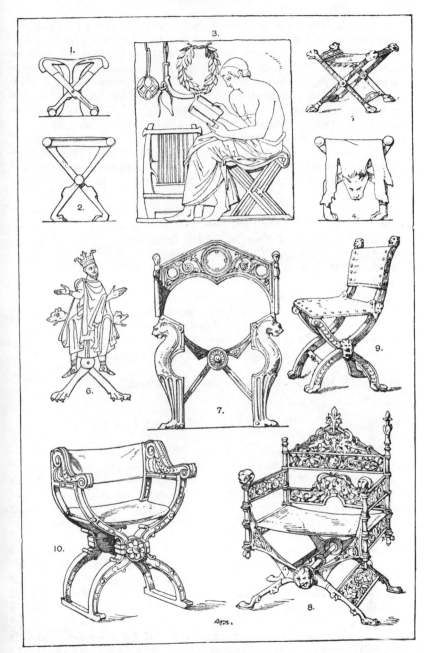

The Folding-Chair. Plate 248.

The Folding-chair may be a Stool, a Chair, or an Arm-chair. Sometimes it can be folded-up as it stands, like our iron Folding-chairs for use in the open air; sometimes it must be taken to pieces before it can be folded-up, like the chair shown on fig. 8. The most suitable material is metal (bronze or iron). Folding-chairs of wood are very often so constructed as not to fold at all, but are merely imitations with the purpose overlooked (fig. 10). The seat is frequently of bands, either textile or leather. Where the seat is not flexible, it must be arranged to be moveable by means of hinges.

Thrones have been sometimes made like Folding-chairs. We may also mention: the Camp-stools for tourists, sportsmen, painters, &c. The principles of decoration are sufficiently elucidated by the figures of the Plate.

PLATE 248. THE FOLDING-CHAIR.

1. Egyptian, tomb of Chambali, 18th dynasty.
2. Antique, (Diphros okladias).
3. Greek, tomb of an agonothetes, found in Krissa, (Delphi).
4. Antique.
5. Mediaeval, Nonnenberg, (Mothes).
6. Mediaeval, miniature painting, representing King Nabuchodonosor, 9th or 10th century, (Viollet-le-Duc).
7. Mediaeval, bronze gilt, Throne of Dagobert, restored.
8. Mediaeval, bronze, 12th century, (Viollet-le-Duc).
9. Renascence.
10. French Renascence, Sens cathedral, (Raguenet).

THE BENCH. (Plate 249.)

The Bench is an elongated seat, usually intended for several persons. In its simplest form, as a board with four legs, it was already known in Antiquity. In the Middle Ages and the Renascence, it was in general use; and was employed not only as a seat, but as a table, as is shown by such terms as "work-bench", &c. The Bench-seat was afterwards furnished with a back and arms, the back being frequently formed like the canopy over stalls (fig. 7). It was upholstered with cushions and draped with textiles. The material is generally wood; but in public buildings there are also Benches made of stone. This latter material and iron, frequently combined with wood, are the most suitable for benches in the open air. A further variety is formed by the Double-bench, with a back in the middle; this back is moveable, as shown in the example (fig. 3).

As the Bench, in most cases, is intended for every-day use, it is generally undecorated. Those of the Middle Ages are more the

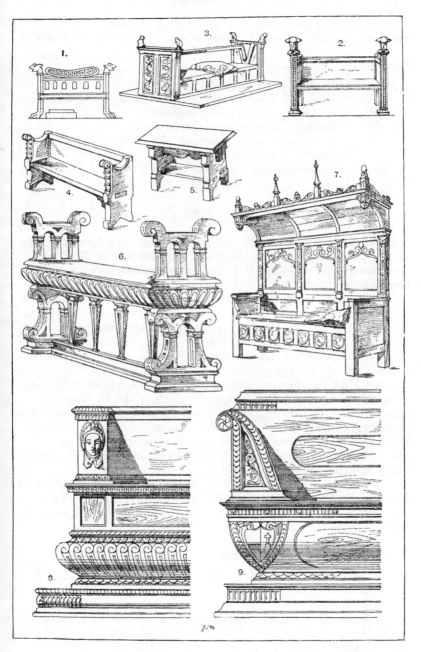

The Bench. Plate 249.

work of the carpenter than that of the cabinet-maker, but the Renascence, especially in Italy, has created some finely-decorated examples.

PLATE 249. THE BENCH.

1, 2, 4 and 5. Middle ages, (Viollet-le-Duc).
3.   Mediaeval, double with moveable back, for use in front of the fireplace, (Viollet-le-Duc).
6.   Renascence, with arms, (Ducerceau).
7.   Renascence, with canopied back, church at Flavigny, French, (Viollet-le-Duc).
8—9.   Renascence, with podium, Italian, (Teirich).

THE SOFA, AND THE COUCH. (Plate 250.)

The Sofa and the Couch are among upholstered furniture what the bench is among wooden furniture. By the side of forms which are nothing more than elongated Chairs, occur others which have more the character of the Bed. The intention of these pieces of furniture is therefore to be found in their availability for both lying and sitting. According as the one or the other object becomes predominant, the symmetrical form (figs. 4—7), or the unsymmetrical form with strongly marked head (figs. 1 and 8), is employed. In accordance with the double object, the arms are frequently treated as cylindrical cushions (fig. 7), or upholstered with cushions (fig. 6).

Although furniture of this nature was not unknown to the Antique, as shown by the Roman examples (figs. 1 and 2), these articles cannot be said to have come into common use before the last three centuries; and now-a-days the sofa is found in every middle-class household. What enormities our Modern times have perpetrated in this direction is evidenced by the S-shaped Ottomans for two persons, which are sometimes to be found in our Saloons.

We may here briefly mention the transitional form which is found in Waiting-rooms, and Public vehicles; and the circular Ottoman with centre-piece for flowers, which occupies the centre of the floor in Galleries.

PLATE 250. THE SOFA, AND THE COUCH.

1.   Roman bedstead (lectus cubicularis) in the form of a sofa, (Ménard et Sauvageot).
2.   Ditto.
3.   Mediaeval bench, with cushions and drapery, (Viollet-le-Duc).
4—7. Modern forms of the Sofa, (Gewerbehalle, &c.).
8.   Modern Couch.

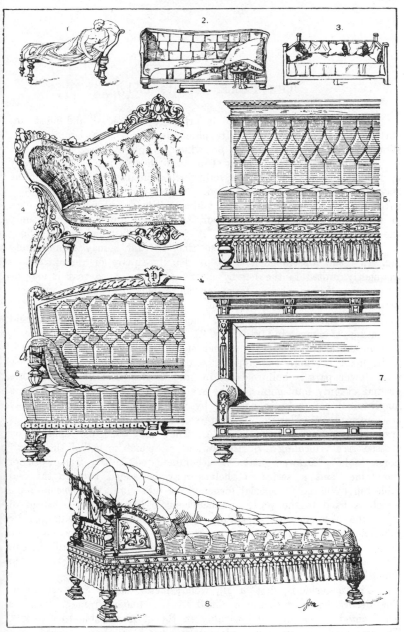

The Sofa, and the Couch. Plate 250.

b. Tables.

THE TABLE. (Plate 251.)

Next to the seat, the Table is probably the oldest and most important piece of furniture. Its chief uses are as a Dining - table, Work - table, and Fancy - table on which to place vases, utensils, &c. Its principal parts are the flat Top, and the Frame. The top may be square, rectangular, circular, elliptical, semicircular, &c. The frame may be very variously constructed. There are tables with one leg, with three, four, and more legs, and sometimes tables with two legs, in which case the Top rests upon two side - supports. Where only one leg is used as a support, it is either fastened to the floor or the lower end is spread - out so that the table may stand firmly (fig. 4). The top, in such cases, is usually square or round, and is frequently united to the leg by means of a screw, so that it may be taken - off. Where three, four, or more legs are used as supports, they are often connected by means of a framework, on which the table - top then rests (fig. 8). The legs may further be rendered rigid by means of connecting rails (fig. 9). The legs are prismatic, turned, or sometimes curved. They either stand upright, or slope outwards as in fig. 9. Where the top rests upon two side-supports (fig. 5), their lower part is hollowed-out in such a way that they touch the ground at only four points. They are connected with each other by a longitudinal bar, held in position by wedges (fig. 5). Sometimes they are replaced by pillars or balausters (figs. 6 and 10), or other legs are employed in addition (fig. 11). They may also be replaced by crossed struts forming a S. Andrew's cross, which is called the "Sawhorse table". Drawers may be accommodated in the framework of the table; and a series of shelves may be added beneath the real table-top (Whatnot). Special forms of the table are: the Console-table, which is fixed to the wall, and has console - like supports instead of legs; the Telescope or expanding table, which may be enlarged by different kinds of mechanism; the Folding-table which may be made larger or smaller by means of flaps (chiefly used for card tables); the Occasional - table for a variety of purposes; the Writing - table, to which a special Plate will be devoted, and many more.

The material is, first of all, wood; metal, stone, &c., are rarer. The decoration is specially confined to the under - frame, which is ornamented by carving and turning in the style suitable to supports. The top is frequently left undecorated, as it is often covered with a table - cloth; and the objects placed upon it would not permit the decoration to be properly seen. Where the top is decorated, the ornamentation is flat, consisting of intarsia-work, incising, painting, &c.

The size of the table varies according to the purpose for which it is intended; its height, on the contrary, is subject to little variation, and is about 2 ft. $4\frac{1}{2}$ ins. for ordinary tables. Tables, with legs which could be adjusted to varying heights, were in use in the Antique period, being required by the social life of that time; a similar arrangement may also be seen on some modern artists' tables, which can not only be adjusted to different heights, but also allow the top to be slanted.

The following remarks are from the point of view of history and style. The Egyptian, Assyrian, and Persian tables, chiefly known to us from the representations of altars, have legs terminating in claws. This motive was also popular among the Greeks and Romans, with the difference that the latter nations permit the claws to rest directly on the ground, while the former support the claws upon small circular plinths. The legs of Antique Tables are frequently of bronze; they have a similar form with those of the Tripod; and like them are adjustible, as already observed (fig. 1). The table-tops are often of stone or wood. Large rectangular tables with stone supports of rich workmanship, and round tables with three legs of marble, a considerable number of which are given on Plates 143 and 144, are well known to us from the excavations at Pompeii. They were not Dining-tables but State-tables which stood in the tablinum and atrium of Roman houses. Dining-tables of the modern form were unknown to the Antique; even in the Early Greek period, while it was still the custom to sit at dinner, each diner had his own separate table; and the same custom continued in the later period when meals were taken in a recumbent posture. These little tables were lower than ours. We also find them in similar forms among the Romans (fig. 3), along with larger Banqueting-tables, around three sides of which the Sofas were ranged as shown ⊔. The Late Roman period was one of lavish luxury; we are told, for example, of tables with legs of silver and ivory, and with Table-tops of rare woods, &c. Incredible prices, up to £ 14,000, were paid for a single choice top.

The Tables of the Middle Ages were generally rectangular or semicircular, rested on posts or trestles, were plain, and rather cumbrous. It is said of Charlemagne, however, that he possessed three of silver, and one golden (?) table. Beautiful and richly-designed Tables of very different kinds have been preserved from the time of the Renascence. Of particularly frequent occurrence, are richly-carved side-trusses (fig. 7), simpler forms of which were already in use in the Gothic period (fig. 5). In the Barocco and Rococo periods, the legs are curved, and the tops are of bold, arbitrary design (fig. 8). The Console-table is an invention of this period. It was also at this

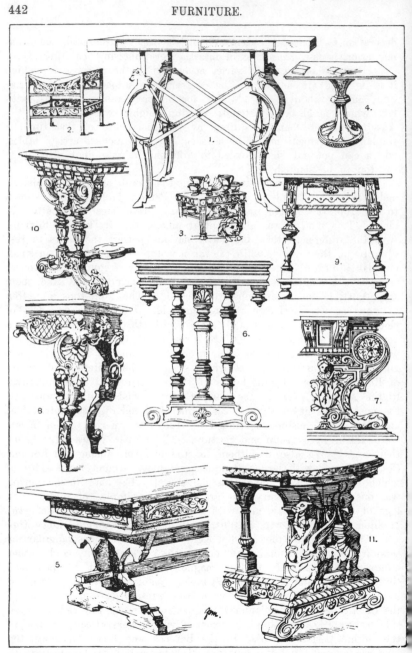

Plate 251.　　　　　　The Table.

time that the Dumb-waiter, came into general use. As far as art is concerned, our modern Tables are mostly copies of old models.

Plate 251 gives a small selection from the copious material.

PLATE 251. THE TABLE.

1. Antique, bronze, Museum, Naples, (Raguenet).
2. Antique, bronze, (Ménard et Sauvageot).
3. Roman, (Kantharos of Ptolemy).
4. Mediaeval, Chronicle of Louis XI, (Viollet-le-Duc).
5. Late Gothic, Municipal Collection of Antiquities, Freiburg, (Schauinsland).
6. Renascence, with turned legs, French, Castle of Bussy - Rabutin, (Côte d'or).
7. Renascence, with carved side-trusses, French, (Ducerceau).
8. French, 18th century, Garde-meuble, Paris, (Raguenet).
9. Modern, Renascence style.
10. Modern.
11. Modern, French, Paris, (Raguenet).

THE WRITING-TABLE. (Plate 252.)

The peculiar construction of the Writing - table removes it from the category of ordinary Tables. In a certain sense it forms the transition to the Cabinets, in the form in which it is now manufactured. The Writing-table is a product of modern civilisation. In earlier times, when writing was the privilege of the select few, the common table evidently served the purpose. It is also true that the old caligraphers, used special writing apparatus, either desks which could be rested on the knees (fig. 1), or small tables, an example of which is given in fig. 2. But it was reserved for our much-writing Modern time to invent special furniture for business and private use. The Writing - table must not only serve for writing, but also as a receptacle for stationery, correspondence, writing-materials, &c. Hence it is furnished with cupboards, drawers, pigeon-holes, and shelves. It is often furnished with side-cupboards below the table-top having a space between them for the legs of the writer. Where the table has an upper part, which admits of a variety of constructions, as may be seen from the few examples of the Plate, it is usually of lesser depth than the surface of the table so as to leave the necessary room for writing. The same end is attained by leaving a space equal to the whole depth free between it and the table - top, as shown by fig. 6. The table-top is often covered with some textile material or with leather, to afford a soft surface for writing - upon.

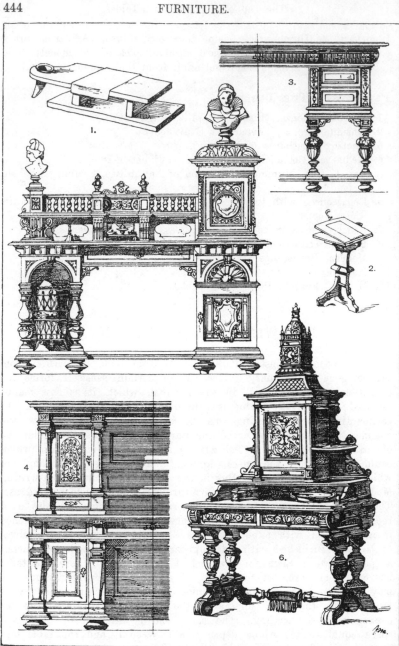

Plate 252. The Writing-Table.

Special varieties are formed by the Double-writing-table for office use, the Cylinder-desk, which can be closed after use by letting down a cylindrical flap, the Secretaire, in which the table-top may be lifted up or locked, the Lady's-writing-table, &c.

PLATE 252. THE WRITING-TABLE.

1. Mediaeval, (scriptionale) with inkhorn, intended to be placed on the knee, 11th century, portal of the church, Vezelay, (Viollet-le-Duc).
2. Mediaeval, with double top, for raising, 15th century, Abbey of Saint-Michel-en-Mer, (Viollet-le-Duc).
3. Modern, with eight legs and side drawers, (Max Schulz).
4. Modern.
5. Modern.
6. Modern, by W. Hanau, (Gewerbehalle).

c. Cabinets.

THE CABINET.   (Plate 253.)

Cabinets were evidently a rare phenomenon in Antiquity. The Egyptians and the Greeks were probably not acquainted with them at all; the Romans seem to have possessed simple Cabinets with two doors, if we may judge from occasional paintings; in any case, however, they were of no artistic importance. Chests, of which we shall speak later on, were no doubt more frequent, and took the place of cabinets. It was the same in the early Middle Ages, in which we certainly find Cabinets in churches and monasteries, but seldom in private houses. Where they do occur, they show the hand of the carpenter rather than that of the skilled cabinet-maker. "The cardinal feature of Romanesque furniture is practicability; that the slow moving, serious spirit of that time paid but little regard to elegance was only natural: men had their virtues and their vices, but they were free from affections of the nerves" (Georg Hirth). Cabinets became more common in the Gothic period; and although the matched-board-work and the simple carving generally give the products of this time a certain rude appearance; still the architectural disposition of the members, and the bands and mounts, are effective. Later Gothic led to all kinds of extravagances, one of which is the lavish use of geometrical tracery, called "flamboyant" from its flame-like character. The revolutionary process, which marks the transition from Gothic to Renascence, finds striking expression in the group of Cabinets. Georg

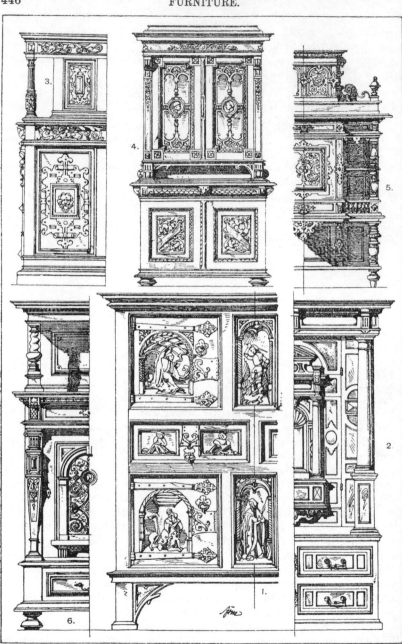

Plate 253.

The Cabinet.

Hirth, whom we quoted above, describes the revival of decoration in the transition period, in the following words: "In their (wood carvers', cabinet-makers', and others') hands the prismatic bead was transformed into the living vine, the stone leaf-work of the minster was metamorphosed into lifelike flowers and rich sweeping branches, wrested with astounding skill from an immense variety of materials. In contrast to the lofty and imaginative but severe creations of the Gothic masons this developement of art in the sphere of ornament seems to me like a picturesque revolution, like the song of the German lark in the rosy dawn of a new day of humanity. The chimes of spring rang from the Lower Rhine to our snow-capped giant peaks, a loud cry for the All-mother Nature, for freedom of heart and imagination. And then what childlike naivete, what devout, blissful hopefulness in these modest men! In truth, the more we strive in vain to imitate them, the more we ought to love them, to draw inspiration from their works and to bless their memory."

Astounding and of high importance, are the achievements of the Renascence in Cabinets and Shrines. They are of all imaginable sizes, from small Caskets to large Cabinets occupying a whole wall. They are devoted to the most different objects: linen, clothes, books, jewels, &c. A rich wealth of form is evolved; architectural systems of columns and pilasters mark the divisions of the ever-alternating doors, drawers, and opens spaces. Add to this the charming play of the coloured woods, grainings, wood-mosaics, and intarsia-work, set-off by the use of all kinds of mounts. The place of the prismatic and bevelled posts is taken by richly-profiled and twisted columns and terminal-figures; instead of matchboard-work we find mortised frame-work, and panels decorated with figures and ornaments. The revolution produced a happy and lasting effect. We do well when we build further on this tradition, and construct our modern Cabinets on the good models of this epoch. Unhappily the few examples of our Plates can only give a faint idea of this group.

PLATE 253. THE CABINET.

1. Late Gothic, end of the 15th century, oak, with tinned iron mounts, Germanisches Museum, Nuremberg, (Kunsthandwerk).

2. Renascence, variegated woods, South German, 16th century, (Formenschatz).

3. Renascence, side-view, German, (Formenschatz).

4. Modern, by Prof. Schick, Carlsruhe.

5. Modern, black wood with copper intarsia, by A. Balcke.

6. Modern, in two woods.

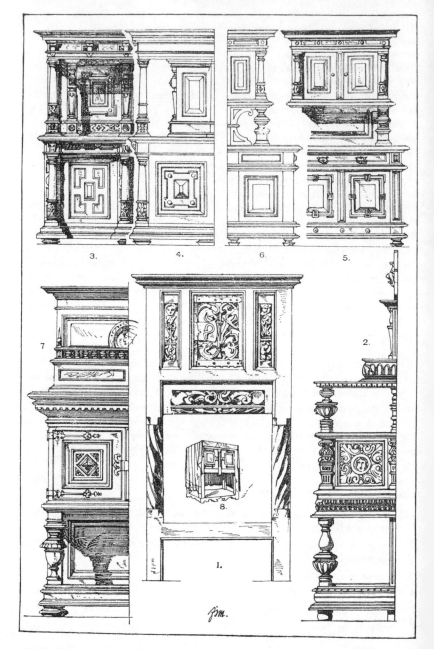

3.   4.   6.   5.

7.   2.

8.

1.

Plate 254.   The Sideboard.

THE SIDEBOARD. (Plate 254.)

Sideboards are a separate division. They are intended for the reception of articles used in the service of the table. Vases and ornaments may also be placed upon them; and in many cases they are themselves decorative objects. In the Middle Ages they are comparatively plain, and of invariable form; the ground-plan being an oblong or semi-octagon; they stand on legs, and have of an open space beneath, over which are the cupboards, with a flat top, (figs. 1 and 8). During the Renascence, this traditional plan gave way to richer and more complicated constructions; the lower recess was frequently retained; instead of it or along with it, further recesses were added at the middle height or still higher; the top is constructed as an independent member, often of smaller dimensions and recessed; and terraces of shelves with balaustered galleries for glasses and plates, form the conclusion of the whole.

Here, too, our Modern times follow the old models. Special requirements have given birth to special forms, such as the Buffets in hotels, and waiting-rooms, which frequently form an integral part of the wainscot or architecture of the wall.

PLATE 254. THE SIDEBOARD.

1. Renascence, German, with reminiscences of Gothic, Bavarian National Museum, Munich.
2. Renascence, side-view, St. Lo, Normandy, 1580, South Kensington Museum, (Musterornamente).
3—4. Modern, front and side-view, designed in the School of Industrial Art, Carlsruhe.
5—6. Ditto.
7. Modern, by Ph. Niederhöfer, Frankfort.
8. Mediaeval, (Viollet-le-Duc).

THE HANGING-CABINET. (Plate 255.)

Hanging-cabinets also form a special subdivision. They differ from other Cabinets in being of more modest dimensions, by being, for practical purposes, of less depth, and, as they are intended for suspension, by terminating in a console instead of in legs and base. For the rest, what has already been said of Cabinets in general, will hold good of Hanging-cabinets also.

These are adapted to hold books, tobacco, &c., medicine, keys, correspondence, &c.

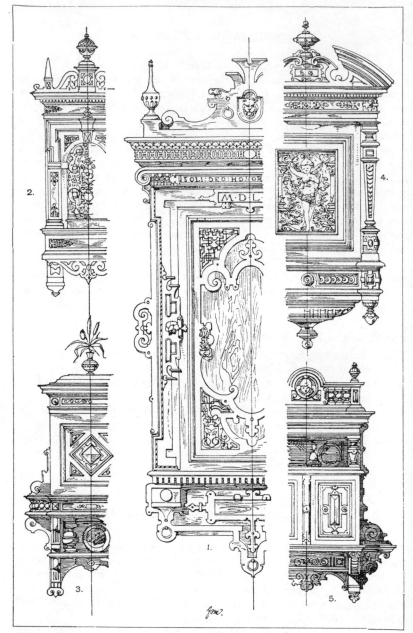

Plate 255.

The Hanging-Cabinet.

PLATE 255. THE HANGING-CABINET.

1. Renascence, German, (Formenschatz).
2. Modern, with intarsia panels, by Dir. Hammer, Nuremberg.
3. Modern, architect Crecelius, Mainz.
4. Modern, by Dir. Götz, Carlsruhe.
5. Modern, by Prof. Haas, Lucerne.

THE CHEST. (Plate 256.)

Chests are of older date than Cabinets. We meet with them on Antique vase-paintings, and among the objects found in Pompeii. They have the form of boxes, prismatic or widening towards the top, with short legs and with rich mountings, of nailheads, &c. (fig. 1).

In the Middle Ages, the Chest was a very popular piece of furniture. Its form was mostly that of a prismatic box without feet, with delicate iron mounts, and all kinds of carving (figs. 2—5). Very often Chests were at the same time used as benches. The same form was retained by the Renascence but differently decorated in accordance with the style of the time. Besides this, we have numerous examples of smaller Chests with feet and lids of pyramid form, richly decorated with carving, intarsia, ivory, and metal reliefs. These small Caskets were chiefly used for jewelry, and as work-boxes, etc., for which purposes similar caskets are still manufactured.

PLATE 256. THE CHEST.

1. Antique, Pompeii, (Ménard et Sauvageot).
2. Mediaeval reliquary, (Viollet-le-Duc).
3. Mediaeval bench-chest, 13th century MS. (Viollet-le-Duc).
4. Gothic, carved chestnut wood with iron mounts and handles, 15th century, (Viollet-le-Duc).
5. Mediaeval, Brampton church, England, (Viollet-le-Duc).
6. Renascence, Dutch, (L'art pour tous).
7. Renascence, Italian.
8. Renascence, Flemish, 17th century, (L'art pour tous).

d. Miscellaneous.

THE DESK, &c. (Plate 257.)

The Desk is a stand with a sloping top, on which books and other things may be placed. Passing over Reading-desks, Music-desks, and other desks for secular use, which as a rule are left undecorated; we have the desks used in churches, e. g. the "Prie-dieu", the Lectern, &c., which are to some extent found of rich workmanship as early as

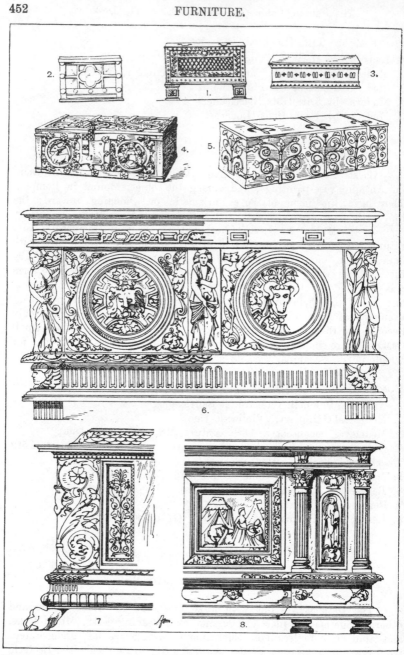

Plate 256.   The Chest.

beginning of the Middle Ages. They are made of wood, or metal, of both combined. We distinguish between single and double ⸱sks. The Lectern is frequently supported on the back of an Eagle ⸱ith outspread wings, a design which is supposed to contain a ⸱eference to the Evangelist S. John, whose symbol in the eagle. Ecclesiastical desks eiter have a fixed position in the choir or chancel, or they are moveable. These latter were sometimes like a Saw-horse and could be folded-up; in which case the slope was replaced by bands (fig. 6). The upper part of fixed desks frequently revolves, and is furnished with sconces for lights.

The Easel is a sloping frame with three or four legs. The front and rear are often connected by hinges to enable the angle of the slope to be altered at will. The front is provided with a small board, which can be adjusted to different heights by pins or other mechanism. It is an invention of modern times; and in its usual undecorated, form is employed by painters, sculptors, &c. But it is often made as a decorative piece of furniture of superior finish, to hold pictures, portfolios, &c. The decoration in this case may consist of the symbols of art, as shown in fig. 7.

PLATE 257. THE DESK, &c.

1. Gothic, 15th century, base of wood, slope of wrought-iron, eagle and ball gilt, dragon painted green, S. Simphorien, Nuits, (Viollet-le-Duc).
2. Mediaeval, San Stefano, Venice, (Mothes).
3. Renascence, marble, Pisa Cathedral, Italian, (Kunsthandwerk).
4. Mediaeval, Double-desk with revolving shaft, end of 13th century (Viollet-le-Duc).
5. Mediaeval, Upper part of Double-desk, (Viollet-le-Duc).
6. Renascence, Folding stand, cathedral, S. Gimignano, Italian, (Kunsthandwerk).
7. Modern decorative Easel, architect Durm, (Gewerbehalle).

THE CLOCK-CASE, &c. (Plate 258.)

The Clock-case, as a piece of furniture, is of comparatively recent date, for the invention of the clock with a train of wheels is itself not old; and for some time after their introduction clocks were manufactured without cases or, at any rate, without cases of artistic importance. In the 17th century, cases for protecting the works against dust and for giving the clock a more pleasing aspect, begin to appear. The forms at first manufactured were chiefly two. The first is that of the old-fashioned tall Hall-clock, something like the toilet-stands (figs. 5 and 6), the upper part accommodating the clock

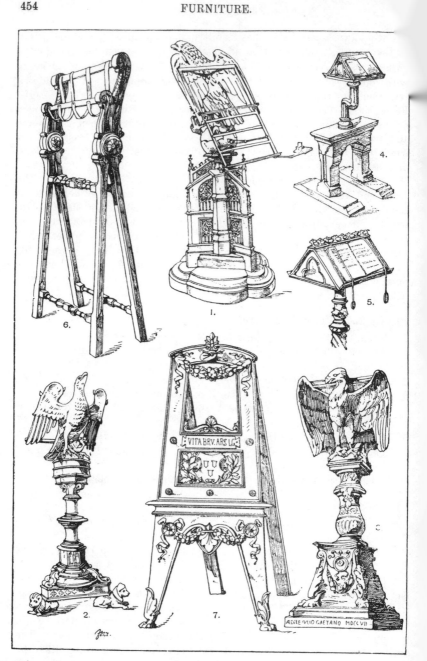

Plate 257. The Desk, &c.

and the lower part being destined for the weights. The other form is that of the dwarf drawing-room clock, the weights being replaced by springs, so that the case does not need to be so tall, and is only dependent on the length of the pendulum. These clocks are placed on chimney - pieces, cabinets, &c., or on pedestals (fig. 1). A third form, which was added at a later date, is the hanging - case, intended for both weight and pendulum clocks. With more or less alteration these forms, together with a number of innovations, are in use at the present time. Pendules and similar constructions are not taken into account here. Clock - cases are mostly of wood, frequently decorated with gilding, and metal mounts. A special division, in respect of material, is formed by the clocks in Buhl - work. The dials, of lacquered wood, porcelain, metal, enamelled, in niello-work, &c., are often bordered by a metal ring and closed by glass doors. Pendulum and weight-cases may be either open or closed; sometimes they have only a slit for the bob. The sides of the case are often of fret-work, in order that the sound of the striking - work may be better heard. Dome - shaped clocks are sometimes crowned by a small bell - turret (fig. 3). Calendar-clocks, Cuckoo-clocks, Trumpeter-clocks, and similar fancy forms, also require special construction. In general, we may assume that the get-up of our modern regulator and other clocks is perfectly familiar to the reader. The starting - points in designing a clock case are the diameter of the dial, the depth of the works, the distance from the centre of the dial to the centre of the bob and the extent of swing of the pendulum, and (in the case of Weight-clocks) the length to which the weights run.

It is possible that Toilet-stands may have been met-with in the Middle Ages; but they were not treated as decorative furniture till the Renascence. A number of really magnificent examples from this period have been preserved (fig. 5). The usual form is that of a slender, tall Cabinet, the upper and lower parts of which are provided with doors, and serve to hold various necessary objects, while the centre takes the form of a niche. In this niche hangs a metal water-reservoir with a lid and a cock; at the lower end of the niche is a basin to receive the waste water. Elegant wrought-iron towel-holders are attached. The two figures (5 and 6) will give an idea of the arrangement of these pretty pieces of furniture, which are now becoming popular again, after they had been supplanted and fallen into disuse.

PLATE 258. THE CLOCK - CASE, &c.

1. Barocco, with pedestal, by Daniel Marot.
2. Modern, with roof, by Hans Steimer, Furtwangen.
3. Modern, with metal ornaments, architect Lauter, Carlsruhe.
4. Modern, by Fr. Miltenberger, Nuremberg.

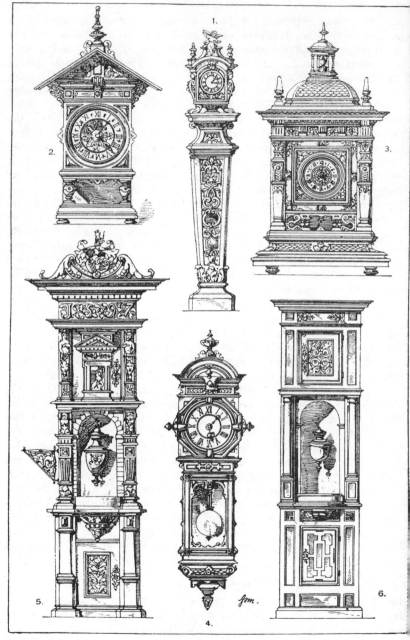

Plate 258. The Clock-Case, &c.

5. Toilet-stand, German Renascence, 1597, Town-hall, Ueberlingen, (Gewerbehalle).
6. Toilet-stand, various coloured woods, German Renascence, (Formen-schatz).

THE BEDSTEAD, AND THE CRADLE. (Plates 259—260.)

From the earliest to the present time, the Bedstead has passed through many changes. In the Egyptian and Assyrian styles: we find metal Bedsteads imitating the forms of animals (Plate 259. 1, 2); and sometimes arranged to fold up like a Camp-bed (Plate 259. 2). Those of the Greeks and Romans, which served partly as Beds, and partly as Couches, are of manifold forms. In addition to the four-legged bench (Plate 259. 3), we have benches with a head-board (Plate 259. 1), with head and foot board (Plate 259. 4), the latter being usually lower than the former, and others with head, foot, and back boards, like our modern Sofas (Plate 260. 2). The materials are wood and metal, sometimes more precious materials, ivory, &c., as we learn from the examples found in Pompeii.

The same fundamental idea may be seen in the Bedsteads of the earlier Middle Ages, which show traces of Byzantine influence, and have richly-decorated, turned posts, and carved sides. The front was often furnished with an opening to allow of getting into the bed (Plate 259. 5, 6). At a later period the Bedstead was furnished with canopied hangings suspended from special rods fixed to the wall. The Renascence considerably enlarged the size; placed it on a podium; raised the head-board; and carried the legs higher to receive the tester or canopy-frame, which was then adorned with drapery and hangings. Examples of this period have been preserved (Plate 260. 1 and 2). In the Barocco and Rococo periods: textile materials predominate, and the wooden frame is neglected. Then the so-called "Parade-beds" (Plate 260, 3) became fashionable.

Modern times again have generally simplified the form. The commonest is that with high foot and head-boards (the latter often to excess), and low sides. Tester-bedsteads have passed out of fashion.

The Cradle seems to have been an invention of the Middle Ages. By means of pins the little box or trough-shaped Bedsteads were fixed in a frame in which they were moveable; or the legs of the Bedstead were replaced by curved battens which admitted of rocking (Plate 259. 8 and 9). The Cradles of the Renascence are of similar form, often with raised end-boards, and rich carving. Owing to sanitary objections, Cradles have almost gone out of use. Some-

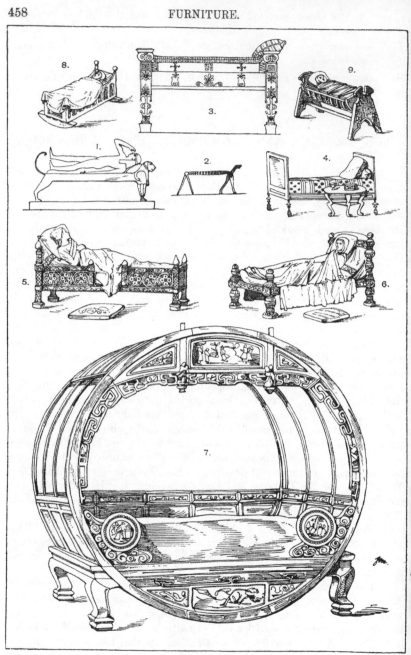

Plate 259. The Bedstead, &c.

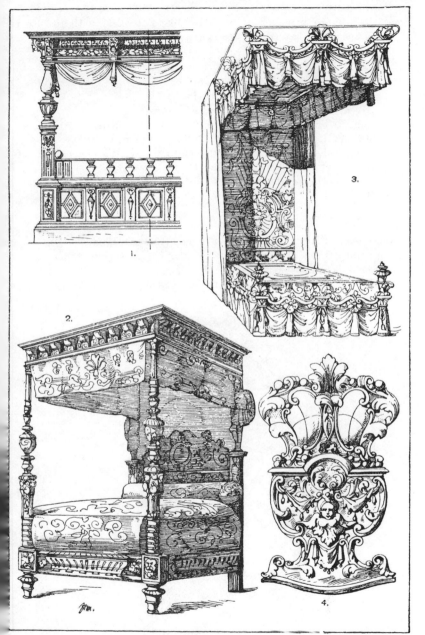

The Bedstead, &c. Plate 260.

times Cradles are made of metal rods, like a basket, with the head
of the frame raised to support a canopy.

PLATE 259. THE BEDSTEAD, &c.

1. Egyptian, (Ménard et Sauvageot).
2. Egyptian collapsible Camp-bedstead.
3. Greek, vase-painting, (Ménard et Sauvageot).
4. Roman, Pompeian vase-painting, (Ménard et Sauvageot).
5. Mediaeval, MS. of the 13th century, (Viollet-le-Duc).
6. Mediaeval, MS. of the 12th century, (Hortus deliciarum of
    Herrad of Landsberg), (Viollet-le-Duc).
7. Chinese, (L'art pour tous).
8—9. Mediaeval Cradles, (Viollet-le-Duc).

PLATE 260. THE BEDSTEAD, &c.

1. Renascence, Plantin Museum, Antwerp, (Gewerbehalle).
2. Renascence, French, Cluny Museum, Paris, (L'art pour tous).
3. Barocco, Parade-bedstead, by Daniel Marot.
4. Renascence, Head-board of Cradle, French, gilt ornaments on
   red ground (L'art pour tous).

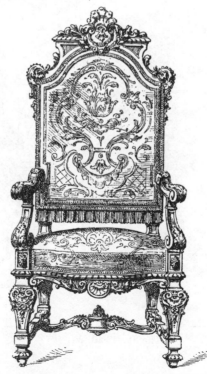

D.

FRAMES, &c.

The term "Framework" is a very inclusive one. Every edging, border, and every rim of a plate, belongs to this group; but the following ten plates will contain only those features in which the Frame is, to a certain extent, an end in itself, and a definite, characteristic whole. Framework is useful in every branch of applied art; it is used in an immense variety of materials, and is treated in many different ways. Plates 261—270 contain some important subdivisions selected from the entire group: these are frames of Architectural character; frames (strictly so-called) for Pictures, Mirrors, &c., Tablets, Typographical borders, and the borders of Dials, Plates, &c.

It is highly interesting to pursue the rise of Framework on an architectural basis, its gradual transformation and its adaptation to the products of art industry. For this, however, we refer the reader to the remarks of Semper (*Der Stil*, §§ 130 et seqq.). We will only make the following observations from the point of view of style: Framework, in the sense in which it is here understood, only occurs rarely and sporadically in the older styles, the Antique and the Middle Ages. It was reserved for the Renascence to cultivate this field, and to attain the highest possible results. It cannot, however, be denied that occasionally it was exaggerated and illogical. A Frame must, above all things, have some relation and proportion to the object to be framed. To make a frame, and put it where there is nothing to be framed, is illogical. And yet we find in the late Renascence, and in the Barocco and Rococo periods, countless examples which, so far as their application goes, have no other object than the decoration of empty spaces.

THE ARCHITECTURAL FRAME. (Plate 261—262.)

By Architectural Frames we mean those which are used in Architecture, and those which, although applied in other branches, such as furniture, show an architectural derivation. These are: the framings of doors, windows, panels, tablets, medallions, niches, soffits, &c. In Furniture they are the border-like ornaments which serve as a framing to panel-ornaments; but which are also very often used merely as decoration, without having any object to frame. There are two classes of Frames: one which is mon-axial, with external ornaments at the top and bottom, to emphasize the vertical attitude; and one which is bi-axial, for application on horizontal surfaces. In the former class: the lower ornament has the general shape of a suspended triangle. This expresses the idea of supporting like a Console; and is a free-ending down-wards. The other of these has the general shape of the erect triangle; making a cresting feature, and is the free-ending upwards. Frames of this class are shown on Plate 261, figs. 2, 8, 9, 10 and 11. In the second class of Frames: the space to be enclosed, be it a circle, square, or oblong, is surrounded by an ornament which is symmetrical on all sides without regard to top and bottom. Frames of this class are shown on figs. 4—7 of Plate 261, and figs. 5, 8 and 9 of Plate 262. These two principles are not always so strongly marked as in the examples given; and sometimes they are combined; but as a rule the one or the other will always predominate.

PLATE 261. THE ARCHITECTURAL FRAME.

1. Gable-opening of a Dormer-window, Rouen, French, 17th century, (L'art pour tous).
2. Tablet, modern, in the style of the Italian Renascence.
3. Pedestal, Italian Renascence, Genoa, (Owen Jones).
4. Door-panel, (Architektonisches Skizzenbuch).
5. Stove-tile, Castle of Wülfingen near Winterthur, 17th century, (Kunsthandwerk).
6. Desk in S. Giorgio maggiore, Venice, Italian, Renascence.
7. Coffer, cupola of the Dagobert Tower, Baden-Baden, German, Renascence.
8—9. Pulpit, Magdeburg cathedral, German, 1595—1597, (Gewerbehalle).
10. Door of cabinet, in the style of the German Renascence, (Formenschatz).
11. Door of a sideboard, Louvre, Paris, Renascence.

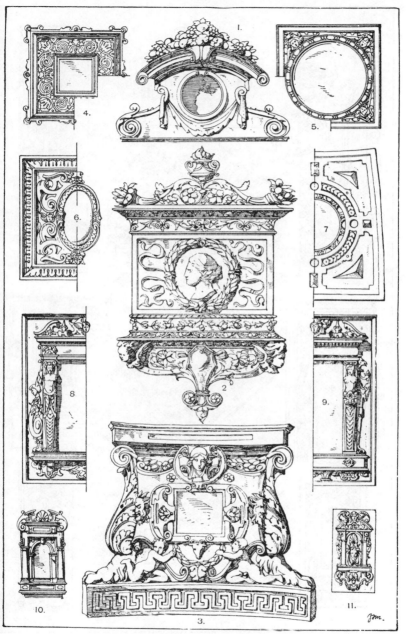

The Architectural Frame.

Plate 261.

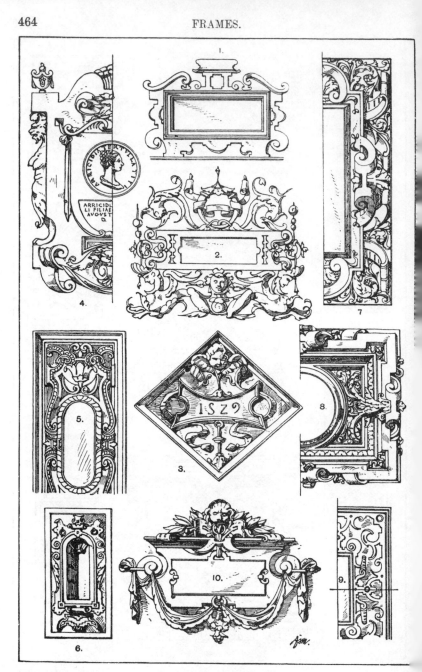

Plate 262.   The Architectural Frame.

PLATE 262. THE ARCHITECTURAL FRAME.

1. German, 17th century, Stalls, Stiftskirche, Aschaffenburg, (Gewerbehalle).
2. Italian, Renascence, (Formenschatz).
3. French, 1529, Lozenge panel, choir of Chartres cathedral, (Raguenet).
4. Renascence, by Enea Vico, (Formenschatz).
5. Italian, Renascence, Panel of the stalls, S. Giorgio maggiore, Venice.
6. German Renascence, Frame of small niche, Dagobert Tower, Baden-Baden.
7—8. Modern, French, Hotel Mirabaud, Paris, Architect Magne, (Raguenet).
9. Modern, in the style of the German Renascence.
19. Modern, French, Paris, (Raguenet).

THE MIRROR-FRAME, &c. (Plates 263—264).

The moveable Mirror-frames, which are designed and made to be hung-up, might have been classed among the Furniture; but they are more conveniently treated here. The Middle Ages framed Altarpieces and the Pictures of the saints; but the universal use of frames begins with the Renascence; and it is particularly Italy which has preserved the most numerous examples of this period. At first we meet with Architectural-frames; but simultaneously with the transition from the Mural-picture of the Middle Ages (which had been a part of the wall), to the Table-picture (which was portable), the treatment becomes freer and less constrained. And when the architectural members were afterwards blended-together in scroll-work, the fundamental architectural idea generally remained visible, as may be seen from the Barocco and Louis XVI frames in Plates 263. 1, 2, 6, and 10; and 264. 3 and 4. It was reserved for Modern times to cut-up factory-made mouldings into lengths, to produce frames of any required size, without regard to the proportion which should exist between the frame and the enclosed space. Cheap and practical! but Art has gained nothing by it. Still, we would not be understood to say that our time does not occasionally produce frames which completely satisfy the demands of both technique and taste.

The chief material is wood; but bronze is used for frames of small size. The old custom of painting and gilding the carved-wood frames, led to the manufacture of the so-called "gilt frame", which is made of stamped brass. Opinions may differ as to the justification of these frames from an aesthetic point of view; but there is little

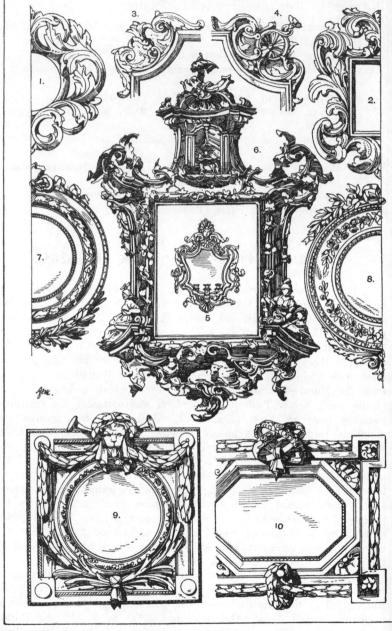

Plate 263. The Mirror-Frame, &c.

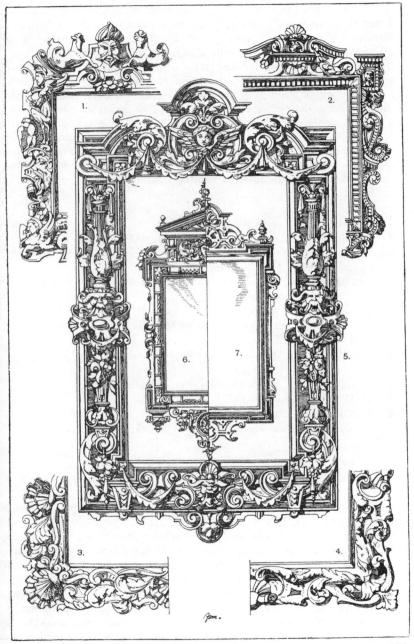

The Mirror-Frame, &c.   Plate 264.

doubt that the metallic frame tends to enhance the effect of coloured pictures. Porcelain and glass have also been used as materials for frames; but their propriety will always be questionable.

In addition to outline and style of decoration: an important part is played by the amount of projection of the Frame. The effect of a picture, which appears to be recessed behind a Bevel-frame, is very different from that of one which seems to be brought into relief by a Torus - moulding. The fundamental form of the frame is usually oblong, either figure-wise or landscape-wise; circular, elliptic, or square frames, are rarer. Sometimes the outer shape of the Frame differs from the inner shape (Plate 263. 9, 10). In the Barocco period, frames received a number of arbitrary curved forms; as shown in on Plate 263, fig. 5.

PLATE 263. THE MIRROR - FRAME, &c.

1—2. German, 18th century, Berlin, (Kunsthandwerk).
3—4. French, angle - ornaments of wall - panels, old castle of Bercy, near Paris, 18th century, (Raguenet).
5. Barocco, with bracket, by Paul Decker, (Formenschatz).
6. Rococo, (Formenschatz).
7—8. French, Louis XVI., by La Londe, (Wessely).
9—10. French, Louis XVI., by Delafosse, (Raguenet).

PLATE 264. THE MIRROR - FRAME, &c.

1—2. Renascence, (Raguenet).
3—4. Italian Renascence, Florence, (Gewerbehalle).
5. Modern, (Gewerbehalle).
6. Modern, by Prof. Schick, Carlsruhe.
7. Modern, by the architect Huber, Frankfort.

THE STRAP-WORK FRAME. (Plates 265—266.)

When the Frame is cut into fantastic shapes and bands, which interlace and curl, like leathern Straps; then it is termed the Strap-work Frame. It is much used, in the later Renascence, for Shields, Tablets, &c.; and is a characteristic of the Elizabethan style. Foliage, palmettes, festoons and garlands of fruit, fluttering ribbons, cherub-heads, &c. are frequently added. Strap-work was an invention of the Renascence; and it is extremely common, especially in the later years of that period. This kind of Frame-work is frequently used, not as a Frame, but for mere decorative purposes, so that the fields to be framed are left as empty spaces. Strap-work appears in architecture, sepulchral monuments, and epitaphs; on medals and coins; in cabinet-

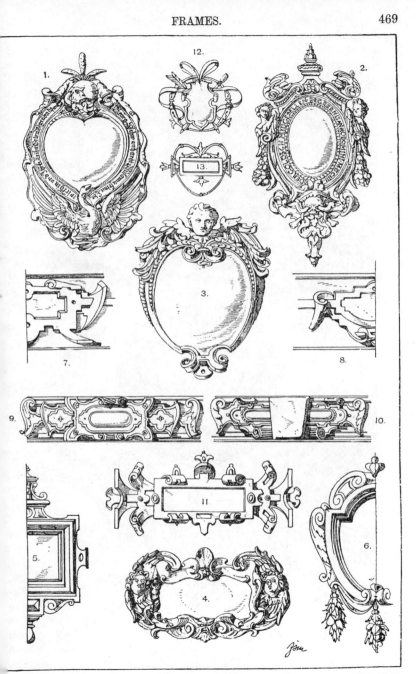

The Strap-work Frame.   Plate 265.

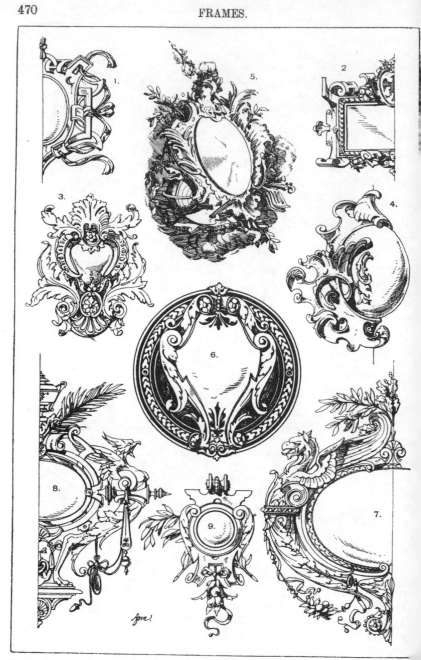

Plate 266. The Strap-work Frame.

work, heraldry, jewelry, the decoration of books, &c., and the minor arts in general. The arrangement is usually symmetrical; but this was abandoned in the Rococo period in favour of unsymmetrical and picturesque arrangements, as shown in Plate 266, fig. 5.

PLATE 265. THE STRAP-WORK FRAME.

1—4.   Renascence, bronze tablets, cemetery of S. John, Nuremberg, (Gewerbehalle).
5—6.   Renascence, 17th century, French, (L'art pour tous).
7—10. Renascence, new castle, Baden-Baden, 1576—1577.
11.   Renascence, National Library, Paris, (Raguenet).
12.   Modern, French, book ornament.

PLATE 266. THE STRAP-WORK FRAME.

1.   Renascence, French.
2.   Renascence, from "Civitates orbis terrarum", published by P. von Brackel, Cologne, 1573, (Ysendyck).
3.   Rococo, Louvre, Paris, (Raguenet).
4.   Rococo, French, corner of a wall, (Raguenet).
5.   Rococo, French.
6—7.   Modern, by Dir. Kachel, Carlsruhe.
8.   Modern, French, (Liénard).
9.   Modern.

THE TYPOGRAPHICAL FRAME. (Plates 267—268.)

We find numerous Framework - motives in the decoration of books and documents; and though they have become more general since the invention of printing, we find them in the Manuscripts of the Middle Ages. The Title-pages were framed or bordered; it was also a favourite practice to border the headings; Initials are sometimes treated in this way; and Printers'-marks, and Head and Tail-pieces are often designed with Strap - work. Old books are often richly decorated with such things; and artists of the highest rank often lent their aid to this style of decoration. After the sobriety which ruled in the first half of this century, our modern times have devoted increased attention to this branch. Breaches of taste are still committed in this direction, principally because factory - made Blocks, Borders, and Rules, are combined without judgment in Typography. Not only books, but also diplomas, addresses, ball-programmes, dinner and business-cards, labels, book-plates, and similar things are furnished with artistic borders. The principles of decoration, and the motives employed, are very varied; and great freedom is al-

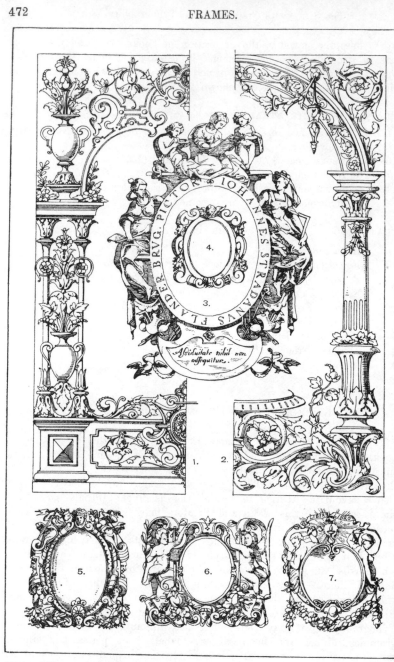

Plate 267.   The Typographical Frame.

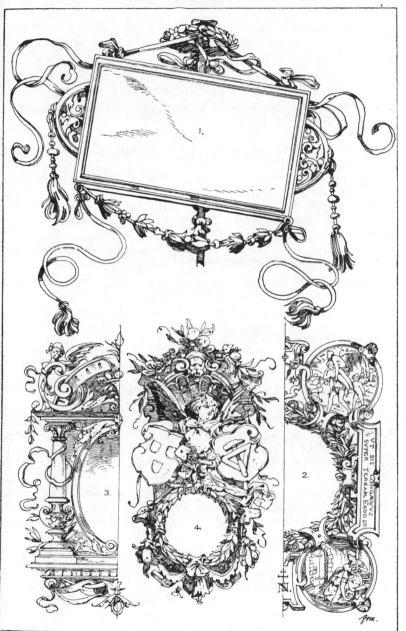

The Typographical Frame. Plate 268.

lowed. When architectural forms appear, they are treated lightly and playfully; and are often resolved into all manner of strap-work (Plate 267. 1, 2).

PLATE 267. THE TYPOGRAPHICAL FRAME.

1. Border, by Johann Sadler, 1550—1560, Flemish, Renascence, (Guichard).
2. Border, by Hans Holbein, (Guichard).
3. Border, by J. Wiericx, 16th century, Flemish, Renascence, (L'art pour tous).
4. Printer's-mark, (Giacomo Cornetti of Venice), Italian, Renascence, 1586, (L'art pour tous).
5. Ditto, (Giovanni Guarisco, Venice, 1575).
6. Ditto, (Ex typographia Jacobi Staer, 1585).
7. Ditto, (A. Quantin, Paris, 1882).

PLATE 268. THE TYPOGRAPHICAL FRAME.

1. German, Tablet from the triumphal entry of the Emperor Maximilian by Hans Burkmair, (1473—1531).
2. French, Renascence, 16th century, Lyons, (L'art pour tous).
3. Modern, by Max Läuger, Carlsruhe.
4. Modern, by Rudolf Seitz, Munich.

THE STRAP-WORK TABLET.   (Plate 269.)

Examples of Strap-work, designed for use in some of the Minor Arts, which serves not as a frame but as the actual Tablet, are shown in the Plate. Figures 1 and 2 are clock-cases; 3 and 4 are for goldsmiths' work; 5 and 6 are wrought-iron signs; 7 and 8 are suitable ornaments for stamped-leather, and inlaying; fig. 10 is an escutcheon; and Nos. 9 and 11 are book-mounts. The series might easily be increased; but these examples will suffice, as it would lead us too far to treat each of these classes in detail.

PLATE 269. THE STRAP-WORK TABLET.

1.   Clock-case, hammered metal, French, Renascence.
2.   Clock-case, stamped metal, Modern.
3—4. Decoration of escutcheons, snuff-box lids, &c., by Wilhelm Visscher, 17th century.
5—6. Wrought-iron signs, Modern.
7.   Book-cover, 16th century, French Renascence, (L'art pour tous).
8.   Modern, (Gewerbehalle).

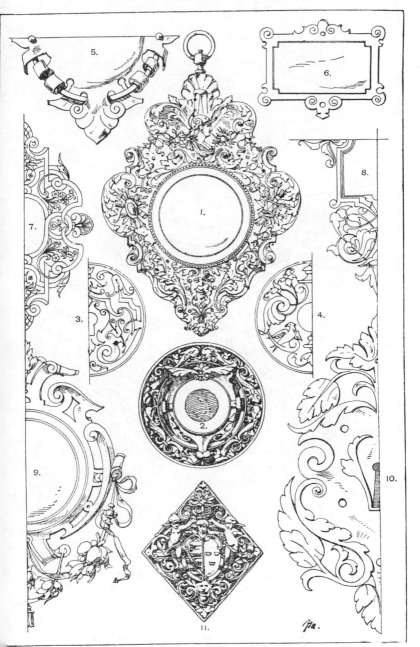

The Strap-work Tablet.

Plate 269.

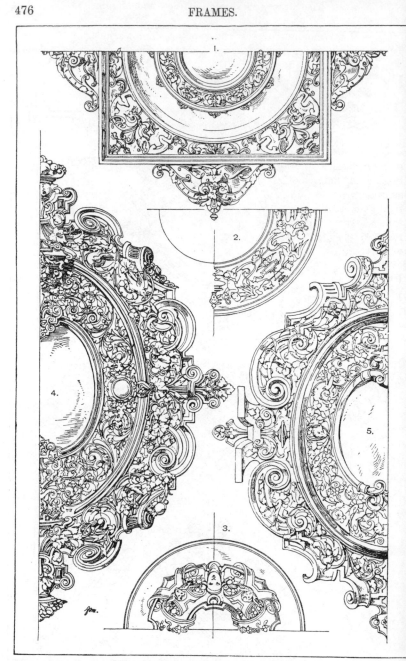

Plate 270.   The Strap-work Border, and Margin.

9.   Metal mounts for the cover of an album, Modern.
10.   Wrought-iron escutcheon, German, 16th century, National
      Museum, Munich.
11.   Centre-piece of bookbinding, by Dir. C. Graff, Dresden.

THE STRAP-WORK BORDER, AND MARGIN. (Plate 270.)

To those products of art, which frequently receive an additional
exterior border or Margin, must further be reckoned plates and dishes.
So far as they are included under pottery, the border usually has a
smooth unbroken edge; the material scarcely admitting of a freer
treatment of the rim. It is different when the object is of metal; in
this case, the rim may be decorated with pierced-work; and the outlines
may undergo a richer and more vigorous treatment (figs. 4 and 5), in
which the framework forms a free-ending outwards.

PLATE 270.   THE STRAP-WORK BORDER, AND MARGIN.

1.   Renascence, Majolica, Gewerbemuseum, Berlin, (Gewerbehalle).
2.   Renascence, Majolica, Italian, (Racinet).
3.   Renascence, Limoges, by Pierre Raymond, 16th century, (Racinet).
4—5. Modern, by Placido Zuloaga, Eibar, Spain, (Gewerbehalle).

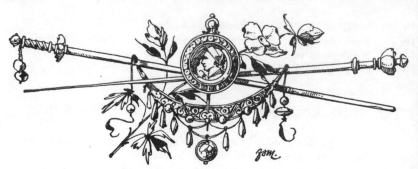

E.

JEWELRY.

The love of personal adornment is as old as mankind itself; as is proved by the relics which have been preserved from the earliest times. Personal adornment, broadly taken, is a somewhat extensive domain; it includes the Painting and Tattooing of the body, Clothing, as soon as this exceeds what is required to meet practical needs, Armour, &c.; but this section will be confined to adornment by Jewelry.

The following 10 plates will deal with this group so far as their chief representatives are concerned. These are: Pins, Buttons, Finger-rings, Chains, Necklets, Bracelets, Belts, Clasps, and Buckles, the various kinds of Chatelaines, and Ear-rings.

The plan of this book requires that we should chiefly direct our attention to the decorative aspect of these objects; but we will here offer a few general observations on the subject.

Trinkets, which are not indispensable, but rather an object of luxury, are closely connected with dress and costume; and like them, subject to fashion. This explains the different transformations which trinkets have undergone in the course of centuries. On the other hand, technical considerations have also played a part: the art of working the materials has passed through various stages of development in the different periods; so that the form and finish were governed not only by the fashion, and taste of each period, but also by the technical skill of the workman.

The principal materials of trinkets are the precious metals. From the state in which the metals are found in Nature, it is easy to see that the first metal to come into general use would be Gold, which is found in a pure state almost all over the world; and is easy to work. It can easily be beaten into plates, and drawn out into wire; and the earliest style is consequently that of plate-gold and filigree work. This is abundantly proved by the objects belonging to primitive times whether they are found on Greek, Oriental, Scandinavian, or American ground. The common metals, and bronze, are also occasionally used as well as gold and silver. Among non-metallic materials, we have: gems, and other valuable stones, pearls, enamels, amber, shells, mother-of-pearl, &c.

In addition to the arts of punching and hammering metal plates, and filigree work, the latter consisting chiefly of soldering-together wire and beads, there arose, in process of time, the further arts of: casting, chiselling, niello, enamel, damaskeening, inlaying, gilding, silvering, oxidising, and die-sinking. For other than metallic materials, the principal processes are: cutting, facetting, setting, the production of tints, and foils, and the engraving of gems, and cameos. As it is impossible here to go into details of the history or technique of these processes, we will refer the reader to the special works on this subject, among them: Semper, *Der Stil,* Hauptstück XI. Metallotechnik; Luthmer, *Der Goldschmuck der Renaissance* (from which excellent work we have taken a number of our figures); Bucher, *Geschichte der technischen Künste;* Mathias, *Der menschliche Schmuck.*

Taken on the whole, trinkets are an article of Womans' toilet, although certain objects have also been worn by Men, either at all times, like the Finger-ring, or only at certain periods and among certain nations, like the Bracelet. On the other hand, there are certain objects of personal adornment, like Orders, Badges, and Medals, which are a speciality of the male sex. Trinkets which presuppose an injury of some part of the body, such as Ear and Nose-rings, are a relic of barbaric manners. An excessive indulgence in adornment is usually characteristic of the primitive stage, and of the decay of the civilisation of a nation; while the golden ages of civilisation and style are marked by restraint in the quantity of trinkets, and by a chaste moderation in the use of the effects of bright gold and cut gems — "The later empire (Roman), Byzantium, the entire early period of the Middle Ages, swim in gold" — says Semper. The best periods of personal adornment are the Antique and the Renascence: but it is impossible to praise too highly the attempts which are being made, at the present time, to improve the style of Goldsmith's-work and Jewelry, by a recurrence to the models of those times. For the rest, certain traditional and standard forms of trinkets have been preserved for centuries, in some national costumes, such as those of Switzerland, Italy, Sweden, and elsewhere.

The Pin. (Plate 271.)

The Pin is a toilet article of very general use, particularly in primitive times. According to its application, it is either a Hair-pin or a Dress-pin. Its form may be referred to three fundamental types. The first has a cylindrical or slightly conical stem, pointed like a thorn at one end, and terminated at the other by a knob or some other finial (figs. 1—16); it is used principally as a hair or breast pin, the stem in the former case being sometimes split like a fork (figs. 23—24). The materials are chiefly metals, bone, and horn; the head and the stem may be of different materials, as in the modern glass-headed pin. The handsomest examples of this class are to be found in the Antique, which gave this simple object a great variety of form. The East also furnishes us with original forms, as shown by the Japanese examples (figs. 22—26).

The second class is that of the Fibula, the Brooch or Safety-pin. These pins consist of two parts, a disc or hoop - shaped upper - part connected with the actual pin by elastic spirals or by a hinge, the point of the pin being held and secured by a catch like a hook or sheath. Brooches are always used for garments; and, in the antique, supplied the want of Buttons. They were in common use up to the Middle Ages, as shown by the numerous finds in Greece, Italy, and Scandinavia. The hoop is commoner than the disc; and more practical, as it afforded room for the gathered - up folds of the garment. The decoration is of the utmost variety; certain forms, such as the spiral (fig. 36), are conventional. The material is always metal, mostly bronze, more rarely a precious metal. Modern times make use of these pins only in the form of the plain wire Safety-pin, and the Brooch, in which latter the disc replaces the hoop (fig. 37). Double-pins form a third class. Two or three (and occasionally more) pins of the first class are connected by means of chains or spangles, usually to serve as an ornament for the bosom (fig. 17). This form, was popular in ancient Scandinavian art; and is in use up to the present day in some national costumes.

Plate 271. The Pin.

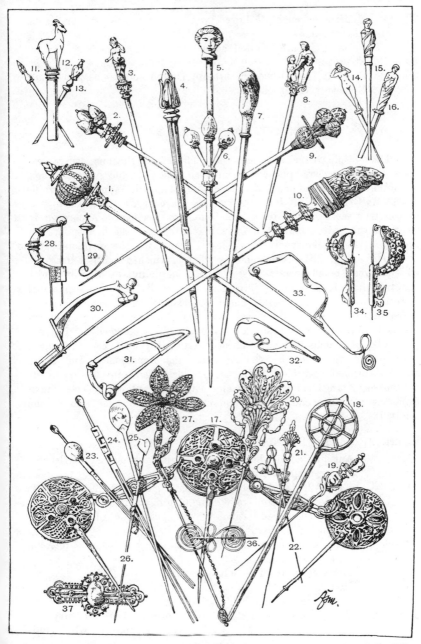

The Pin.   Plate 271.

27.   Modern, French, Filigree work with pearls and brilliants, (Gewerbehalle).

28—33.   Antique, bronze, United collections, Carlsruhe.

34—35.   Etruscan, Gold.

36.   Etruscan, spiral-brooch, bronze, United collections, Carlsruhe.

37.   Modern, (Gewerbehalle).

The Button. (Plate 272.)

The objects, which we have here classed as Buttons, serve various purposes. They appear as Pendants to necklets and similar things, as Bullæ (an antique pendant like an amulet with symbolic significance), as Ornaments of Belts, Garments, Harness, &c., and as Buttons, in the strict sense of the term, for fastening garments. According to its uses, the Button takes the form of the sphere, the hemisphere, or the disc. As a Pendant it resembles a drop with the character of a free-ending (fig. 26). One end is then furnished with a ring by which it may be suspended or sewed-on. The double-buttons or Links, shown in figs. 1, 14 and 27 form a special subdivision. The principal materials are again the metals, enamelled, damaskeened, set with gems, or as filigree-work. Buttons are also manufactured in ivory, mother-of-pearl, amber, glass, and similar materials; discs of wood are covered with silk, and metal threads, adorned with gold-foil, &c. Standard examples are furnished by the Antique, the Renascence, and many Modern national costumes, while the modern wholesale factory-made Button has scarcely any artistic value. Our examples have been taken from the periods named above; and are mostly the same size as the originals.

PLATE 272. THE BUTTON.

1.   Antique, double-button, gold, United collections, Carlsruhe.

2—3.   Etruscan, gold with gems and pearls.

4, 5, 6, 7, 11, 12, 14, 15, 16, 17, 19, 27, 28 and 29.   Buttons and double-buttons of various origin, of metal, with filigree-work, enamelled, &c. In the possession of Prof. Marc Rosenberg, Carlsruhe.

8—9.   Renascence, gold, enamelled and set with pearls, Regalia, Berlin, (Luthmer).

10.   Renascence, from a belt.

13.   Modern, filigree.

18.   Renascence, enamelled, National Museum, Munich.

20 and 23. Buttons by a Frankfort maker of the 18th century, in the collection of Mr. J. Werneck, Frankfort, silk, gold-thread and foil, (Kunsthandwerk).

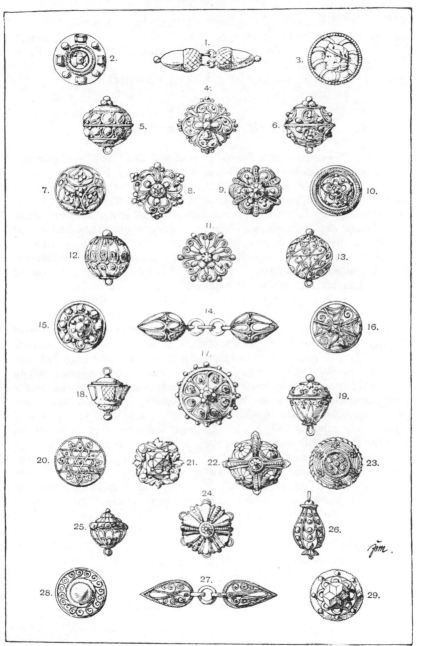

The Button.

Plate 272.

21.   Renascence, the gallery, Schleissheim, (Luthmer).
22 and 24. Renascence, from pictures in Wörlitz and Gotha, (Luthmer).
25.   Indian, silver filigree, from Sumatra, United collections, Carlsruhe.
26.   Modern, pendant of a necklet, (Gewerbehalle).

THE RING. (Plate 273.)

The Finger-ring is universally employed as an article of personal adornment; and it is one which has been worn by both sexes at almost all times, and in almost all countries. The manner of wearing it was determined partly by fashion, partly by edicts. Sometimes it was considered good taste to wear only a single ring, at other times both hands were covered with rings; it is worn sometimes under, and sometimes over the glove; plain, comfortable forms give way to monstrous shapes; sometimes it is purely ornamental, sometimes it has a symbolic significance, as in the wedding ring (a legacy of heathendom to Christianity); sometimes it is a token of dignity, as in the fisherman's ring of the Pope, and of Emperors, Kings, &c.

The form is manifold. The Signet - ring, formed partly of a single piece (fig. 4), partly of a hoop in which a cut gem revolves (fig. 1), occurs in the Egyptian style. Spiral rings with the serpent motive (figs. 7 and 8), and rings opening on one side (fig. 12), are not rare in the Antique. Besides these: other forms appear, which are still popular. Sometimes the upper side was broadened to receive some ornament or a gem (figs. 5, 9, 10, 13), a method which was used in the Renascence (figs. 20—29), while the Middle Ages preferred cylindrical, ribbon - like bands (figs. 14 and 16), and architectural motives (fig. 17). It was reserved for Modern times to give the Wedding-ring its smooth, convenient, but artistically unimportant form. The predominant material is gold. Niello, enamel, pearls, and gems, are used for its further decoration. The ring has frequently given rise to artistic freaks, e. g. where two or three separate rings are so constructed that they may be interlocked.

PLATE 273. THE RING.

1—3.   Egyptian, signet, (Ménard et Sauvageot).
4.   Roman, signet, found in the Crimea.
5.   Egyptian, with enamel and two horses in free relief.
6.   Egyptian, with pierced work, (Racinet).
7—8.   Greek.
9—10.   Roman, found in the Crimea.
11.   Etruscan, gold, Vulci, (Blümner).

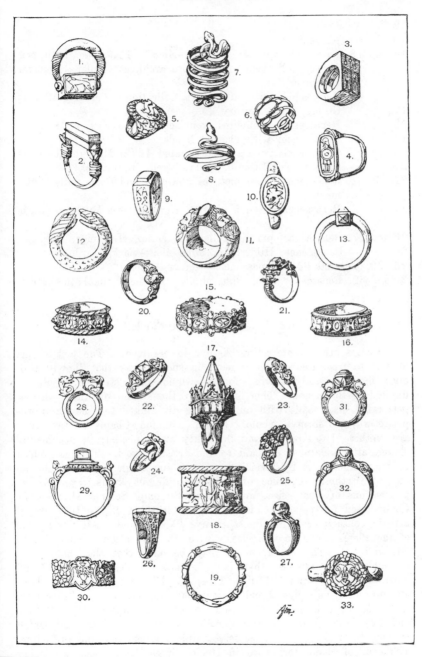

The Ring.   Plate 273.

12.   Pompeian.
13.   Ancient Italic.
14 and 16.   So-called "Jewish wedding-rings", 15th and 16th cen-
              turies, collection of the late architect Oppler, Hanover,
              (Luthmer).
15.   Renascence, with cut onyxes, Collection in Cassel,(Luthmer).
17.   Gothic, 13th century, (Mothes).
18.   Renascence, enamelled, representing the Fall of Man.
19.   Renascence, with clasped hands.
20.   Renascence, from a picture, dated 1572, Museum, Cologne.
21.   Renascence, Museum, Sigmaringen, (Luthmer).
22—23.   Renascence, from pictures at Gotha and Darmstadt, (Luth-
              mer).
24.   Renascence, from a picture, Germanisches Museum, (Luth-
              mer).
25 and 27.   Renascence, private collection, Mainz, (Luthmer).
26.   Renascence, Hildesheim, with niello-work, (Luthmer).
28, 29, 31, and 32. Renascence, (Hefner-Alteneck).
30 and 32.   Renascence, after Hans Mielich, Middle of the 16th century.

THE CHAIN.   (Plate 274.)

Chains are an interesting chapter in ornament. The task of art
here is to treat the stubborn metal in such a way that it will produce flexible, easily-moving forms, which shall still be absolutely
unyielding to tension. This is done by the system of links. Rings,
perforated discs, balls with an eye, &c., are linked together in appropriate ways to form a whole. In the common Chains of everyday
use, nothing but strength and flexibility are expected; in ornamental
chains, attention must be paid to the artistic effect. This is sought
to be attained, less by lavishing care on the single link, than by an
elegant rhythmic sequence of links of different kinds, by effective
alternations of form, size, and treatment (comp. Semper II, p. 497).
Chains used for personal adornment, at least as far so they are of
artistic consequence, are almost always like a Band. All the figures
of the Plate belong to this class, with the exception of figs. 5, 8,
11, and 16. The arrangement may be such that the chain, held
horizontally, is neutral, that is, of the same design upwards and
downwards, right and left (figs. 1, 4, 15, 17, 18); or it m.ay have
an "up and down" (figs. 9 and 13); it may also have a lateral direction,
in which case it is chiefly used to suspend objects (figs. 3, 10,
and 12). Chains are sometimes made tapering towards the end, which
is done by making each successive, link smaller than the preceding.
The ends of chains terminate in Hooks, Eyes, Rings, &c., according

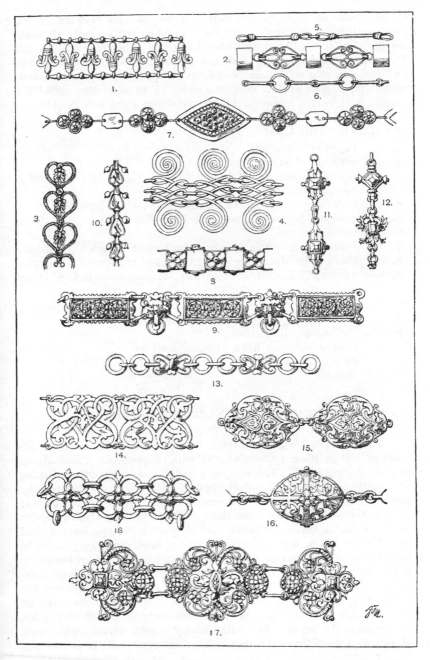

The Chain. Plate 274.

to their use, as Necklets and Belts, or to suspend Watches, Bags, Smelling-bottles, and similar articles. Heraldic and symbolic elements are often found on Chains of Orders and Office, something like fig. 12. The size and material vary with the purpose. The materials are the precious and ordinary metals, sometimes with gems and pearls, enamel, niello, and filigree-work. This last seems to be especially suited for chains, as it readily conveys the idea of being light and flexible.

PLATE 274. THE CHAIN.

1.   Egyptian, (Racinet).
2.   Etruscan, Louvre, Paris, (Racinet).
3.   Greek, filigree, found in the Crimea, Hermitage, St. Petersburg, (Kunsthandwerk).
4.   Etruscan, bronze spirals, United collections, Carlsruhe.
5.   Antique, bronze, United collections, Carlsruhe.
6.   Gallic, bronze.
7.   Indian, silver filigree, from Sumatra, United collections, Carlsruhe.
8.   Small prismatic, from Sumatra, United collections, Carlsruhe.
9.   French, Chain-belt, 16th century, Sauvageot collection, (L'art tous).
10.   Renascence, from a Chatelaine, with enamel and pearls.
11—12. Renascence, gold, Grünes Gewölbe, Dresden.
13—15. Renascence, H. Holbein.
16.   Pierced ellipsoid links, Grünes Gewölbe.
17.   Renascence, exhibition, Carlsruhe, 1881.
18.   Modern.

THE NECKLACE, OR NECKLET. (Plate 275.)

The Necklace has always been a favourite article of feminine adornment. It is worn either alone or with a pendant. Three classes may be distinguished. The first is a ring, consisting of a clasping hoop with or without a pendant (figs. 7 and 8), and mostly used by savage peoples. The second is formed of links in a similar manner to the chain-belt (fig. 10). The third, and at the same time the most perfect form, is that in which a row of pendants hangs from a cord or a slender chain, and encircles the neck, thus giving expression to the idea of a free pendant ending as well as to that of an encircling band. Striking artistic effects may be obtained by the rhythmic alternation of the links, and by a tapering from the middle towards the ends. Egyptian and Antique necklets are frequently constructed on this principle; as are also the neck ornaments of primitive peoples, who replace the pendant by shells, shining insects, corals, or the teeth of animals. Sometimes the three classes are combined; it is not rare

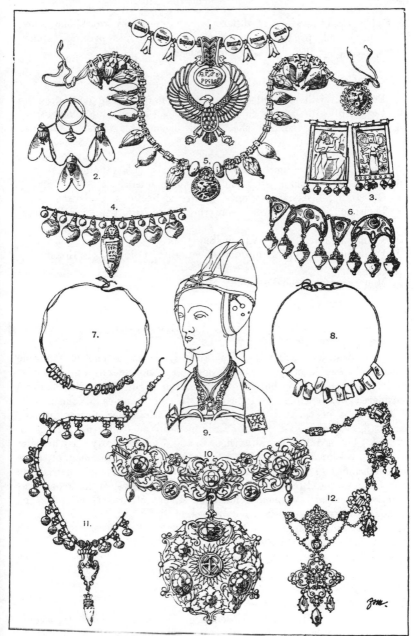

The Necklace. Plate 275.

to find several necklets of different circumferences worn one above the other; and producing a good effect. Metal, precious stones, pearls, &c., play the chief part in Necklaces.

PLATE 275. THE NECKLACE.

1. Egyptian, with enamelled pendant, (Ménard et Sauvageot).
2. Egyptian, with golden flies (symbolic), (Ménard et Sauvageot).
3. Antique, with stamped sheet-metal ornaments, found in Rhodes, (Ménard et Sauvageot.)
4. Egyptian, (Ménard et Sauvageot).
5. Etruscan, gold, Campana collection, Paris, (L'art pour tous).
6. Oriental, gilt silver filigree, (L'art pour tous).
7. Old Italic, Neck-ring, bronze, United collections, Carlsruhe.
8. Barbaric, Neck-ring, iron, from the White Nile, United collections, Carlsruhe.
9. From portrait, Henry VI, of England.
10. From portrait, 1572, municipal museum, Cologne, (Luthmer).
11. Filigree.
12. Modern, (Gewerbehalle).

THE BRACELET. (Plate 276.)

The Bracelet, which is now exclusively an article of feminine adornment, was formerly worn by men also, not merely on the wrist as at the present day, but on the arm too. But even the Antique considered this custom, and that of wearing bangles on the ankles, to be a relic of barbaric times. Bracelets are either closed rings or bands (figs. 9 and 11); or they are open on one side (figs. 2, 6, 8, 13 and 14); or rolled spirally (figs. 3 and 7); or, finally, the bracelet may be a closed chain with a greater or lesser number of links (figs. 10 and 16). Another division is formed by the twisted example (fig. 5). As the Bracelet is an object of some size, it is, more frequently than other ornaments, made of silver rather than of gold; the Antique shows a preference for bronze.

PLATE 276. THE BRACELET.

1.   Egyptian, pierced-work, (Ménard et Sauvageot).
2.   Assyrian, bronze, Louvre, Paris, (Blümner).
3—4.   Roman, found in Pompeii.
5.   Antique, (Ménard et Sauvageot).
6.   Bronze, found near Ladenburg, United collections, Carlsruhe.
7.   Spiral wire, United collections, Carlsruhe.
8.   Bronze, United collections, Carlsruhe.

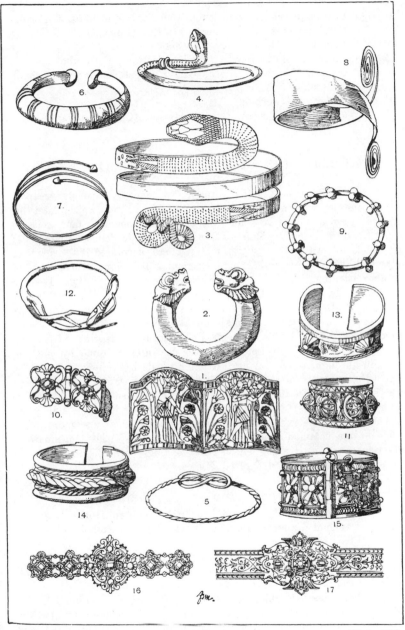

The Bracelet.

Plate 276.

9.   Bronze, found near Ladenburg, United collections, Carlsruhe.
10.   From portrait, 16th century, Gotha, (Luthmer).
11.   Venetian, 16th century, (Mothes).
12.   Javanese, black wood, United collections, Carlsruhe.
13—15. Modern Egyptian, silver, Grand Ducal Landesgewerbehalle, Carlsruhe.
16.   Modern, (Gewerbehalle).
17.   Modern, by Dir. A. Ortwein, Granz, (Gewerbehalle).

THE GIRDLE, THE BUCKLE, AND CLASP. (Plate 277.)

The Girdle was originally used by men to suspend weapons from; and by women to confine the clothing at the waist; later-on, it was worn merely as an ornament, or to carry pouches, fans, scissors, &c. Its form is either that of the Chain-girdle (comp. Plate 274), or Bands of leather or textile material are decorated by ornaments of metal sewed or threaded-on. Particular attention is usually given to the fastening, which is generally a Clasp or Buckle (figs. 1, 7, 8 and 15). The Agraffe (Lat. *agrappa*) or Hook, and the Buckle are applied to other purposes besides fastening Girdles; the former are used as fastenings for garments; the latter on the straps of weapons, harness, &c. The Buckle is complete in itself, consisting of a ring or hoop with a movable pin; and the fastening is done by pushing the pin through a hole in the leather or textile band (figs. 2, 4 and 5). The Clasp consists of two parts, generally symmetrical, one of which can be hooked into the. other (figs. 9—13). Clasps and Buckles are both old inventions; and are found in very early times. As they are objects of practical use rather than ornament, they are more often made of the common than of the precious metals. The terminations of clasps are mostly designed as free-endings, which gives them a certain similarity with decorated hinges.

PLATE 277. THE GIRDLE, THE BUCKLE, AND CLASP.

1.   Greek Girdle, gold and hyacinths, tomb in Ithaca.
2.   Ancient Italic or Roman Buckle, bronze, United collections, Carlsruhe.
3.   Roman Clasp, silver, (Ménard et Sauvageot).
4.   Alemannic, Buckle, bronze, found near Mosbach, United collections, Carlsruhe.
5.   Mediaeval Buckle, Scandinavian, (Weiss, Kostümkunde).
6.   Gallic Girdle, St. Germain Museum, (L'art pour tous).
7.   Gothic Buckle, 15th century, from a picture, municipal museum, Cologne, (Luthmer).

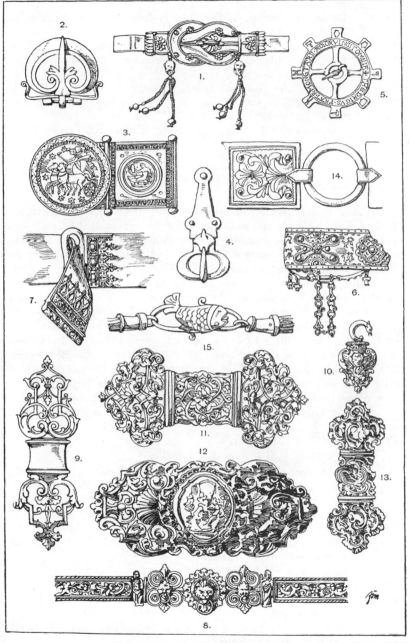

The Girdle, the Buckle, and Clasp.   Plate 277.

8.   Renascence Girdle, 17th century, National Museum, Munich.
9.   Renascence Clasp.
10.   Renascence Clasp, National Museum, Munich.
11.   Renascence Clasp, Kunstgewerbemuseum, Berlin, (Gewerbe-
          halle).
12—13.   Barocco and Rococo Clasps, National Museum, Munich.
14.   Modern Norwegian Girdle, brass and leather, United collec-
          tions, Carlsruhe.
15.   Sumatran Girdle-fastening, silver, United collections, Carls-
          ruhe.

THE PENDANT. (Plate 278.)

Pendants are among the most beautiful of articles of adornment. Their forms and uses are manifold. We find them as Lockets, with and without symbolic meaning; as Ornaments for the hat and the biretta; as "Charms" on watch-chains, and, less richly finished, on Harness. The Pendant is naturally designed on the principle of the free-ending. Sometimes it assumes the form of the Cross, the Medallion, the Votive-tablet, or the Monogram. It serves as a setting for gems, miniatures, coins, &c. It offers the proper field for all kinds of little hanging ornaments; and for the full display of the goldsmith's versatile skill. Examples of exceptional beauty have been transmitted to us by the Antique, and still more so by the Renascence. Not only did the first artists of this period occupy themselves practically with such things; but they designed numerous patterns for them, e. g. Hans Holbein, in his sketchbook for Henry VIII, of England.

We can only offer a small selection from the copious material.

PLATE 278. THE PENDANT.

1.   Egyptian, gold and enamel, (Racinet).
2.   Gold, found in Rhodes, Louvre, Paris, (Ménard et Sauvageot).
3.   Greek, gold filigree, found near Kertsch, Hermitage, St.
          Petersburg, (Kunsthandwerk).
4.   Etruscan, gold, Campana collection, (L'art pour tous).
5.   Ancient Italic, bronze, United collections, Carlsruhe.
6.   Turkish, harness in the Booty of Prince Ludwig of Baden,
          United collections, Carlsruhe.
7—9.   Renascence, (Hefner-Alteneck).
10.   Renascence, 1637, Exhibition, Carlsruhe, 1881.
11.   Empire period, gold filigree, collection of Prof. Marc Rosen-
          berg, Carlsruhe.
12.   Renascence, Antique cameo set in enamelled gold and jewels,
          Paris, (L'art pour tous).

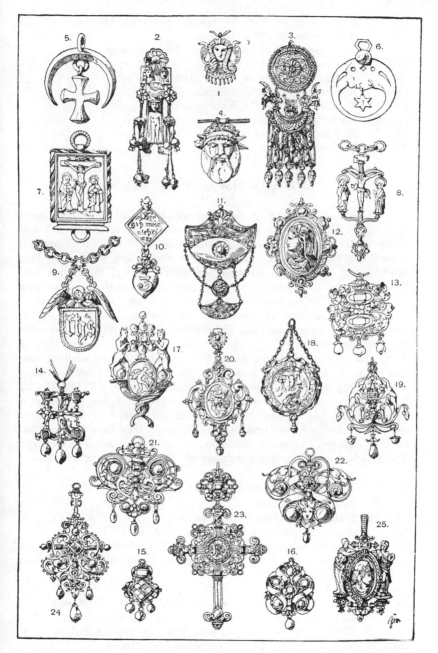

The Pendant. Plate 278.

13.   Renascence, by Hans Brosamer, (Formenschatz).
14.   Renascence, by Hans Holbein.
15—16.   Renascence, by Hans Holbein, (Formenschatz).
17.   Renascence, (Luthmer).
18.   Renascence, 17th century, Silver coin, set.
19.   Renascence, by Julius Bernic, (Luthmer).
20.   Modern, (Blätter für Kunstgewerbe).
21—23.   Modern, (Zeitschrift des Kunstgewerbevereins).
24.   Modern, (Gewerbehalle).
25.   Modern, French.

THE EAR-RING.   (Plate 279.)

The custom of wearing Ear-rings as articles of adornment seems to be of ancient oriental origin; and to have penetrated through Asia Minor to the civilised countries of the West. It has been practised from the earliest times by the Arabs, in Spain, and in Sicily. Both sexes, among the ancient Germans and Gauls, decked themselves with Ear-rings. As the wearing of them implies either that the ear must be pierced or the ornament hung on to the ear, neither of which processes are particularly aesthetic; the custom has fallen out of fashion, and become obsolete. The forms in general are two: the Ring and the Drop. The Rings are either not quite closed (figs. 1, 3, 9, and 10); or they are fastened by a catch of one kind or another (figs. 7, 14, 20, 21, and 31). Drops usually terminate in a wire loop by which they may be suspended (figs. 6, 15, 16, 26, 27, 29, and 30). As these objects must be light, they are generally of delicate form, and modest dimensions, manufactured of the precious metals, in sheet or wire-filigree. As Pendants they have the character of free-endings, frequently consisting of different moveable members. The standard examples are furnished by the Antique and the East.

PLATE 279.   THE EAR-RING.

1—3.   Egyptian, (Racinet).
4—12.   Etruscan, Louvre, Paris, (Racinet).
13.   Greek, in the form of a siren, gold, found in Ithaca.
14—21.   Roman, National Library, Paris, (L'art pour tous).
22.   Bronze, found near Niedereggenen, Baden, United collections, Carlsruhe.
23.   Old Frankish.
24.   Renascence, from portrait, castle at Gotha, (Luthmer).
25.   Louis XVI, gold of various colours, (Racinet).
26—27.   Modern, by Dir. A. Ortwein, Graz, (Gewerbehalle).
28—29.   Modern, Tunis, United collections, Carlsruhe.

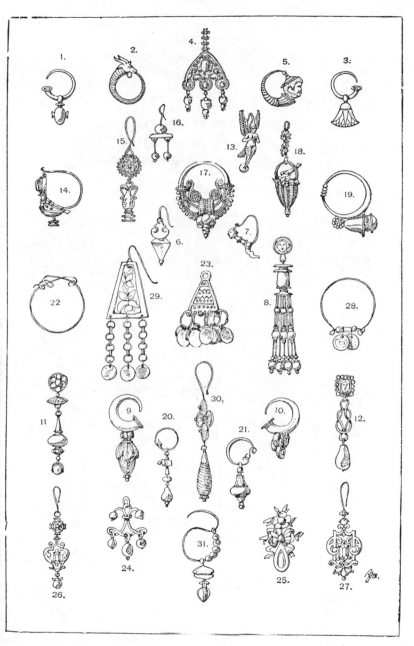

The Ear-ring. Plate 279.

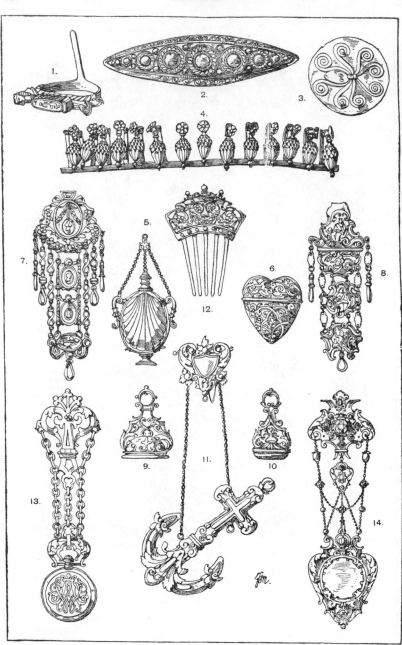

Plate 280.   Miscellaneous Jewelry.

MISCELLANEOUS JEWELRY. (Plate 280.)

Finally, we may mention a number of articles of adornment which, from their nature, are less generally used; either because they are worn only by certain persons, or that, as objects for daily use they only fall within the category of decorative objects when they are richly finished. Among them are decorations for the head, for example, the Diadem, Bridal and other Chaplets, Insignia of Orders of Knighthood, Combs, Scent-bottles, Seals, Needle-cases, &c. The so-called "Chatelaine", was in common use in the Middle Ages; and has been revived lately. It is suspended from the belt or some other part of the dress; and is furnished with hooks, from which Bags, Keys, Fans, Scissors, Watches, Scent-bottles, &c. may be hung (figs. 7, 8, 13 and 14). We may also add Spangles, which were sewed as a decoration on garments in the Antique; and sometimes in later periods (fig. 3).

We give a few examples of these objects, without any pretension to system or exhaustiveness.

PLATE 280. MISCELLANEOUS JEWELRY.

1. Egyptian Diadem, gold incrusted with gems and enamel, with the badge of King Amesis.
2. Greek Head-dress, gold-plate, found in Mykenae, (Blümner).
3. Greek Spangle, ornament of a dress from Mykenae, (Blümner).
4. Greek Diadem, gold, found near Kertsch, Hermitage, St. Petersburg, (Kunsthandwerk).
5. Renascence, Smelling-bottle, as Pendant.
6. Barocco, Smelling-bottle.
7—8. French Chatelaines, 18th century, (Racinet).
9—10. Barocco, Seals, Exhibition, Carlsruhe, 1881.
11. Modern, Needle-case, in anchor-form as a Pendant, private collection, Carlsruhe.
12. Modern, Comb, (Gewerbehalle).
13. Modern, French, Chatelaine, (Gewerbehalle).
14. Modern, Chatelaine, by Dir. A. Ortwein, Graz, (Gewerbehalle).

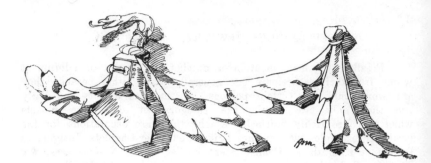

F.

HERALDRY.

Heraldry has so many points of contact with Ornament that it cannot be omitted from a work that deals with the whole art of Decoration. Heraldry includes both the science and the art of armorial bearings. The former contains the rules of framing and bearing coats of arms; the latter is the practical art of "blazoning" or designing and depicting such coats. Armorial bearings are distinct Badges, fixed according to certain principles, which individuals, families and corporations are entitled to bear in perpetuity. Armorial bearings arose during the crusades, towards the end of the 11th century. The elevation of the nobles into a corporation, the addition of the family or surname to the baptismal name, the peculiar usages of Chivalry, the custom of military games and tournaments, are all closely connected with the introduction of armorial bearings. Heraldry as a science did not arise till a later time (about the 13th century). Armorial bearings, whose origin is contemporary with the custom of wearing such Badges, and whose right to be borne was afterwards tacitly recognised, are distinguished from the later bearings, the right to bear which was granted by Letters-patent from princes or their plenipotentiaries. Besides the nobles, the right of armorial bearings was possessed by other patrician, though not noble, families. Their bearings have frequently arisen from monograms, family tokens, and trade-marks. The inscription on a coat of arms of the Fuggers of the year 1382 runs: "Dises zaichen, wirt Vlrich Fugger, vorbemelten Hansen Fuggers Bruder, gepraucht haben, Welchs hernach Jacob Fugger, des namens der erst, angenommen, und das sambt seinen

Sünen, bis auf aufpringung des Wappens, gefiert hat" (This token
was no doubt used by Ulrich Fugger the brother of the above-named
Hans Fugger: it was afterwards adopted by Jacob Fugger, the first
of the name, and borne by him and his sons until the assumption
of the coat of arms). The marshalling of armorial bearings was the
duty of the Heralds, whose official badge was the tabard and the staff.
The Heralds' Colleges still exercise control over armorial bearings on
behalf of the State. Including the coats of families, towns, corporations,
and offices, there are probably about 200,000 coats of arms in
existence. Coats are called allusive or punning when they suggest,
(in whole or in part), the name of the bearer. The pikes on the coat
of the Lucy family, the hirondelles of the Arundells of Wardour, are
familiar instances in English heraldry.

We may distinguish three principal epochs of armorial bearings:
(1) The period from the 11th to the 13th century, in which the
shield alone with its badge formed the Arms, which is the period of
the evolution of Heraldry; (2) The period from the 13th to the 15th
century, in which shield, helmet, and crest formed the Arms, in which
painted shields and helmets were really worn, which was the golden
age of heraldry; (3) The period from the 16th century to the present
time, in which the wearing of shields and helmets with badges was
discontinued; and Heraldry creased to be a living art, which is the
period of decay, in which arbitrariness, ignorance, and a pedantic ad-
herence to antiquated principles have taken the place of the living
art. From the point of view of style we may distinguish: — Early
Gothic, Late Gothic and Renascence Arms; as also those of the Barocco and Rococo periods; and Modern times. The general direction
of style has always had an influence on Heraldry; but the developement
of architecture is on the whole always some twenty years in advance.
The developement of heraldry was different in different countries; and
even the modern English, French, German, and other systems, differ
from one-another in several essential points.

Here, of course, we cannot go minutely into the details of the
subject. We shall only give, in all brevity, what is absolutely
necessary. The Plates will deal with the colours or Tinctures, the
Shapes and Divisions of the Shield, the Charges, the Helmet and its
accessories; the badges of Rank and Dignity; and Pageantry. Those
who wish to study Heraldry more deeply, will find an ample literature at their disposal; since Bartolus de Saxoferrato took up the
subject in the middle of the 14th century, more than enough has
been written about heraldry. As accompaniments and supplements
to study and teaching we may recommend the excellent work of
F. Warnecke: *Heraldisches Handbuch,* illustraded by Doepler the
younger; the *Anleitung zur praktischen Darstellung und Ausführung
heraldischer Ornamente für das gesamte Kunstgewerbe,* by Detlav

Freih. von Biedermann, with illustrations, in the *Zeitschrift des Münchener Kunstgewerbevereins,* 1885; and the *Katechismus der Heraldik* by Dr. Ed. Freih. von Sacken. These works have been followed in this chapter, and our illustrations are taken from them. Heralds have invented a special language of their own, that is always used in Blazoning, which is the technical description of a coat of Arms; and it should always be as correct and concise as possible, so that the coat may be drawn from it. This language will be used, as far as possible, in the explanations of the following plates.

Finally, we may observe that anyone, who has to deal practically with Heraldry, will scarcely ever succeed in satisfying all those who have laid-down and still lay-down rules on the subject. Although, on the one hand, it seems advisable that on the whole a certain order should be maintained and arbitrariness excluded, still, on the other hand, a good deal of antiquated rubbish might be eliminated from the rules without doing any harm. On this point real heralds like Warnecke are all agreed. The safe path is in the middle; that artistic freedom is quite consistent with observance of heraldic rules is shown by the masters of the Renascence: Dürer, Burckmair, and others. For our present purpose: the most suitable sources for the study are the drawings of these Masters; and next to them: old Seals, Windows, and Monuments. Heraldic ornaments may be applied to thousands of things; in Architecture, in Mural painting, on Furniture, in Textiles, in Documents, on Harness, &c. But they should only be applied where they have a representative character; and then only with moderation and purpose, and in due proportion to the object.

Tinctures, and Divisions of the Shield. (Plate 281.)

In the good old days of Heraldry there were six Tinctures, which were almost exclusively used, two metals and four colours. The metals are gold (or), and silver (argent); which for practical reasons were often replaced by yellow, and white. The original colours are red (gules), blue (azure), black, (sable), and green (vert). Full, strong shades were employed: vermilion or minium for red, cobalt or ultramarine for blue, Paris green, emerald green, or some other striking shade for green. The original scale of colours was afterwards enlarged by the addition of the so-called "Proper" or natural colour of the object, purple (purpure), ash-gray (which is not used in English Heraldry), blood-colour (murrey), and tawny (tenne). Natural objects, men, animals &c. were represented "proper", that is, in their natural tints; whereas the older heraldry depicted these objects in one of the nearest original tinctures: e. g. the lion was golden or red, the eagle was black or red, and so on. Purple is not used on the Shields, but only on Crowns, Caps of estate, and Mantlings. Murrey and Tenne are tinctures that might well have been dispensed-with; as they conflict with the original principle, which was to make the shield clear and distinct at a distance.

Where coats of Arms are depicted uncoloured, as is frequently the case in books: the tinctures in the oldest period were indicated by their initial letters. Afterwards they were indicated by dots and hatchings. Silver was left plain, gold was indicated by dots, red by perpendicular lines, blue by horizontal lines, black by crossed horizontal and perpendicular lines, and the other tinctures were also marked as shown on the Plate.

The Furs are also generally reckoned among the tinctures. Ermine has black tails or tips on a white or silver ground; Erminois has the same tints reversed. On robes, mantlings, and coronets: ermine is depicted in its natural form. The fur known in German heraldry as *kürsch* is denoted by strokes arranged like scales. Vair, with its varieties "vair per pale" and "countervair", is of silver and blue in the shapes shown on the Plate. Vair has obviously arisen from an arbitrary division of the field, like the check and fusil, of which we shall have to speak later on.

Damaskeening (see also p. 281.) is the name given to minute decoration intended to enliven the various tinctures without interfering with the effect of the colours or altering the coat. The design is arbitrary: originally geometrical patterns were preferred, afterwards scrolls and curves were added.

In the case of relief-work, when it is not painted: the damaskeening and the dots and hatchings of the tinctures, may also be plastic, but the height of the relief must be moderate if the effect is not to be spoilt. On seals and similar objects: the effect is produced by engraving. Where the coat, instead of standing upright, is in a slanting position, the lines of the hatchings follow the axis of the shield, as otherwise confusion would be inevitable.

According to good heraldic rules, colour should not be laid upon colour, nor metal on metal. Coats which transgress this rule are said to be false. The principle cannot, however, be always maintained in the case of composite coats (comp. Plate 283).

In the divisions of the shield: the expressions "dexter", and "sinister" (right, and left) refer to the bearer of the shield; they are to be understood as if one were standing behind the shield and holding it in front of the breast; hence it follows that the expressions mean just the reverse of what they do in ordinary life. If we divide the shield by lines: we have Fields, which are termed "quarters" when they are rectangular. The example in the Plate divides the shield into nine quarters. The names of the different quarters are given, so that it is unnecessary to repeat them here.

The Heraldic Colours or Tinctures.

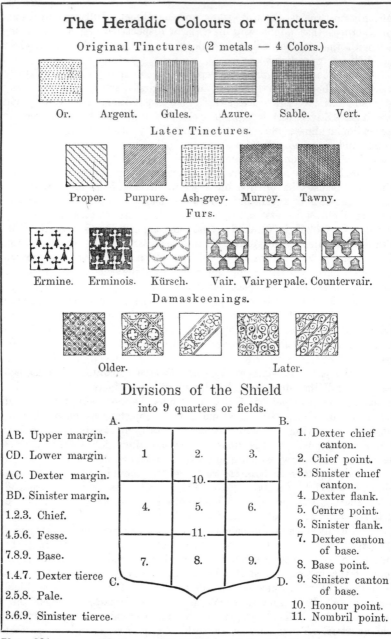

Original Tinctures. (2 metals — 4 Colors.)

Or.   Argent.   Gules.   Azure.   Sable.   Vert.

Later Tinctures.

Proper.   Purpure.   Ash-grey.   Murrey.   Tawny.

Furs.

Ermine.   Erminois.   Kürsch.   Vair.   Vairperpale.   Countervair.

Damaskeenings.

Older.   Later.

Divisions of the Shield
into 9 quarters or fields.

AB. Upper margin.
CD. Lower margin.
AC. Dexter margin.
BD. Sinister margin.
1.2.3. Chief.
4.5.6. Fesse.
7.8.9. Base.
1.4.7. Dexter tierce
2.5.8. Pale.
3.6.9. Sinister tierce.

1. Dexter chief canton.
2. Chief point.
3. Sinister chief canton.
4. Dexter flank.
5. Centre point.
6. Sinister flank.
7. Dexter canton of base.
8. Base point.
9. Sinister canton of base.
10. Honour point.
11. Nombril point.

Plate 281.   Tinctures, and Divisions of the Shield.

The shield sometimes bears a smaller shield. The large shield which bears the smaller is called the Escutcheon. The smaller shield in the centre is termed the Inescutcheon. The Inescutcheon sometimes bears a third shield which is then said to be "sur le tout du tout". The smaller shields have the same shape as the large shield.

The chief and the dexter side of the shield are the most honourable parts; and preference is given to the angle of the dexter chief or canton. In blazoning a coat: the description always starts from this point.

SHAPES OF THE SHIELD. (Plate 282.)

The shape of the shield is very varied; and is chiefly determined by the period in which it originated. The oldest shape is the triangular or "heater-shaped" shield (fig. 1). It was in use in the 12th, 13th and 14th centuries. On seals, it is first one-half and at a later time one-third the height of a man; the ratio of its height to its breadth is about 10 : 7. In the 14th century shields straight at the top and rounded at the bottom (we may term them half-round) began to appear; and after them shields pointed at the bottom (fig. 2). This shape, and the 16th century shapes which were developed from it (figs. 4—6), were probably never actually borne; but are merely heraldic. At the end of the 14th century the Tilting-shields begin to make their appearance, their shape being based on that of the shields used in tournaments (figs. 7—10). The indentations in the sides of these are suggested by the "bouche" or place for the lance on shields intended for actual use. The Tilting-shield is considerably smaller than the Triangular-shield; it is about one-fifth the height of a man. At the end of the 15th century the old shapes disappear, and make way for the German or strap-work shields. These latter were never in actual use, but are ornamental inventions mostly based on the Tilting shield. Figs. 19—26 give a number of such shields belonging to different periods of the Renascence epoch. Shapes like figs. 11 and 12 are very common in Italy at that time. Elliptic, circular, and almond-shaped shields are not rare, especially in the Barocco period, a time in which Heraldry was treated in a somewhat arbitrary fashion. Of shapes that are specifically modern, we may mention: figs. 16 and 17, the former of which was used for the Arms of Great Britain & Ireland; and of France; while the latter is the best adapted for the blazoning of complicated coats. The Lozenge-shape (fig. 18) is especially the shield of ladies; in France, where it has been common since the 13th century, it is frequently surrounded with a knotted twisted girdle.

PLATE 282. THE SHAPE OF THE SHIELD.

1—3.   Triangular, pointed, and half-round.
4—6.   Simple shapes, Renascence.
7—10. Simple shapes, Tilting-shields.
11—12. Italian Renascence.
13—15. Elliptical, almond, and circular.
16—17. Modern.
18.   Lozenge-shaped.
19.   German, Michel Müller, 1564.
20.   German, unknown master of the 16th century.
21.   German, Daniel Lindtmair, 1595.
22.   German, Jost Amman, end of 16th century.
23.   German, school of Holbein, 16th century.
24.   German, Hans Wägmann, 1565, (Warnecke).
25.   German, 16th century.
26.   German, 16th century, (Formenschatz).

ORDINARIES. (Plate 283.)

Heraldic representations may be divided into Ordinaries, and Charges.

The Ordinaries are the geometrical figures which are formed when the shield is divided into different fields by straight or curved lines which extend to the margin of the shield. The number of such figures is infinite. Plate 283 contains a collection of the ordinaries which most commonly occur. We shall not discuss each figure in detail. The following blazoning or description of the figures on the Plate will, no doubt, give the reader all he requires to know. The blazoning begins from the upper dexter angle of each shield.

PLATE 283. THE ORDINARIES.

1. Per pale, sable and or.
2. Paly of four, argent and sable.
3. Argent, the dexter tierce gules.
4. Gules, a pale or.
5. Argent, a pallet (narrower than a pale) sable.
6. Per fesse, or and gules.
7. Barry of five, azure and argent.
8. Or, a chief azure.
9. Argent, a base gules.
10. Argent, a base vert.

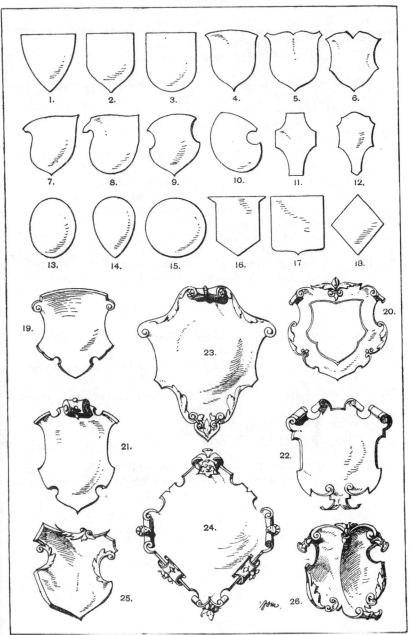

Shapes of the Shield.

Plate 282.

11. Or, a fesse gules.

12. Argent, a barrulet sable.

13. Per pale; the dexter half argent, the sinister half per fesse azure and or.

14. Per fesse; the upper half per pale sable and gules, the lower argent.

15. Quarterly, or and azure.

16. Checky of nine, vert and argent.

17. Checky of twenty, or and gules.

18. Quarterly: the 1st and 4th per pale, argent and gules; the 2nd and 3rd or.

19. Per fesse, gules and argent, a pale counterchanged.

20. Per pale, barry of five, or and azure, counterchanged.

21. Paly of six, argent and sable, a fesse counterchanged.

22. Or, a cross gules.

23. Argent, a dexter canton sable.

24. Azure, a chief point vair.

25. Per bend, or and vert.

26. Per bend sinister, argent and azure.

27. Or, in the dexter chief a triangle sable.

28. Argent, in the sinister base a triangle gules.

29. Or, a bend gules.

30. Bendy sinister of six, azure and argent.

31. Per saltire, vert and argent.

32. Per bend, the dexter half argent, the sinister per bend sinister, vert and or.

33. Per bend sinister, bendy of six, sable and argent, counterchanged.

34. Lozengy, argent and azure.

35. Fusilly, argent and azure.

36. Or, a pile azure.

37. Azure, a pile argent, issuing from the sinister side.

38. Gyronny of four, argent and gules, issuing from the dexter chief point.

39. Or, a chevron vert.

40. Chevronny of six, azure and argent.

41. Party per pale and saltire, gules and argent.

42. Gyronny of eight, or and azure.

43. Argent, a gyron azure, moving from the dexter side.

44. Per pall, sable, argent and gules.

45. Per pall reversed, or, argent and azure.

46. Argent, a pall gules.

47. Pily barwise, argent and azure.

48. Per fesse angled, argent and gules.

49. Per fesse escartely, azure and or.

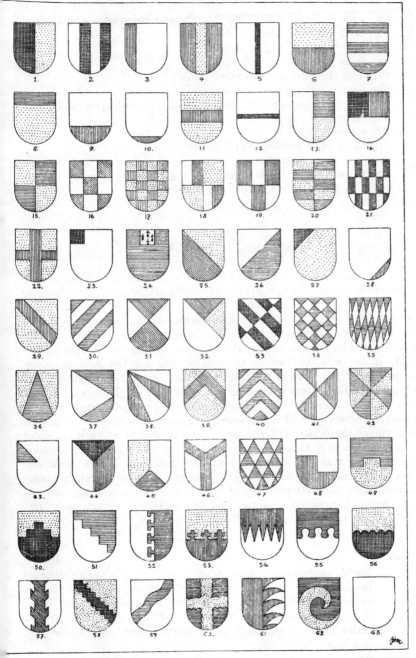

Ordinaries.

Plate 283.

50. Or, a pile indented sable, also Per chevron indented, or and sable.
51. Per bend indented, azure and argent.
52. Per pale potented, argent and azure.
53. Per fesse potented, or and gules.
54. Per fesse dentilly, gules and aregnt.
55. Per fesse nebuly, azure and argent.
56. Sable, a chief engrailed or, also Per fesse engrailed, or and sable.
57. Argent, a pale raguly.
58. Or, a bend indented.
59. Argent, a bend sinister wavy azure.
60. Azure, a cross engrailed ór.
61. Gules, four wolf's teeth argent, moving from the sinister side.
62. Azure, a gurge issuing from the sinister base.
63. Argent.

CHARGES. (Plates 284—285.)

The second class of heraldic representations are Charges. We distinguish natural, imaginative, and artificial charges, according as they belong to the kingdoms of nature, the heavenly bodies, phenomena of nature, or to fantastic forms; or again to art, trade, mechanics, &c. Contrary to the Ordinaries, whose outlines usually touch the edge of the shield, the charges usually stand free in the field, at any rate, on two or three sides, and fill the field as much as possible. The charges are all more or less conventionalised; and show conventional forms agreeing with the style of the times. Attention must be paid to this point, so that the unity of style may be preserved between shield and charges They are mostly shown in profile, and vigorously drawn and outlined. The tinctures, at least in older heraldry, are not those of nature, but one of the nearest heraldic tinctures, so that the idealisation extends not only to the form but also to the colour. Complicated objects are often comparatively simplified; trees, for example, appear with few leaves and fruits, &c.

Some charges, such as the lion and eagle, are of extremely frequent occurrence; others the following are rarer.

Among animals the following are represented: —

PLATE 284.

1.   The Lion (rampant) with open jaws and protruding tongue; the body lean, especially towards the hinder quarters; the tail curled upwards, natural or split, but not arbitrarily; the teeth, claws, &c. are gules on metal, or and argent on colors; the entire figure is generally or or gules, more rarely sable, and still more rarely azure.

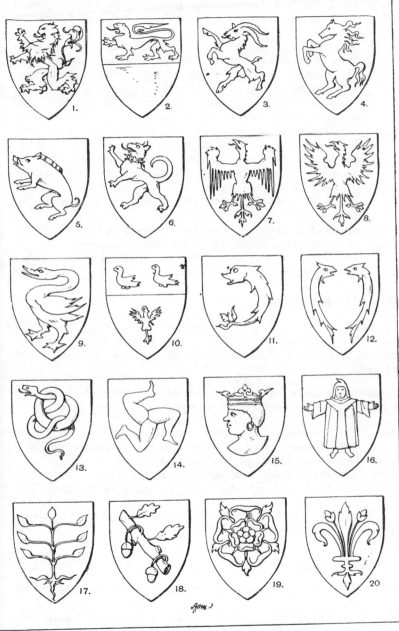

Charges.   Plate 284.

2. The Leopard, a lion walking (passant), the head frequently turned to the spectator (guardant); the tail curled over the back, (see also Plate 44).

3. The Ibex jumping (salient), the horns large, and (like the claws) of a different colour to the body, which is usually sable.

4. The Horse (rampant), mostly without saddle and harness; mane and tail flying; generally sable, argent or gules.

5. The Boar (rampant), bristles erect, and (like the tusks and claws) of a different tincture to the body.

6. The Dog (rampant), generally with a collar, with ears erect.

7—8. The Eagle (displayed), the talon spread; the head usually turned to the dexter side, the beak open; the tongue protruding; frequently barbed; the tail is sometimes ornamentally treated; generally sable, gules, or or, (see also Plate 53).

9. The Goose (like the swan) with reverted neck, generally argent, or sable.

10. The Martlet (which is a Swallow without beak and feet,) the two upper are passant, the lower one is displayed.

11. The Dolphin (rising), often with dorsal crest and ornamental tail.

12. Two Dolphins (rising and respecting each other), with open mouths.

13. The Serpent (nowed), generally argent, azure, or vert.

Other animals of frequent occurrence are the Stag, Bear, Wolf, Fox, Bull, Cock, Raven, Dove, Stork, Crane, Pelican, Crab, Whelk, &c. Parts of animals are also not infrequent, such as the wings, head, and claws.

Both the entire human body and its several members are used in heraldry; we may mention as examples:

14. The Triquetra, 3 legs with bent knee, conjoined, and regularly disposed round a point; a badge on antique shields in Greek vase-paintings, and the Arms of Isle of Man.

15. The Moor's-head, with ear-rings and crown.

16. The Monk with extended arms, the Arms of München.

In addition to the above: arms, hands, legs, trunks, clasped hands, &c.; also angels, saints, deities, fools, maidens, knights, kings, savages, &c.

Among plants are:

17. The Lime, uprooted, with few leaves, (also fruit-trees, the oak, fir, &c.).

18. The Oak-branch, gnarled, with few fruits and leaves, (also withered branches, or logs, &c.).

19.   The Rose, idealised as a rosette, single or double, in five to eight parts.
20.   The Lily or Fleur-de-lis, conventional, consisting of three petals, with or without stamens; used in art long before the birth of heraldry; common in French coats.

In addition to the above: Clover, Nettle, Water-lilies, Grapes, Pomegranates, Fir-cones &c.

Plate 285. Charges.

The most frequent imaginary figures and monsters are:

1. The Griffin (rampant), with eagle's head and wings, lion's body, tail curved upward or downward, the upper and lower halves often of different colors.
2. The Panther, similar to the griffin, but without wings, usually spitting flame (turned towards the sinister side).
3. The Dragon, a winged reptile with two lion's paws or eagle's claws. (The wivern is similar, but with hinder feet.)
4. The Dragon with wolf's jaws, serpent's body and fish-tail.
5. The two-headed Eagle (an ordinary eagle with two heads turned away from each other, each with nimbus), the coat of the Holy Roman Empire.
6. The Seiren (an eagle with the bust of a virgin), the arms of Nuremberg.
7. The Mermaid (a naked female figure, terminating below the breast in a fish - tail), the figure is also found without arms and also symmetrical, with two tails curved upwards.
8. The Sea-lion, with the fore-part of a lion terminating in a fish - tail.

Of the heavenly bodies there occur:

9. The Sun, with face and sixteen rays, straight and wavy alternately; always gold.
10. The Moon, waxing or waning, with or without face (in the first case the crescent is argent and the face or).
11. The Star, with rays of five to eight points; or.

Less common are: Comets, and the Earth, with the lines of latitude and longitude.

Among the phenomena of nature we have:

11. The Cloud, very conventional, argent or azure.
12. The Rainbow, gules, or, and azure (shown in the Plate above a triple hill).

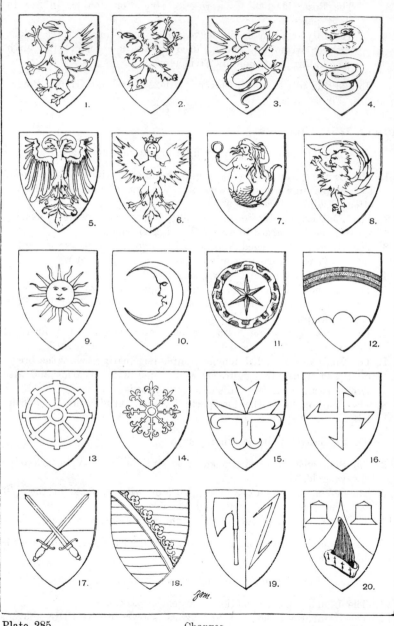

Plate 285. Charges.

In addition: Storm and Wind, depicted by heads blowing; Lightning, depicted by a bundle of flames.

To the artificial objects which are employed belong: Architectural constructions (towers, gates, castles, churches, bridges, fountains, ships); Utensils (tools, instruments, weapons, anchors, keys, banners); Vessels (kettles, goblets, mugs); articles of attire (hats, caps, belts, crowns, mantles, shoes); family and trade Tokens, Monograms and Crosses of all kinds. Some examples are:

13. The Wheel, with eight spokes projecting beyond the felloe.
14. The Wheel of Cleves, a rosette terminating in eight lilies.
15. The Maltese Cross, and the cross ancrée (the Plate shows one half of each).
16. The Cross cramponée.
17. Two crossed Swords.
18. The Crancelin, a wreath of rue, resembling the hoop of a crown.
19. The Axe, and the two-headed Axe.
20. The Hat, and the Cap of maintenance.

Several charges may be combined in the same coat, or one charge may be placed over another. The same charge may also be repeated in a coat. The blazoning of the charges is not so simple as that of the ordinaries; and, when the technical language of heraldry fails, we must have recourse to the language of every-day life. We will here give a few of the commonest of these technical expressions with brief explanations:

accompanied: the main figure is surrounded by smaller figures.

accosted: a figure has other figures by its side.

armed, beaked, membered: an animal is furnished with claws, beak, members, &c., of a different colour from the animal itself.

charged: when one figure bears another.

counterchanged: when the different tinctures alternate with one another.

couped: when a part of a figure appears to have been cut-off clean.

erased: when a part of a figure appears to have been torn-off.

issuant: when a figure rises out of the bottom of an ordinary or shield.

flanked: when one figure stands by the side of another.

naissant: when part of a figure rises from the centre of an ordinary.

passant: when an animal is represented as walking with one foot raised.

rampant: when an animal rises on its hind feet; the usual position for wild animals.

statant: when all four feet of an animal touch the ground.

semé or powdered: when an arbitrary number of one figure is scattered over the shield.

2 and 1: three figures, placed thus `. .`

2, 2 and 1: five figures, placed thus `. .`

1, 3 and 1: five figures, placed thus `. . .`

2, 1 and 2: five figures, placed thus `. .`

and so on.

FORMS OF THE HELMET.   (Plate 286.)

In the earliest days of Heraldry the shield by itself formed the coat; and it is, down to the present time, sufficient for the presentment of the bearings. To a complete coat, however, belong further the Helmet, and the Crest. Sometimes, particulary on seals, the Helmet and Crest are used alone as a badge. But just as we saw that all shields are not suitable for heraldic purposes, so here, too, there are only a few helmets which have found acceptance in heraldry; such as the Tilting-helmets. We have to consider four forms. The oldest is the Salade, (fig. 1). The Heaume, the lower half of which is cylindrical and the upper half a truncated cone, rests on the shoulders, (figs. 2—4). The Tilting-helmet (figs. 6—9), is more elegant than the heaume; it fits better to the form of the head, and has a slit for the purpose of vision, (fig. 5 shows an intermediate form between the Heaume and the Tilting-helmet). The latest form is that with the barred Visor (figs. 10—11). This fits closer to the head than the Tilting-helmet; the slit has been enlarged to a broad opening, guarded either by vertical bars or by a grating. The Armet (fig. 12), and other helmets, like the Burgonet, are unheraldic; and are seldom seen in Arms.

Speaking generally: the Salade belongs to the 13th; the Heaume to the 14th; the Tilting-helmet to the 15th and 16th centuries; the Vizor also belongs to the two latter centuries. The first three helmets are known as "closed", the Vizor-helmet as "open".

PLATE 286.   THE HELMET.

1.   Salade, first half of 14th century, Armory, Berlin, 11 $^3/_4$ ins. high.

2—3.   Heaume, front and side view, 14th century.

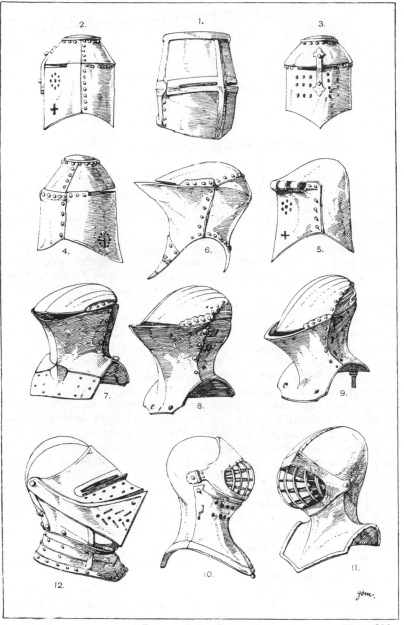

Forms of the Helmet. Plate 286.

4.   Heaume, second half of the 14th century, from the collec-
          tion of Gustav von Decker, Berlin, 14 1/2 ins. high, (Warnecke).
5.   Heaume, approximating to the form of the Tilting-helmet,
          14th century.
6—9.   Tilting helmets.
10—11.   Helmets with barred Vizors.
12.   Armet.

HELMET TRAPPINGS.   (Plates 287—288.)

Plates 287 and 288 show the Helmet in conjunction with the
coat of Arms. As the Helmet was only worn by knights, it belongs,
strictly speaking, only to the coats of knightly families; towns and
corporations, the clergy, and ladies, do not bear the helmet, although
there are exceptions.

As regards style, the Helmet should match the form of the Shield.
The Salade and the Heaume belong to the Triangular - shield: the
Tilting - helmet also belongs to these and still more to the Tilting-
shield. Helmets with barred Vizors are most suitable to Half-round-
shields. The size should also be in proportion to that of the Shield.
The height varies between $1/2$ and $2/3$ the height of the Shield.
The usual position is over the centre of the upper margin of the
shield, and resting upon it (not free), so that it covers a little of
the field (Plate 287, 5). If the shield is represented in a slanting
attitude; the helmet rests on the highest angle (Plate 287. 6, 7, 8).
When the coat is composite, several Helmets may be placed upon the
Shield; they are then proportionately smaller in size. When the
number of Helmets is 2, 4, or 6: they turn their profile to each
other; when the number is uneven, the central one is shown in full
face. Only one helmet can be placed on a slanting shield. Helmets
may also be placed at the side of the shield, or borne by the supporters. The helmet is coloured as if made of polished iron, frequently
with decorations of silver or gold; or the entire helmet may be gilt
or silvered. If the bearer was entitled to wear any Collar, he might
show it on the Helmet (Plate 287. 5); but these appendages are non-
essential; and are not met - with before the 15th century. The Helmet
is usually depicted as lined with red cloth.

The essential trappings in a complete coat of Arms are: 1. the
Crest, 2. the Mantling.

The Crest probably originated from the custom of painting
heraldic figures on the helmet. At a later date, plastic ornaments
were added to the helmet; they have some figurative connection with
the coat. If the coat is blazoned with heraldic figures: these are
repeated either wholly, or partly, in a simple manner, as a crest

(Plate 288, figs. 1—4); if the blazoning is with ordinaries: these are repeated on certain objects selected as Crests. The principal of these objects are:

Horns, in pairs, curved as a crescent or a lyre, in later times broadened out at the ends like a mouthpiece, painted with the tinctures or ordinaries of the coat, surmounted with branches, &c. (Plates 287. 4, 288. 4 and 5).

Wings, natural or artificial, singly or in pairs, displayed, or in profile; painted with the tinctures or ordinaries of the coat (Plates 287. 1 and 7; 288. 6).

Cushions and screens, round or square discs, painted with the blazoning of the coat, hung and surmounted with tassels, bells, and peacock's feathers (Plate 287. 6).

Caps, pointed and turned up, showing the colours and blazoning of the shield, the tips decorated with coronets, plumes, &c. (Plate 287. 5).

Quivers, cylindrical or conical tubes, painted with the colours of the shield, crowned with coloured feathers (Plate 287. 8).

Human beings, animals, and all kinds of artificial objects; the former often depicted as half-figures. We must refrain from entering into detail into the various relations, often full of meaning, between the crest and the shield; as an example we may refer to Plate 287, 2, where the blazon of crossed arrows and pitcher on the shield are repeated as a quiver and a goblet in the hands of the maiden who forms the crest.

The Mantling is the connecting-link between the Helmet and the Shield. In the oldest times it was formed of cloth: at a later date covers of stiffened material, leather, metal-plate, &c., were used, the edges being cut-out into ornamental shapes. The same materials were also employed for the Crest. During the Renascence period: the Mantling was cut into ribbon-like strips, each strip being treated independently like an Artificial-leaf. The Wreath is interposed between the Crest and the Helmet, (Plate 288. 1, 3, 6). It rarely has more or less than two tinctures. Where the Crest is directly connected with the Helmet: the tinctures of the Shield are correspondingly continued on the Wreath. The Mantling shows the tinctures of the coat counterchanged in such a way that the colour is usually visible outside, the metal inside. If it have four colours: the chief ones are on the dexter, the others on the sinister side. It should correspond in style with the rest of the Arms: Salades and heaumes require simple edges (Plate 287. 7); while Tilting and Vizored helmets require jagged or scalloped edges.

PLATE 287. THE HELMET TRAPPINGS.

1. Tilting-helmet, with rich Mantling, and Crest of double wings, Albrecht Dürer, coat of arms of Death, 1503.
2. Coat, with Tilting-helmet, rich Mantling, and Crest of a virgin, German Renascence, (Formenschatz).
3. Half-round-shield, with Vizored-helmet, Mantling like ribbons, and Crest two swans' necks.
4. Tilting-shield, inclined to the sinister side, Vizored-helmet, Mantlling like ribbons, and Crest two horns decorated.
5. German shield, with Vizored-helmet, and Crest a Cap-of-maintenance.
6. Shield, inclined to the dexter side, with Vizored-helmet, Mantling, and Crest a cushion.
7. Triangular-shield, inclined to the dexter side, with Salade, Mantling, and Crest double wings.
8. Half-round-shield, inclined to the sinister side, with Vizored-helmet, and high Crest and Mantling, (Dietz).
(Figs. 3 to 8 are from Siebmacher's Wappenbuch.)

PLATE 288. THE HELMET TRAPPINGS.

1. Tilting-shield, with Vizored-helmet, Mantling, and Crest an eagle.
2. Tilting-shield, with Vizored-helmet, Mantling, and Crest of a naissant figure, German Renascence, (Formenschatz).
3. Tilting-shield, inclined to the dexter side, with Tilting-helmet and naissant bull as Crest, Italian Renascence, palace in Florence.
4. Tilting-shield, inclined to the dexter side, with Tilting-helmet, Mantling, and crest of horns.
5—6. Coats, by Hans Sebald Beham, 1544.
7. Modern coat, on seal, by A. von Werner.

CROWNS, &c. (Plate 289.)

The principal heraldic badges of rank and dignity are: the Crown, Hat, Cap-of-maintenance, Wand, Sword, Key, &c., and the insignia of the various Orders of Knighthood.

The Crown-of-rank, which is not to be confounded with the crown of the shield, is placed above the shield in the place of the Helmet; the same holds good of the Coronets, and Caps (figs. 11—14). These latter have partly a conventional form, appertaining to the dignity; and they have special forms for special cases.

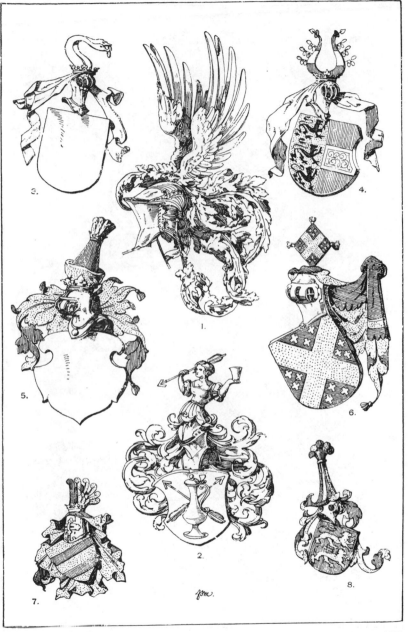

Helmet Trappings.   Plate 287.

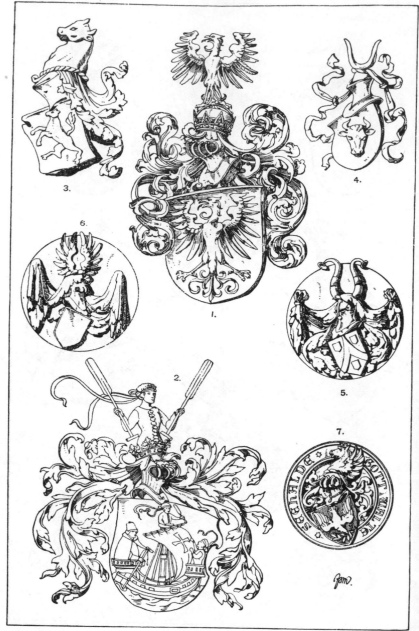

Plate 288.

Helmet Trappings.

PLATE 289. CROWNS, CORONETS, &c. [according to German Heraldry].

1. The German Imperial-crown: a circle of gold, set with brilliants and formed of eight shields, with four gold arches, surmounted by the imperial mound and cross, lined with gold brocade, with two decorated waving ribbons of gold.

2. The Austrian Imperial-crown: a jewelled circle with eight leaves, three arches curving from front to back; closed at the sides, lined red; crowned with a cross.

3. The Regal-crown: a jewelled circle with eight leaves; eight arches set with jewels or pearls; mound an cross.

4. The Grand-ducal-coronet: a royal crown, lined red.

5. The Ducal-coronet; faced with ermine, eight leaves, red lining, with mound and cross.

6. The Princely-coronet: faced with ermine, four leaves, red lining, mound and cross.

7. The Coronet of a Serene Highness: circle with eight leaves, red cap, with ermine tippet.

8. The Count's Coronet: gold circle with sixteen pearls (nine are visible).

9. The Baron's Coronet: twelve pearls (seven are visible).

10. The Nobleman's Coronet: eight pearls (five are visible).

11. Arms with Crown, by Albrecht Dürer.

12. Papal coat of Arms, with tiara and keys.

13. Arms, by Hans Burckmair, with mitre and crozier.

14. Archbishop's Hat: green with ten tassels (on each side). Cardinal's hat: red with fifteen tassels. Bishop's hat: green with six tassels.

Orders and Decorations are either the badges of certain brotherhoods (the Knights of Malta, the Temple, S. John, the Teutonic Order, &c.); or they are distinctions conferred by sovereigns. The former are blazoned on the shield, quarterly with the personal bearings (fig. 16), or they are placed beside or behind the shield so that the ends of the cross project beyond the edge of the shield. The latter are almost without exception suspended from collars or borne below the shield (Plate 290. 4, 7).

15. The Order of the Golden Fleece (founded by Philip of Burgundy in 1429).

16. Shield, with the Maltese order quarterly.

17—18. Pennons, or Standards: they are either placed as a background to the shield, or borne by the supporters; they are therefore a part of Heraldic pageantry.

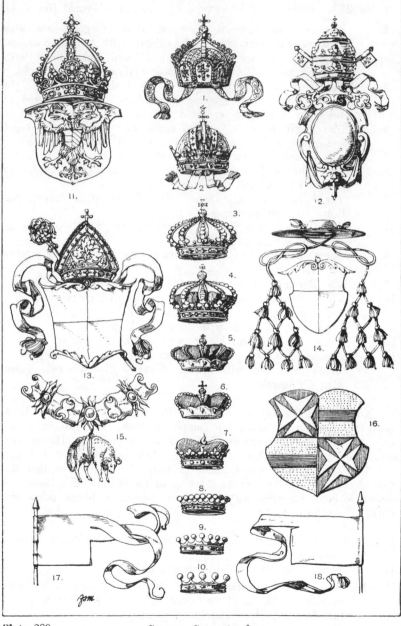

Plate 289. Crowns, Coronets, &c.

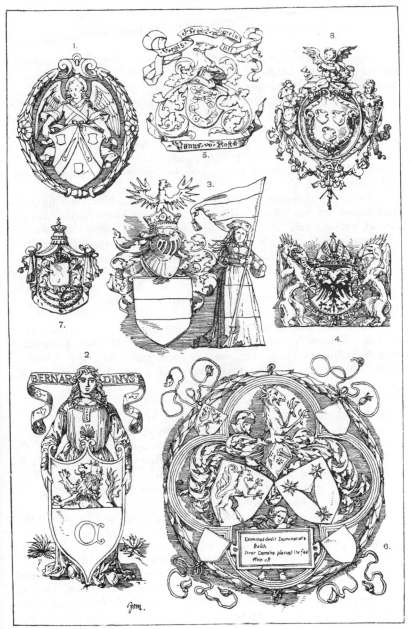

Heraldic Accessories.

Plate 290.

HERALDIC ACCESSORIES. (Plate 290.)

Under this title, we group such decorations as form do not an essential part of the Coat, but rather give an artistic finish to it. The principal are: Supporters, Tents, Mottoes, &c.

Supporters are figures of human beings, or animals: angels, knights, ladies, savages, lions, griffins, &c. On old tombstones and the seals of knights, the possessor of the coat appears as the bearer of it. Supporting angels are usually placed behind the shield (figs. 1 and 2). Ladies, knights, savages, &c., stand at the side of the shield, either singly, or in pairs; and the same rule applies to animals (figs. 3 and 4).

Tents are draperies in the form of a Baldacchino, serving as a background for the Shield. The outside is generally purple, the inside of ermine, and they are hung with golden tassels and fringes. Such accessories are only suited to the coats of Sovereigns, and States; and are of comparatively Modern introduction.

Mottoes, War-cries, &c. are written on fillets or bands beneath or round the shield (fig. 5). Examples of such mottoes are the English "Honi soit qui mal y pense", the American "E pluribus unum", or the Wurttemberg "Furchtlos und treu".

There are also definite rules for the heraldic composition of a number of coats in one (for example, in a double coat the figures must be affronted, &c.); but we need not enter into, the details of these. The artistic execution is very various and arbitrary (fig. 6).

PLATE 290. HERALDIC ACCESSORIES.

1. Angel, as Supporter, by H. J. Gantinn, 1628, (Warnecke).
2. Angel, as Supporter, Italian, 16th century, (Formenschatz).
3. Lady, as Supporter, H. Burckmair, Triumphal Procession of the Emperor Maximilian, (Observe the repetition of the tinctures on the lady's dress, the crest, and the banner).
4. Griffins, as Supporters, by Hans Burckmair, (Formenschatz).
5. Coat, with Mottoes, 1529.
6. Composite coat, within a quatrefoil, Dürer's school, (Formenschatz).
7. Modern Tent.
8. Coat of Arms of the Artists, designed by L. Lesker. In consequence of an affront offered by the lords of Rappoltstein to the artists employed in the building of Strassburg minster, it is said that the Emperor Sigismund granted the artists, called the "Yunkers of Prague", permission to bear the same coat of arms — or, three escutcheons azure — (Martin Crusii, Schwäbische Chronik).

G.

WRITING, PRINTING, &c.

(ORNAMENTAL LETTERS.)

The invention of Writing dates back thousands of years before our era. To which nation it is to be assigned, cannot at present be fixed with any certainty. Greek writing was developed from the Phenician; and served, in its turn, as a basis for Roman writing. From the Roman writing, arose the Occidental and Scandinavian writings, as well as the Runic. The Latin script was introduced into Germany contemporaneously with Christianity. The early Middle Ages treated the shapes of letters in a some what arbitrary manner. By the side of the Majuscles (or capital letters) appear the Minuscles (or small letters, produced by the contraction and simplification of the former), (compare the letters E and M in alphabet 1 on Plate 291). By the side of the upright and angular Capital letters, appear the Uncial letters with their round and freer shapes (compare E, M and U in alphabet 2 on Plate 291). Alongside of the perpendicular letters, the more convenient slanting or Cursive letters begin to be employed. Beside the Uncial writing, the Gothic period brought Text-hands into use (Plates 294, 295, and 296). By this time the gradual transformation was so far advanced that at the first glance it is often impossible to recognise the original connection. The more complicated the Text-hands became, the more difficult they were to read; so that it must be considered a happy circumstance that the Renascence period strove in many ways to simplify the texts, and to revive the old Latin alphabet, (1 on Plate 297). The invention of printing in the year 1440 had an important influence on the developement of the shapes of letters. The period of the decadence of the Renascence brought with it the decadence in the forms of letters, which is most clearly seen in the middle of the 18th century. Since then, and especially in recent days, a gratifying progress has been made to something better, although it cannot be said that every attempt at improvement has been successful. It must not be forgotten that practical needs should be considered, quite as much as aesthetic aspirations, especially in a domain of such great and general importance as letters. It should always be borne in mind that the first requirement is easy reading; and that this is dependent on simplicity and characteristic shape in the letters.

As regards the decorative effect, for in this work we have chiefly to deal with decoration, it has first to be observed that the Antique did not recognise the principle of ornamental writing, either because no one thought of the possibility of ornamenting writing, or because they intentionally preferred the greater legibility, or for some other now unknown reason. At a later date almost all civilised nations and periods have occupied themselves more or less with the decorative effect of writing. This may take two different directions: either the letter may be decorated in its component parts, which eventually leads to the extravagance that fishes, birds, human forms, &c., in all' imaginable contortions, form the outline of the letters; or the letter in its ordinary form may receive a decorative finish by means of decorative accessories, by being set in a frame which theen appears as a free ending, or as a picture. The second treatment is especially suitable for Initials; and has led to very ingenious combinations; e. g. the background will frequently be an illustration of the subject of the· chapter which the initial begins, (Fig. 2, Plate 298). Both kinds of decoration may be combined. The first mode of decoration frequently leads to the loss of the real character of the letter; in the second mode it not infrequently happens that the letter cuts the picture, or vice versa, in an unpleasant manner. Colour is an important factor in the decoration of writing. Gold, silver, and a great variety of colours, but above all, gold and red, along with black, play an important part in writing in the miniature painting of the Calligraphists, as well as in Typography. In the present work we are unhappily compelled to leave this aspect out of consideration.

In the Middle Ages: it was principally monks and nuns who devoted themselves to the art of Writing; from the 13th century onwards, it was also practised by laymen. A long series of celebrated Calligraphists might be named. Calligraphy retrograded gradually with the introduction of Printing; but on the other hand the best artists of the Renascence, such as Holbein and others, did not disdain to design Initials 'and other letters for printers, as may be proved from a countless number of old books. As Christianity was introduced into Germany by the Irish, northern influences may also be traced in writing. Up to the 10th century the decorations of Writing have almost exclusively the character of interlaced-work and fantastically interlaced figures of animals; but from this period a vigorous plant decoration begins to be developed, eventually terminating, in later Gothic, in the endless interlacing of confused lines. The Renascence period prefers to set its initials in square frames; and these creations are among the most beautiful that writing has ever produced. The interlaced and artificial ornaments which afterwards became so common in Typography, especially in the 17th and 18th centuries (Plate 294. 2, 3 and 5), are either the invention of the Calligraphists of this period, or are the transfer of their archievements to Typography. Here, too, as in so many other things, Modern times revert to the models of the most different older periods; rightly when good is selected, and wrongly when the objectionable is revived. Over those sins of Modern Writing, which culminate in deforming our houses and the titles of our books with rows of shaded letters in all manner of possible and impossible places and positions, it is best to draw the charitable veil of silence. Compared with these sins of style, those sentimental garlands of roses and forget-me-nots, into which the last century formed its lines, are tolerable.

As regards the technical names of the kinds of letters now in general use: we can only say that they are so arbitrary that we shall do best to refrain altogether from attempting to enumerate them. Whoever wishes for information on this point may be recommended to consult the Specimen-book of some good Type-foundry.

Attempts were early made to construct Alphabets on a definite system; to base them on network, to determine the height and breadth of the entire letter, the dimensions of its component parts, &c.; among others Dürer devoted himself to this task. Space has not permitted us to reproduce all these constructions; but as a specimen we have given on Plate 300 the constructions of a few.

The notation of Numbers was introduced at the end of the Middle Ages. Our Numerals are an Arabian invention, whence their name. Plate 300 shows two collection of numerals of old times which are not sensibly different from those now in use. It is well known that, before Numerals were generally employed, recourse was had to the Latin letters (Roman numerals) for the indication of numbers. It is really remarkable that this latter apparatus, in spite of its unpractical character, has remained in use down to the present day.

Finally we may say a word or two about the Monogram. This name is given to letters and interlacings of letters intended to replace or to indicate a name. It may be formed either by single ornamented letters, usually the initials of the first and family name (Plate 300. 5—7), or by all the letters contained in the word (Plate 300. 10). It is not imperative that all the letters should be of the same size or style; and if necessary some of them may be reversed. A Monogram should be well arranged, and clear, so that it need not require to be guessed-at like a riddle. A good effect is produced by adding attributes and badges of dignity to monograms. Artistic sense and feeling must here supply the place of rules. Numerous and excellently ornamented monograms will be found in Gerlach: *Das Gewerbemonogramm*.

There are various books on Writing, as well as numerous collections of Initials and Alphabets. Prof. Hrachowina's *Initialen, Alphabete und Randleisten* (Vienna: Graeser) will be found very useful in teaching. Dr. Lamprecht's *Initial-Ornamentik des 8—13. Jahrhunderts* (Leipzig: A. Dürr) is an exhaustive study of the older styles of writing.

PLATE 291. ROMANESQUE LETTERS.

1.   Alphabet, beginning of the 8th century, S. Cuthbert's evangeliarium, British Museum, (Shaw).
2.   Alphabet, 10th century, MS. British Museum, (Shaw).
3.   Initial, 12th century, Berlin Museum.
4.   Initial, 12th century, Breviarium Cassinense, Bibliothèque Mazarine, Paris, (L'art pour tous).
5.   Initial, 9th or 10th century.
6.   Initial, 12th century, Berlin, Museum.
7.   Initial, 12th century, (Arnold & Knoll).
8.   Initial, 12th century.
9—10. Initials, 990, Echternach evangeliarum, Gotha, (Lamprecht).

PLATE 292. GOTHIC UNCIAL LETTERS.

1.   Alphabet, 1349, S. Margaret's, King's Lynn, England, (Shaw).
2—5. Initials, 1480, Rouen.
6—7. Letters, stalls of S. George's chapel, Windsor, end of 15th century, (Shaw).
8.   Gothic initial.
9.   Gothic initial, 1494.
10—17. Initials, 1480, Pontificale of Johann II., Archbishop of Trier, (Shaw).

PATE 293. GOTHIC UNCIAL LETTERS.

1.   Alphabet, 14th century, (John Weale).
2—3. Initials, 15th century, (Hrachowina).
4—7. Initials, 14th century, 1330.
8—9. Initials, end of 15th century, (Formenschatz).

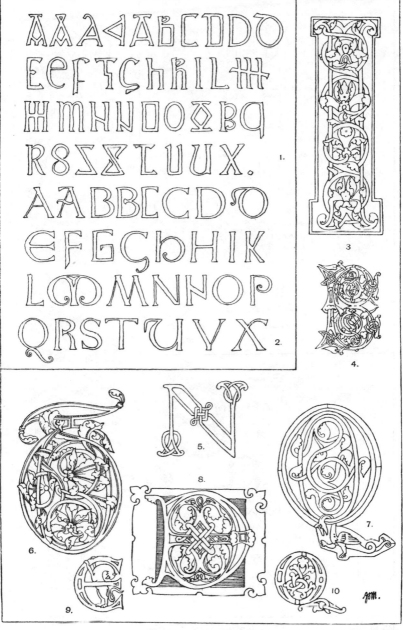

Romanesque Letters.

Plate 291.

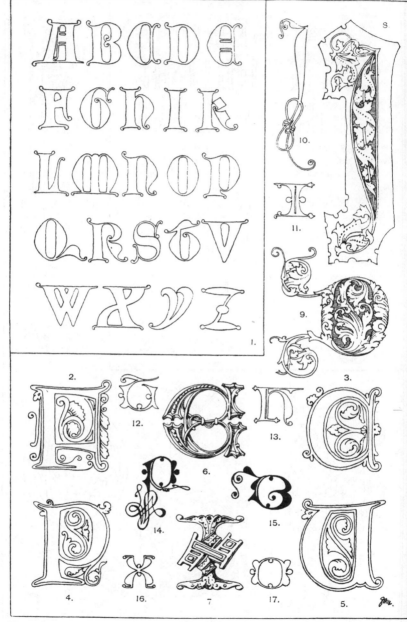

Plate 292. Gothic Uncial Letters.

Gothic Uncial Letters.   Plate 293.

PLATE 294. OLD ENGLISH LETTERS, &c.

1. Old English text, tomb of Richard II, Westminster Abbey, about 1400, (Shaw).
2—4. Initials, 16th century, Plantin Museum, Antwerp, (Ysendyck).
5—8. Initials, 16th and 17th centuries, (Raguenet).
9. Modern initial, Dir. Götz, Carlsruhe.

PLATE 295. OLD GERMAN LETTERS.

1. German text, 1467, (Hrachowina).
2. German text alphabet, composed from several documents.

PLATE 296. MODERN TEXT.

1. Schwabach type.
2. Gutenberg Gothic.
3. Fr. Thiersch, (Malerjournal).
4. Ribbon ornament, as Typographical Tail-piece.

PLATE 297. RENASCENCE LETTERS.

1. Roman Renascence alphabet, 1547, specimen-book of John of Yciar, Durango, Biscaya.
2. Renascence alphabet, lower-case Roman letters, specimen-book of Wolfgang Fugger, Nuremberg, 1553, (Hrachowina).
3. Renascence initial, 1531.
4. Renascence initial, 1500, (Formenschatz).
5. Initial, 1534, Lucas Cranach the elder, (Formenschatz).
6. Renascence initial, "Gedruckt Zu Augspurg Durch Jost De Necker" (Wessely).
7. Renascence initial, Italian, (Formenschatz).
8. Initial, 17th century, Elzevir printing office, (Ysendyck).
9. Initial, 17th century, specimen-book of Paul Fürst of Nuremberg, (L'art pour tous).
10. Initial, Barocco period, French, (Hrachowina).
11. Modern initial, by P. Koch.
12. Modern initial, by Dir. C. Hammer.

PLATE 298. ROMAN INITIALS.

1. Renascence, 1537, (Hrachowina).
2. Renascence, 17th century, Plantin printing office, Antwerp, (Ysendyck).
3. Modern, French.
4—13. Modern, Paris.

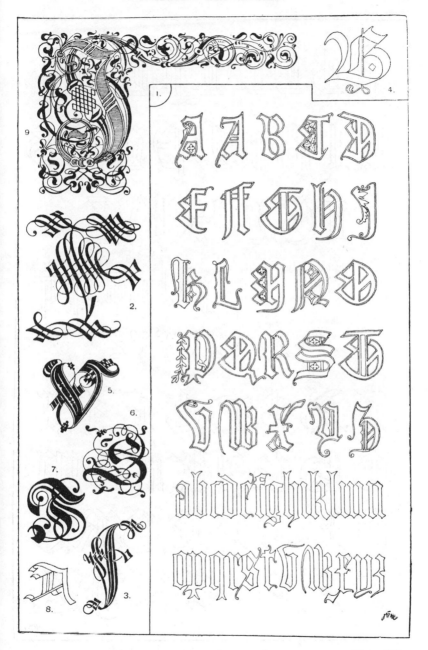

Old English Letters, &c.   Plate 294.

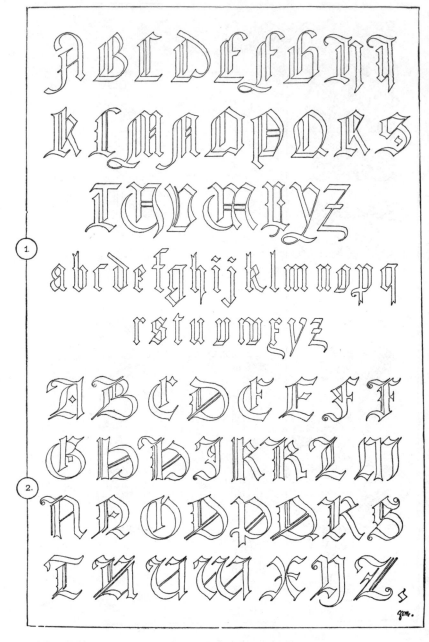

Plate 295. Old German Letters.

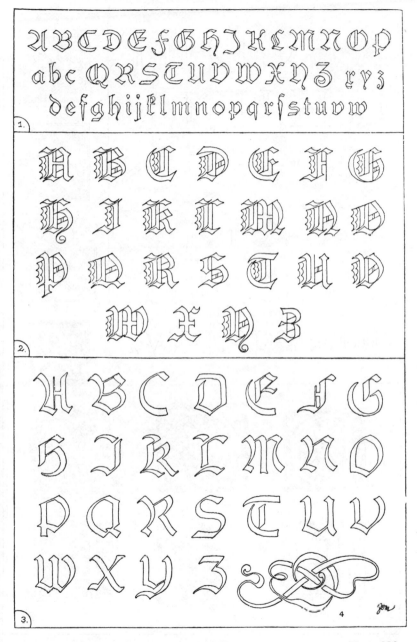

Modern Text.

Plate 296.

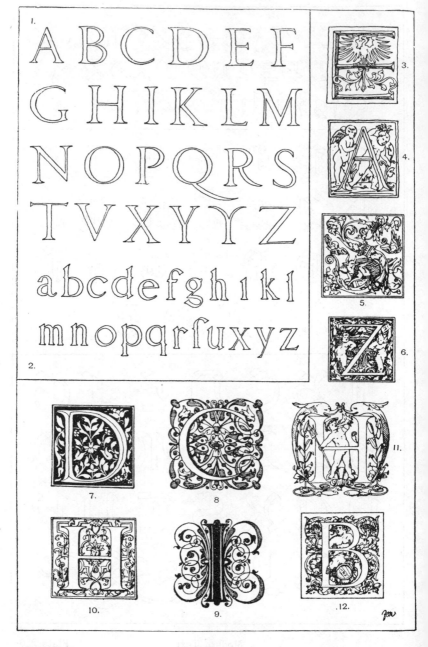

Plate 297. Renascence Letters.

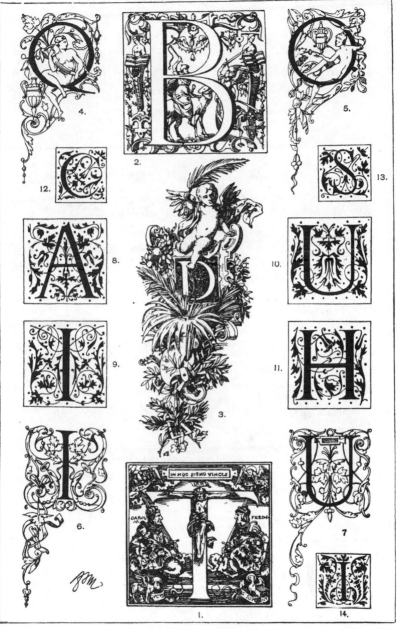

Roman Initials. Plate 298.

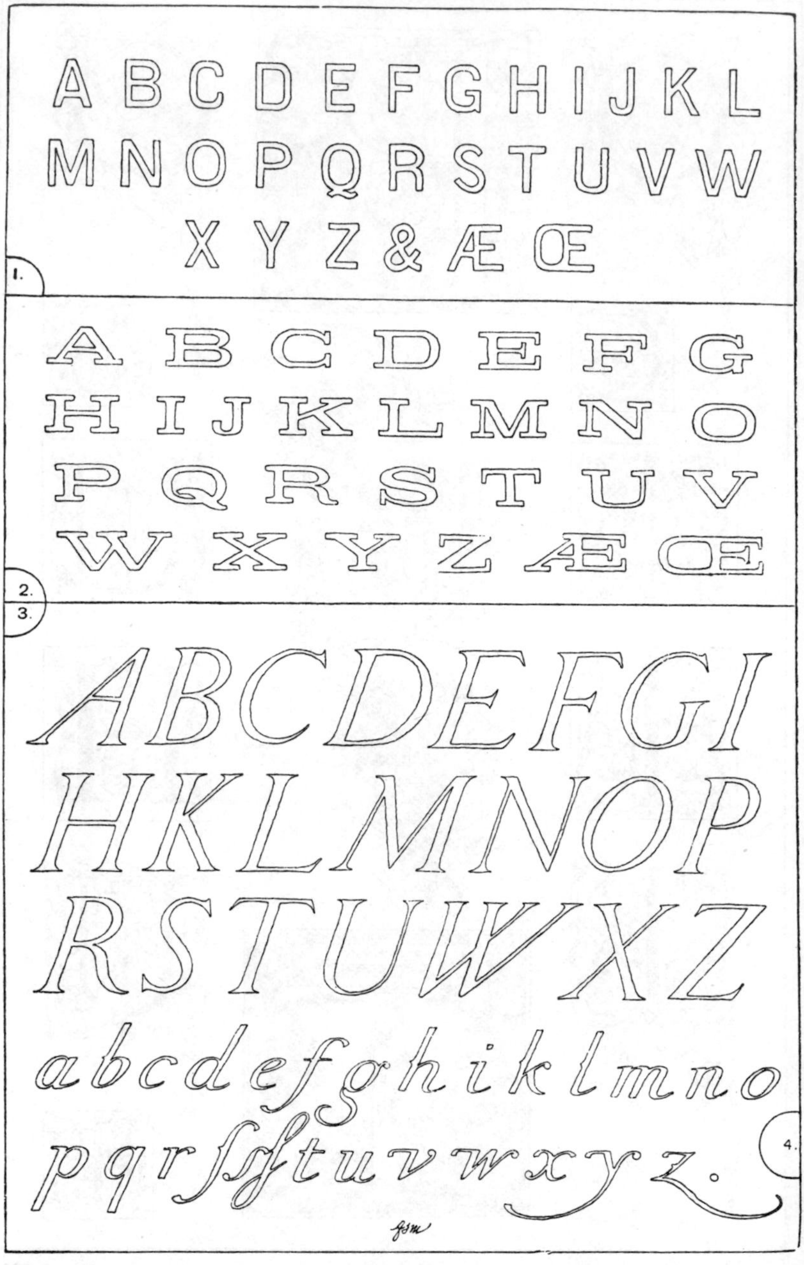

A B C D E F G H I J K L
M N O P Q R S T U V W
X Y Z & Æ Œ

1.

A B C D E F G
H I J K L M N O
P Q R S T U V
W X Y Z Æ Œ

2.
3.

ABCDEFGI
HKLMNOP
RSTUWXZ

abcdefghiklmno
pqrſsstuvwxyz.

4.

Plate 299.   Roman Letters.

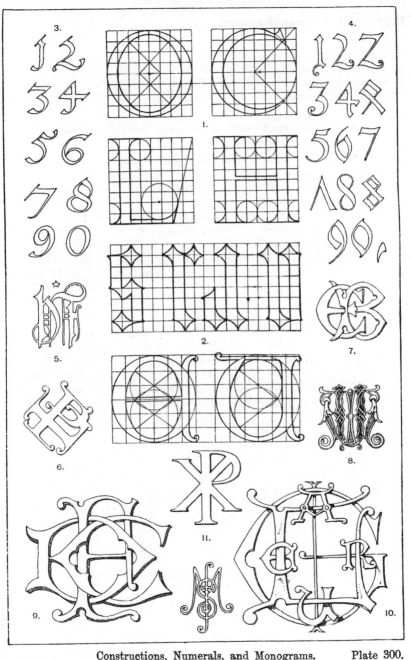

Constructions, Numerals, and Monograms.   Plate 300.

PLATE 299.   ROMAN LETTERS.

1. Modern.
2. Modern.
3. Renascence italic, Gottlieb Münch, Ordnung der Schrift, 1744.
4. Renascence lower-case italic, Michael Bauernfeind, Nuremberg, 1737, (Hrachowina).

PLATE 300.   CONSTRUCTIONS, NUMERALS, AND MONOGRAMS.

1.   Roman capitals.
2.   German text, and large Gothic uncial letters.
3—4.   Arabic numerals, 15th and 16th centuries.
5, 6, 7 and 9. Modern monograms of two and three letters, (Raguenet).
8.   Modern monogram, Dir. Götz.
10.   Monogram of a name: "Laugier", (Raguenet).
11.   Monogram of Christ; formed of the Greek initials of
                 the name of Christ, found in the Catacombs. It is
                 frequently combined with the letters $A \, \Omega$, in allusion
                 to Rev. XXII. 13: "I am Alpha and Omega" (compare
                 Plate 213. 13). Of later date is the monogram IHS,
                 the first three letters of the name Jesus, $IH\Sigma OY\Sigma$,
                 when written with Greek letters, which was afterwards
                 selected by the Jesuits as the badge of their order. It
                 has been variously explained as meaning: "Jesus
                 hominum salvator" (Jesus the saviour of men); "In Hoc
                 Salus" (in Him is salvation); "Jesus Habemus Socium"
                 (we have Jesus for our companion); or: "In Hoc Signo
                 vinces" (in this sign thou shalt conquer).

INDEX.

The numerals refer to the Pages in all cases. Where they are enclosed in Brackets:
the page is a Plate; and the small numerals refer to the Figures in the Plate.

A CATALOGUE OF SELECTED DOVER BOOKS
IN ALL FIELDS OF INTEREST

A CATALOGUE OF SELECTED DOVER BOOKS
IN ALL FIELDS OF INTEREST

THE NOTEBOOKS OF LEONARDO DA VINCI, edited by J.P. Richter. Extracts from manuscripts reveal great genius; on painting, sculpture, anatomy, sciences, geography, etc. Both Italian and English. 186 ms. pages reproduced, plus 500 additional drawings, including studies for Last Supper, Sforza monument, etc. 860pp. 7⅞ x 10¾.   USO 22572-0, 22573-9 Pa., Two vol. set $15.90

ART NOUVEAU DESIGNS IN COLOR, Alphonse Mucha, Maurice Verneuil, Georges Auriol. Full-color reproduction of Combinaisons ornamentales (c. 1900) by Art Nouveau masters. Floral, animal, geon -tr interlacings, swashes — borders, frames, spots — all incredibly beautiful. G place. hundreds of designs. 9⅜ x 8¹/₁₆ .   22885-1 Pa. $4.00

GRAPHIC WORKS OF ODILON REDON. All great fantastic lithographs, etchings, engravings, drawings, 209 in all. Monsters, Huysmans, still life work, etc. Introduction by Alfred Werner. 209pp. 9⅛ x 12¼.   21996-8 Pa. $6.00

EXOTIC FLORAL PATTERNS ⁻ COLOR, E.-A. Seguy. Incredibly beautiful full-color pochoir work by great F: nch designer of 20's. Complete Bouquets et frondaisons, Suggestions pour étoffes. Richness must be seen to be believed. 40 plates containing 120 patterns. 80pp. 9⅜ x 12¼.   23041-4 Pa. $6.00

SELECTED ETCHINGS OF JAMES A. McN. WHISTLER, James A. McN. Whistler. 149 outstanding etchings by the great American artist, including selections from the Thames set and two Venice sets, the complete French set, and many individual prints. Introduction and explanatory note on each print by Maria Naylor. 157pp. 9⅜ x 12¼.   23194-1 Pa. $5.00

VISUAL ILLUSIONS: THEIR CAUSES, CHARACTERISTICS, AND APPLICATIONS, Matthew Luckiesh. Thorough description, discussion; shape and size, color, motion; natural illusion. Uses in art and industry. 100 illustrations. 252pp.
21530-X Pa. $2.50

TEN BOOKS ON ARCHITECTURE, Vitruvius. The most important book ever written on architecture. Early Roman aesthetics, technology, classical orders, site selection, all other aspects. Stands behind everything since. Morgan translation. 331pp.
20645-9 Pa. $3.50

THE CODEX NUTTALL. A PICTURE MANUSCRIPT FROM ANCIENT MEXICO, as first edited by Zelia Nuttall. Only inexpensive edition, in full color, of a pre-Columbian Mexican (Mixtec) book. 88 color plates show kings, gods, heroes, temples, sacrifices. New explanatory, historical introduction by Arthur G. Miller. 96pp. 11³/₈ x 8½.   23168-2 Pa. $7.50

THE ART DECO STYLE, ed. by Theodore Menten. Furniture, jewelry, metalwork, ceramics, fabrics, lighting fixtures, interior decors, exteriors, graphics from pure French sources. Best sampling around. Over 400 photographs. 183pp. 8⅜ x 11¼.
22824-X Pa. $4.00

THE GENTLEMAN AND CABINET MAKER'S DIRECTOR, Thomas Chippendale. Full reprint, 1762 style book, most influential of all time; chairs, tables, sofas, mirrors, cabinets, etc. 200 plates, plus 24 photographs of surviving pieces. 249pp. 9⅞ x 12¾.
21601-2 Pa. $6.00

PINE FURNITURE OF EARLY NEW ENGLAND, Russell H. Kettell. Basic book. Thorough historical text, plus 200 illustrations of boxes, highboys, candlesticks, desks, etc. 477pp. 7⅞ x 10¾.
20145-7 Clothbd. $12.50

ORIENTAL RUGS, ANTIQUE AND MODERN, Walter A. Hawley. Persia, Turkey, Caucasus, Central Asia, China, other traditions. Best general survey of all aspects: styles and periods, manufacture, uses, symbols and their interpretation, and identification. 96 illustrations, 11 in color. 320pp. 6⅛ x 9¼.
22366-3 Pa. $5.00

DECORATIVE ANTIQUE IRONWORK, Henry R. d'Allemagne. Photographs of 4500 iron artifacts from world's finest collection, Rouen. Hinges, locks, candelabra, weapons, lighting devices, clocks, tools, from Roman times to mid-19th century. Nothing else comparable to it. 420pp. 9 x 12.
22082-6 Pa. $8.50

THE COMPLETE BOOK OF DOLL MAKING AND COLLECTING, Catherine Christopher. Instructions, patterns for dozens of dolls, from rag doll on up to elaborate, historically accurate figures. Mould faces, sew clothing, make doll houses, etc. Also collecting information. Many illustrations. 288pp. 6 x 9. 22066-4 Pa. $3.00

ANTIQUE PAPER DOLLS: 1915-1920, edited by Arnold Arnold. 7 antique cut-out dolls and 24 costumes from 1915-1920, selected by Arnold Arnold from his collection of rare children's books and entertainments, all in full color. 32pp. 9¼ x 12¼.
23176-3 Pa. $2.00

ANTIQUE PAPER DOLLS: THE EDWARDIAN ERA, Epinal. Full-color reproductions of two historic series of paper dolls that show clothing styles in 1908 and at the beginning of the First World War. 8 two-sided, stand-up dolls and 32 complete, two-sided costumes. Full instructions for assembling included. 32pp. 9¼ x 12¼.
23175-5 Pa. $2.00

A HISTORY OF COSTUME, Carl Köhler, Emma von Sichardt. Egypt, Babylon, Greece up through 19th century Europe; based on surviving pieces, art works, etc. Full text and 595 illustrations, including many clear, measured patterns for reproducing historic costume. Practical. 464pp.
21030-8 Pa. $4.00

EARLY AMERICAN LOCOMOTIVES, John H. White, Jr. Finest locomotive engravings from late 19th century: historical (1804-1874), main-line (after 1870), special, foreign, etc. 147 plates. 200pp. 11⅜ x 8¼.
22772-3 Pa. $3.50

THE MAGIC MOVING PICTURE BOOK, Bliss, Sands & Co. The pictures in this book move! Volcanoes erupt, a house burns, a serpentine dancer wiggles her way through a number. By using a specially ruled acetate screen provided, you can obtain these and 15 other startling effects. Originally "The Motograph Moving Picture Book." 32pp. 8¼ x 11. 23224-7 Pa. $1.75

STRING FIGURES AND HOW TO MAKE THEM, Caroline F. Jayne. Fullest, clearest instructions on string figures from around world: Eskimo, Navajo, Lapp, Europe, more. Cats cradle, moving spear, lightning, stars. Introduction by A.C. Haddon. 950 illustrations. 407pp. 20152-X Pa. $3.50

PAPER FOLDING FOR BEGINNERS, William D. Murray and Francis J. Rigney. Clearest book on market for making origami sail boats, roosters, frogs that move legs, cups, bonbon boxes. 40 projects. More than 275 illustrations. Photographs. 94pp. 20713-7 Pa. $1.25

INDIAN SIGN LANGUAGE, William Tomkins. Over 525 signs developed by Sioux, Blackfoot, Cheyenne, Arapahoe and other tribes. Written instructions and diagrams: how to make words, construct sentences. Also 290 pictographs of Sioux and Ojibway tribes. 111pp. 6⅛ x 9¼. 22029-X Pa. $1.50

BOOMERANGS: HOW TO MAKE AND THROW THEM, Bernard S. Mason. Easy to make and throw, dozens of designs: cross-stick, pinwheel, boomabird, tumblestick, Australian curved stick boomerang. Complete throwing instructions. All safe. 99pp. 23028-7 Pa. $1.75

25 KITES THAT FLY, Leslie Hunt. Full, easy to follow instructions for kites made from inexpensive materials. Many novelties. Reeling, raising, designing your own. 70 illustrations. 110pp. 22550-X Pa. $1.25

TRICKS AND GAMES ON THE POOL TABLE, Fred Herrmann. 79 tricks and games, some solitaires, some for 2 or more players, some competitive; mystifying shots and throws, unusual carom, tricks involving cork, coins, a hat, more. 77 figures. 95pp. 21814-7 Pa. $1.25

WOODCRAFT AND CAMPING, Bernard S. Mason. How to make a quick emergency shelter, select woods that will burn immediately, make do with limited supplies, etc. Also making many things out of wood, rawhide, bark, at camp. Formerly titled Woodcraft. 295 illustrations. 580pp. 21951-8 Pa. $4.00

AN INTRODUCTION TO CHESS MOVES AND TACTICS SIMPLY EXPLAINED, Leonard Barden. Informal intermediate introduction: reasons for moves, tactics, openings, traps, positional play, endgame. Isolates patterns. 102pp. USO 21210-6 Pa. $1.35

LASKER'S MANUAL OF CHESS, Dr. Emanuel Lasker. Great world champion offers very thorough coverage of all aspects of chess. Combinations, position play, openings, endgame, aesthetics of chess, philosophy of struggle, much more. Filled with analyzed games. 390pp. 20640-8 Pa. $4.00

DECORATIVE ALPHABETS AND INITIALS, edited by Alexander Nesbitt. 91 complete alphabets (medieval to modern), 3924 decorative initials, including Victorian novelty and Art Nouveau. 192pp. 7¾ x 10¾. 20544-4 Pa. $4.00

CALLIGRAPHY, Arthur Baker. Over 100 original alphabets from the hand of our greatest living calligrapher: simple, bold, fine-line, richly ornamented, etc. —all strikingly original and different, a fusion of many influences and styles. 155pp. 11⅜ x 8¼. 22895-9 Pa. $4.50

MONOGRAMS AND ALPHABETIC DEVICES, edited by Hayward and Blanche Cirker. Over 2500 combinations, names, crests in very varied styles: script engraving, ornate Victorian, simple Roman, and many others. 226pp. 8⅛ x 11. 22330-2 Pa. $5.00

THE BOOK OF SIGNS, Rudolf Koch. Famed German type designer renders 493 symbols: religious, alchemical, imperial, runes, property marks, etc. Timeless. 104pp. 6⅛ x 9¼. 20162-7 Pa. $1.75

200 DECORATIVE TITLE PAGES, edited by Alexander Nesbitt. 1478 to late 1920's. Baskerville, Dürer, Beardsley, W. Morris, Pyle, many others in most varied techniques. For posters, programs, other uses. 222pp. 8⅜ x 11¼. 21264-5 Pa. **$5.00**

DICTIONARY OF AMERICAN PORTRAITS, edited by Hayward and Blanche Cirker. 4000 important Americans, earliest times to 1905, mostly in clear line. Politicians, writers, soldiers, scientists, inventors, industrialists, Indians, Blacks, women, outlaws, etc. Identificatory information. 756pp. 9¼ x 12¾. 21823-6 Clothbd. $30.00

ART FORMS IN NATURE, Ernst Haeckel. Multitude of strangely beautiful natural forms: Radiolaria, Foraminifera, jellyfishes, fungi, turtles, bats, etc. All 100 plates of the 19th century evolutionist's Kunstformen der Natur (1904). 100pp. 9⅜ x 12¼. 22987-4 Pa. $4.00

DECOUPAGE: THE BIG PICTURE SOURCEBOOK, Eleanor Rawlings. Make hundreds of beautiful objects, over 550 florals, animals, letters, shells, period costumes, frames, etc. selected by foremost practitioner. Printed on one side of page. 8 color plates. Instructions. 176pp. 9³/₁₆ x 12¼. 23182-8 Pa. $5.00

AMERICAN FOLK DECORATION, Jean Lipman, Eve Meulendyke. Thorough coverage of all aspects of wood, tin, leather, paper, cloth decoration — scapes, humans, trees, flowers, geometrics — and how to make them. Full instructions. 233 illustrations, 5 in color. 163pp. 8⅜ x 11¼. 22217-9 Pa. $3.95

WHITTLING AND WOODCARVING, E.J. Tangerman. Best book on market; clear, full. If you can cut a potato, you can carve toys, puzzles, chains, caricatures, masks, patterns, frames, decorate surfaces, etc. Also covers serious wood sculpture. Over 200 photos. 293pp. 20965-2 Pa. $3.00

150 MASTERPIECES OF DRAWING, edited by Anthony Toney. 150 plates, early 15th century to end of 18th century; Rembrandt, Michelangelo, Dürer, Fragonard, Watteau, Wouwerman, many others. 150pp. 8⅜ x 11¼. 21032-4 Pa. $4.00

THE GOLDEN AGE OF THE POSTER, Hayward and Blanche Cirker. 70 extraordinary posters in full colors, from Maitres de l'Affiche, Mucha, Lautrec, Bradley, Cheret, Beardsley, many others. 9⅜ x 12¼. 22753-7 Pa. $4.95
21718-3 Clothbd. $7.95

SIMPLICISSIMUS, selection, translations and text by Stanley Appelbaum. 180 satirical drawings, 16 in full color, from the famous German weekly magazine in the years 1896 to 1926. 24 artists included: Grosz, Kley, Pascin, Kubin, Kollwitz, plus Heine, Thöny, Bruno Paul, others. 172pp. 8½ x 12¼. 23098-8 Pa. $5.00
23099-6 Clothbd. $10.00

THE EARLY WORK OF AUBREY BEARDSLEY, Aubrey Beardsley. 157 plates, 2 in color: Manon Lescaut, Madame Bovary, Morte d'Arthur, Salome, other. Introduction by H. Marillier. 175pp. 8½ x 11. 21816-3 Pa. $4.00

THE LATER WORK OF AUBREY BEARDSLEY, Aubrey Beardsley. Exotic masterpieces of full maturity: Venus and Tannhäuser, Lysistrata, Rape of the Lock, Volpone, Savoy material, etc. 174 plates, 2 in color. 176pp. 8½ x 11. 21817-1 Pa. $4.00

DRAWINGS OF WILLIAM BLAKE, William Blake. 92 plates from Book of Job, Divine Comedy, Paradise Lost, visionary heads, mythological figures, Laocoön, etc. Selection, introduction, commentary by Sir Geoffrey Keynes. 178pp. 8½ x 11. 22303-5 Pa. $3.50

LONDON: A PILGRIMAGE, Gustave Doré, Blanchard Jerrold. Squalor, riches, misery, beauty of mid-Victorian metropolis; 55 wonderful plates, 125 other illustrations, full social, cultural text by Jerrold. 191pp. of text. 8⅛ x 11. 22306-X Pa. $5.00

THE COMPLETE WOODCUTS OF ALBRECHT DÜRER, edited by Dr. W. Kurth. 346 in all: Old Testament, St. Jerome, Passion, Life of Virgin, Apocalypse, many others. Introduction by Campbell Dodgson. 285pp. 8½ x 12¼. 21097-9 Pa. $6.00

THE DISASTERS OF WAR, Francisco Goya. 83 etchings record horrors of Napoleonic wars in Spain and war in general. Reprint of 1st edition, plus 3 additional plates. Introduction by Philip Hofer. 97pp. 9⅜ x 8¼. 21872-4 Pa. $3.00

ENGRAVINGS OF HOGARTH, William Hogarth. 101 of Hogarth's greatest works: Rake's Progress, Harlot's Progress, Illustrations for Hudibras, Midnight Modern Conversation, Before and After, Beer Street and Gin Lane, many more. Full commentary. 256pp. 11 x 14. 22479-1 Pa. $7.00
23023-6 Clothbd. $13.50

PRIMITIVE ART, Franz Boas. Great anthropologist on ceramics, textiles, wood, stone, metal, etc.; patterns, technology, symbols, styles. All areas, but fullest on Northwest Coast Indians. 350 illustrations. 378pp. 20025-6 Pa. $3.75

MANUAL OF THE TREES OF NORTH AMERICA, Charles S. Sargent. The basic survey of every native tree and tree-like shrub, 717 species in all. Extremely full descriptions, information on habitat, growth, locales, economics, etc. Necessary to every serious tree lover. Over 100 finding keys. 783 illustrations. Total of 986pp.
20277-1, 20278-X Pa., Two vol. set $9.00

BIRDS OF THE NEW YORK AREA, John Bull. Indispensable guide to more than 400 species within a hundred-mile radius of Manhattan. Information on range, status, breeding, migration, distribution trends, etc. Foreword by Roger Tory Peterson. 17 drawings; maps 540pp.
23222-0 Pa. $6.00

THE SEA-BEACH AT EBB-TIDE, Augusta Foote Arnold. Identify hundreds of marine plants and animals: algae, seaweeds, squids, crabs, corals, etc. Descriptions cover food, life cycle, size, shape, habitat. Over 600 drawings. 490pp.
21949-6 Pa. $5.00

THE MOTH BOOK, William J. Holland. Identify more than 2,000 moths of North America. General information, precise species descriptions. 623 illustrations plus 48 color plates show almost all species, full size. 1968 edition. Still the basic book. Total of 551pp. 6½ x 9¼.
21948-8 Pa. $6.00

AN INTRODUCTION TO THE REPTILES AND AMPHIBIANS OF THE UNITED STATES, Percy A. Morris. All lizards, crocodiles, turtles, snakes, toads, frogs; life history, identification, habits, suitability as pets, etc. Non-technical, but sound and broad. 130 photos. 253pp.
22982-3 Pa. $3.00

OLD NEW YORK IN EARLY PHOTOGRAPHS, edited by Mary Black. Your only chance to see New York City as it was 1853-1906, through 196 wonderful photographs from N.Y. Historical Society. Great Blizzard, Lincoln's funeral procession, great buildings. 228pp. 9 x 12.
22907-6 Pa. $6.00

THE AMERICAN REVOLUTION, A PICTURE SOURCEBOOK, John Grafton. Wonderful Bicentennial picture source, with 411 illustrations (contemporary and 19th century) showing battles, personalities, maps, events, flags, posters, soldier's life, ships, etc. all captioned and explained. A wonderful browsing book, supplement to other historical reading. 160pp. 9 x 12.
23226-3 Pa. $4.00

PERSONAL NARRATIVE OF A PILGRIMAGE TO AL-MADINAH AND MECCAH, Richard Burton. Great travel classic by remarkably colorful personality. Burton, disguised as a Moroccan, visited sacred shrines of Islam, narrowly escaping death. Wonderful observations of Islamic life, customs, personalities. 47 illustrations. Total of 959pp.
21217-3, 21218-1 Pa., Two vol. set $10.00

INCIDENTS OF TRAVEL IN CENTRAL AMERICA, CHIAPAS, AND YUCATAN, John L. Stephens. Almost single-handed discovery of Maya culture; exploration of ruined cities, monuments, temples; customs of Indians. 115 drawings. 892pp.
22404-X, 22405-8 Pa., Two vol. set $8.00

VISUAL ILLUSIONS: THEIR CAUSES, CHARACTERISTICS, AND APPLICATIONS, Matthew Luckiesh. Thorough description and discussion of optical illusion, geometric and perspective, particularly; size and shape distortions, illusions of color, of motion; natural illusions; use of illusion in art and magic, industry, etc. Most useful today with op art, also for classical art. Scores of effects illustrated. Introduction by William H. Ittleson. 100 illustrations. xxi + 252pp.

21530-X Paperbound $2.50

A HANDBOOK OF ANATOMY FOR ART STUDENTS, Arthur Thomson. Thorough, virtually exhaustive coverage of skeletal structure, musculature, etc. Full text, supplemented by anatomical diagrams and drawings and by photographs of undraped figures. Unique in its comparison of male and female forms, pointing out differences of contour, texture, form. 211 figures, 40 drawings, 86 photographs. xx + 459pp. 5⅜ x 8⅜.

21163-0 Paperbound $5.00

150 MASTERPIECES OF DRAWING, Selected by Anthony Toney. Full page reproductions of drawings from the early 16th to the end of the 18th century, all beautifully reproduced: Rembrandt, Michelangelo, Dürer, Fragonard, Urs, Graf, Wouwerman, many others. First-rate browsing book, model book for artists. xviii + 150pp. 8⅜ x 11¼.

21032-4 Paperbound $4.00

THE LATER WORK OF AUBREY BEARDSLEY, Aubrey Beardsley. Exotic, erotic, ironic masterpieces in full maturity: Comedy Ballet, Venus and Tannhauser, Pierrot, Lysistrata, Rape of the Lock, Savoy material, Ali Baba, Volpone, etc. This material revolutionized the art world, and is still powerful, fresh, brilliant. With *The Early Work,* all Beardsley's finest work. 174 plates, 2 in color. xiv + 176pp. 8⅛ x 11.

21817-1 Paperbound $4.00

DRAWINGS OF REMBRANDT, Rembrandt van Rijn. Complete reproduction of fabulously rare edition by Lippmann and Hofstede de Groot, completely reedited, updated, improved by Prof. Seymour Slive, Fogg Museum. Portraits, Biblical sketches, landscapes, Oriental types, nudes, episodes from classical mythology—All Rembrandt's fertile genius. Also selection of drawings by his pupils and followers. "Stunning volumes," *Saturday Review.* 550 illustrations. lxxviii + 552pp. 9⅛ x 12¼.

21485-0, 21486-9 Two volumes, Paperbound $12.00

THE DISASTERS OF WAR, Francisco Goya. One of the masterpieces of Western civilization—83 etchings that record Goya's shattering, bitter reaction to the Napoleonic war that swept through Spain after the insurrection of 1808 and to war in general. Reprint of the first edition, with three additional plates from Boston's Museum of Fine Arts. All plates facsimile size. Introduction by Philip Hofer, Fogg Museum. v + 97pp. 9⅜ x 8¼.

21872-4 Paperbound $3.00

GRAPHIC WORKS OF ODILON REDON. Largest collection of Redon's graphic works ever assembled: 172 lithographs, 28 etchings and engravings, 9 drawings. These include some of his most famous works. All the plates from *Odilon Redon: oeuvre graphique complet,* plus additional plates. New introduction and caption translations by Alfred Werner. 209 illustrations. xxvii + 209pp. 9⅛ x 12¼.

21966-8 Paperbound $6.00

JEWISH GREETING CARDS, Ed Sibbett, Jr. 16 cards to cut and color. Three say "Happy Chanukah," one "Happy New Year," others have no message, show stars of David, Torahs, wine cups, other traditional themes. 16 envelopes. 8¼ x 11.
23225-5 Pa. $2.00

AUBREY BEARDSLEY GREETING CARD BOOK, Aubrey Beardsley. Edited by Theodore Menten. 16 elegant yet inexpensive greeting cards let you combine your own sentiments with subtle Art Nouveau lines. 16 different Aubrey Beardsley designs that you can color or not, as you wish. 16 envelopes. 64pp. 8¼ x 11.
23173-9 Pa. $2.00

RECREATIONS IN THE THEORY OF NUMBERS, Albert Beiler. Number theory, an inexhaustible source of puzzles, recreations, for beginners and advanced. Divisors, perfect numbers. scales of notation, etc. 349pp. 21096-0 Pa. $4.00

AMUSEMENTS IN MATHEMATICS, Henry E. Dudeney. One of largest puzzle collections, based on algebra, arithmetic, permutations, probability, plane figure dissection, properties of numbers, by one of world's foremost puzzlists. Solutions. 450 illustrations. 258pp. 20473-1 Pa. $3.00

MATHEMATICS, MAGIC AND MYSTERY, Martin Gardner. Puzzle editor for Scientific American explains math behind: card tricks, stage mind reading, coin and match tricks, counting out games, geometric dissections. Probability, sets, theory of numbers, clearly explained. Plus more than 400 tricks, guaranteed to work. 135 illustrations. 176pp. 20335-2 Pa. $2.00

BEST MATHEMATICAL PUZZLES OF SAM LOYD, edited by Martin Gardner. Bizarre, original, whimsical puzzles by America's greatest puzzler. From fabulously rare Cyclopedia, including famous 14-15 puzzles, the Horse of a Different Color, 115 more. Elementary math. 150 illustrations. 167pp. 20498-7 Pa. $2.50

MATHEMATICAL PUZZLES FOR BEGINNERS AND ENTHUSIASTS, Geoffrey Mott-Smith. 189 puzzles from easy to difficult involving arithmetic, logic, algebra, properties of digits, probability. Explanation of math behind puzzles. 135 illustrations. 248pp. 20198-8 Pa. $2.75

BIG BOOK OF MAZES AND LABYRINTHS, Walter Shepherd. Classical, solid, and ripple mazes; short path and avoidance labyrinths; more — 50 mazes and labyrinths in all. 12 other figures. Full solutions. 112pp. 8⅛ x 11. 22951-3 Pa. $2.00

COIN GAMES AND PUZZLES, Maxey Brooke. 60 puzzles, games and stunts — from Japan, Korea, Africa and the ancient world, by Dudeney and the other great puzzlers, as well as Maxey Brooke's own creations. Full solutions. 67 illustrations. 94pp. 22893-2 Pa. $1.50

HAND SHADOWS TO BE THROWN UPON THE WALL, Henry Bursill. Wonderful Victorian novelty tells how to make flying birds, dog, goose, deer, and 14 others. 32pp. 6½ x 9¼. 21779-5 Pa. $1.25

HOUDINI ON MAGIC, Harold Houdini. Edited by Walter Gibson, Morris N. Young. How he escaped; exposés of fake spiritualists; instructions for eye-catching tricks; other fascinating material by and about greatest magician. 155 illustrations. 280pp.   20384-0 Pa. $2.75

HANDBOOK OF THE NUTRITIONAL CONTENTS OF FOOD, U.S. Dept. of Agriculture. Largest, most detailed source of food nutrition information ever prepared. Two mammoth tables: one measuring nutrients in 100 grams of edible portion; the other, in edible portion of 1 pound as purchased. Originally titled Composition of Foods. 190pp. 9 x 12.   21342-0 Pa. $4.00

COMPLETE GUIDE TO HOME CANNING, PRESERVING AND FREEZING, U.S. Dept. of Agriculture. Seven basic manuals with full instructions for jams and jellies; pickles and relishes; canning fruits, vegetables, meat; freezing anything. Really good recipes, exact instructions for optimal results. Save a fortune in food. 156 illustrations. 214pp. 6^1/$_8$ x 9^1/$_4$.   22911-4 Pa. $2.50

THE BREAD TRAY, Louis P. De Gouy. Nearly every bread the cook could buy or make: bread sticks of Italy, fruit breads of Greece, glazed rolls of Vienna, everything from corn pone to croissants. Over 500 recipes altogether. including buns, rolls, muffins, scones, and more. 463pp.   23000-7 Pa. $3.50

CREATIVE HAMBURGER COOKERY, Louis P. De Gouy. 182 unusual recipes for casseroles, meat loaves and hamburgers that turn inexpensive ground meat into memorable main dishes: Arizona chili burgers, burger tamale pie, burger stew, burger corn loaf, burger wine loaf, and more. 120pp.   23001-5 Pa. $1.75

LONG ISLAND SEAFOOD COOKBOOK, J. George Frederick and Jean Joyce. Probably the best American seafood cookbook. Hundreds of recipes. 40 gourmet sauces, 123 recipes using oysters alone! All varieties of fish and seafood amply represented. 324pp.   22677-8 Pa. $3.50

THE EPICUREAN: A COMPLETE TREATISE OF ANALYTICAL AND PRACTICAL STUDIES IN THE CULINARY ART, Charles Ranhofer. Great modern classic. 3,500 recipes from master chef of Delmonico's, turn-of-the-century America's best restaurant. Also explained, many techniques known only to professional chefs. 775 illustrations. 1183pp. 6^5/$_8$ x 10.   22680-8 Clothbd. $22.50

THE AMERICAN WINE COOK BOOK, Ted Hatch. Over 700 recipes: old favorites livened up with wine plus many more: Czech fish soup, quince soup, sauce Perigueux, shrimp shortcake, filets Stroganoff, cordon bleu goulash, jambonneau, wine fruit cake, more. 314pp.   22796-0 Pa. $2.50

DELICIOUS VEGETARIAN COOKING, Ivan Baker. Close to 500 delicious and varied recipes: soups, main course dishes (pea, bean, lentil, cheese, vegetable, pasta, and egg dishes), savories, stews, whole-wheat breads and cakes, more. 168pp.
USO 22834-7 Pa. $1.75

EGYPTIAN MAGIC, E.A. Wallis Budge. Foremost Egyptologist, curator at British Museum, on charms, curses, amulets, doll magic, transformations, control of demons, deific appearances, feats of great magicians. Many texts cited. 19 illustrations. 234pp. USO 22681-6 Pa. $2.50

THE LEYDEN PAPYRUS: AN EGYPTIAN MAGICAL BOOK, edited by F. Ll. Griffith, Herbert Thompson. Egyptian sorcerer's manual contains scores of spells: sex magic of various sorts, occult information, evoking visions, removing evil magic, etc. Transliteration faces translation. 207pp. 22994 7 Pa. $2.50

THE MALLEUS MALEFICARUM OF KRAMER AND SPRENGER, translated, edited by Montague Summers. Full text of most important witchhunter's "Bible," used by both Catholics and Protestants. Theory of witches, manifestations, remedies, etc. Indispensable to serious student. 278pp. 6⅝ x 10. USO 22802-9 Pa. $3.95

LOST CONTINENTS, L. Sprague de Camp. Great science-fiction author, finest, fullest study: Atlantis, Lemuria, Mu, Hyperborea, etc. Lost Tribes, Irish in pre-Columbian America, root races; in history, literature, art, occultism. Necessary to everyone concerned with theme. 17 illustrations. 348pp. 22668-9 Pa. $3.50

THE COMPLETE BOOKS OF CHARLES FORT, Charles Fort. Book of the Damned, Lo!, Wild Talents, New Lands. Greatest compilation of data: celestial appearances, flying saucers, falls of frogs, strange disappearances, inexplicable data not recognized by science. Inexhaustible, painstakingly documented. Do not confuse with modern charlatanry. Introduction by Damon Knight. Total of 1126pp. 23094-5 Clothbd. $15.00

FADS AND FALLACIES IN THE NAME OF SCIENCE, Martin Gardner. Fair, witty appraisal of cranks and quacks of science: Atlantis, Lemuria, flat earth, Velikovsky, orgone energy, Bridey Murphy, medical fads, etc. 373pp. 20394-8 Pa. $3.50

HOAXES, Curtis D. MacDougall. Unbelievably rich account of great hoaxes: Locke's moon hoax, Shakespearean forgeries, Loch Ness monster, Disumbrationist school of art, dozens more; also psychology of hoaxing. 54 illustrations. 338pp. 20465-0 Pa. $3.50

THE GENTLE ART OF MAKING ENEMIES, James A.M. Whistler. Greatest wit of his day deflates Wilde, Ruskin, Swinburne; strikes back at inane critics, exhibitions. Highly readable classic of impressionist revolution by great painter. Introduction by Alfred Werner. 334pp. 21875-9 Pa. $4.00

THE BOOK OF TEA, Kakuzo Okakura. Minor classic of the Orient: entertaining, charming explanation, interpretation of traditional Japanese culture in terms of tea ceremony. Edited by E.F. Bleiler. Total of 94pp. 20070-1 Pa. $1.25

Prices subject to change without notice.
Available at your book dealer or write for free catalogue to Dept. GI, Dover Publications, Inc., 180 Varick St., N.Y., N.Y. 10014. Dover publishes more than 150 books each year on science, elementary and advanced mathematics, biology, music, art, literary history, social sciences and other areas.